FRANZ SCHUBERT AND *THE MYSTERIUM MAGNUM*

BY

FRANK RUPPERT

RoseDog Books

PITTSBURGH, PENNSYLVANIA 15222

ISBN: 978-1-4349-9324-3
Printed in the United States of America

First Printing

For more information or to order additional books, please contact:
RoseDog Books
701 Smithfield Street
Pittsburgh, Pennsylvania 15222
U.S.A.
1-800-834-1803
www.rosedogbookstore.com

For Betty, Claire, and Liz,
the women who make the mystery real for me.

Table of Contents

Forward

Every writing has its unquestioned assumptions. Axiomatic to this book is that we live in a world that is both an expression and a betrayal of a higher existence that seeks incarnation. I cannot prove that this is true nor will I try to do so. If personal experience and the hopes and strivings of mankind throughout history have not already convinced the reader of the validity of this axiom, I shall surely fail in my attempt. According to this assumption, wisdom is the guide in the incarnation process.

This wisdom assumes a broad and paradoxical metaphysical universe. The building blocks of this expansive universe are values as well as facts. Quality reigns supreme. Power is its handmaid. Implied by this metaphysics is an ontology, theology, epistemology, cosmology, and heuristic structure for problem solving, more broad than those to which we are accustomed. The importance of this bi-polar wisdom cannot be exaggerated. It opens the door to a new age, a better world. It guides us towards union with God. A supreme artistic expression of this wisdom in the works of Franz Schubert is what this book is all about.

This wisdom unites opposites in ever more inclusive unities. One set of opposites that is relevant to our topic is a pair of antithetical philosophies. One focuses upon judgments concerning factual relationships; the other focuses upon an ideal harmony of values in a higher world, traces of which are found in the shadow-land of value experience. The wanderer is the hero-subject who must unite these opposites. The wanderer is you, me, every man, every woman. In response to life's core invitation, he or she ascends through the actually existing world of fragmented value towards a better world of harmony that must be created according to patterns generated by the imagination of the wanderer. The actual universe of diverse and competing value fragments can only be united through the creative power of the wanderer. The cosmic journey is out of existing fragmentation (man-woman, self-other, heaven-earth, life-death) towards a harmonious whole, a wedding of sorts. The path of wisdom leads creatively out of alienation through life and death towards a mysterious, frightening, inviting, thrilling destination.

This wisdom demands revolutionary creativity of the wanderer and ascends towards the wedding of opposites not primarily by belief and obedience but by creatively and imaginatively reconciling the opposites in ever greater unities. The wisdom fosters an expansive yet discriminating religion in which the wanderer is called to be a problem solver who must creatively exercise a higher consciousness in making the kingdom come. The true drama of life according to this wisdom is a romance between a stranger adrift in a foreign land of value conflicts and an imperfectly incarnate "beloved" symbol of a barely imaginable new age of harmony between the self and the other and between the larger, universal Self and God. The romance of the Beloved leads the wanderer beyond alienation, beyond wars, and beyond death to a dream unity with the multiple others, and, through that unity, to an unimaginable unity with God.

This dramatic life-view has had a long and stormy history. I shall briefly review that history to make more accessible to the reader one of the most sublime mystical expressions of this wisdom in all of art. Then I will analyze the expression of this life-view in the art of Franz Schubert. The key to this analysis is the identification of correlations between the instrumental works and poetry already set by the composer as Lieder. Experience of these correlations is computer accessible. It is precisely these correlations of poetry and music in the instrumental compositions that open the door to the Schubert treasure. They give a fuller, deeper understanding of the man and his art in all its facets. They enable us to share his wisdom.

Schubert, an Austrian Catholic, celebrated this wisdom musically and symbolically. Always his celebrations express the central concern of Islam, Judaism, and Christianity: the sacralization of life. His creativity in expressing this sacralization underlies all of his music, giving it its spiritual depth. In his celebrations he sometimes used the language of traditional Roman Catholicism, sometimes the language of the Cabala, sometimes the language of pagan mythology. Concepts are sometimes expressed in the inspiring poetry that are common to Catholicism like the Trinity, the Incarnation, and redemption by Christ. At other times he employed ideas common to the Cabala like the hidden God self-revealing through a romance between a messianic light bringer and the light collector or Shekhinah. Islamic mysticism is everywhere. The divine suffuses the human._But for Schubert no idea, no belief is an absolute. Each is only a springboard into an experience of the great mystery that is the ground of the life experience. For him as for many Jewish cabalists and Sufi mystics the artistic approach to the *mysterium magnum* is universal, created for Everyman/Everywoman (whom we will call "the wanderer") who yearns for an ascent through yet beyond each narrow religious sect towards divine illumination and the hidden God.

The ascent to wisdom as it is revealed in the instrumental works trumps all ideas about it. All mystical formulas and ideas, all beliefs and laws, all human achievements and political systems, all philosophies and religions, all myths and parables are only partially successful efforts to grasp the drama of romances that are the heart of life's great mystery. They are all a middle ground between higher and lower worlds. They should be used in the ascent; but they must each be transcended. Everything in this middle ground is ambivalent, both expressing and betraying the sacred drama. Everything in this middle ground is split apart, divided into contradictions. This creates value conflicts, the fertile if painful springboard for the wanderer's ascent to higher worlds. The wanderer must pick his or her way carefully through this thicket.

Schubert's art is from beginning to end a celebration of this *magnum mysterium* of intercourse between worlds. The celebration transcends both fundamentalism and nihilism by replacing their clear ideas with the openly and intentionally ambivalent language of poetry. The words that everywhere inspire this art are graphic enough to suggest universal experiences yet are never a dogmatic prison demanding uncritical acceptance. In this art Schubert's wanderer, his alter-ego and ours, awakens to a mysterious invitation to a better world, an invittion incarnate in a woman. Her allure awakens the wanderer to the_need to leave home, the self, to discover a larger universe through union with the other. Yet the invitation that she mediates calls the wanderer beyond even her. Though she awakens him to the higher life she also betrays it. For Schubert's wanderer life's great challenge is to respond to the invitation by creatively interlacing two worlds, one transcendental and impossibly distant, the other close by but unreliable.

Unlike religious fundamentalism, this wisdom finds beliefs and laws poor substitutes for the experience of the romance. And unlike nihilism this wisdom finds the life experience meaningless apart from transcendental invitation. Paradise lies beyond the walls of the contradiction. Wisdom demands of each wanderer a reasoned and self-directed ascent through yet beyond orthodox religious ideas and beyond a superficial love of life and the earth to the transfiguration of earth by love.

Schubert's wanderer, the hero of the instrumental works and the subject in all his art, is himself, you, me, romancing the hidden God in and through the lower world, but simultaneously called to transcend and then re-discover that world in an experience of divine harmony. To truly taste this art is to dine on the food of the gods. It is to ascend to a higher wisdom. In Schubert's art the sweet mystery of life finds utterly sublime expression. If art of this sort interests you then profit from going further and enjoying the romance of the *magnum mysterium* as it has been so uniquely expressed through the musical magic of this composer who lived in Vienna from 1797 to 1828 and in those thirty-one years created a truly unique liturgy for the ascent of the soul.

PART ONE:
SCHUBERT AND THE MYSTERY

Towards a New Age

Oh world of beauty, where are you? Will you return?
Lovely, ancient blossom of nature!
Now only in poetry and song can we know you.

Even the fields mourn your passing;
No longer do divine spirits live here;
What was once alive and spirited
Is now a lifeless shadow.

Die Götter Greichenlands by Friedrich Schiller, D.667

The art of Franz Schubert expresses through poetry-inspired music an ascent into an ancient wisdom that beckons society towards a new and better world. Central to this wisdom is the belief that life is a journey of awakening to an invitation from a hidden God, an invitation leading out of chains and imprisonment to an undefined but variously imagined, promising, and trustworthy triumph of love. The pathway to that triumph leads through union of the self with the other, a union of opposites, ultimately passing through death to a mysterious transfiguration.

Schubert expresses this ancient wisdom through musical stories of a wanderer who represents each of us. The wanderer seeks a better world, following a divine call through life's joys and sorrows. Through poetry-inspired music Schubert expresses this paradoxical invitation in both its beauty and pain with consummate authenticity.

For Schubert the core life experience is one of indirect divine invitation. His wanderer's experience of the invitation is mediated through the value polarities of life. This middle ground consists of conflicting dynamic realities that attract the wanderer in opposing directions. Paradoxically in this universe of competing values there is also an attraction to unity. The divine harmony that attracts through these polarities has been called the Divine Sophia. She is true wisdom, the ideal spirit of the earth. Her imperfect incarnations take the form of men, women, children, lovers, the self and the other, the God of revelation and the divinely beautiful world, different religions, nations, and races, each a revelation, each a betrayal of their transcendental source.The incarnations shine and shimmer in the wanderer's life with an other-worldly radiance, refracting, reflecting the "distant star" that they imperfectly express. These contradictory incarnations, these values in conflict, attract and repel us with overwhelming power.

The universe of values is then the field upon which the romance between the hidden God and the wanderer is played. Each value properly seeks full self expression. Paradoxically it finds it only through union with other values.. Like the wanderer each value must both assert and transcend itself to find paradise. Like the wanderer each value must pass through life and death to reach the divine "home".

The wanderer encounters this sweet mystery of life, the *mysterium magnum,* in the reconcililiation of value conflicts. There is divine invitation in the tensions between the hidden value harmony, Sophia, and the fractured universe of divine incarnations. It is in these tensions that we encounter the living invitation of the hidden God. We are calling call this encounter the "rose cross mystery", the *mysterium magnum*.

The power of the *mysterium magnum* impressed Friedrich Schlegel:

Fülle der Liebe
Friedrich Schlegel D.854
On earth, the eyes are moist with tears,
Yet I am bathed in the heavenly apparition!
Its magic overcomes me;
It orders everything in my life!

The wisdom to embrace this mystery is paradoxically both rare and universal. It is missed by the fundamentalists and nihilists but underlies the mysticism of Judaism, Christianity, and Islam. The great Sufi mystic Umar Ibn al-Fărid expresses this as if it were splendid wine:

Ode To Wine
They tell me: "Describe it,
For you know it well!"
Indeed I do know it:

Purity that is not water;
Lightness that is not air;
Light that is not fire;
Spirit that is free of the body.

Be drunk from this wine, if only for an hour;
And you will make of time your slave.

Without this wine there is no life;
Be intoxicated with it,
Or be a fool!

The wisdom touching the *mysterium magnum* and celebrated by Umar Ibn al-Fărid is rare and elusive. Some distort it by thinking it nothing but a reasoned analysis of sensory experience. They reject any notion of an experience of a divine, personal invitation. Accordingly, they make an absolute out of science, power, pleasure, etc.

Others reduce the mystery to an ideology. They characterize it as an idea, a belief in an infallible church, a sacred book, a person, etc. The medium becomes the message. They fail to recognize that true wisdom, the *mysterium magnum*, the point at which the human touches the divine, embraces yet transcends every idea and feeling about religion, politics, science, and everything else.

The *mysterium magnum*_can be imperfectly experienced by uniting disparate experiences into a dramatic unity. The *Book of Ecclesiastes* puts it this way:

There is an appointed time for everything,
And time for every affair under heaven;
A time to be born and a time to die;
A time to plant and a time to uproot the plant;
A time to kill and a time to heal;
A time to tear down and a time to build;
A time to weep and a time to laugh;
A time to mourn and a time to dance.

The wisdom that touches the *mysterium magnum is* an awakening to the "now", i.e. to the deep meaning of what is happening. The awakening can be visualized in the form of a rose cross. The horizontal bar of the cross represents the romance between values in conflict in the bi-furcated experience of the wanderer. The vertical bar represents the intensely personal and life-giving invitation to the wanderer from the hidden God. The invitation is not direct. Rather it is mediated by ideas that try to unite the opposites. The imaginative and creative efforts of the wanderer to reconcile value conflicts condition the experiences of divine invitation. And divine invitation is experienced in the movement out of contradiction towards unity. The rose at the center of the cross is the "now" moment of the wanderer, who must reconcile the contradictions. The wanderer is called to resolve earth's contradictions and so romance the hidden God. The wanderer touches the *mysterium magnum* in awakening to the interlacing of earth and heaven in what actually is happening, a sometimes thrilling, sometimes painful, often challenging, always hope-filled "now".

We are calling the image of the hidden God that subtly attracts the wanderer the Divine Sophia. She is a distant star, the vague and unarticulated ideal of divine harmony that conditions the wanderer's creative efforts to synthesize contradictions. Awakening to her secrets and responding appropriately to her demands is the definition of wisdom. Schubert's art might be characterized as a series of love songs to this enigmatic Sophia. Schubert's wanderer pursues the romance of Sophia through efforts to create a better world by reconciling value conflicts. This is a painful challenge. The pain is intense enough to tempt the wanderer to abandon the ascent and escape its challenge. But the romance of Sophia is the way to freedom and the wanderer sings of the sadness and joy of the ascent.

The romance of Sophia in and through various life experiences is an accurate characterization of Schubert's art. Sufi mystics wrote of the romance of Sophia like this:

Because she appeared through incarnations,
Everyone thought that the incarnations were not her.
She emerged veiled, hidden from their eyes,
Each incarnation shaded and shaped differently.
......

She would appear and disappear in every age,
According to the needs of the time,
Appearing to lovers in many guises,
In shapes rare and beautiful.
Umar Ibn al-Fărid

In the eighteenth and nineteenth centuries German poets and dramatists, mightily influenced by Islamic mysticism, were celebrants of this romance. Their poetry anticipates a new age, a "land where roses bloom", where "the dead rise to new life", a land of "eternal May", "heaven", a "triumph of love". For most of these poets the new age meant life after death. But in addition it meant a new humanity, a new way of living and resolving value conflicts. It was an interlacing of opposing worlds. The new age would be an awakening of society expressed in part in the transformation of problem solving, a transformation achieved by rejecting neither religion nor science, rejecting neither a personal deity who is the divine "other", nor the divine spirit of the earth. It would embrace both God and goddess. But it would transcend each vision of the hidden God. It would seek that God not through a false absolute, whether that absolute be revelation, a church, science, technology, or any of the modern divinities. It would seek that hidden God in the transcendence of contradictions.

At the end of the eighteenth century one of history's explorers of the rose cross mystery and one of the fonts of German romanticism, Novalis, thought that a truly universal religion was just around the corner. It was soon to be the "heartbeat of the new age". He envisioned that new age as a dream maiden. She depended upon the emergence of a profoundly reformed Christianity raised above its tendency towards the tyranny of little absolutes. Society was spinning "a new veil for the virgin, revealing her heavenly shape". A feminine image of God was to take its proper place beside the traditional masculine one and be recognized as an equally sacred counterpoint to the traditional western idea of God. In that higher world religion and science would embrace. A new politics would be possible as the world awakens to the invitation to embrace the harmony that it had heretofore shunned.

This expectation of an ascent to a new age had been celebrated in Grail legends and in the seventeenth and eighteenth centuries Rosicrucian/Masonic lodges. It affected not only German romantics but also the creators of the United States of America. When would it appear? Novalis counseled patience to an impatient world:

> *When? When? That must not be asked. Just be patient. It will come.*
> *Christianity or Europe*

When Novalis wrote these words, a religion and a political system expressive of the rose cross mystery was a promising aroma in the air. A great awakening to divine harmony made possible by the spiritual adulthood of each wanderer seemed to be inviting from just around the corner. Economics and politics were in flux, becoming something new. But something essential was missing, something so important that without it the new age would dawn misshapen and poisoned. The reform of the religious orthodoxies that was expected did not happen. They had no recognition of their own limitations in expressing the *mysterium magnum*. Instead the orthodoxies preferred their limited ideas to the mystery. In response came an equally absolutistic rejection of religion. Although the "re-mystification" of religion through an encounter with the *mysterium magnum* was implicit in some of the most important art and political documents of the eighteenth and nineteenth centuries, both religious fundamentalism and nihilism rejected a mystery-centered religion, preferring their idols.

Yet the life-giving and peace-bestowing wisdom, so prized by Novalis, would not completely disappear. It can be experienced through the works of a Viennese composer of music who died in 1828 at the age of thirty-one. Nowhere did the ascent to this wisdom find more profound and radiant artistic expression than in Schubert's art. Through the interplay of heaven and earth his wanderer experiences the mystery that gives meaning to life, its triumphs, its failures, guilt, tragedy, and death. This encounter with the cosmic *mysterium magnum* was expressed by one of Schubert's poets like this:

The cool breeze blows softly over darkened fields.
The heavens alone are smiling from a thousand eyes!
One soul in-spirits the rolling waters,
Whispering its words through the forest trees.
Wave follow wave where spirits quietly mourn.
Word follows word wherever there is life.
For the mystic only the one sound is heard,
Underlying the manifold splendor of earth's great dream!
Friedrich Schlegel

and:

The small birds, high in the sky...
The towering mountains and the silver river
Winding like a snake through the valley...
The poet knows their true meaning!
They all sing like a choir,
One singer with many songs!
Friedrich Schlegel

The encounter with the *mysterium magnum* celebrated in Schubert's para-liturgies had by 1820 become politically incorrect. It was too revolutionary in its empowerment of the wanderer and gave too great an importance to "the world" for Roman Catholicism. At the same time it was and is too intensively spiritual for materialists. The twin poisons of fundamentalism and nihilism were on the rise. The paradoxical mystery became politically incorrect and remains so today. Yet the awakening of the wanderer to the rose cross wisdom through which contradictions are rconciled is our hope for a new age of peace and a deeper grasp of life's meaning.

Yes, but...... Franz Schubert... the heroic celebrant in music of an ancient tradition of transcendental invitation! Franz Schubert, the creator of a body of art that implies a profound reform of religious orthodoxy and a transformation of problem solving throughout society! Is Schubert not the most spiritually controversial of composers? He is called a moral pervert by some, an injudicious setter of laundry lists by others. This assertion of the mystical and profound nature of Schubert's art and of its relevance to our twenty-first century search for life's meaning is far outside of the mainstream of modern musicology. Is the claim not outrageous?

The more important books on Schubert include splendid works by Maurice Brown, Alfred Einstein, Brian Newbould, Dietrich Fischer-Dieskau, John Reed, Christopher Gibbs, Peggy Woodward, Elizabeth Norman McKay, Joseph Wechberg, George Marek, and the excellent notes by Graham Johnson appended to the Hyperion Lieder discs. All focus primarily upon facts about the composer's life. All rely heavily upon the *Thematic Catalogue* and *Memoirs by His Friends* by Otto Erich Deutsch. Occasionally they raise questions concerning the "meaning" of the music, but as a rule avoid the issue because it cannot be approached according to the rules of strict science. This has resulted in a diffidence concerning Schubert's inspiration that has not marred all of the writings on Mozart and Wagner.

In the effort to transcend this fact-centered approach to Schubert's intensely mystical art it has been necessary to enter into the touchy and misty area of inspiration. What was Schubert doing with his art? Is that art really understood when all we speak of are musical technicalities and historical facts? What actually inspired or drove the man to create what he did? What in his inner life found expression in his art? Maynard Solomon tackled these questions in his 1989 article *Franz Schubert and the Peacocks of Benvenuto Cellini* and in his response to Rita Steblin's critique of the article in the Summer, 1993 edition of *19th Century Music*. The 1989 article contained speculations concerning Schubert's sexuality and developed a Freudian understanding of his art. Solomon interpreted the considerable documentation of the heterosexual nature of Schubert and his circle of friends as an effort to conceal not only homosexuality, but something even less substantiated, child abuse. Schubert's art, Solomon guessed, was the product of irrepressible, irrational and subhuman drives. His personality was that of a helpless victim of these drives. His appetite for sex was characterized as "unorthodox" and "insatiable". His hedonism was "compulsive", an irresistible demand to act irrationally. His personality was gluttonous for food, drink, pleasure, rapture, beauty, and music. His "prodigious creativity" was "obsessive", a word suggesting the control of his mind by irrational forces. He had an overpowering drive towards "physical extinction". His "immersion in the sensuous moment" was his way of achieving that end. What Solomon characterized as Schubert's decision to die was, he thought, the "ultimate sign" of his exercise of free will. In 1989 Solomon considered this suicidal sexual compulsivity as "possibly the heroic region of Schubert's personality".

Not surprisingly this analysis elicited a heated response and a tense dialogue. Solomon's intimations of a near-psychotic Schubert and an art determined by psychosis were in conflict with tradition and sparked a hot debate. While some musicologists, especially Americans, found the thesis compelling, many others did not. In the Summer 1993 edition of *19th Century Music,* the respected music historian Rita Steblin, echoing and developing writings from the Viennese *Durch die Brille*, found Solomon's hypotheses "highly questionable". "To put it bluntly" she wrote, "there is no evidence that Schubert or members of his circle were homosexuals. Solomon has mistranslated several key documents, quoted selected passages out of context, and misrepresented the cultural and artistic context of society in Biedermeier Vienna. It does not speak well of our critical faculties that we are blind to the deficiencies of his argument. Schubert deserves better."

The controversy effected hints of a significant change of course by Solomon. In his 1993 response to Steblin (*19th Century Music*, Summer 1993) he defended portions of his original thesis but wrote that Schubert's art, presumably no longer irrational and determined by hedonistic compulsion, is rather the product of "a supreme mind" and of a "many sided human being". Rather than proposing a Freudian dictation by sexuality Solomon seemed almost Jungian in his suggestion of spiritual dimensions of the composer that counterbalanced and sublimated whatever his instincts prompted him to do. He underscored his recognition that his thesis concerning those instincts could not be proven and was highly speculative. He suggested that he merely wanted to throw something new into the mix on Schubert, and perhaps deepen a shallow understanding of this composer by suggesting new and theoretically possible explanations of his amazing art. In the wake of the controversy respected musicologists like Newbould and Gibbs have found many of Solomon's guesses non-compelling, questionable at best. Schubert's inspiration, recognized by all as complex, has remained a puzzle.

Insight into Schubert's inspiration is what this book is about. My interest is only obliquely in the "facts" of Schubert's life. This book is meant as a complement to names, dates, and technical insights provided by most other writers. I am interested primarily in Schubert's art as an expression of his encounter with the *mysterium magnum.* And yet I will base my thought upon a very fundamental fact: the inspiration of Schubert's instrumental compositions by poetry. That poetry will be the source of whatever value our thoughts have with respect to the unique art produced by this "supreme mind".

Nowhere is the mystery that inspired Schubert more completely revealed than in his instrumental works. Poetry that the composer set first as Lieder and then as movements of the instrumental compositions will be our guide. The inspiring poems can be identified with considerable security for most of the masterworks. (See the chapter "Magical Immersion in the Mystery.") These poems point, but only indirectly, to the adventures and misadventures of Schubert's real life, encouraging some hesitant speculation concerning the "facts" of that life. But they point directly to the Grail-like romance between higher and lower worlds that is everywhere expressed in the inner life adventures of a wanderer who is the subject of his musical tales. They reveal to us Schubert's priceless understanding of the rose cross mystery and an uncanny, magician's ability to give the mystery expression in music. The poems are sometimes radiant with the light, joy, and hope for a new age. Sometimes they are intensely darkened by the cruelty of fate in actual life. The light is almost blinding. The darkness is terrifying. But the divine invitation is never lacking.

Schubert's expression of the rose cross mystery was rare and precious, an experience of the Rosicrucian, German-Jewish, Christian-Islamic symbiotic wisdom that was having an impact upon Europe at the end of the eighteenth and beginning of the nineteenth centuries, promising a union of races, nations, and religions in the spiritual ascent. Schubert's art stands together with the music of Bellini, Donizetti, Verdi, Mozart, and Beethoven, the paintings of romantics like Runge, Friedrich, and the Hudson River School, literary works such as those by Mendelssohn, Lessing, Schiller, the brothers Grimm, and the political events in the New World, all celebrating a divine invitation to a paradoxical transfiguration of our war-torn and fragmented world.

I respect the giant steps that musicology has already taken in analyzing Schubert's art. My approach is different from most of these efforts. I strongly suggest that my perspective is a valid and essential complement to them, and no less based upon fact. This book hopefully will enable the reader to experience more deeply the life-transforming mystery suggested by the fourth movement of the unfinished *Seventh Symphony*, inspired by this poem by Novalis:

The world is radiant with a new light.
At last it is home!
Down to the bottom of the sea
The fear of death is gone
And we embrace life with joy.

My decision to focus upon the rose cross mystery as "liturgically" expressed in Schubert's art is unusual to say the least and should be explained. I was a Roman Catholic priest in the Archdiocese of Washington, D.C. I was ordained in Rome, December, 1958. I received from the Gregorian University a license to teach Roman Catholic theology. Ten years later, in 1968, together with a number of other priests in Washington, D.C., I took public issue with the papal encyclical *Humanae Vitae* that continued the ban on birth control, denying the rights of conscience. With most of these others I was transferred and suspended. Shortly afterwards I left the priesthood, married, and had my life enriched by my wife and two daughters. The priesthood that I have left and my married life combine to influence my choice of perspective. I suggest however that they do not distort but may enhance my perceptions on the matter I have chosen for discussion.

I write this book for wisdom addicts, seekers of the Grail, agonized lovers of an ultimately indefinable and wildly improbable new age to be expressed both internally in a higher consciousness of the mystery and externally in its expressions in society. The mystery will always mean an embrace of the divine invitation which appears both in the incredible hope and beauty and in the chaotic darkness and bone-numbing terror of our conflicted lives. Such a call assumes a broad and somewhat unfamiliar metaphysics, creating a divine harmony out of the opposites of intuition and reason, facts and drama, matter and spirit, messianic and sophianic figures, the human and the divine, heaven and earth, God and creation, joy and sorrow, life and death. Reverence for the *mysterium magnum* creates a hunger for religious and political reform that could facilitate society's ascent to a new age.

The interplay between heaven and earth that Schubert celebrates hovers like a distant but powerful star above our war-torn world. I suggest that through this art we can touch that star and experience more completely its attraction. For we are called, even now as our nations and churches sink ever more deeply into the horrors of fundamentalism and nihilism, to make the impossible dream real and bring the light of the distant star to earth. In the face of religious wars, racial hatreds, national paranoia, barbaric insensitivity to human values on the part of both governments and citizens, in the face of the massive failures of all forms of government including democracy and the unprecedented power of the greedy and the stupid to destroy the earth, in the face of mass death and destruction, wisdom calls us silently and powerfully to ascend creatively to a better world. It calls us to a reverential embrace of the *mysterium magnum.*

In celebrating the *mysterium magnum* as it appears in Schubert's art I write not to bury the orthodoxies or modernity but to save them. Although it will not seem so to some, I am both profoundly Catholic and enthusiastically of my age. I do not want to harm either my church or modernity. I do want to reform them. The church and the world that I seek are the church and the world sought by millions of others of all faiths, races, and nations. The unique values of each orthodoxy must not be lost. Each should reach its apotheosis ... in a higher unity with others than is now possible. Now is the hour for Catholic, Protestant, Jew, and Muslim to prize above all else the transcendental mystery that seeks incarnation in beliefs and laws which both express and betray it. Now is the hour to experience the missing soul of the new age: the romance of the hidden God through creative immersion in the rose cross wisdom. For many of us Schubert can help.

A Larger Metaphysical Universe

Through all the harmonies of
earth's many colored dream...
One faint sound permeates all...
For one attuned to the mystery!
Friedrich Schlegel

The quest for the secret wisdom which unlocks the mysteries of life and opens the gate to a new and better age is perennial. Getting the paradoxical secret right is the challenge. Simplification has been the problem. Goethe equated the secret with nature. Hegel equated it with historical process. Hitler equated it with race. Stalin equated it with the power of the masses. Some Americans have decided that the secret is democracy. Others think it is free trade. The secret according to some Jews is the state of Israel. While these visions of the *mysterium magnum* are exclusively worldly, religious fundamentalists make the opposite mistake. The mystery for many Evangelical Protestants is a personal relationship with Jesus Christ. The mystery for many Roman Catholics is belief in and obedience to church teaching. The mystery for many Muslims is the Koran. There can be no doubt that such expressions/distortions of the rose cross mystery are empowering windows to the divine. Yet each of them also limits the mystery. Unless the limitation is acknowledged it creates a hatred for portions of the world and thus for the hidden God whose life radiates through them all. Limitations of the mystery that are unrecognized as such are a poison with immense destructive power.

The art of Schubert is a celebration of his nuanced and liberating grasp of the meeting point between the divine and the human that we are calling the *mysterium magnum.* For this composer the liberating mystery meant a romance, both between opposites and between the transcendental and partially hidden God and the soul. His wanderer embraces life as a journey, a dramatic becoming, an adventure in which both joy and sorrow have a part. A wanderer is sent into a foreign land, exiled from his heavenly home. There he becomes aware of being alien, a stranger. He begins to find himself in a romance of a woman. He and his beloved ascend/descend through life/death to a transcendental homecoming. Throughout his life Schubert gave artistic expression to this world-transfiguring drama that leads through life and death to a mysterious transfiguration. For example Schubert once used as poetic inspiration these words of Franz Schober concerning the end of the journey:

> ***Todesmusik D758***
> Franz Schober
> *Then will the sweet and heavenly harmonies envelop me!*
> *My chains will become light and fall away!*
> *I will see all the wonders of my life which brought me joy;*
> *All the beauty that bloomed in my life will stand…transfigured before me!*

This ascent to world transfiguration was so important to the composer that he used the same poem to inspire the following masterworks:

- o The *"Unfinished" Symphony*, D.759 in its entirety;
- o The *"Wanderer" Fantasy,* D.760, the third section;
- o The *Piano Trio in B Flat,* D.898, the first movement.

In the *mysterium magnum* divine life erupts everywhere. But nowhere is it more stupendous than in the wedding of divine invitation and the spark of hope in the wanderer.

> **Die Allmacht**
> Ladislaus Pyrker D.852
> *Great is Jehovah the Lord!…*
> *Hear divine life in the whisper of the green forest;*
> *See it in the golden fields of corn;*
> *And in the splendor of the spring flowers.*
> *But still more does your heart reveal that life,*
> *When it looks longingly up towards God,*
> *And trusts in divine love and mercy!*

This poetry inspired not only a, Lied D.852, but also portions of two masterworks:

The *Ninth Symphony* (D.944), fourth movement
The *Piano Trio in E Flat* (D.927), fourth movement

Embracing the mystery the wanderer is one with nature in a shared journey. But there is a difference. Nature is at home, already fulfilled in her journey.

The wanderer is still far from home. This alienation of the wanderer, his status as a stranger in a foreign land, was a constant theme of this composer's art. The first two movements of the *Ninth Symphony* celebrate it. It was beautifully expressed in the following Lied:

> **The Wanderer to the Moon**
> Johann Gabriel Seidl D.870
> *I wander about, alien in a strange land, homeless, unknown;*
> *You, however, wander all over, from eastern cradle to western grave,*
> *You visit and leave many a land,*
> *But wherever you are you are home.*

Schubert, celebrating the *magnum mysterium*, the earth-transfiguring romance of heaven, tells the story of an alter-ego, a wanderer, a stranger in a foreign land who wants to go "home". He is tired of a "land strange to ideals". He thirsts for his true homeland where love is queen. But 'going home' is inextricably tied to his romance of an imperfect incarnation of Sophia, the divine image, a dream maiden. The goddess is sometimes a mystical presence, sometimes absent, sometimes nature, sometimes the mother of Jesus, sometimes Theresa Grob, sometimes Karoline Esterhazy. In her the loving invitation of God to come home is both made incarnate and betrayed. In her eyes is divine allure and deception. Her powerful spirit at times fills the earth, transfiguring nature. Often, tragically, she disappears, leaving the wanderer's life a sorrow. But always there is the promise of a triumphant return, a mysterious love fulfillment, a mystical wedding that mysteriously transcends death. It is "on the other side" where all will be well. For Schubert God is inconceivable apart from these experiences of the *magnum mysterium*. Worship of God, "Going home", and union with the purified dream maiden are all mysteriously connected.

The allure of the dream maiden is to a sometimes puzzling, sometimes frustrating, sometimes terrifying, sometimes awesomely beautiful ascent to the stars. That ascent with its transfiguration of the wanderer's life assumes a metaphysics that has profound implications for theology, epistemology, and problem solving. In that metaphysics there is but one Absolute, the hidden God. Everything else is a mix. This changes religion from a matter of belief and obedience into a discerning and responsible ascent through the compromised mists of the actual towards the uncompromised but ever-elusive ideal. That ascent is in response to the personal but indirect divine invitation experienced through divine images found in the creative and intuitive experiences of the wanderer and imperfectly enunciated in revelation. This romance is the core experience of life. It changes politics from a rule by the powerful to the creation of a problem solving society where individual wanderers are empowered to transfigure their portions of society in a flexible accord with both the past and present experience. It demands the empowerment of the individual. The new age is seen as a time when catatonic subservience to the powerful and paranoid is transcended in a kingdom where freedom and love are triumphant.

In the triumph of love that beckons in the *mysterium magnum* nothing remains the same.

The *magnum mysterium* as seen by Schubert challenges the *status quo*. It transcends every institution. In this politically incorrect tradition the hidden God attracts indirectly through the goddess. Heaven attracts through the earth. The divine other and the self must unite to discover the hidden God. "Home" is where opposites are united. There neither heaven nor earth disappear but are mutually enhanced. The ascent to a higher consciousness of the "Now" is a discriminating but inclusive ascent through ideologies and the multitude of human experiences. Nothing of value is lost. In this mystery there is a radically intensified but discriminating embrace of the bi-polarity that both reveals and hides the source of the divine invitation.

We read about this mystery in Jewish writings when they celebrate the Divine Sophia. In her is captured the truly sublime splendor of creation transfigured by the light of God. She is the Mother of creation. She pre-existed creation as we know it, and somehow is the goal of its becoming. She speaks as follows:

The Lord begot me, the firstborn of his ways...
From of old I was poured forth, at the first, before the earth...
While as yet the earth and fields were not made...
He who finds me finds life, and wins favor from the Lord.
Book of Proverbs

Genesis One celebrates the mystery of the great romance between heaven and earth. God is known through the divine image, Sophia. God is known in terms of sexual love, the reconciliation of contradiction that generates new life. The image of God as a romance is the model for the love union of man and woman and is the ultimate model for the Christian Trinity.

God created man in his image:
in the divine image her created him;
male and female he created them.
God blessed them saying:
Be fertile and multiply...

In the *Book of Wisdom* of the *Old Testament* the image of God has a feminine face. She is the Divine Sophia. She learns from God and teaches the wanderer. The spirit of this dream maiden is to permeate all of creation, making it the perfect image of God.

She is an aura of the might of God and a pure effusion of the glory of the Almighty...
In her is a spirit...all-powerful, all seeing...pervading all spirits...
She is the refulgence of eternal light,

> *The spotless mirror of the power of God.*
> *She who is one can do all things...passing into holy souls from age to age...*

The Divine Sophia, the dream of creation, is the goal of our Becoming. She is what we are called to be. She is what is highest and best in us and in the cosmos. And she is our link with God. The intoxicating wine of the Sufi mystic Umar Ibn al-Fărid gave us a taste of her. Through her gradual and often painful incarnations a new age is being prepared. That new age is the "Holy City", "the new Jerusalem", the "bride ready for her husband" all mentioned in the New Testament Book of Revelation.

> *Then I saw a new heaven and a new earth...I also saw the Holy City, a new Jerusalem, coming down out of heaven from God, prepared as a bride adorned for her husband.*

This beloved in a romance with God and the Christ-like lover in a romance of the wanderer is far more than a creature of the imagination. She is in and of our world. She is the deepest, partially hidden, elusive Truth that beckons through experience. Sophia through her various incarnations is the alluring middle ground between the hidden God and the wanderer. In that middle ground Being inhabits and attracts becoming. She is the treasure underlying and partially hidden in divine revelation. And she can be found in the depths of the experience of nature, spouse, children, friends, job, etc. She both fills the earth and yet is the earth-transcendence hidden there. Until she is discovered and loved God remains hidden and unknowable. The awakening of the wanderer to her means an awakening to the divine invitation that is present but partially hidden in every part of the life experience.

The search by Christian Europe for this dream maiden who brings heaven to earth has a history. At the beginning of the thirteenth century the search for her took the form of a hunt for the Holy Grail. Grail legends were written by Chrétien de Troyes and Robert Boron in France and Wolfram von Eschenbach in Germany. The search was prompted by agonies caused by the stupidity of religious wars. What had once seemed to be wise now appeared to many as foolish. The *magnum mysterium* was evidently not to be found in a self-aggrandizing war against Islam. And yet the elusive but redemptive mystery was surely hidden in the interweaving of the dramas of religious and daily life. The symbol of this elusive secret was the Grail, the holder of the Eucharist. Wisdom, it was thought, consisted somehow in a blend of experiential mysticism and philosophy, religion and science, heaven and earth, the divine and the human. The mystery was to be experienced at the point at which the opposites are reconciled. Finding that point would be a key to a new age.

In the first of these Grail stories Chrétien suggested that the Grail, a feminine power, a dish holding the messianic Eucharist, could bring peace and honor to the knight Perceval. The search for the Grail involved the hero in an effort to transform his brutish knightly life in accord with the love/death of

Jesus Christ. This implied a challenging integration of divine invitation and the daily struggles of life.

Wolfram gave us a German version of the wisdom myth. His wisdom was symbolized by a heavenly stone that had the power to shower every joy and blessing upon its possessor. The stone was attainable only by way of an intellectual search, a reasoned challenging of the actual order of ideas in quest of a new order that could embrace the new experiences.

For both Chrétien and Wolfram the Grail meant a new religious and political order that would not destroy, but rather complement and fulfill tradition. The new order would demand a creative re-arrangement of the actual world, a reconciling of contradictions, to be effected by the wanderer. Understanding this interplay implied a metaphysical revolution that rejected a simple truth-error paradigm derived from church authority in favor of an organic one of reconciling value conflicts according to a subtle experience in the concrete situation of the invitation to a better world. This implication suggested a reframing of tensions between religions, between men and women, between power groups, between opposites at every level. It suggested that Truth can and often must be discovered by transcending simple ideas. It suggested that the individual problem solver has a puzzling but real empathy with the divine image and must courageously and creatively seek the incarnation of this image through the reconciliation of contradictions. Conseuently this Grail wisdom implied the social empowering of the individual wanderer as a unique problem solver.

But is this metaphysical sea-change valid? Is the resolution of value conflicts not a choice between truth and error? Should value positions not resolve their contradictions by a power contest as if one value is right, the other wrong? Fifteen hundred years before the Grail stories this question was given some attention by Greek philosophers. Some thinkers saw value conflict as an opposition between perfection and imperfection in the expression of Being. A case in point was the tension between masculinity and femininity. In an arbitrary selection between the opposites one side, man alone, was deemed fully human. What was fully present in a man was thought to be only partially present in a woman. The ethic followed. Morally, politically, socially woman must be subordinate to man. The man-woman tension was the microcosm through which the macrocosm of problem solving in the case of value conflicts was seen. In a particular value conflict one value was chosen as an absolute. The other value was seen only as its inadequate expression or even its enemy. Pythagoreans and Sophists adopted this position.

Variations on the tyranny of an "absolute" value over a conflicting value followed. Parmenides and Plato resolved sexual conflict in a kind of political compromise. They suggested treating men and women as if man were not superior to woman. This was a practical compromise to bring peace and not a theoretical breakthrough. They held that in fact man is superior to woman. A variation of this "practical approach" to the Being/Becoming tension is the American system of majority rule in which a working and workable ethic is sought through a low common denominator compromise between a governing ideology and enough of its enemies to produce a winning coalition.

More promising implications for the resolution of value conflicts emerged in the writings of Sappho and Empedocles. With respect to the man/woman tension the opposites were judged to be equal in dignity but in important but undefined ways different and complementary. The complementarity contributed to the "journey", the production of an offspring. Becoming was to be realized through the creative union of the opposites. True humanity lies above and beyond the distinction, beyond the parts, in a creative union which is far more than the sum of its parts. The values in conflict should be reconciled in a higher unity, not subordinated one to the other. The name often given to this creative union is love.

At stake was the use of war as the preferred problem-solving mechanism. With Aristotle this hope for a more vast and truly liberating understanding of value conflicts, was throttled. His response to the man/woman value conflict was a return to the inferior metaphysics of a linear truth-error paradigm. A principle to particular application was the preferred way to resolve value conflicts. This meant the subordination of woman to man. Woman, defined only as an imperfect man, was inferior. Man's seed was defined as the sole determinant of the child's makeup. Woman was only a limiting principle. Implied was the subordination of race to race, of nation to nation, of religion to religion. Opposites were condemned to a paranoid-catatonic relationship. Sexual tyranny was legitimized.

This reality-distorting resolution of value conflicts that is graphically expressed in the tension between man and woman was and is tragically flawed. It is blind to the bi-polarity that characterizes every human understanding of the divine. It is blind to the simultaneous expression and limitation of Being that every value, every expression of Becoming, is. It is blind both to the Being realized in all Becoming and to the limitation of Being present in every Becoming. It is the antithesis of the rose cross mystery. In this mystery a divine harmony between opposing values invites the wanderer, every wanderer, both into and beyond ideologies, into and through every religious and political system. This is because true wisdom means a romance of the wanderer not with some ideas about God but with the hidden source of divine invitation.

The romance between the hidden God and the wanderer through the romance of a unity of opposites has a long history. Hermes Trismegistus was the ancient Egyptian god of wisdom who was reputed to be the author of all the sacred hermetic books. Some of them survive in the form of the *Corpus Hermeticum*, writings compiled in perhaps the third century A.D. that combine Christian and far more ancient pagan visions. The *Corpus Hermeticum* was an important inspiration for the Renaissance. The most famous of its books is the *Poimandres*. In it we find an archetypal myth dealing with the romance between the *Nous,* God, and the wanderer made incarnate through a romance between the opposites, man and nature.

> *Now the Nous, the Father of all beings, being life and light, brought forth a man similar to himself, whom he loved as his own child. For the Man was beautiful, reproducing the image of his Father; for it was indeed with his own form that God fell in love and gave over to him all his works. ...*
>
> *The man who had full power over the world of mortal beings and animals, leant across the armature of the spheres, having broken through their envelopes, and showed to the Nature below the beautiful form of God. When Nature saw that she had in him all the inexhaustible beauty and energy of the Governors joined to the form of God she smiled with love, for she had seen the features of that marvelously beautiful form of man reflected in the water and his shadow on earth. And he, having seen his image in Nature, reflected in the water, loved her and wished to dwell with her...Nature, receiving her beloved, embraced him and they were united, burning with love.*

Reality in the myth is not simply a web of factual relationships. It is a creative love drama, a bi-polar romance of opposites, an ascent through their reconciliation. The relationship between man and God is realized through the reconciliation of opposites, symbolized and realized in the loving union of man and woman, humanity and nature. Love replaces belief and obedience as the preferred human ethic.

This insight into Truth as an experiential ascent through contradictions towards a divine harmony had a powerful impact upon fifteenth and sixteenth century Europe. According to Frances Yates of Oxford, the translation into Latin of the *Poimandres* in 1453 awakened the yearning for a new age expressive of this respect for the goddess (i.e. for the image of God in the world) and produced a vigorous search for her secrets. The immediate result of the search challenged Europe's best minds to purify and transcend the simplistic beliefs and laws derived from church and scripture in new and higher visions that demanded the exercise of creative reason. They sought new idea syntheses that could accommodate their rapidly changing life experiences. To gain this freedom from religious fundamentalism they established secret societies. This triggered a reaction from Rome which in turn triggered an opposite and ominous reaction within the secret societies. The societies gradually changed from being celebrants of the *magnum mysterium* into being agents of nihilism. Their power for both good and evil is underscored in a book by James Billington. He wrote in *Fire in the Minds of Men* that the secret societies have had a profound effect upon virtually every major geo-political movement of our time, both good and bad.

JUDAISM AND THE MYSTERY

The Jewish approach to the *magnum mysterium* had a powerful influence upon Schubert. A study of the opera *Alfonso und Estrella* suggests that the Cabala with its unique grasp of the rose cross mystery was a dominant formative force for the Viennese composer. This account of Jewish mysticism is by a non-Jew and is offered with necessary apologies. But a non-Jewish appreciation of the immense splendor of Judaism was an essential part of Schubert's approach to the mystery and remains today a limited but irreplaceable element in the creation of a new age.

Franz Schubert was a Catholic who was aware of his profound enrichment by Judaic mysticism. His tales of the wanderer are everywhere inspired by the Cabala. Catholicism and Judaism were complementary and critically important sources of his inspiration, so much so that it is possible to characterize his work as the artistic crown of the monumentally important symbiosis of Judaic and Christian mysticism that occurred in Germany during the eighteenth and early nineteenth centuries. From Catholicism Schubert was enriched by the central mystery of the invitation to definitively transcend the lower world through union with the Messiah in passing through death. From Jewish Cabalism he was enriched by the sacred meaning of life. This intersection of Judaism and Catholicism determined his grasp of the *magnum mysterium*. These complementary/contradictory mysticisms in Schubert's art are essential and irreplaceable components.

The Jewish mystic sometimes approaches the mystery through myth. The Tree of Life is a mythical analysis of the manifestation of divine light in creation. The manifestation is realized progressively through the issuing of light from the hidden God, light that is realized in a series of opposites. The final manifestation of divine light, the tenth Sefirot, is the Shekhinah. Her responsibility is to change the darkness of the world of diminished and fragmented light into radiant harmony. This is done by re-uniting the lower world of contradictory values, gradually transfiguring it. The fragmented lower world is the *Qelippah* into which she has fallen. The process of changing the lower into the higher world is called *Tiqqun*. Once awakened to her task and empowered by Kether, the first sefirot and the primal light-bringer, she seeks to become the perfect image of God, separating light from darkness. She begins her task enchained, a prisoner of hostile forces in the *Qelippah*. She finishes her task in the fullness of divine light. In cabalistic mythology she is the Jewish people. The parallel between the Shekhinah and Estrella in the opera *Alfonso und Estrella* is too compelling to ignore.

In Judaism's Tree of Life the divine manifestation in the Shekhinah is slowly formed as she gathers into one the light fragments. Kether, the bearer of the divine light of the hidden God, seeks out his Beloved, the Shekhinah in every corner of creation. Creation becomes the image of God through their creative inter-working. Becoming ascends towards Being. There is here a romance between God's bride on one hand and a messianic light-bringer, a romance which defines the contact with the otherwise hidden God.

The ideal harmony of light fragments that is the goal of the process or Tiqqun is sometimes called the Divine Sophia. Hers is the kingdom of love, the ultimate achievement in *Alfonso und Estrella*.. She stands above the actual order as its ideal, a channel of divine invitation who is experienced obliquely in all value. Her attraction is through dimly sensed reconciliations of the tensions encountered in value experience and symbolized in the Tree of Life. Sophia is above history, above the Jewish people, above every thing. Yet she demands incarnation in history, in the Jewish people, in every thing. Jewish mysticism suggests an ascent to a new age of value harmony. The invitation is to create a gradual incarnation of the divine image. This invitation lies at the heart of the rose cross mystery and is a constant theme in Schubert's musical art.

The redemptive myth of the ancient Jews tells of their symbolic selection to be the Beloved of God, the one in whom creation reaches its zenith. The *Torah* is a record of a people's awareness of this life-altering invitation. The history of this people has ever been a series of re-awakenings to it. It has also been an effort to transcend tribalism in a universal and cosmic vision of divine invitation. Prominent in their consciousness is God's romance of his people. They experience the divine call to a new age. For example, Isaiah was aware of this invitation:

The spirit of the Lord is upon me;
He has sent me to bring tidings to the lowly,
To heal the brokenhearted,
To proclaim liberty to the captives
And release to the prisoners...

God is powerful and angry with the enemies of this new age.

Here is your God.
He comes with vindication;
With divine recompense he comes to save you.

He promises success in the venture.

Those whom God has ransomed will return and enter Zion singing, crowned with everlasting joy!

Isaiah

For millions of Jews this invitation to lead the world in a romance with God has given life its meaning. It has been their hold upon the *magnum mysterium.* The interplay between heaven and earth, between God and his people, is played out daily. Its goal is the day of grace that ends Schubert's great opera. The culmination of the drama lies in the nebulous but trustworthy future. But even in the present each person plays a part.

One of the great treasures that the Cabala brings to Jews and through them to the world is a higher consciousness of the role individuals play in this romance. Messianic figures (like Alfonso) bring divine light into the world. Sophianic figures (like Estrella) attract these messiahs and make the new light their own. This bi-polarity assumes a quasi-sexual nature of the romance between heaven and earth as we have already observed in the *Book of Genesis.* God made human beings in his image, male and female. The command he gave was to unite, produce offspring, and create in the image of the Creator. Values in conflict are polarized. They must unite. Man and woman are godly precisely in their romance of one another.

God created man in his image; in the divine image he created him; male and female he created them...and he found it very good...

...and God blessed them saying: Be fertile and multiply; fill the earth and subdue it.

In the *Book of Wisdom* we read of the bi-polar relationship between the wanderer and the Divine Sophia. She is both beloved of God and the beloved of man.

I loved her and sought her from my youth. I wanted her for my bride. In her is companionship with God.

The Book of Wisdom

Sophia, the perfect image of God, is at once heavenly and earthly wisdom, the key to the mystery. She is the Being that lures all Becoming. She is heavenly harmony as it relates to the earth. And although she is a distant star far above the wanderer she fills the earth with her beauty; she is everywhere, the ideal towards which earth ascends.

> *Indeed she reaches from end to end mightily, governing all things well.*
> *The Book of Wisdom*

The romance of Sophia is the aim of the man who is truly wise. Union with God is realized through union with her.

> *Her I loved and sought after from my youth. I sought to take her for my bride and was enamored of her beauty. She brings with her the splendor of companionship with God. ...The Book of Wisdom*

God is known indirectly but really through Sophia. She guides the romance of opposites; she is the alluring goal of that romance.

> *All that is created by the Ancient of Ancients can live and exist only by a male and a female.*
> *The Zohar*

Sophia is the divine harmony that sounds throughout creation. She can be heard in the hero and in the recluse. She is the pearl beyond price, the hope of all mankind. She is God's bride. She is the love union, the cosmic harmony that unites opposites. And she is the force that moves the opposites towards union. The Judaic Sophia is not a feminine God. She is the sweet, gentle invitation to become what the wanderer can and will be. She is the way that he or she knows God. Graced by her the soul is led to union with God. In priceless Judaic poetry this mythical feminine dwelling place of God is celebrated.

> *She (Wisdom, the divine Sophia) is an aura of the might of God...*
> *And a pure effusion of the glory of the Almighty...*
> *She is the refulgence of eternal light,*
> *The spotless mirror of the power of God.*
> *The Book of Wisdom*

Sophia stands between man and God as the point of contact of the wanderer with the mystery. Through her God loves man and man experiences divine invitation. The Jewish bard sings simultaneously of two romances, one a love tryst between the Divine Sophia and God, the other a love tryst between the wanderer and his Beloved, the Divine Sophia.

> *My lover is like a gazelle or a young stag;*
> *Here he stands behind our wall gazing through the windows,,*
> *Peering through the lattices.*
> *My lover speaks; he says to me,*

"Arise my beloved, my beautiful one,
And come!

Oh my dove in the clefts of the rock...
Let me see you and hear your voice,
For your voice is sweet and you are beautiful!
Song of Songs

In the *Song of Songs,* the mystical incarnation of a relationship to God is the man-woman romance.

More delightful your love than wine...Draw me! I follow eagerly! Bring me to your chambers!

The Divine Sophia is as real as the experience of the mysterious invitation which lies at the root of all consciousness. Yet she is ever beyond us, a transcendental ideal that attracts yet is never possessed. Her call is always to ascend. Yet that call is received within the context of value conflicts in the life situation. The vertical and horizontal bars of the rose cross must intersect. So the Divine Sophia must be distinguished from the Earthly Sophia, the incarnate Shekhinah, who struggles to realize her divine identity within the context of value conflicts. Through the reconciliation of contradictions she is painfully preparing for her wedding. This happens gradually, with many reverses.

The symbolic romance through which the Shekhinah painfully assumes her proper glory as the bride of God is important because men and women have been exiled from their true home of love's unity. They are wanderers in a strange land, yearning to return home. The earthly Sophia has feet of clay. She must be helped by a divine lover. She does not always accept this help. The theme of an often-tragic romance between the Lord God and Sophia's incarnation in the Jewish people is developed by the prophet Ezekiel.

I swore an oath to you and entered into a covenant with you, says the Lord God...You were exceedingly beautiful, with the dignity of a queen. You were renowned among the nations for your beauty, perfect as it was, because of my splendor which I had bestowed upon you, says the Lord God. But you...played the harlot.

In order to come to this elusive wisdom of knowing the Divine Sophia, the Bride of God, a Cabalist in Spain, probably Moses de Leon, in 1280 composed the main parts of the *Zohar* or *Book of Splendor* as commentaries upon the ascent into what we are calling the rose cross mystery, the *magnum mysterium*. This work was to be a source of doctrine and revelation for Jews equal in stature to the Bible and Talmud for the three hundred years leading up to the Enlightenment. It guided Jews in their reading of Scripture. It took the illuminated reader beneath the surface of stories and laws, beneath the concepts articulated in the scripture, to a more spiritual, hidden mystery, an experience of the Divine Sophia. It thereby enabled the reader to ascend more effectively to a higher consciousness.

> *Woe to the sinners who look upon the Torah as simply tales pertaining to things of the world, seeing thus only the outer garment. But the righteous whose gaze penetrates the very Torah, happy are they! Just as wine must be in a jar to keep, so the Torah must be contained in an outer garment. That garment is made up of tales and stories; but we are bound to penetrate further.*
> *The Zohar*

According to the Zohar the wanderer must stand astride the chasm separating the partial myopia of ideas from the living but limited experience of divine invitation. He is the quintessential wanderer who straddles two imperfect worlds in tension, one the world of ideas, the other the world of experience. The responsibility gives him a great dignity. This is made obvious in chapter thirty-two of *Genesis.* Here we find an extension of the human nobility theme sounded in the first chapter. Jacob, a symbol of the experience of transcendental invitation, wrestles all night with an angel of God, symbol of religious tradition, who cannot defeat him. For this Jacob is praised and rewarded! He is from that point on to be called "Israel", one who wrestles with God's angel (religious orthodoxy) in loyalty to a higher truth. Here is celebrated once again the divine dignity of man made in God's image, who has the personal and individual responsibility and the power to ascend through the contradictions of life and the limitations of orthodoxy to a new and higher cosmic harmony, the Kingdom of Love.

Sophia, the hidden wisdom, transcends this world and all her incarnations in it. But she is met through worldly incarnations like the Torah, the Jewish people, sexuality. The romance of Sophia through one of her incarnations is a thing of the moment. It is a glimpse of sa higher sysnthesis that makes sense of presenting contradiction.

Schubert's art of suggesting transcendental reality through a screen of myth emanates out of the Cabala. Cabalistic wisdom drives deeper, beyond surface meanings, literal meaning of scripture to what trranscends the written word. It compares the experience of finding Sophia in scripture to that of catching a glimpse of

> *...a beautiful and stately maiden ... She is aware that her lover is hovering about the palace, and what does she do? She thrusts open a small door in her secret chamber, shows her face to her lover, then quickly withdraws it...So it is with the Torah. — The Zohar.*

For the wisdom-rich *Book of Splendor* or *Zohar* Sophia lies beyond and above the contradiction between words and experience. She is grasped when words and experience unite in a reflective and willing sensitivity to and participation in the living romance between heaven and earth. She is the true meaning of the moment, the truth of the "Now". This elusive truth may be thought of as being cut out by the opposing blades of a scissors, one blade an imaginative and creative abstraction of creation's story, the other blade the ongoing life experience. The wanderer/mystic does the cutting. The *Zohar* encourages the reader to pray for wisdom with King David:

> *Open thou mine eyes that I may behold wondrous things out of thy law.*

Reason and revelation, the divine and the human, man and woman, are instances in an ocean of opposites that must be united through the creative imagination of the truly wise. Midrash is just such an imaginative exposition of biblical texts by learned Jewish scholars. The expositions are often deeply spiritual and intended to develop a sense of divine immanence and piety, i.e. a sense of the attraction that Being exercises upon Becoming. They seek to transcend the limitations of ideas and tradition in the living experience of divine Being. The Jewish cabalist does not seek to replace reason with revelation or orthodox tradition with new insights but rather to unite these opposites. The Creator is not experienced directly, but rather indirectly as wisdom, Sophia, the hidden source of attraction in the process of transfiguring a world of opposites in luminous unity. In the ascent to Sophia actual contradiction and limitation are transcended in a creative and imaginative ascent towards the ideal.

The meaning of history is a movement towards the full incarnation of the Divine Sophia and the coming divine wedding between heaven and earth. The earthly incarnations of Sophia include both man and woman, both lightbringers and light incorporators. They must become the perfect manifestation of God through the romance of opposites. The "not yet" of Becoming must be brought into relationship with the "now" of Being as the husband and wife become complete through one another. Without this holy union each remains imperfect. Without Sophia "Heaven" is a bloodless ideal. "Earth" is absurd. Sophia's life, love, is a sacred duty. And the incarnation of Sophia can be carnal.

> *There are two reasons for the duty of cohabitation. First this pleasure is a religious one, giving joy also to the Divine Presence; Second, it is an instrument for peace in the world...Hence a man should be as zealous to enjoy this pleasure as to enjoy the Sabbath. The Zohar*

With the full incarnation of the Divine Sophia a new age dawns. The reader can recognize here the well-spring of the romantics' yearning, so much at the heart of Schubert's art.

> *She is fairer than the sun, surpassing even the stars.*
> *She is superior to light for she cannot be vanquished by darkness.*
> *She who is one can do all things renewing everything!*
> *Book of Wisdom*

In the Book of Proverbs she is celebrated:

> *Happy the man who finds wisdom (Sophia)......*
> *Not one of your most choice possessions compares with her.*

Yet the yearning is never fully satisfied in life. Schubert's art celebrates the wanderer's victories over his own weakness and mistakes. The people of God make mistakes. Jews, like Christians, reach upwards towards Sophia and through her to the *magnum mysterium*, but never perfectly. Life inevitably falls short of this perfection, often with overtones of tragedy and guilt. Inevitably life betrays this star-like mystery. Fundamentalists defend the mistakes. Wisdom finds life through them. Wisdom finds life in an awareness of one's own weakness. Is the *Tree of Life* myth to be understood as pertaining exclusively to Jews, or are the Jewish wise men really advance pioneers for the rest of humanity? What or who is the *Qelippah,* the kingdom of darkness in which the Shekhinah must live? Is it other religions, other races, other nations, or is it that segment of every religion including Judaism that is incapable of recognizing divine inviation in one's own weakness. And what is to be done with the *Qelippah*? Is it to be saved or destroyed by a God who loves only a sliver of his creation? Jews are faced with the challenge of creatively and spiritually embracing their heritage while simultaneously embracing contradictory experiences that unite them with other peoples, all of whom reach imperfectly for what lies above and beyond them. Opening to the mystery means transcending the limitations of old understandings in richer, broader new ones. The life-enhancing *mysterium magnum* at the heart of the Cabala transcends every rationalization of it.

Schubert's cabalistic wanderer ascends to the higher life out of the tragedies of life.So too does Judaism. Cabalists have never hidden the fact that the ascent of the Jewish people begins in darkness but ends in light. The challenge to transcend the darkness of the past in the reach for wisdom led some Jews in the seventeenth century to a commitment to the transcendence of the Judaic law. Reacting to the sorrows of Jewish life and inspired by the Lurianic Cabala Jewish mystics experienced a strong urge to see the Shekhinah, the Beloved of God, brought to a new and higher state. The Jewish people had endured much pain. The contradiction between divine promises and history's sorrows had to be resolved. Some Jewish mystics thought that the messianic time had arrived. The people had suffered enough and Jews were ready for the new age. The world would become a true home. Their dream of a new age of the reconciliation of contradictions seemed for a while to become real in a way that few expected, thanks in part to Shabbetai Zevi.

Shabbetai was born in 1626 in Smyrna. At an early age his talents were recognized, but he had to deal with cyclic psychological aberrations. Periods of depression were followed by times of "illumination" during which he felt compelled to act against religious laws and engage in bizarre rituals. In the melancholic periods he retired into seclusion to wrestle with what he thought were demonic powers. His psychic victories somehow were transmogrified into a messianic self-awareness. In 1665 the influential Jewish wise man, Nathan of Gaza had an ecstatic vision of Shabbetai as the Messiah and consequently convinced Shabbetai that his "illumination" experiences were real and not a malady. Nathan's support gave Shabbetai credibility among many thousands of Jews worldwide. Shabbetai announced that he was the Messiah and that a new day was dawning. The messianic news spread quickly, triggering fervent support from many orthodox Jews. Shabbetai initiated a mass movement, demanding repentance, prescribing fasting and abstinence, and demanding pure faith in the coming new age. He claimed to be God's presence on earth. After initial skepticism the claim met with widespread acceptance in the Judaic world which was quivering in its anticipation that something of utmost importance was about to happen. To further prepare his followers for the expected redemption Shabbetai developed liturgies and mystical prayers. He demanded that his followers disobey the Jewish Law in order to reverence the spiritual presence that was now uniquely among them. In his eyes the blindness of anyone to this presence condemned them. He proclaimed himself the "anointed of the God of Jacob" and excommunicated anyone who doubted it. For Shabbetai and his followers the Shekhinah, the Bride of God, God's people, were finally ready; the Messiah had come. Throughout Asia Minor and then Europe Jews flocked to this new Messiah. In 1666 pamphlets appeared in Dutch, German, English, and Italian expanding the sympathy with him among Jews and appealing to the apocalyptic expectations of some Christians. The movement was so pervasive in Germany that people in small towns and hamlets and the urban centers as well recognized Shabbetai as the Messiah and themselves as prepared to meet him. But the messianic movement took a sharp turn in 1666 when Shabbetai renounced his Judaism and became a Muslim. The clash with orthodoxy was inevitable and sharp. Some Jews saw this apostasy as indefensible. But for other Jews the apparent weakness became his strength. They thought that the mystery of God's presence on earth required transcending the Law, transcending the limitations of Judaism itself. His followers, encouraged by Nathan, saw his apostasy as an entrance into a new age in which the old rules, the Law, Jewish exclusivity, were left behind in favor of a new freedom and openness. They saw it as the triumph of true wisdom over the fundamentalist idolatry into which orthodoxy had fallen. The contradiction between the Law and the ongoing life experience could be resolved by a spiritual awareness of the divine invitation in the moment, the "Now". They saw Shabbetai not as a traitor to Judaism, but as the realization of its soul. That soul was and is the rose cross mystery.

Jewish messianism was focusing more and more upon that mystery. It also was becoming more challenging to orthodoxy. Shabbetai thought that this was the time for a new incarnation of the divine harmony. The contradictions of the various religions must now be transcended in a higher, more spiritual unity. He fashioned doctrine to this end. He made a distinction between *Ein Sof,* the unknowable God, the hidden Cause of Causes, and the God of Israel. The God of Israel along with the Shekhinah are the two emanations of *Ein Sof.* Together with *Ein Sof* they constitute a kind of Trinity. One of his important theological doctrines was the recognition of a romance between the two divine emanations, one masculine, the other feminine. Before his death in 1676 Shabbetai suggested a kind of divine trinity in which a romance between the masculine and the feminine pertains to the nature of God. He saw himself as an incarnation of the God of Israel and the long-awaited messiah. In his mind the mystery that was the soul of Judaism was being realized, not destroyed, by a more universal understanding of the great romance between God and his people.

This expression of the Jewish higher consciousness of the rose cross mystery stemming from Cabalistic messianic expectations reached a new high in the next century in Jacob Franck. Franck claimed to be the messianic re-incarnation of Shabbetai Zevi. Following in Shabbetai's footsteps he led other Jews into a kind of Jewish Catholicism. He saw this not a supplanting of Judaism by Catholicism, but rather as a sign of the transcendence of both in a still richer expression of the mystery. Like Shabetai he insisted that a new, more spiritually vibrant age had dawned. Now was the time to transcend the laws of both Judaism and Christianity. The old orthodoxies are now to be spiritually enriched, not destroyed, by embracing one another. He would lead the way. The enrichment would be the ground for new and higher unities, a divine harmony. The bride of God, the Jewish people, were being called to a richer life than Jewish orthodoxy alone could provide. God's bride would be enriched and adorned through a larger unity, a more magnificent harmony. The *mysterium magnum* was calling the Many towards the unimaginable splendor of the One.

Franck proclaimed himself God's voice on earth, superior to the Law. His God was a trinity, similar to that of Shabbetai, consisting of the unknown God, a good God or "Big Brother", and an amalgam of the Shekhinah and the Virgin Mary. His mystical vision was a very personal synthesis of Cabalism and Catholicism. He saw both Shabbetai and himself as incarnations of the second member of the Trinity, the God of Israel or the "Big Brother". He was the Christ-figure who was to inspire the Shekhinah, the chosen people, to prepare for the goal of history. That Shekhinah cannot be defined. She is above every law, every religion, every race as spirit is above matter. The contradiction is reconciled, not in any law or mere belief, but in creative unities that men and women exercise with wisdom and freedom. The truly wise are those who both honor the mystery discovered in their orthodoxy and refuse to cut themselves off from the mystery due to the limitations of that orthodoxy. They insist upon transcending those limitations in new and higher syntheses. Franck attracted Jews of the new age to become men and women of wisdom who discriminate, taking what expresses the mystery in each religion, rejecting what does not. Organized religion, including Judaism and Catholicism, is an imperfect incarnation of the mystery, a cloak to be put on and taken off according to the insights of the wise wanderer.

In the minds of the Franckists Jacob Franck had not "left" Judaism and converted to another religion. Rather he had transcended a legalist and narrow form of Judaism for another, higher form. As was the case one hundred years earlier a "conversion" to another religion was evidence to his followers of strength rather than weakness. For them it was not an abandonment of the heart and soul of Judaism, the mystery, but its more complete incarnation. In the new age they anticipated there would be freedom from sectarian limitations. Now was the time for the mystery that was the soul of Judaism to shine as a light illuminating the world. Citizens of this new age were above the Law, above any belief. True religion for them was the ascent of Becoming towards Being, an ascent realized in a romance of opposites. They were to personify the new Shekhinah. Jacob Franck and Shabbetai were in their own eyes incarnations of the Messiah in the new age, light-bringers to the world. For the great romance to be complete and the wedding of the Messiah to the Shekhinah to take place the world must be changed. It must be rescued from its prison of absolutes, idols, and raised to the freedom demanded by the mystery. The life of the spirit must replace the written Law and laws. The life of the spirit sometimes requires disobedience to the law. So in a given instance breaking the Law could mean an ascent to life for Jews of the new age. Laws, teachings, and practices which constrict the spiritual liberation of the Bride must be challenged, but secretly at first. Orthodox religion, be it Judaism or Roman Catholicism, is but a piece of clothing for the soul, to be donned or discarded with responsibility and freedom. The clothes are entirely secondary to the divine spirit that can never be seen. The great moral imperative is the commitment to the rose cross mystery that at times is both expressed and betrayed by orthodoxy.

Franck was leading thousands of Jews into the new age by relishing the mystery expressed diffrerently by the Jewish and the Catholic orthodoxies and trying not to be limited by the distortions of the mystery that were endemic to each orthodoxy. In Austria his followers included the very influential Hoenig and Dobruschka families. Some families followed him into Roman Catholicism practically en bloc. The Franckists both as Catholics and as Jews had an impact upon Vienna and the world. Some were connected with the upper bourgeoisie and higher Austrian administration. Several served as officers in the Austrian army. Moses, the son of Schoendel Dobruschka, Franck's cousin, became known as Franz Thomas von Schoenfeld. He was a writer and participated in the founding of a Masonic mystical order, the Asiatic Brethren, committed to the wedding of Jewish and Christian mysticism. Members of this group were responsible for enlisting Mozart into Freemasonry. According to the profound and reliable Gershom Sholem many of these followers of Jacob Franck were men of deep faith and moral integrity who sought not to betray either their Judaism nor later their Catholicism. Rather with Catholics of like mind they were committed to the mystery that underlies them both. Their fidelity to the mystery led them both into and yet beyond their orthodoxies in an effort to participate more fully in the great romance between heaven and earth. As a result they were viciously opposed by those orthodoxies. Their flowering, though influential and immensely effective, was short-lived. Sparked by their cabalistic expectations of a new age secret societies in Austria and Bavaria brought much of the eighteenth century German world to life. Novalis' essay *Christendom oder Europa* is an expression of this life. For a few years the reform and unification of the great orthodoxies, Catholic, Protestant, and Jewish, were thought to be the soul of the new age. Our world would be transfigured. These hopes for a fresh new garb for the earthly Sophia had an immense impact in late eighteenth and early nineteenth century Austria. They affected first Mozart and twenty-five years later Schubert.

The impact of such Jewish wisdom upon German thought in the eighteenth century and especially upon Schubert in the early nineteenth century was so profound that this age and Schubert's art which is its crown might be viewed as a symbiosis of Jewish and German genius in its reach towards the *mysterium magnum*. Implicit in Schubert's dream maiden is a hidden invitation to transcend this lower world of chaos and value conflict, an invitation parallel to the cabalist's duty to penetrate beneath the surface of the *Torah*. The invitation is at times terrifying, at times thrilling. The importance of this cabalistic romance to Schubert's experience of the *mysterium magnum* was such that two later chapters will be devoted to it..

Catholicism and the Mystery

The hour is coming and is now here when true worshipers will worship the Father in spirit and in truth.

The Gospel of John

Our professed faith in precisely the God of Jesus should convince us that openness to other churches and other religions is a proper Christian spiritual attitude. New times and new theologies call for new forms of spirituality. — *Roger Haight, S.J.* Lessons from an Extraordinary Era, *America Magazine*

The reform of Roman Catholicism in accord with an ever-changing experience of the *mysterium magnum* has been a cause dear to the hearts of many Catholic intellectuals for centuries. For the past sixty years theologians from all over the world have followed the lead of Karl Rahner, S.J. in questioning the metaphysical framework through which the Catholic Church has understood itself. The conflict between these theologians and Rome has been bloody. The outcome is still very much in doubt. Schubert's significant if unrecognized contribution to this reform is his mythology of the wanderer. At a time when a reformed Catholicism is politically incorrect Schubert's visionary liturgy is for rebellious dreamers.

The eighteenth and nineteenth centuries hosted in Germany an intense effort to transcend Roman Catholic fundamentalism in a more intense immersion in the rose cross mystery.Schubert created out of poetry and music a liturgy for this transcendence that is Protestant, Jewish, and Islamic while remaining Catholic. A largely Protestant pietistic movement had swept through all of Germany and was followed by the Great German Awakening among theologians like August Tholuck and Theodor Fliedner. They responded to the secularization of large segments of the population, a result of industrialism.

People were leaving the small towns and moving to the cities. The spiritual uprooting was devastating to traditional experiences of the *mysterium magnum*. Nihilistic rationalism became a theat to religion. The anti-religious movement found expression in the secret societies. In response Protestant and Catholic intellectuals sought a new understanding of the mystery that could facilitate a harmonious synthesis of modern experience and revelation. Ascending to this higher ground necessitated both a transcendence of religious fundamentalism and a recognition of the limitations of human reason. Catholic and Protestant reformers distinguished between immersion in the mystery and intellectual submission to dogma and moral law. They demanded a respect for the individual wanderer who is charged with the responsibility for this Gnostic ascent. Friedrich Schlegel, Novalis, Joseph Schelling and many others created a powerful movement towards recognizing the unique wisdom of the individual wanderer. Schubert gave to this focus upon the wanderer its ultimate artistic form. To better understand the relationship between Schubert's music and what was happening in German lands and throughout Europe during the first part of the nineteenth century we must analyze what the Catholic Church brought to the table.

Repentance is for Catholicism as for Judaism the condition of life. History means a constant dealing with mistakes. Repentance does not come cheaply for anyone. In particular it has been almost impossible for this institution. The problem of repentance has been compounded for the Catholic Church by the fact that it has solemnly defined itself as infallible. It cannot even recognize its most serious dogmatic and ethical inadequacies because such inadequacies have been "infallibly" declared to be impossible. The correction of very basic theological and philosophical betrayals of the Truth is essential if the Church is to do what the world needs it to do.

Schubert's art expresses an ascent to a new age, assuming movement towards a reformed Catholicism that can be complemented by similar movements within Protestantism, Judaism, etc. The outlines of the Catholic reformation can be described as follows. The Catholic Church has at various times solemnly demonized its supposed enemies like the "self", sexuality, sensual pleasure, women, personal, political, and religious freedom, Jews, Protestants, Islam, "Americanism", "modernism", democracy, other ways of life. In contrast it has esteemed as little absolutes obedience, the intellectual assent of faith, chastity, poverty, humility, perseverance in the faith, and courage in suffering. This selective focus upon passive virtues has led many Catholic mystics to make an absolute of only a part of what is human. It has set the obedient Catholic at war against portions of nature, against portions of himself or herself. In place of a higher consciousness counterbalancing institutional ideas and ongoing experience there often is a warlike hatred for parts of the universe. Both good and evil are concrete realities. The *mysterium magnum* disappears. Consequently the Catholic Church has denied the validity of alternative experiences of divine invitation. It has wrongly sent good people off to fight unnecessary and self-damaging wars against other good people. It has hindered its mystics and intellectuals in their effort to transcend the limits of ideas and enter the larger universe that embraces value experience. Only by repenting of its preference of ideas over the mystery and radically expanding its metaphysical vision of life can the Catholic Church re-discover its true soul and enrich the world.

Catholic reform should take the form of a reconciliation with Judaism, primarily with respect to the divine incarnation in Jesus Christ. Jesus Christ is a unique hypostasis of the Divine Sophia... but not the only one. Because of the insistence by Catholicism (and many Protestants as well) upon creating dogmatic and ethical absolutes there has been an excessive focus upon the divine incarnation in Jesus Christ and a missing recognition of the divine beauty that sparkles in other hypostases of Sophia throughout the vast universe of value experience. This universe of divine beauty is divine revelation and a protection against the fundamentalism endemic to ideologies. In value experience there is the encounter with the *mysterium magnum* that has its core in the invitation of the sacred "Other". Jesus is a symbol and incarnation of that mystery, an awakener to it, a model in responding to it. But as its incarnation Jesus limits the mystery even as he expresses it. The death and the resurrection of Jesus give hope to the wanderer in the face of being mortal. But his life is a valuable but inadequate guide for the lives of other people. Each wanderer must create his or her own ascent into the mystery. God has not rejected the infinitely varied creation of *Genesis One*. Religion must not become an escape from the reconciliation of contradictions that are unique to each individual. Jesus Christ is but a partial revelation of the hidden God. Christianity must focus not primarily upon the Jesus of history but upon the wanderer today.

Schubert's art celebrates a wanderer's ascent to a higher world that is experienced in a woman. The man is a messianic Christ figure; his bride is sophianic, a Shekhinah-like incarnation of the Divine Sophia. Together they are the perfection of creation. Together they are a sacrament of the *mysterium magnum*. Their romance is a symbolic reconciliation of contradiction. The rose upon the cross is the quintessential wanderer, a Christ figure whether Christian or Jew or Muslim. The art is always the work of a poet who yearns for immersion in the mystery and captures the yearning in music. It is never the work of a theologian who tries to express the mystery in words. The yearning needs words but is always dissatisfied with them.

In a remarkably insightful book. *Constantine's Sword* (Mariner Books, 2002), James Carroll argues forcibly that a reformation of Catholicism is necessary, not merely in practice but in beliefs, in dogma. Carroll thinks that the "atonement theory" is an example of what must be rethought. According to this damnable theory God is angry at his creation. He demands a blood sacrifice of a god/man as the price for pardoning the wanderer for Adam's "Original Sin". According to this theory man has become so loathsome to God that he must be damned unless rescued through attachment to Jesus Christ. Attachment to Jesus Christ is won solely through the Roman Catholic Church. God condemns every man, woman, and child to exclusion from God's kingdom unless mollified through the mediating services of the Church. This theory amounts to a complete reversal of Genesis with its creation judged by God as "good". It assumes that the experiences of the goodness of family, friends, and nature are not to be trusted. Loveable creation has been forever replaced by a damned mass with the highly selective rescue of a few. There is an utter centrality now both to the suffering and death on the cross as the point of rescue and to the Church as the channel by which the benefit of that suffering and death comes to the saved. Everyone who is not in some way washed white in the blood of the Lamb through the services of the Church is believed to be condemned to eternal exclusion from God's kingdom. There have been efforts to downplay this longstanding position of Roman Catholicism during the past fifty years. But more than a verbal re-shuffle is necessary. Infallibility is implicated. Pope Boniface VIII (1294-1303) solemnly proclaimed this doctrine:

> *We are obliged to believe and maintain that the Church is one, holy, catholic, and also apostolic. We believe in her firmly and we confer with simplicity that outside of her there is neither salvation nor the remission of sins.*

This sub-human atonement theory which has its echoes within Protestantism dismisses the universal experience of divine invitation as purely subjective. It rejects the goodness of creation that is experienced uniquely in a child, in each man and woman. It was preached by St. Anselm at the beginning of the twelfth century. Of it Carroll writes:

> *The first result of Anselm's theology of salvation (soteriology) was...to solder the faith to the cross, and to make the death of Jesus more important than anything he had said despite his clear statement that "the words that I have spoken to you are spirit and life". His death counted for more than his having been born, having lived as a Jew, having preached a gospel of love in the context of Israel's covenant with a loving God, having opposed the imperium of Rome, having even been brought to the new life of Resurrection. The death obsession of the flagellants was deemed holy, and the blood lust of the Crusaders was sanctified. God too had blood lust.*

Carroll is sure that the discerning spirit of the wanderer that romances the *mysterium magnum* is wiser than the institutional Church. The experience of love transcends every imperfect dogma.

> *All that exists, and in particular all persons who exist, participate by virtue of mere existence in the existence of God. There is no question here of an unbridgeable gulf between the human and the divine. Christian Platonism yields to biblical faith. In this view the creation, more than salvation, is the pivotal event of being and of history, because the creation is nothing less than God's self expression. As Rahner explained, "God does not merely create something other than himself-he also gives himself to this other. The world receives*

> *God, the infinite and ineffable mystery, to such an extent that he himself becomes its innermost life. Human beings are the creatures who respond to that innermost life. "This mystery", Rahner writes, "is the inexplicit and unexpressed horizon which always encircles and upholds the small area of our everyday experience. We call this God, however hard and unsatisfactory it may be to interpret the deepest and most fundamental experience at the very bottom of our being. Man does experience in his innermost history this silent, infinitely distant, holy mystery, which continually recalls him to the limits of his finitude and lays bare his guilt and bids him approach; the mystery enfolds him in an ultimate and radical love which commends itself to him as salvation and as the real meaning of his existence."*

Rahner describes here the rose cross mystery that is the homing beacon for all true religion and the touchstone for valid reform.

Innovative Catholic thinkers from the time of the Gnostics have sought to break free of the "believe and obey" mentality and embrace the mystery that lies at the core of the human experience by way of a kind of Christian cabalism. Their ideas were usually suppressed. For example, early Jesuits, especially Rosicrucians like Athanasius Kircher, led the way in an interlacing of revelation and the human experience. Then the movement was stopped. The Jesuits' history in the matter is mixed. They have been both praised and damned for their reputed and disputed role in creating, controlling, and then trying to destroy the highly imaginative secret societies which complemented revelation with a reverence for the divine treasure within Creation. Umberto Eco in his novel *Foucoult's Pendulum* wrote:

> *Neo-Templarism was all right at the beginning of the eighteenth century, Belso said, and it was all wrong at the end of the century; first because it had been taken over by revolutionaries, for whom anything served, the goddess Reason, the Supreme Being, even Cagliostro, provided they could cut off the king's head; and second because the German princes were now putting their thumbs in the pie, especially Frederick of Prussia, and his aims surely did not correspond to those of the Jesuits. When mystical Neo-Templarism, whoever invented it, began producing things like "The Magic Flute", Loyola's men naturally decided to wipe it out. Its like high finance: you buy a company; you sell off its assets; you declare bankruptcy; you close it down; and you re-invest its capital. The important thing is the overall strategy, not what happens to the janitor. Or its like a car; when it stops running you send it to the junkyard.*

But if the Catholic Church betrayed the *mysterium magnum* that was its life in some ways, in other ways it sparkles with the beauty of that mystery. And it was in catholicism that Schubert first encountered that beauty. The Catholic Church, often a sinner against the rose cross mystery, paradoxically gives to it some of its most splendid expressions. Catholics are nourished by a heightened sense of the divine invitation to transcend this life in a personal but mysterious transfiguration. This awakening of consciousness is the invigorating core of the Catholic life experience. The divine invitation calls each wanderer to transfigure this life through an overlay of God's call. The call comes to the Catholic uniquely through the Eucharistic liturgy. Day after day the divine invitation to a higher life is articulated in the "Take and eat, Take and drink" core of the Roman Catholic Mass. This invitation is to more than a bright new day. It is to the *mysterium magnum*, the profound mystery of the transfiguration of one world by another. It is to union with the Cosmic Christ. It is to an incarnation of the Divine Sophia. The earthly Sophia is being prepared for a radically new union with God.

> *And I, John, saw the holy city, the new Jerusalem, coming down from God out of heaven, prepared as a bride, dressed for her husband*
> *Book of Revelation*

The great mystery as it appears in Catholicism is union with Christ, the Christian hypostasis of the Divine Sophia, in the passage through death to life. In Christ the messiah and the bride form a great romance, one preparing for a final union between the human and the divine.

> *Alleluia! The Lord is King, our God, the Almighty! Let us rejoice and be glad and give him glory! For this is the wedding day of the Lamb;His bride has prepared herself for the wedding. She has been given a dress to wear, made of finest linen, brilliant white. Book of Revelation 19*

There is much in this grasp of the mystery that is inspired by Judaic mysticism. History is a preparation for this wedding. The earthly Sophia, the Shekhinah, will become the Divine Sophia. He/She will unite past and present, divine and human, man and woman, life and death. He/She has appeared already in history. And He/She invites even now. Preparation is a thrilling but pain-filled responsibility.

> *A great sign appeared in the sky, a woman clothed in the sun, with the moon under her feet, and on her head a crown of twelve stars. Because she was with child she wailed aloud in pain as she labored to give birth.*
> *Book of Revelation 12*

The coming of the Lord Jesus meant the completion of the dramatic romance between heaven and earth. Paul wrote:

> *Christ is now raised from the dead, the first fruits of those who have fallen asleep. Death came through a man; hence the resurrection of the dead comes through a man also. Just as in Adam all die, so in Christ all will come to life again.*
> *First Epistle to the Corinthians*

The romance between heaven and earth is made incarnate in the romance between Christ and his followers.

> *How can wedding guests go in mourning so long as the groom is with them...*
> *Gospel of Matthew*

The theme of a romance between heaven and earth and an earthly wedding is repeated.

> *The reign of God can be compared to ten bridesmaids who took their torches and went out to welcome the groom.*
> *Gospel of Matthew*

In response to a query about his relationship to Jesus John the Baptist said:

> *I am not the Messiah. I am sent before him. It is the groom who has the bride.*
> *Gospel of John*

The *Epistle to the Ephesians* refers to a great mystery of romance with God through the romance between man and woman.

> *For this reason a man shall leave his father and mother and shall cling to his wife and the two shall be made into one.*

The theme of the incarnation of the romance between God and the wanderer in the romance between the messiah and God's people is sounded:

> *Husbands love your wives as Christ loved the church...This is a great foreshadowing; I mean that it refers to Christ and the church..*
> *Epistle to the Ephesians*

Paul, like the author of *Genesis* is interested in the rose cross mystery that unites man to God indirectly through the union of earthly opposites. Immersion in the mystery means making it incarnate. For the author of the *Epistle to the Colossians* the union of opposites is realized in the person of Jesus Christ. In him heaven transfigures the earth.

> *In Christ the fullness of deity resides in human form.*

The author of the gospel and epistles of John, like Paul, celebrated divine life as a reconciliation of opposites. The Prologue of the gospel suggests that the transfigured experience of the wanderer has its prototype in the life of God. The Logos is described as erotically loving God much as Sophia does in the Wisdom literature of the Old Testament:

> *In the beginning was the Word (Logos) and the Word loved God, and the Word was God.*

The original Greek words describe the relationship between the Logos and God as *pros ton theon*. This has sexual overtones. Opposites are reconciled and united in love. John's Logos is the perfect emanation of God, identical in many ways with the Divine Sophia of the wisdom literature. This Logos is not merely "with" God, or "in God's presence", but rather seeking, loving God as a spouse. The Logos, a masculine word and a masculine presence vis-à-vis creation, is presented in a feminine context vis-à-vis God, as the Divine Spouse, a hypostasized Sophia. Both within and between God and Creation there is a romance ending in a generative wedding. Relative to God the Logos is feminine. But that same Logos, the face that God shows to the world, is both masculine and feminine in that world. This gospel conceives of God in terms of a romance of opposites. This is its introduction to the rose cross mystery.

God is One, but hidden and comprehensible to us only through the "divine" experience of penetrating the wall of contradiction, i.e. in an interaction of love. The human ascent to God is made in the movement out of contradiction with its chaos and paranoia towards the universal harmony of the higher consciousness. Man and woman through their romance with one another and through their romance with their world are symbols of the romance within God and between God and creation. The pathway to the stars is a ladder consisting of incarnations of divine harmony.

The divine life within each wanderer conditions the wedding of heaven and earth. Christ said to Nicodemus:

> *I solemnly assure you, no one can see the reign of God unless he be begotten from above.*

The symbol of this wedding of heaven and earth is Jesus Christ.

> *The Word became flesh.*

God is experienced indirectly through the incarnation.

> *Whoever has seen me has seen the Father.*
>
> *Gospel of John*

The wanderer is invited into that mystery of divine harmony.

> *Dearly beloved we are God's children now; what we shall later be has not yet come to light.*
>
> *First Epistle of John*

The star-reach of John's insight into the contradiction-reconciling mystery is awesome. Christ Jesus, the archetypal wanderer as well as the Word of divine light, unites in himself the Shekhinah and the Messiah. He is both a sophianic incorporation of that light and a messianic, light-bringing force. Like the Jewish Cabalists' Adam Kadmon he is all things, female and male. He is the unity, the harmony, the triumph of love, the wedding that Creation craves. He prays that that unity of the Divine Sophia be formed in Creation. All men and women are called to be part of this divine harmony by living the great romance.

> *I pray...that all may be one as you, Father, are in me and I in you. I pray that they may be one in us...I have given them the glory that you gave me that they may be one as we are one, I living in them, you living in me, that their unity may be complete. That they may be one as we are one, as you, Father, are in me and I in you, that they may also be one in us......I have given them the glory that you gave me, so that they may be one as we are one.*

The author of John's Gospel invites his readers to something far higher and richer than ideas about Jesus Christ and obedience to church law. Ideas are necessary. But they are always reformable. When they are out of touch with experience they interfere with the rose cross mystery into which the wanderer is invited. John's universe provisionally embraces ideas but transcends them. He calls his readers beyond mere ideas into a transfigured life experience. Ideas are essential to the experience, but must not be regarded as absolute. They have a job to do, namely to bring heaven to earth for the wanderer. But they betray the truth even as they express it.

Love, not belief, is the command:

> *As the Father has loved me so I love you. Live on my love...This is my commandment: Love one another as I have loved you.*

According to this sometimes flawed but amazingly sublime author creation is to be caught up in a cosmic symphony. Empowered by the Messiah the Shekhinah, present in each of us, unites the world, finding divine sparks everywhere, and drawing them into a unity. Love then is the sweet mystery of life, transfiguring the earth by heaven.

> *Beloved let us love one another because love is of God; everyone who loves is begotten of God and has knowledge of God. The man without love knows nothing, for God is love.*

The triumph of love that is so central to Catholicism and Christianity inspires Schubert's art. In that art the romance between heaven and earth is transcendentally realized in a wedding of worlds. This gives character to Schubert's liturgical and more openly religious settings of poetry. His great *Mass in E*

(D.950) is an example. We find ourselves wanderers, aliens in a foreign land. The *Kyrie* is full of painful Gnostic yearning, the yearning of the wanderer exiled in chaos, fear, and hatred, for the divine harmony of a lost home. The yearning arises out of real experience. The *Gloria* is a triumphant celebration of the God who shatters the darkness of our separation and calls us home. The *Credo* celebrates with awesome beauty the redemption mystery that weds the wisdom of the human experience with the divine promise of revelation. The Messiah descends into the land of the dead, into the harsh dissonances of this world. He does not reject the world with its value conflicts. He is the lightbringer awakening and empowering the Shekhinah. His messianic presence means the dawning of a new age. Musically this is announced through a mystical incantation of *"Et incarnatus est.."*, a celebration of life as a romance between an inviting God and a divine Beloved, expressed amazingly but appropriately in a waltz. This is followed by a dramatic recitation of the passage of Christ and the wanderer through death to rebirth, and the celebration of new life. In the *Sanctus* we find a solemn celebration of the divine life that is hidden everywhere, filling the earth with the hope of transfiguration. And in the *Agnus Dei* we have an almost grotesque, crushingly powerful expression of the wanderer's struggle as he makes his way through his exile, battling the dark and terrifying force of the *Qelippah.* The composer realizes in this incomparable song of the wanderer both the pain of the wanderer's exile and the heights to which he or she is invited.

Franz Schubert celebrated the wanderer's romance of the *mysterium magnum* often and profoundly in his art. In the Lied *Im Walde* D.708, a musical setting of a poem by Friedrich von Schlegel, the same divine power as that celebrated in the Mass is realized in the counterpoint between nature's wild power and all-conquering love:

The wind roars like mighty wings of God
Deep in the cool forest night.
Like a hero mounting his steed
Do man's thoughts ascend to the heavens!
Splendid the crimson light of dawn!
Awesome the flashing and deadly lightning,
Exploding and disappearing as if ordered by God!

But the gentle sound of the spring water
Attracts the yearning flowers,
A yearning that sweetly speaks to our hearts
Of a distant Beloved.
The fierce desire to escape life's prison
In surrender to the wild life force
Is made human by love's triumph.

In the poetry inspiring the *Piano Trio in E Flat* (D.927), the wanderer is at first submerged in the darkness of despair.

I have been abandoned by everyone, bound only to death.
I stand on the brink of life, holding a cross,
And stare with desire into the deep grave.

But the wanderer is given a mystical foretaste of divine life.

Oh homeland of peace, world of the blessed,
I am bound to you with a mystical tie.

For this mystical Catholic composer that foretaste transfigures the entire human experience. The mysticism reaches beyond what "is" towards the "not yet", beyond the actual prison towards a distant star, a new age of creative freedom that invites us all. Schubert began singing of this mystery that is the very soul of Catholicism early in life. When he was eighteen his wanderer sang of dying as a triumphant ascent to love's kingdom where divine harmony reigns supreme. The following poetry is part of the Lied *Auf Einen Kirchhof* (D.151) by Franz Xaver von Schlechta, set as a Lied in 1815 and probably set again in the form of the third movement of the early *Piano Sonata in E Major*. In it the wanderer and through him the composer speak of creating music as a kind of swan song, an emanation of the divine harmony, celebrating the life-transcending ascent to a better world. The wanderer hopes that like a sunset his music, created in his dying, will ascend as light-rays towards the heavens.

Like a flame will you shine in your dying,
Giving light like a sunset,
Radiant light-beams,
Reaching' like music, into the heavens.
And you, life within me,
Will you be prey to worms?
All that uplifts and delights me,
Are you too but empty dust?
No! What I sense in my own experience,
What in joy raises me to the stars
Is of God's own doing!
It is his spirit that lives in me!

Are the first four lines an eerie prophecy that the ending of this wanderer's life would be a unique musical celebration of the mysterious passage through death to transfiguration? The poem *Todesmusik D.758*, composed in 1822, inspired not only a Lied, but also several instrumental works, including the "*Unfinished" Symphony* D.759 and portions of the "*Wanderer" Fantasy* D.760. The wanderer sings of a special pairing of his own music and divine harmony in the expression of the higher consciousness.

Todesmusik
Franz Schober D.758
At the sacred hour of death,
When I shall leave this earth and in pain fight my last battle,
Holy spirits, bless me a final time with your peaceful melodies, your pure harmonies;
…………
Then will the sweet heavenly harmonies envelop me.
The chains I have escaped will become light and fall away.
I will see all the wonders of life which brought me such joy,
All the beauty which bloomed in my life will stand transfigured before me…

Two years later in 1824 Schubert set a poem by Mayrhofer to music both as a Lied and as the last movement of the *Grand Duo D.815*, envisioning his wanderer's definitive ascent to divine life. He sang of a transfiguration of consciousness. This transfiguration applies surely to the inner life. But this composer's allegories are not limited to psychology. They express the core mystery of Catholicism, the ascent through death to a mysterious and transcendental transfiguration.

D.805
The clouds of life are gone!
Pure, deep, clear, powerful dreams drift amid the enchanting flowers.

The spirit breaks free from its body prison…
It soars on high!

Thoughts are enlivened by heavenly food.
The body's ancient curse is gone.

Whatever pain I have borne now the triumph is mine!
My deepest yearning is stilled at last.

The muse sing the sphinx to final peace.

And my own arm is raised in triumph!

Still later, in 1827, Schubert had on his mind his unique artistic commitment to singing his swansong in celebration of the wanderer's ascent to transfigured life when he gave *Todesmusik* yet another instrumental setting in the first movement of the *Piano Trio in B Flat* D.898. Here the wanderer re-affirms a transfiguration by love that he saw as the real *Truth* that gives meaning to dying. This is quintessential Christianity, but a Christianity that is harmonious with Islam, Judaism and paganism.

Schubert's wanderer is a music maker telling tales about the spiritual ascent. He ascends to the divine harmony of his higher consciousness by making that harmony incarnate in his life and in his music. He is then both a mystic and a magician. Above all he is a celebrant of wisdom, the soul of the new age. Through poetry-transcending music the wanderer transfigures all things, even dying, by love. For example the composer turned in his last months of life to singing the swansong of the wanderer, not in self pity, but in celebration of the triumph of love in the face of death. Here was the ultimate contradiction and the ultimate reconciliation. In the *Piano Sonata in A Major D.959* the wanderer's downward drive towards depression and death in the first two movements has its mirror image in the Third and Fourth Movements with their joyful and hope-filled anticipation of love's fulfillment and new life. Both the third and fourth movements are inspired by poetry that speaks of transfiguration. The death to resurrection passage of the Catholic Holy Week has here an ultimate artistic expression.

Third movement:

Hark! Hark! The lark at heaven's gate sings!
Shakespeare

Fourth movement:

And deep in the dark mountain spring
I saw heavenly beauty…
And there I saw her!
Ernst Schulze

Immediately following the above setting of the central Catholic mystery the composer turned from his wanderer's vision of death and transfiguration to the reality of dying. In the opening movement of the *Piano Sonata in B Flat D.960*, the wanderer, inspired by *Mignon's Song*, solemnly announces that he is on his way, leaving this beautiful earth for the mysterious afterworld. He follows this proclamation with a meditation upon the imminent end of his life. A part of this meditation is the psalm of praise that he sings in the third movement celebrating the Divine Source of life's invitation. That God is a God of Harmony, to be praised with music:

Psalm 92
D.953
How wondrous it is to thank you eternal God,
To sing your name, Most High!
In the morning we extol your kindness.
In the evening we extol your faithfulness.

Our lyre and psaltery sing their praise.
We thank you with our harps.
Lord and God, your works give me delight,
Happily I sing of your works.
How great they are!

The fourth movement of this last sonata is a setting of the poem *Auf der Brücke* D.853 by Ernst Schulze. Its last words reveal poetically the sublime disposition that is everywhere so evident in this work. The drama of the spiritual ascent, which is simply everywhere in Schubert's work, is coming to its triumphant conclusion.

Though the way is dark and full of mystery
My longing is awake and watchful,
And I race ahead in sweet anticipation!

The same myth in which the wanderer ascends to God as he creates his own music that reaches up to the heavens underlies the *String Quintet in C Major D.956,* composed in August of 1828, three months before Schubert's death. This is perhaps the most sublime swansong ever composed. The first movement is a prayer of the dying wanderer, torn between fear and hope.

Hymn to the Holy Spirit
Alois Schmidl D.948
Lord and God, hear this prayer...
Which longingly reaches up to you in your goodness......
Lead us to what is good and just!

The third movement suggests that the hunt for the better world is nearing its triumphant end. It is inspired by some of the poetry already quoted from the Lied *Der Hirt auf dem Felsen D.965.*

The Finale of this sublime quintet is a rollicking, yet intensely serious adieu to art and to life, bringing the mythical drama of the wanderer's search for the new age to its conclusion. The warrior/mystic is going home and singing about it. Now the song is ending. The double meaning here is obvious. The inspiring poem is *Zur guten Nacht* by Johann Friedrich Rochlitz set as D.903.

Listen, the hour chimes
To end our party.
It tells each to go home
After he has emptied his glass,
Thanked our host,
And sung this song to its end.

Schubert's wanderer experienced the mysterium magnum in the core mystery of Christianity, the passage through death to new life. His own sickness and dying was for him a time to sing of the spiritual ascent. The ascent approached its climax with the approach of death. This conviction conditioned Schubert's art just as a similar conviction had conditioned the Egyptian and Greek mysteries. In the unfinished *Symphony in D Major D.936*, the completion of which was prevented by the composer's death, we find once again the poetry that he set also as one of his last songs, *Der Hirt auf dem Felsen*. The Gnostic wanderer stands atop the mountain of his life and sings of the mystery of transfiguration. Each of the three movements are inspired by poetry that anticipates an imminent and joyful conclusion to life's dramatic journey beyond death in search of the Beloved. The wanderer is a singer of songs so sublimely tragic that they open the gates of heaven.

> *D.965*
> *So plaintive is the song in the woods,*
> *So tortured the voice in the night,*
> *That the heart speeds the prayer to Heaven...*
> *...with divine power!*

Schubert's wanderer is profoundly Catholic not in a way that excludes others, but rather in a way that unites him with all other awakened wanderers from other faiths as they ascend out of life's conflicts to transfiguration. He endures intense pain and enjoys sublime beauty as he wrestles with the contradictions of his life. He is on a journey that leads first to immersion in the world, then to an often frustrated effort to transfigure that world, and finally to itstranscendence in a higher world. An invitation from Being to Becoming underlies this sublime Catholic mysticism. Schubert's wanderer has been exiled from his true home and wants to return. He seeks a higher consciousness of what he is about. A messianic visitation awakens and empowers him. Through time the strange and foreign land is painfully transfigured by the wanderer who is now himself messianic. But the pace of the transfiguration is glacial. Death approaches. The re-creation of the earth must be left unfinished.

Schubert set the following lines of Novalis in May of 1819 as a song celebrating the transfiguration of the earth by a love that was incarnate in Christ:

> *Few know love's secret, its hunger, its thirst! The true meaning of the Last Supper is a puzzle to the materialist mind. The wanderer has experienced real life in the passionate embrace of love and felt his heart enflamed in love's sacred fire. He has searched the heavens, measuring their infinite distances. That wanderer will eat eternally this body of unity and drink this blood of passionate freedom!*
>
> *Who could guess the noble purpose of the body? Who could guess at the true meaning of the blood? Someday all will be one body! Someday all will be united in the same fire of love, the sacred blood! Yes, the ocean will be-*

come crimson in love! The rock will erupt in blossoms if life! Never will the banquet of love end! Never will the heart be satisfied! Never will the unity of lover and beloved be complete! Always the beloved is being transformed, always being more perfectly possessed!

The heart grows ever more thirsty, ever more hungry through love's passion. The joy of loving never wanes. If only the fundamentalists could taste it! Then they could sit with us at the table of boundless love! They would recognize the supremacy of love and rejoice transfiguring power.

The words above interlace sexuality and sublime mysticism. There is no demonization of parts of creation by Schubert. His rose cross mysticism both embraces and contradicts Catholic orthodoxy. In the mystery of the Eucharist Schubert finds a pure symbol of life's meaning, a symbol that leads beyond institutional theology. All those who yearn for life are invited. Sexual love is not antithetical to the mystery. It is its prized sacrament. The body and blood mysteriously become vessels of eternal light and love.

Schubert's Catholicism, while challenging to the sectarian exclusivity preferred by Catholic orthodoxy, was indeed genuine in its celebration of the rose cross mystery. In Schubert's time as in our own there was a demand for the reformation of Christianity and especially of the Roman Catholic Church. The world, it was thought then as now, needed a church that it did not have. The higher consciousness of the rose cross mystery seemed to demand an opening of windows in that church to the fresh air of experience, fresh air that would demand flexibility in dogma as well as morals. Something was needed to raise Catholics above their church's institutional torpor, its prison in beliefs that contradicted the experience of the sacred. The church then as now needed a deeper and richer immersion in the rose cross mystery. Reformed Roman Catholicism seldom appears more attractive, more truly universal than in this unique art.

GNOSTICISM AND THE MYSTERY

The form...will vanish in the fusion of unity; for now their works lie scattered. In time Unity will perfect the spaces. It is within Unity that each one will attain himself; within knowledge he will purify himself from multiplicity into Unity, consuming matter within himself like fire, darkness by light, death by life.

The Gospel of Truth

The metaphysical universe of the pietists and the Great German Awakening, of Novalis, Friedrich Schlegel, Josef Schelling, Mozart, Schubert, and other German thinkers, poets, painters, and composers of the eighteenth and nineteenth centuries, was in some ways a re-incarnation of the metaphysical universe of early Gnosticism. It was a romance of the *mysterium magnum*. The mystery had had a unique expression in first, second, and third century gnosticism. Gnostics were aware of both the necessity for and the limitations of religious orthodoxy. Jewish and Christian orthodoxy were for them a spectacular pie in which the fruit, the mystery, is covered by a crust of ideas that both protect and hide it. The crust must be penetrated by wisdom to get to the fruit. What divided the Gnostics from orthodox Jews and Christians was at root metaphysics. The Gnostics highly esteemed the ascent to unity in experiential knowing and saw intellectual discrimination as the handmaid of that ascent. Their orthodox enemies mistrusted individual experience as a threat to communal order and central power. Orthodoxy sought to correct this error by blind obedience to church law and unquestioning belief in church doctrine. For orthodoxy experience was the enemy. Gnostics were despised for preferring their intuitions to church teaching.

The Gnostics constituted a large and influential segment of early Christianity. They were persecuted by rationalists in the fourth century. Until the Nag Hamadi discoveries in 1954 their story came to us mainly through the writings of their persecutors. Christian orthodoxy succeeded in gaining political power and used it to suppress the Gnostics. Yet thanks to the Nag Hamadi literature the Gnostic story and with it intimations of a far broader metaphysics and a more liberal, tolerant religion have been fleshed out from authentic Gnostic documents.

The Christian Gnostics, following the Egyptian and Greek mystery religions and the Jewish mystical tradition, saw themselves as wanderers, awakened by divine invitation and challenged to make the spiritual ascent into the mystery through an interplay of intuitive experience and reason. Their journey was a romance with the hidden God through divine images in the world. The outer world of nature could not fulfill the wanderer's dreams. The Divine Sophia invited the wanderer to transcend the world's limits, including the limitations of religious orthodoxy. Those who prefer the ideas of orthodoxy to the intuitive invitational experience of Sophia were thought to be guilty of idolatry.

This foolish idolatry has long been the original sin of religious orthodoxy. Timothy Freke and Peter Gandy mock the idiocy of this confusion of divine truth and its literal expression in human ideas in their book *Jesus and the Lost Goddess:*

> *Fundamentalists hold up the barbarous Old Testament as a divinely inspired account of the works of the one and only god Jehovah. Lets just have a look at the sort of god they are worshipping. In the Book of Genesis Jehovah destroys all living things on the earth by flood, but somehow also manages to find the time to specifically execute one individual man for letting his semen spill on the ground when having sex. In the Book of Exodus he inflicts hideous plagues on Egypt for not letting the Israelites leave, despite the fact that it was he himself who 'hardened the Pharaoh's heart'. He also kills all the firstborn Egyptian children, assists the Israelites in slaughtering an entire tribe of Amalekites, makes it allowable to beat a slave to death and, after rumors that Israelites have worshipped a rival god, orders faithful Israelites to kill their friends and relatives leading to the death of 3,000 people. Not content with this in the First Book of Samuel Jehovah takes vengeance on the people of Gath by giving all the men a fatal dose of haemerrhoids. In the Book of Leviticus he condones human sacrifice. In the Book of Deuteronomy he orders the Israelites to utterly destroy the people of the cities that he bequeathes to them as their ' inheritance', commanding them "not to leave anything that breathes alive'. In the Book of Numbers he orders a man to be stoned to death for gathering sticks for fire on the Sabbath, and sends a plague which kills 14,000 people. He also gives the Israelites the power to utterly destroy the Canaanites and exterminate the people of Og, advising with regard to the captured women and children: 'Kill every male among the little ones and kill every woman who has known a man intimately. But keep alive for yourself all young girls who have not*

> *known a man intimately.' You can see why the Gnostic Marcion nicknamed Jehovah 'the Exterminator'.*

The Gnostics despised the notion that the truth can be captured and not betrayed by human ideas. For them only intuition can reach through ideas to the hidden truth. A limited wisdom of ideas must respect the inner life experience of divine invitation. The Gnostics were originally Jews and Christians who despised the cheapening of the faith experience that fundamentalism implied. Ideas are only the ante-chamber of true wisdom. The true God for them was not the anthropomorphic God of Genesis II, but rather the hidden source of divine invitation reached by intuitive experience. This true God could be known...but only imperfectly... from past revelations. True knowledge of the true God was in part a matter of personal experience. Orthodox religion with its preference for idea relationships was for the Gnostic a distorted pathway to the true God. The ideas of orthodoxy betray as well as express the invitatory romance between the true God and the wanderer. The Gnostics thought that it was as important to face squarely the betrayals by orthodoxy as it was to be enriched by its treasures. Only by embracing this paradox could they ascend to the higher consciousness of the mystery. Many Gnostics fostered a creative and world-enriching counterbalance between the inner and outer worlds of the wanderer. Unfortunately other Gnostics created an alternative form of fundamentalism.

For most Gnostics the higher consciousness meant that the Gnostic wanderer does not simply possess ideas about divine invitation. He experiences the call personally, dramatically. He feels the invitation as he pursues his own unique life drama. This affects what he does and how he sees himself. The experience is but a glimpse, brief, imperfect, incompletely understood. But it is real and it transcends *knowledge about* God and religion. It transcends conceptual knowing. The *Apocryphon of John* describes the higher consciousness as a helper, a creative, inventive consciousness that is present in every person, but is often hidden and unrecognized. But when recognized it can work to restore him or her to full being and works to benefit all of creation. It is a dramatic grasp of life which vaguely teaches something about origins and destination.

This higher consciousness inevitably challenged some of the conclusions made by the Jewish and Christian orthodoxies. Many Gnostics distinguished the real God of the inner world who invites but remains hidden, i.e. cannot be conceptualized, from Jehovah, the God of the outer world. There is then a true God, the God of the Gnostics who transcends the God of Revelation, and a false God, the Jehovah of orthodoxy. Some Gnostics saw in Jesus one who was similarly aware of the distinction between the God-distortion of religious fundamentalism and the true but hidden God who invites through both revelation and the experience of value. For them each "now" is in the final analysis sacred invitation. Valentinian Gnostics thought that the true God can be reached only by respecting but transcending ideas of God and ascending higher through intuition. Elaine Pagels writes insightfully:

> *Heracleon explains that most Christians tend to take literally the images they find in the scriptures. They see God as the creator who made this present world, the lawgiver who gave the tablets to Moses on Sinai, the divine Father who begot Jesus. But those who experience God's presence come to see the traditional images of God for what they are - human creations. One need not reject such images, Heracleon says, since they provide an essential way of pointing towards divine reality that words cannot express; but one may come to see that all religious language - and much other language - consists of such images. Whoever values this comes to worship God, as Jesus said, in "spirit and in truth".*
>
> *Beyond Belief*

The Valentinian Gnostics did not think of themselves as heretics or lesser Christians any more than ninety percent of today's American and European Catholics think themselves less Catholic because they disdain the Roman teaching on birth control. On the contrary the Gnostics, like today's free thinking adult Catholics, considered themselves elite Christians precisely because they encountered divine invitation personally and freely. They felt that they possessed a higher consciousness of that invitation that did not dismiss Christian orthodoxy as meaningless, but saw in it a launching pad for the spiritual ascent that reached yet higher. It found inspiration and life in that orthodoxy. But it did insist upon the limitation of orthodoxy and the occasional necessity to transcend and correct it. This awakening to the divine presence was celebrated in the Valentinian *Gospel of Truth*.

> *The Gospel of Truth is joy to those who have received from the Father of Truth the gift of knowing him by the power of the Logos, who has come from the pleroma and who is in the thought and the mind of the Father. He it is who is called the Saviour.*
>
> *The Gospel of Truth*

The wanderer, once awakened, can ascend to a higher consciousness. This meant a new appraisal of beliefs and laws, not rejecting them as invalid, but rather refining them qualitatively and harmonizing them with experience. Life in this higher and better world meant a special way to know, a special way to be. And at the core of the new knowledge was *epinoia*. *Epinoia* was based upon an indirect but real and powerful experience of divine invitation, mediated through value. It embraced the metaphysics of drama as well as the metaphysics of ideas. It was controlled by a manager-magician, the wanderer. He or she ascends out of the contradictions both in the exterior and interior worlds to recreate the outer world by reconciling its value conflicts. The wanderer must create his own universe. He can look up to the stars and see divine splendor. He can experience the storm and feel divine power. He can see divine beauty in the flowery meadow, and feel the gargantuan force of the cascading waters. But in human affairs this divine harmony, so evident in the outer world of nature, is often contradicted and must be creatively brought into being in the unique life of each wanderer. Each wanderer must rise above the war of opposites that imprisons him or her and make of life a unique and priceless unity. So each wanderer seeks a new age that is both personal and communal, in which contradictions are reconciled. God's harmony, imaged in nature, must find a yet more noble expression through godly human creativity.

For every wanderer the outer world remains inescapably imprisoned in shadows of darkness. Victories over the darkness can be only partial and temporary. In cabalistic terms the world remains in the *Qelippah.* And yet hidden within the darkness, often in orthodox religion, is a freedom-promising light. Gnosis, the experience of that light, is life-transfiguring. Only *gnosis*, a harmony of reason and experience, raises the wanderer above the *Qelippah*.

In conflicts between ideas of orthodoxy and *gnosis... gnosis* was trump. Gnostics adjusted to the mind-deadening "absolutizing" of judgments by church orthodoxy in their own way. Church judgments were respected but not considered final. No magisterium, no book, nothing in history replaced the mystery of an experiential/rational inner life encounter between the soul and God.

Valentinian Gnosticism, reflecting Jewish wisdom, recognized the wanderer as properly a wrestler with the God known through the outer world. In order to remain in contact with the hidden God of the *mysterium magnum* the wanderer had to interpret revelation in the light of actual experience. The wanderer subjected laws and beliefs to the experiential light derived from uniting opposites. Sometimes sexual liberties were taken. Moral teachings and dogmas were not regarded as absolute. As a consequence Gnosticism was condemned by Christian orthodoxy as a dangerous and immoral heresy.

Gnosticism alerted mystics for centuries to the bi-polarity, the dividedness, the essential imperfection of the "now". The resolution of bi-polar tension can be reached only through spiritual creativity in the face of opposites. The awareness of bi-polarity and the response to it is what we are calling immersion in the rose cross mystery. According to the *Gospel of Thomas:*

> *The kingdom is inside you, and it is outside of you. When you come to know yourselves, then you will become known and realize that it is you who are sons of the living Father...*
>
> *The Gospel of Thomas*

The *Gospel of Thomas* challenges its readers to act wisely, in accordance with an inner, divine light, transforming the earth. It warns against one-sidedness, counseling instead the wisdom that creates a heaven on earth. The higher consciousness ascends to the hidden God as it reconciles conflicts in the inner life and the outer world.

> *When you make the two one, and when you make the inside like the outside, and the outside like the inside, and the above like the below, and when*

> *you make the male and the female one and the same... then you will enter into the kingdom.*
>
> *The Gospel of Thomas*

Soon after the death of Jesus, followers of Menander and Simon Magus took this fundamental principle one step farther. God must be understood in terms of the reconciliation of contradiction. God can best be understood as a divinely fruitful bi-polarity, a Father and a Mother (Ennoia, the feminine thought of the Father). Together bthey generate the offspring of this contradiction, the Son. This divine romance is the prototype for the archetypal experience of the fruitful union of earthly opposites. God can be understood and approached through the sacred and sacramental sexual experience. In stark contrast to Christian fundamentalists these Gnostics rejected a polarized, masculine, monolithic, legalistic, logical, rationalistic nature in God, in creation, and in redemption. They celebrated instead the divine life that can be known best through the archetypal and generative love ascent of man and woman.

> *I shall praise and glorify thee and...the three: Father, Mother, and Son, the perfect power.*
>
> *The Apocryphon of John*

The wanderer must awaken to the mystery of the self, becoming that true self according to the divine image.

> *When you come to know yourselves...you will realize that it is you who are the sons of the living Father.*
>
> *The Gospel of Thomas*

The awakening promises a higher life in a new age.

> *I shall give you what no eye has seen and no ear has heard and no hand has touched and what has never occurred to the human mind.*
>
> *The Gospel of Thomas*

An example of how the Gnostics could make a silk purse (something spiritual) out of a sow's ear (the literal text) consider how some of them radically re-interpreted *Second Genesis*. For the Gnostics the God of *Genesis II* was a creature of the outer world, not the true God but a pretender, the *demiurge*. He was the false god of fundamentalism, tragically limited, commanding slavery, not freedom. Sometimes this god had to be disobeyed. So *Genesis II* was not to be rejected but re-interpreted. This re-interpretation was a springboard to a richer experience of "now". Eve, archetypal woman, responds wisely to the serpent. She is Sophia, incarnate. In following her Adam finds salvation. Adam and Eve's rebellion against the tyrannical false god in the name of wisdom was symbolic, not of a "fall" in the sense of a moral collapse, but rather of a graduation to moral adulthood.

Gnostic wisdom meant immersion in the rose cross mystery. Many Gnostics sought the true God in the reconciliation of the duality between the patriarchal God of the Jews on one hand and Sophia the perfect image of God celebrated in the Jewish wisdom literature on the other. Gnostic writing celebrated the romance between God and Sophia (perfect creation) and called it a marriage. This romance is the prototype for earthly love. In the Gnostic gospels Jesus and Mary Magdalene are symbols of that marriage. Sexual love, an analogue of that union, could be intensely sacred.

> *Marriage in the world is a mystery...it belongs not to the darkness and to the night, but to the day and to the light.*
>
> *The Gospel of Phillip*

That romance of earthly opposites unites the world to God.

> *Great is the mystery of marriage for without it the world would not exist.*
>
> *The Gospel of Phillip*

The Judaic vision of the ascent of the Shekhinah to unity with creation and with God recognizes a unique value in woman. She together with man constitute the ideal Anthropos. Woman's ascent to her proper queenship is the symbol of the coming of the new age.

> *When Eve was still in Adam death did not exist. When she was separated from him death came into being. If he enters again and attains his former self, death will be no more.*
>
> *The Gospel of Phillip*

A spiritualized sexual love is the light-bringing sacrament, the symbol of the great romance between heaven and earth that leads to love's triumph.

> *Everyone who will enter the bridal chamber will kindle the light...if anyone becomes a son of the bridal chamber he will receive the light..*
>
> *The Gospel of Phillip*

Gnosticism at its best united heaven and earth not by escaping the outer world but by transfiguring it by an inner light. The clashing values of both inner and outer worlds must be reconciled first of all in the inner life, in *gnosis.*

> *It is within unity that each one will attain himself; within knowledge he will purify himself from multiplicity into Unity, consuming matter within himself like fire, darkness by light, death by life.*
>
> *The Gospel of Truth*

The romance between God and Sophia illuminated the love between the living, sexual, resurrected Christ, the incarnation of God, and Mary Magdalene, the incarnation of the Divine Sophia. The symbolic incarnation of the rose cross mystery in the relationship between Jesus and Mary Magdalene is an important theme in the *Gospel of Phillip.*

> *(Jesus) loved her more than all the disciples and used to kiss her often ...*
> ... .
> *The rest of the disciples asked him, Why do you love her more than all of us?*

But Gnostics could betray the mystery as grievously as did the orthodoxies. Some, infected by Greek rationalism and its consequent dualism, fell into a monolithic rejection of bi-polarity. They despised portions of the outer world. According to this dualism creation is split between good and evil parts. In each case one part is good, the other evil. One part of reality is irreconcilably pitted against another. This metaphysical poison, the ugly part of our inheritance from the Greeks and Persians, pits experience against reason, nation against nation, sex against sex, race against race, religion against religion. Value conflicts are resolved by arbitrary selection and not by an ascent to higher unity. Objects like stones, stars and places, as well as religious and philosophical systems can be categorized as "good" or "evil" in the name of a capriciously cruel god who arbitrarily selects the saved and delights in destroying the damned. Out of such dichotomies came the demonizing of large categories of things like the flesh, sex, women, competing religions, races, and nations. Such distortions of transcendental reality paint portions of the worlds (national, racial, religious, etc.) in demonic colors as a matter of course, making a higher unity impossible.

The gnostics at their best were celebrants of a great mystery that transcends every idea about it. Their celebrations have had great influence upon the Renaissance and upon the spiritual awakening in Europe in the eighteenth century. Schubert in particular was a beneficiarty of their wisdom. His art embodied their recognition of the need for symbols in approaching the *mysterium magnum*. Poetry that never pretends to be an ideology inspired his creations. He expressed himself in music that transcends even poetry in a far richer language of the heart. The art for those capable of penetrating beneath its surface is a kind of neo-gnostic ladder to the stars.

Traces of The Mystery

Then I saw a new heaven and a new earth. The former heaven and the former earth had passed away, and the sea was no more. I also saw the holy city, a new Jerusalem coming down out of heaven from God, prepared as a bride adorned for her husband.

Book of Revelation

The *mysterium magnum* means a paradoxical immersion in the dramatic tension between two great romances, one between heaven and earth, the other a romance between earthly opposites. The wanderer encounters this rose cross mystery experientially at the point where the romances meet, i.e. in the "now", the present moment. Immersion in the mystery means an intuitive embrace of the "now". The embrace demands first an awakening by the wanderer to his or her plight, i.e. to being where he or she does not want to be. Then it demands an awakening to the divine invitation to an ascent to a better world. The ascent leads through living and dying, through hope and despair, through triumph and defeat to a mysterious, transcendental triumph. Immersion in the mystery gives meaning to life. This life-altering experience is the soul of the great religions and the spiritual core of an ideal harmony between them. It is also the most basic ground for harmony within and between races and nations, sexes and generations, groups and individuals, and opposing parts of the self. It suggests the key to the ideal resolution of value conflicts. This chapter presents a highly selective overview of appearances of this mystery.

From the time of the ancient Egyptians and Greeks the *mysterium magnum* has meant creative personal participation in a romance between worlds and not service to an ideology. The wisdom that embraces this romance has sometimes envisioned life as a process in which a universe of light fragments, split and separated in darkness, are slowly and laboriously united in an ascent to a better world. This movement is one of qualitative expansion and quantitative contraction. It demands courage and creativity of the illuminated wanderer in uniting the fragments. The higher world is reached by transcending, not rejecting, the lower one. Fidelity to this task of transcending gives direction to the life of Schubert's wanderer and underlies Schubert's art. The challenge of fidelity to the rose cross mystery is expressed many times in the poetry that inspired that art as this book will show. In meeting that challenge the composer followed in the footsteps of many other cultural leaders. An awareness of some of these earlier celebrants of the mystery will be helpful in gaining an appreciation of what Schubert has accomplished.

The role of the wanderer in the interplay between worlds is crucial and has a history. The wanderer is filled with divine life. Adam Kadmon of the Cabala, the Divine Sophia of the wisdom literature, the Logos of Plato, the "Word" of the *Fourth Gospel* all suggest that the wanderer is charged with a divine responsibility, one of conducting a romance between higher and lower worlds. Some higher consciousness of that responsibility is latent in everyone.

This noble responsibility of the wanderer was given expression in Hermetic writing from the third century which reflects an ancient awareness of the thrilling miracle that exists in a higher consciousness of the mystery:

> *What a great miracle is Man, O Asclepius, a being worthy of reverence and honor. For he passes into the nature of a god as though he were himself a god. He has familiarity with the race of demons, knowing that he is issued from the same origin. He despises that part of his nature that is only human, for he has put his hope in the divinity of the other part.*
>
> *The Asclepius*

This divine spark of the wanderer does not make him or her self-sufficient. The divine self has an absolute need of the divine other. This was expressed in the following quotation from *Celestial Hierarchies* written by the Pseudo Dionysius in the fifth or sixth century. True wisdom means an openness of the wanderer to the ultimate contradiction to the self: the transcendental Other. That Other is beyond the categories of thought familiar to the wanderer.

> *...scriptural imagery proceeds naturally through sacred images like "Word", "Mind", and "Being" to reveal the attributes of God. But there is also the scriptural device of praising the Deity by presenting it in utterly dissimilar revelations. He is described as invisible, infinite, ungraspable, and other things which show not what he is but what in fact he is not. The second way of talking about him seems to me to be much more appropriate, for, as the secret and sacred tradition has instructed, God is in no way like the things that have being and we have no knowledge at all of his incomprehensible and ineffable transcendence and invisibility.*

The wanderer is called experientially to awaken to the invitation to unite with this hidden Other. Only by making the leap beyond self can he realize himself. Elsewhere the Pseudo-Dionysius writes about this incomprehensible God:

> *Again as we climb higher we say this. (God) is not soul or mind, nor does God possess imagination, conviction, speech, or understanding. Nor is God speech per se, understanding per se. God cannot be spoken of and cannot be grasped by understanding. God is not number or order, greatness or smallness, equality or inequality, similarity or dissimilarity. God is not movable, immovable or at rest. God has no power; God is not power, nor light. God does not live nor have life.. God is not a substance nor eternity nor time. God cannot be grasped by the understanding since God is neither knowledge nor truth. God is not kingship. God is not wisdom. God is neither one nor oneness, divinity nor goodness. Nor is God a spirit in the sense in which we understand that term. God is not son-ship nor fatherhood, and is nothing known to us or any other being. God falls within the predicate neither of non-being nor of being. Existing beings do not know God as God actually is and God does not know them as they are. There is no speaking of God, nor name nor knowledge of God. Darkness and light, error and truth-God is none of these. God is beyond assertion and denial. We make assertions and denials of what is next to God, but never of God, for God is both beyond every assertion, being the perfect and unique cause of all things, and, by virtue of a preeminently simple and absolute nature, free of every limitation; God is also beyond every denial.*
>
> *The Mystical Theology*

The God who is the ground of both self and other is often hidden behind contradictions, and can be touched, albeit imperfectly and with transience, in their reconciliations. This is especially true in the relationship between men and women. The wanderer has the divine spark that enables him or her to make the leap beyond the self to find the truest self in union with the other.

The Roman Church has often found the responsible and creative wanderer to be a problem, preferring obedience to church authority. In the twelfth century this disfigurement of the core mystery by Christian orthodoxy was challenged by the Knights Templar. On June 12, 1118 Hughes de Payens and eight other knights pledged themselves to the protection of pilgrims traveling to the Holy Land. The knights established their quarters upon the ruins of the Temple of Solomon. While in the Middle East they discovered a mysterious "treasure". From these beginnings they became extraordinarily wealthy and influential in both secular and mystical affairs in Europe. Their treasure promised a new age of freedom. Richard the Lion-hearted was an honorary Templar. His brother and rival, King John, was forced to sign the Magna Carta, a foundation stone for the political rights of man, by Richard's trusted advisor, Aymeric in 1215. The Templars had a revolutionary understanding of the mystery, one that threatened both the political orthodoxy of France and the religious orthodoxy of Rome. These knights were responsible for the Grail romances that celebrated the wanderer's quest for divine life, a quest suggesting that that divine life and life in the world were intimately connected. Man was to play a creative part in his own redemption. Because of this challenge to the absolute sway of political and religious orthodoxy over the wanderer the Templars were persecuted and driven by Phillip IV out of France in 1314. They found refuge in Scotland where, according to legend, they won the day for the Scots against the English at Bannockburn. In addition to the Magna Carta and the Grail romances the Templars used their mathematical skills, learned in the Middle East, to inspire and direct the building of the great Gothic cathedrals in Europe. But the hidden effects of the counterbalance were more imposing still. Secret societies were created to facilitate the wanderer's immersion in the mystery. European mystics sought a working counterbalance between its vertical (the wanderer and God) and horizontal (the reconciliation of value conflicts) dimensions. Unfortunately Rome in 1314 authorized King Phillip to torture and kill the Templars' grand master, Jacques de Molay and other knights, making this particular expression of the mystery lethally impolitic.

In the eleventh, twelfth, and thirteenth centuries in Languedoq the Troubadours created a new and challenging wedding of the "demonic" and the divine. They sought to experience the wedding of higher and lower worlds through their church-defying experience of sensual love. They celebrated sensual love as a ladder for the ascent from the lower to a higher world. Contradicting the Augustinian damnation of sensual pleasure as sinful they saw sensual and sexual love as a privileged way to the stars.

René Nelli in *Le Roman de Raimon de Miraval, Troubadour* wrote of one of the famous troubadours:

> *Because the beauty of women, ephemeral as it is, exalts the man and makes him better; he never wanted to admit that this world was the work of the Demon (as the Cathar Church believed). He only put his confidence in the supreme love, which is neither of God nor of the devil, but remains the image of the only eternity which nature permitted to men to experience for the duration of an instant.*

For these seekers of the higher consciousness of the wedding of higher and lower worlds that we are calling the rose cross mystery matter was not necessarily the enemy of the spirit. Rather "in-spirited" matter could be the pathway to the stars. Sexuality could be, should be, the special sacrament of the Divine Sophia. The true enemy of the mystery was the grotesque dualism that underlies wars between nations, races, religions, and sexes.

One notable seeker after the elusive harmony between opposites was Johannes "Meister" Eckhart, the first great, speculative Rhineland mystic, born in Hochheim in 1260. Following the Pseudo-Dionysius he held that there is a mystical co-naturing between heaven and earth to which God attracts the wanderer in an experience that stupefies the mind. Poets and mystics more easily recognize this experience. Here is one allusion to this secret wellspring of life within the wanderer:

> *But now perhaps you say: what can God do in the core and essence of the soul without ideas?' I couldn't possible know, for the agents of the soul deal only in ideas, taking things and naming them, each according to its own idea...Since the soul itself does not know, it wonders and, wondering, it seeks, for the soul knows very well that something is afoot. See, as long as it is concealed, man will always be after it. It appears and disappears, which means we shall plead and sigh for it. Saint Paul felt constrained to pursue it within his soul and not without. It was within and never outside, always inward. When he was convinced of that he said: 'I am persuaded that neither death...nor any affliction can separate me from what I find inside me."*
>
> *Meister Eckhart*

For Eckhart, this higher consciousness that calls the wanderer ever higher is God's "insight into himself". It is God's self-awareness that is in some way in the wanderer. In the wanderer it is divine wisdom, the Divine Sophia.

> *God has perfect insight into Himself and knows himself up and down, through and through, not by ideas but directly. God begets His Son through the true unity of the divine nature. See! This is the way. He begets His Son in the core of the soul and is made one with it. There is no other way. If an idea is interposed, there would be no true unity. Man's whole blessedness lies in that unity.*
>
> *Meister Eckhart*

In the fourteenth century another great German mystic, Nicholas of Cusa, spoke of this world-transforming higher consciousness that we are calling immersion in the rose cross mystery whereby man ascends into "Paradise" by reconciling the contradictions presented by nature. He gave us his insight into the nature of this ascent. The ascent to harmony leads through dissonance to a triumph of love. As we reconcile opposites we live the divine life. In *De Visione Dei* we read:

> *I have found the abode wherein you shall dwell without veil, an abode surrounded by the coincidence of contradictions. This coincidence is the wall of Paradise wherein you dwell. The gate of this wall is guarded by a lofty rational spirit. Unless this spirit is vanquished there is no entrance possible. It is only on the other side of the coincidence of contradictions, not on this side, that you, the Divinity, can be seen.*

True wisdom for Nicholas lay in the encounter with God realized through the re-creation of divine harmony out of contradiction on earth, i.e through the reconciliation of opposites. Here the wanderer ascends to his true home. The

Divine Sophia, the beautiful image of God, rather than calling the wanderer away from the world, invites him to ascend through it by resolving its conflicts, not through condemnation and hatred but through aggregation in imaginative new unities. The Pseudo-Dionysius, Meister Eckhart, and Nicholas prepared other thinkers and hopefully ourselves for a cultural movement away from the doctrinal rigidity that sometimes poisoned religious orthodoxy towards idea flexibility and the penetration of the walls of contradiction.

Immersion in the *mysterium magnum* was often enough for the wanderer through a woman. A famous celebrant of wisdom, Dante Aligieri, the greatest Italian poet, lived in thirteenth century Florence. He was born in the same decade as Meister Eckhart. Dante had a profound awareness of the higher consciousness that sees life as a romance with God through his sophianic image. He found in a special woman an incarnation of that image. At the core of his life was a Platonic romance between himself and his Sophia-incarnation, the beloved Beatrice, who mediated for him a romance with God. He first met Beatrice when he was nine years old. She remained the guiding star and inspiration for his life, especially after she died. He wrote of her:

> *It was given to me to behold a wonderful vision, wherein I saw things which determined me to say nothing further of this blessed one until such time as I could discourse more worthily concerning her. And to this end I labor all I can as she in truth knows. Therefore if it be his pleasure through whom is the life of all things that my life continues a few years, it is my hope to write concerning her what has never been written of any woman. Then may it seem good to him who is lord of courtesy that my spirit should rise to behold the glory of its lady, to wit of that blessed Beatrice who now gloriously gazes on the face of him "qui est per omnia saecula benedictus."*

Beatrice was a true image of God, a mediatrix between God and Dante, not separating but uniting them. She was for him Sophia incarnate.

Dante was married (probably happily) and not to Beatrice. He had children. This intensely sacred love was directed towards a woman married to someone else. Dante wrote *The Divine Comedy* and there celebrated the multi-layered and paradoxical great romance. Beatrice, for him an incarnation of the Divine Sophia, the perfect image of God, led Dante in his vision of art, his ascent to God, and to love's triumph.

> *Then I turned my eyes to my lady...and I was amazed for deep within those eyes glowed such a smile that in seeing it I touched the height and depth of my grace and my heaven. Paradiso*

Forty years after Dante's birth, another Christian, cabalist, Francesco Petrarca or Petrarch, was born in Florence. His lyrical poetry helped launch the Renaissance. And, like Dante, he celebrated a mystery-centered wisdom that challenged orthodoxy to a radical expansion. Like Dante he expressed himself in allegory and myth. And like Dante this wanderer found his experience of the *mysterium magnum* through a woman. For him Laura was an incarnation of the Divine Sophia, the bride of the Lamb, and the perfect image and the beloved of God. His romance of her was spiritual, Platonic, and powerful, inspiring him to express his own spiritual ascent in works of the highest beauty. Again we see a higher consciousness that is realized in the interplay between a concrete love relationship of a man with a woman who in a real but limited way makes incarnate his relationship with God.

Such expressions of the rose cross mystery suggest that there is something besides the institutional Church that serves as the ultimate ethical guide of the wanderer. The mystery has always created a tension, sometimes life-giving, sometimes tragic, with religious and political orthodoxy. The tension was intensified in the middle of the fifteenth century when a third century collection of works was translated by Marsilio Ficino. That collection forged new bonds between Christianity and the ancient Indian, Egyptian, Persian, Jewish, and Greek mysteries. In the opinion of the Oxford scholar Frances Yates these works unleashed the spiritual powers of the high Renaissance by introducing Europe to suppressed pagan ideas about the wanderer, revealing them in their organic harmony with the mysteries of Christianity. Driven by the hunger for a fuller life experience intellectual leaders reading these works were awakened to their inherent power to be gods and goddesses. A problem-solving metaphysics that transcends scholasticism was implied.

We speak of the *Corpus Hermeticum*. Through it the wanderer was challenged to godliness and the Judeo-Christian belief system required alteration. The works suggested that the godly life is realized ideally in a love union between a divinely masculine messianic figure and a divinely feminine beloved. This wedding paradoxically weds the wanderer to an earthly beloved and to the otherwise hidden God. Men and women and indeed all pairs of opposites make this romance incarnate, ascending through contradiction in quest of divine life. The wise man or woman whom we are calling the "wanderer" navigates the ascent. He or she is called to be a *magus*, a magician, and facilitate the great romance. He or she must ascend though and beyond the universe of law and authority, the *Truth*-distorting metaphysics of ideas, into a revolutionary experience of himself/herself and the world. Awakened by incarnations of the messiah the wanderer reaches beyond what has been achieved towards the dream-maiden, the Divine Sophia, in whom the image of God is perfected. The spiritually mature wanderer is called to act like the image of God he/she truly is, and act as a messiah and/or Sophia to bring into divine harmony the chaotic and demonic forces of the cosmos. The wanderer is called to be a divine lover of a godly beloved. Men and women can be gods and goddesses. By creatively and imaginatively reaching upwards towards the Divine Sophia they truly image God. In this effort divine worlds touch and transfigure our own. In *Giordano Bruno and the Hermetic Tradition* Yates gives a précis of *Hermes Trismegistus to Tat on the Common Intellect*. The wanderer in his journey has powers beyond expectation:

> *See what power, what swiftness you possess. It is so that you must conceive of God; all that is he contains within himself, like thoughts, the world, Himself, the All. Therefore unless you make yourself like God, you cannot understand God; for the like is not intelligible save to the like. Make yourself grow to a greatness beyond measure; by a bound free yourself from the body; raise yourself above all time; become eternity; then you will understand God. Believe that nothing is impossible for you; think yourself immortal and capable of understanding all, all arts, all sciences, all natures of every living being. Mount higher than the highest height; descend lower than the lowest depth. Draw into yourself all sensations and everything created, fire and water, dry and moist, imagining that you are everywhere on earth, in the sea, in the sky, that you are not yet born, in the maternal womb, adolescent, old, dead, beyond death. If you embrace in your thought all beings at once, times, places, substances, qualities, quantities, you may understand God.*

Here is the romance of world-becoming. The wanderer is called to a higher consciousness, imaging God through an embrace of opposites, expanding himself to divine dimensions. Here the Hermetic wanderer who combines the visions of ancient pre-Christian religion and Christianity is called not merely to laws and beliefs and certainly not to paranoid fear and hatred, but to awaken, think and act like...to become... what in some limited sense he is destined to be, the perfect image of God, the Divine Sophia. This he can do only by uniting contradictions, transcending limitations, creatively becoming what he now is not. He is called to ascend through liberated reason and creative imagination to ever higher harmonies. One symbol of the harmony is a cross, one bar vertical, the other horizontal; one bar the God-wanderer romance, the other bar the reconciliation of worldly contradiction. They meet in the middle where the wanderer must wrestle with the paradox. In the "Egyptian Genesis", the *Poimandres* from the *Corpus Hermeticum,* man, the wanderer, is seen as a divine image of God, ready for participation in a cosmic romance.

> *Now the Nous, the father of all things, being life and light, brought forth a Man similar to himself, whom he loved as his own child. For the Man was beautiful, reproducing the image of his Father...*

The wanderer's challenge is objectified in a myth in which a romance between a masculine messianic figure and a feminine beloved leads through and finally out of the darkness. This is the archetypal drama. In the *Corpus Hermeticum* the masculine hero, a kind of Christ figure, sees the heroine (Nature, the world, creation) in her divine beauty (for she also is an image of God), falls in love with her, and unites with her as with his bride. Here the romance between the hidden God and the wanderer is imaged through unions of opposites. Love, the harmonic binding force, unites heaven and earth as it unites earthly opposites. God is imaged when the divine feminine in Nature and the messianic figure unite. The world-awakening *Poimandres* sings of this romance.

> *Then Man, who had full power over the world of mortal beings and of animals, leant across the armatures of the spheres...and showed to the Nature below the beautiful form of God.; when Nature saw this inexhaustible and divine beauty and power...she smiled with love, for she has seen those features, marvelous and beautiful, reflected in her waters, seen his shadow reflected on the earth. And he, seeing such reflections in the earth and water, fell in love with her and wished to unite with her. Thus did he come into union with an irrational form. She embraced him...and they burned with love for one another.*

The wanderer is not called to be merely a follower of rules. Instead he is called to awaken to his own divine potential. The wanderer has a responsibility, a job to do. He must be creative and imaginative in his ascent. In the words of the *Poimandres:*

> *He who knows himself goes towards himself, that is towards his true nature. You are light and life, like God the Father of whom Man was born. If therefore you learn to know yourself as made of light and life...you will return to life.*

Marsilio Ficino made a monumental contribution to the dawning of a new age by his translation of the *Corpus Hermeticum* into Latin, making its revolutionary focus upon a godly wanderer accessible first to Italy and then to all of Europe. In Ficino's capable hands, the metaphysical contradictions of the inner life invited new vistas. The deceptive clarity of the orthodoxies had to make room for the "shadow-land of the heart", a possession not of any institution but of the wanderer. The Neo-Platonic universe of experience combined with Christian universe of belief in a way that inspired a monumental eruption of culture. Around Ficino men of brilliance gathered, challenging the *status quo* not with a rejection of the past but with its embrace expressed through a transcendence of it. With Ficino they thought that the wanderer, wedding the world of experience to the world of the intellect, could be a magician, opening the pathway to the stars. The wedding led to new and experiences of the beauty of life. For example biblical tradition and personal experience interacted to inspire some of the greatest paintings of all time. In addition transcendental beauty could be imagined through combinations of poetry and music. Paired these opposites could be powerful tools whereby the magician awakens the spirit to the truth of the rose cross mystery.

The powerful nobleman Cosimo di Medici used his influence in Florence to help Ficino bring the *Poimandres* with its challenging view of the wanderer to the attention of Europe. Divine life must become incarnate. The wanderer can and should be godlike. The Christian Cabala in Florence flourished under Cosimo's tutelage. Botticelli, Michelangelo, Leonardo, and Bernini ascended to the higher consciousness and expressed in their creations the illumination that comes with harmonizing religion and the bi-polar mysteries of nature.

Through their art Christianity was changing. It was not being destroyed but enhanced.

The enhancement was a realization of the rose cross mystery. The vertical relationship of the wanderer to God was being enriched by relating opposites. The wanderer was making his ascent to God indirectly, through nature. Christ, for Christians the climactic incarnation of the Divine Sophia, stands at a point where the bars of the cross meet, a rose upon a cross of opposites. He is the prototypical wanderer. The great artist is Christ-like as a master of contradiction. The Italian giants sparked a massive rebellion against religious fundamentalism's tyranny over the wanderer. Expressions of the electrifying light of a new age can be seen in the godlike nude figures that adorn walls in Florence, Sienna, and Rome and in museums throughout the world. The wanderer's joy in being human was illuminated with joy in experiencing the divine invitation to a higher life.

When we speak of the Renaissance we speak of the wanderer's awakening to the paradoxical romance that transfigures the human experience. We speak of the wanderer's awakening to the rose cross mystery. The new man of the Renaissance, inspired by the *Corpus Hermeticum*, wanted to expand to the infinite dimensions of nature and in doing so to more faithfully image God. He was to be a magician, who could, when properly prepared, make nature work for him. In short the wanderer was being awakened to his and her responsibility to paradoxically assert yet challenge tradition in the creation of a new world.

Among these brilliant celebrants of this paradoxical wisdom the name of Pico della Mirandola stands high. In him the Magus, the practitioner of the Christian Cabala, a union of Jewish and Christian mysticism, found a champion. For him the wise man who mastered astronomy and astrology could unite higher and lower worlds. Pico saw the Jewish Cabala as a great aid for the wanderer to understand the Christian mysteries and experience the spiritual ascent to divine harmony. In this he found support from Pope Alexander VI who officially sanctioned and recommended the Christian Cabala to the faithful. Pico's wanderer lived to unite theology and philosophy, religion and science, reason and faith in a new age:

> *We have lived, illustrious friend Ermoleo, and to posterity shall live not in the schools for the grammarians, the teaching places of young minds, but in the company of the philosophers, conclaves of sages, where the questions of debate are not concerning the mother of Andromache nor the sons of Niobe and such light trifles, but of things human and divine.*

In Pico's wisdom-inspired vision contradiction found its resolution in the interpenetration of opposing worlds. Here the infinite and thrilling dimensions of Sophia, the Bride of God and the ideal of mankind, begin to appear. The wanderer is to return to his divine home by uniting opposites. The creative genius, bridging contradictions between clashing groups in society, between philosophies, between arts and science, between religious sects, between rich and poor, can elaborate new systems and solutions and in doing so penetrate to the divine source of life's invitation. The prison of the light fragments, the cabalistic *Qelippah*, is not necessarily the enemy of the wanderer. It is the treasure trove where his future waits. It will be his stairway to the stars.

> *In us will dwell Gabriel, the spirit of the Lord, who will lead us through the wonders of nature, and show us where dwells the virtue and the power of God.*
>
> *Pico, De hominis dignitate*

Are contradictions to be reconciled? Or will there be eternal war between opposites? Is there to be a new age? Frances Yates wrote of Pico who pioneered in the wanderer's new symbiosis of Jewish and Catholic mysticism with science:

> *The profound significance of Pico della Mirandola in the history of humanity can hardly be over-estimated. He it was who first boldly formulated a new position for European man, man as Magus using both magia and Cabala to act upon the world, to control his destiny by science. And in Pico the organic link with religion of the emergence of the Magus can be studied at its source.*
>
> *Giordano Bruno and the Hermetic Tradition*

Giordano Bruno was another in the parade of Italian giants who found their inspiration from immersion in the rose cross mystery. For him the journey to the stars was a romance between the wanderer and a woman in whom divine invitation was incarnate. In *De gli eroici furori* he composed a series of love poems accompanied by commentaries and dedicated to Philip Sydney. In them Bruno turned to the heartland of the *Qelippah*, sexuality. Un fortunately orthodox Christianity, following Augustine, saw Original Sin as sexual pleasure. Catholic mysticism had taken for granted that for man woman was an occasion of sin and sexuality was part of the darkness from which the mystic must emerge. Bruno thought differently. Woman can transfigure the wanderer's life. Sex can hurt. But simultaneously its heavenly beauty invites the wanderer into the sublime.

> *Render yourself, oh Goddess, unto pity!*
> *Open, oh lady, the gates of your eyes,*
> *And look upon me if you would give me death!*

This goddess is a mediatrix between higher and lower worlds, calling the wanderer both to a higher life and to death in making the ascent. The stars, the eyes of the goddess, God's eyes, project the power and the allure of the higher world. Their enigmatic invitation makes the contradiction-reconciling, death-assuring divine invitation incarnate. The invitation to a higher life and the allure of a beautiful woman are differing expressions of the same divine reality. Yates wrote of this mystery:

> *By saying that the eyes should open the lover is praying that the divine light should show itself. And the death that the glance of the eyes can give can signify the mystical death of the soul (which same is eternal life which a man may anticipate in this life and enjoy for eternity.)*

Bruno thought that this enigmatic divine light that is both deadly and life-engendering shines throughout creation. Its acceptance makes all the difference. The acceptance of death is inseparable from the invitation to life. (This principle is a key to understanding Schubert.) The paradoxical invitation can take possession of the soul with stupendous power. The soul is a hunter for this godly light. Bruno's hunter for the higher consciousness, Actaeon, sees in the waters of nature divine beauty, the Goddess, the perfect image of God.

> *Here amid the waters, that is, in the mirror image of the divine, wherein shines the luminous divine goodness and splendor… he sees the most beautiful form and face that it is possible to see.*
>
> *Eroici furori*

For Bruno a new age seemed to beckon. His insistence upon the experiential dimension of man's ascent to the divine through nature sparked hopes for an endless enhancement of life through science and love. The individual man and woman could be godly…to one another. The warring European world would at last break out of the Aristotelian dualism that held it captive. In its place there would be a recognition of a higher order of problem solving that would affect life throughout the world. Unimaginable powers in man were about to be unleashed through the triumph of wisdom. A new problem solving philosophy, a fresh vision of religion, a commitment to science, and a demand for the empowerment of the individual affected many European intellectuals. Dualism with its little absolutes was being set aside in favor of an ascent to true wisdom. At the end of the sixteenth century Giordano Bruno could write:

> *The question which we ought to ask ourselves is whether we are in the daylight with the light of truth rising above our horizon, or whether the day is with our adversaries in the antipodes; whether the shadows of error are over us or over them; whether we who are beginning to revive the ancient philosophy are in the dawn which ends the night or in the evening of a day which is closing. And this is not difficult to decide for these two schools of thought can be roughly judged by their fruits.*
>
> *Cena de la ceneri*

Bruno envisioned a metaphysical universe that was quite distinct from that of Christian fundamentalists. An alternative epistemology! An alternative problem solving paradigm! Implications of a new and richer theology! All based upon a higher consciousness directing a spiritual ascent! For Bruno true wisdom was a romance of the divine image in creation. And the wise individual, the wanderer, must be caught up in that romance. The wanderer must become a magician who embraces the challenge to transfigure a fragmented world. That transfiguration depends upon a luminous inner life, committed to reconciling its contradictions in ever higher unities. Could it be true that a new age was dawning in which the divine harmony obliquely sensed by the wise man would replace the little absolutes of religious fundamentalism?

> *May this dark and gloomy night of our errors pass away, for the dawn of a new day of justice invites us. And let us place ourselves in such a manner that the rising sun does not disclose uncleanness. We must purify ourselves and make ourselves and make ourselves beautiful...we must place ourselves first, I say, in the intellectual heaven which is within us, and then in this sensible and corporeal heaven which presents itself to our eyes...Oh gods, if we thus renew our heaven, the constellations and influences shall be new, the impressions and fortunes shall be new, for all things depend on this upper world.*
>
> *Spaccio della bestia trionfante*

Bruno envisioned a thorough reform of our warring society into a harmonious whole based upon a sympathy between opposing worlds, between the stars and earth, between religions, between science and religion, between the inner man and nature. The implication of this vision was a reform of problem solving. The wanderer had to be awakened to his or her star-reaching power to re-create the world. The illuminated individual could penetrate the walls of contradiction that are the cosmic prison.

This empowerment of the Magus did not mean the denial of God. It did mean the weakening of church control over problem solving. It meant that the intermediary between heaven and earth could at times be the wanderer. The Inquisition raged. People paid with their lives for embracing the responsibility and authority along with the dogmatic flexibility that the higher consciousness of the wanderer implied. Their attitude towards the "other" race, religion, and culture was not sufficiently belligerent for religious and political orthodoxy. Fundamentalism was sure that God's self revelation was exclusively a matter of history and the property of the Catholic church and her approved political conduits of power. God's invitation was to be institutionally determined. Rome's opposition to Bruno's Christian Cabalism forced him to leave Italy and go to the Palatinate in Germany. There he found people schooled in the mysticism of Eckhart and eager to hear his awakening wisdom. Small groups sometimes called "Giordanisti", prototypes of Rosicrucian Freemasonry, welcomed this transcendentalism and spread it. Giordano Bruno ultimately paid for his espousal of the *mysterium magnum* by being burned at the stake in Rome. Along with the Gnostics, the Sufis, the Troubadours, Marsilio Ficino, and Pico della Mirandola he was one of wisdom's heroes, one of Franz Schubert's spiritual ancestors.

In fits and starts and in the teeth of savage opposition a new age based upon a higher consciousness of the *mysterium magnum was* taking form. The earthly Sophia, the Shekhinah, was being prepared by wisdom for her adulthood, her mature exercise of responsibility, and thus for her wedding, even as the determination of her fundamentalist enemies to keep her a child hardened. The preparation of the bride meant the relevance of secular life with its many conflicts to the spiritual ascent. The artist had something to do with the preparation. He could and should be a Magus, creatively suggesting new harmonies between worlds in conflict. Giving him mystical stature in the process was Francesco Patrizi, Professor of Platonic Philosophy at the *Sapienza* in Rome. He attacked Aristotelian theories of art in which *mimesis*, the ancient theory of imitation, was thought to be the only acceptable theory for painting. In conjunction with Frederico Zuccaro, Patrizi insisted upon a different theory, one in which a qualitatively richer reality can imaginatively be created out of unions of opposites. This process is possible because of the divine riches latent in the inner world. Because of that inner world the person, the wanderer, counted in resolving problems of value conflict. He or she was indeed irreplaceable. In a cabalistic development of thought the "thing out there" was seen to stand in creative tension with the inner life of the artist. The divine in art would now be sought in neither the object or in the subject alone, but in a creative wedding of object and subject. The artist could both respect and enrich the objective world by his or her own dramatic experience of value. He or she could transcend...not replace... what is known through the senses by what can be known qualitatively by the intuition of values. He or she could imaginatively depict a higher world that is developed out of the lower one, thereby awakening others to higher possibilities. Presumably because of its recognition of this creative power in the individual wanderer Patrizi's work was placed on the Index of the Inquisition and did not enjoy full publication and circulation.

The great Italians of the Renaissance, products of Catholicism, enthusiasts for the spiritual wealth it offers, yearned for the liberty that could come only through a reform of their church. The reform that they sought was a better expression of what we are calling the *mysterium magnum* or the rose cross mystery, counterbalancing dynamics, one the vertical relationship between man and God, the other the horizontal relationship between worldly opposites. This counterbalance is the responsibility first and foremost of the individual wanderer. Some of these Italians sought the religious empowerment of the wanderer to pursue the universal harmony that transcends an exclusively vertical religion which neglects the chaotic but very real divine thrust in the universe of values. They sought an interplay of a relationship to God and an immersion in the value conflicts of the world. They sought the spiritual ascent through the reconciliation of contradictions. They relished the previously forbidden territory of sexuality, feminine allure, and nudity, thought by many fundamentalists to be incarnations of evil. No longer seen as "the enemy", as distractions from the contemplation of divine ideas, these denizens of the *Qelippah* were transfigured into a ladder in the ascent to harmony, mighty steeds that the wanderer can and indeed must integrate into his spiritual world.

The embrace of such red light areas in new and higher harmonies by intensively spiritual artists became the hated target of fundamentalists who continued and intensified their demonization of everything sensual. With seeming inevitability the fragile unity of spirituality and sexuality that was being fashioned by champions of the rose cross mystery was viciously attacked both by the religious fundamentalists and by the anti-spiritual secularists. The movement within Christian orthodoxy towards the transfiguration of the life of the wanderer through this recognition of the image of God in sensuality was to be tragically opposed by both Protestantism and the Catholic Counter-Reformation. While it was increasingly clear that the wanderer could know God by embracing the eternal feminine, the Divine Sophia, along with her incarnations in religious orthodoxy, it was also clear that often enough religious orthodoxy seemed to prefer the role of Sophia's executioner.

In the face of the Inquisition the effort to make religious orthodoxy more relevant to the life of the wanderer continued in the seventeenth century. In France the movement to integrate the vertical and horizontal mystical dynamics was led by Jean Eudes, Jean Jacques Olier, Charles de Condren, Vincent de Paul, and Louis Marie de Montfort. In seventeenth century France the acts of Jesus Christ (the "mysteries" of his life) were seen as transcending space and time, acts and dispositions, experiences to be united with experiences of others. This was to happen through the mediation of the Roman Catholic liturgy. Berulle, De Condren, and Olier founded what came to be known as the "French School" of spirituality. At its core was the idea that the faithful are sharers in divine dispositions. The Christ disposition becomes their own. The experience of Jesus Christ is one with experiences at other times, in other places. Through the Mass, the experiences of differing times and persons are wed. The point of the liturgy is not merely thanksgiving for a job already done by someone else but primarily an experiential empowerment for the wanderer. Jesus is one in whom the Christ disposition was realized. But so too are others throughout history. The Christ disposition transcends space and time and is incarnate in the life of the wanderer. Union in this experience liturgically can and should mean an awakening to divine invitation as it is uniquely expressed in the life of each wanderer.

What was being unleashed by this expression of the rose cross mystery was a movement correcting a poisonous bias within the Church, away from an exclusively vertical relationship with God with its focus upon belief and obedience towards a cross-like mystery in which the experiences and the judgments of the wanderer were recognized as the focal point of spirituality. This change, only hinted at in seventeenth century Roman Catholicism, contained the implication that the authority for problem solving might rest in the hands of the adult wanderer and not in the hands of the institutional church.

Because Catholic orthodoxy was so opposed to the freedom inherent in the *mysterium magnum* introduction to it was largely in the hands of the secret societies. In the seventeenth century German Palatinate the Rosicrucian Enlightenment began as a Protestant effort to integrate the mystical depth of the Middle Ages with the world-view being developed by science and philosophy. Its focus was upon a self-directed spiritual life that was independent of church authority. It was launched with a series of three publications, first the *"Fama" Manifesto* in 1614, second the *"Confessio" Manifesto* in 1615, and third the *Chemical Wedding of Christian Rosenkreutz* in 1616. The documents treat of the apocalyptic expectation of a new age. The archetypal drama was a uniting of freedom, religion, and science. The *Chemical Wedding* is a narrative divided into seven days, like the *Book of Genesis*. The first day begins by contemplating divine mysteries. Suddenly a tempest arises in the midst of which an angelic woman appears whose garments are like the sky, star-spangled. As she mounts aloft she gives a mighty blast on her trumpet and announces a great wedding feast in which mortal man is to taste of godly delight. The days that follow reveal more about this heavenly wedding. On the fourth day there is a "merry comedy" in which ancient enmities are transformed by love. The power of the "wicked priest", power that freezes the world into contradictions, preventing the divine from transforming them, power that locks economics, politics, and religion into sub-human molds, is finally broken. In the last days of the *Chemical Wedding* the secrets of a mystical philosophy are revealed; fear of death is overcome and the illuminated initiates return to their world to spread the good news. Just as the Book of Revelation anticipated a new dawn of society so did the apocalyptic vision of the Rosicrucians herald the dawning of sophianic wisdom and "true religion" in the life of the wanderer who ascends to the light by uniting opposites in ever higher unities.

In the *Confessio,* another of the founding documents of the Rosicrucians, we find this praise of the forbidden wisdom:

> *No philosophy do we have other than that which is head and sum, the foundation and contents of all faculties, sciences and arts, the which (if we well behold our age) contains much of (the true wisdom of) theology and medicine, but little of the (false) wisdom of the law."*

The *Fama Fraternitatis* speaks of the new age as a synthesis of philosophy, theology, politics, economics, and science, a metaphysical universe harmonizing the divine and the human to be realized and exercised by the wanderer. And it identifies the wanderer's wisdom with an ancient and powerful tradition:

> *Our philosophy is not a new invention, but stands as the fallen Adam received it and as Moses and Solomon used it. That wisdom ought not be doubted or denied. It was embraced by Jesus himself in its completion. As he*

> *is the image of the Father, so is that philosophy his image. One must not distinguish between philosophical and theological truth. In this Plato, Aristotle, Pythagoras and others agree. And in this Enoch, Abraham, Moses, and Solomon were exemplary, and, yet more so, the Bible.*

In the face of political and religious fundamentalism champions of a new age of wisdom sought to change their world, not by eliminating Christian orthodoxy but by reforming it. The religious orthodoxies were not pleased. The push for religious peace and unity was condemned. The savagely bloody Thirty Years War was one response. All over Europe there was an effort to put a halt to the movement towards a new age. In the Rosicrucian documents the mythical hero of true wisdom, Christian Rosenkreutz, arranged to preserve his priceless vision of wisdom and the nobility of the wanderer from those who would do it harm. He constructed a burial place to store symbols of the spiritual ascent.

> *In another chest were little bells, burning lamps, and chiefly artificial songs, generally all done to the end, that if it should happen that after many hundred years the order of Fraternity should come to nothing, they might by this only vault be restored again.*
>
> *Fama Fraternitatis, Founding Literature of the Order of Rosicrucians*

Bells, lamps, artificial songs, mystical ties to the challenging, politically incorrect higher consciousness that reconciled the human and the divine alluded to in a Rosicrucian document written hundreds of years earlier! The mythical Christian Rosenkreutz, a visitor to the world of Islam, had buried a collection of symbols, keys to this wisdom that denied absolute power to any and every earthly judgment, but recognized transcendental power in the wanderer's experience of a divine attraction to a higher harmony. As we have observed this wisdom reached back through Iaslam, the Cabala, and the first fifteen hundred years of Christianity to the most ancient times, linking the spiritual heart of modern religion through its Gnostic and Jewish parents, to a yet more distant, more Oriental past. This wisdom was thought to have the power to break the chains of tyranny, change lives, change society, and bring on a new age. Rosenkreutz saw in this symbolic collection of artifacts a key to the life experience, so empowering and enriching for the wanderer that through it the world might be transformed. Artifacts, or rather the *mysterium magnum* that underlay those artifacts, could change the world. The wisdom tradition symbolized in the artifacts differed so radically from the philosophy preferred by the orthodoxies, both religious and political, that symbolism and secrecy was necessary to protect it. But there was enormous power in that forbidden wisdom. It constituted a recognition of the importance of the individual wanderer, a recognition certain to be challenging both to both religious and secular orthodoxies.

Christian Rosenkreutz is described as both godly and worldly: He is...

...sprung from the noble and renowned German family of R.C, a man admitted into the mysteries and secrets of heaven and earth through the divine revelations, subtle cogitations, and unwearied toil of his life. In his journeys through Arabia and Africa he collected a treasure surpassing that of kings and emperors; but finding it not suitable for his times, he kept it guarded for posterity to uncover; and he appointed loyal and faithful heirs of his arts and also of his name. He constructed a microcosm corresponding in all motions to the macrocosm, and finally drew up his compendium of things past, present, and to come.

Fama Fraternitatis

The effect of the wanderer-empowering, contradiction-reconciling rose cross wisdom was electrical throughout Europe. Comenius in Prague described it:

I beheld one who was spreading out his wares and calling on the people to buy his wondrous secrets. They were, he said, taken from the treasure of the new philosophy, and would content all who were desirous of secret knowledge. And there was joy that the holy Rosicrucian brotherhood would clearly now share its treasure bounteously with them.

Labyrinth of the World

The response in Prague was at first enthusiastic, then muted:

Some rejoiced, not knowing for joy where to go. They pitied their ancestors because during their lifetime, nothing such had happened. They congratulated themselves because perfect philosophy had been fully given unto them... I also began to rejoice...Others openly exposed these things saying they were fraud and deceit...til I myself was grieved seeing no end to it...I said to my guide "Is nothing then to come of all this? Alas for my hopes! For I likewise, seeing such expectations, rejoiced that I had found nurture convenient for my mind.

Labyrinth of the World

The bloody seventeenth century reaction of religious and political orthodoxies to the sophianic bridal preparation dictated by the higher consciousness horrified Comenius. It prompted him to turn inwards for solace. It is in wisdom's refuge in the inner life that he finds the strength to go on:

And now he heard a voice crying "Return". He looked around but could see no one, and again the voice cried "Return". Return to the house of the heart from whence you came. Then close the door behind you.

Labyrinth of the World

The great world-reformer Gottfried Wilhelm Leibnitz, born in Leipzig in 1646, journeyed east from Germany to Saint Petersburg and west to London in an effort to bring into being a world society illuminated by the quality sensitive wisdom by encouraging the illumination of the wanderer in a free and productive society. The influence of Leibnitz upon Queen Ann of England encouraged a politically incorrect industrialism and territorial expansion in the British colonies of Virginia and New England. He insisted upon uniting the human and the divine by the empowered wanderer who loves both the transient world and an eternal God.

> *Your desires are granted (the celestial angel said), "since you desire wisdom rather than the pleasures which the vain spectacles of the world offers to your gaze. But you will lose nothing of what is solid in these same spectacles. You will see them with eyes quite differently enlightened. Your understanding, being fortified from on high, will discover everywhere the brilliant enlightenment of the Divine Author of things; you will observe only wisdom and happiness where men customarily find nothing but vanity and bitterness. You will be satisfied by your Creator. You will be enchanted by the sight of his works. Your admiration will not be the result of ignorance, as is that of the common herd. It will be the fruit of the knowledge of the glories and wonders of God...God will establish his seat in your heart, and the Heavens follow Him everywhere. Go then and lift up your mind above whatever is mortal, and whatever perishes, and bind yourself only to the eternal verities of the light of God.*
>
> *Philosophical Dream*

Many expected that at some point in the future the day for the empowerment of the wanderer would dawn. And then what would become of religious orthodoxy? Some intellectual leaders thought that the new age would require the annihilation of the Roman Catholic Church along with the political institutions protected it. But these rebels were abandoning the tradition of rose cross wisdom that had so often been the bond between religious reformers. Others wanted neither slavery to any orthodoxy nor a nihilistic rejection of them. They were hungry for an inner life capable of transforming the outer one into something beautiful, thrilling, joyful. But they valued highly the spiritual wealth that they found preserved (albeit in a distorted form) by the orthodoxy. As a step towards reconciling that contradiction they sought a profound reformation of the Catholic Church.

While reformers fought over whether to reject or reform the orthodoxies Judaism hosted its own civil war. Jewish Cabalism focused upon its own tension between the rose cross mysticism and dualism. In the sixteenth century Isaac Luria reacted to the expulsion of Jews from Spain in 1492 with a change in focus of Jewish mysticism. The exile and return of the Shekhinah that characterized the mystical vision of Moses de Leon in the thirteenth century began to be understood primarily in terms of the future of the Jewish people and not merely their past. History was being replaced by a richer experience of the

"Now". Luria focused upon the Tree of Life as a way of purifying the living Jewish people for their wedding with the Messiah.

Jewish Cabalism often expressed itself according to a metaphysical universe of dramatic values. The Tree of Life was evocative of a drama in progress and not of concrete things in frozen relationships. The romance between a divine messianic light and its eternal Beloved, the Shekhinah, is the drama hidden among the nouns, hidden in fundamentalist separation, hidden in and behind the uniqueness of race, religion, nationality, sex, etc. The bride must ascend towards a universal harmony. In the seventeenth century many Jewish cabalists thought that now was the time for this to happen. The Shekhinah was ready for a definitive messianic visitation. The new age was at hand. First Shabbetai Zevi and later Jacob Franck, both Cabalists of a high order, announced the new age. The Shekhinah, the light-incorporator, was ready for her light-bringing, messianic spouse. But Judaism was divided over the identity of the Shekhinah. For some Cabalists she was purely and simply the Jewish people. But for others she was mankind of whom the Jewish people were a unique but limited symbol. In either case she was being called to transcend the old ways, the old limitations, the old Law in something new and richer. Led by her messiah she was being invited to a new age.

This new stage in Jewish history had a powerful influence outside of Judaism and can can be found in Christian writings. In the face of political and religious fundamentalism and a growing and ominous nihilism a new age of the higher consciousness of the godly power of the wanderer seemed to be dawning upon Europe in the late eighteenth century. In the mind of many cabalists, Jewish and Christian, the bride had been prepared. She was ready for the Messiah. The romance had entered a new and higher phase. At hand was a transfiguration that would fulfill all anticipations. Through Rosicrucian groups this expectation spread. It was aptly expressed by the great German thinker and founder of German romanticism Novalis in 1799:

> *Everywhere there seems to be stirring a mighty sense of creative will, of limitlessness, of infinite diversity, of holy particularity, and the infinite capacity of the human spirit. Having awoken from the morning dream of helpless childhood, a part of the race is exercising its first powers on the snakes that entwine its cradle and want to rob it of the use of its limbs. All these things are still only hints, disjointed and rough, but to the historical eye they betray a universal individuality, a new history, a new humanity, the sweetest embrace of a surprised young church, and a loving God, and the ardent conception of a new messiah in all its thousand members at once. Who does not feel the sweet shame of being with child? The newborn will be the image of his father; a new golden age with dark, infinite eyes, a prophetic, consoling time, working miracles and healing wounds, and sparking the flame of eternal life-a great time of reconciliation, a savior who like a true genius will be at home among men, who can only be believed in and not seen, and who is visible to the faithful in countless forms, consumed as bread and wine,*

> *embraced like a beloved woman, breathed as air; heard as word and song, and with heavenly delight, among the sharpest pangs of love, taken up in the form of death into the innermost part of the body whose turbulence ceases at last.*
>
> *Christendom oder Europa*

The poetry of Novalis celebrated this evolutionary preparation of a people in Germany. He expected monumental changes in history, changes inspired by a national higher consciousness that united opposites in creative symbioses. This suggested a leap beyond the religious fundamentalism on both sides that focused upon why others must be excluded from love's triumph. Sophia, it seemed, was about to descend in her beauty upon the world whose differences were to be resolved in cosmic harmony. This expectation was expressed by Novalis in a poem set three times twenty years later by Franz Schubert...as a Lied *Hymn IV D.662*, as the third movement of the *Piano Sonata in A Major D.664*, and shortly thereafter as the fourth movement of the unfinished *Seventh Symphony in E Major D.729.*

> *I tell everyone,*
> *And they tell their friends.*
> *Everywhere the new kingdom of heaven is appearing!*
> *The world becomes radiant with a new light!*
> *Now at last it will be home!*

Many German intellectual leaders were ready for the dawning of a new age of freedom that would reconcile the contradiction between a personal God calling the wanderer to a higher world and the universe of value conflicts. Immersion of society into the rose cross mystery beckoned. The wanderer was to be nourished by orthodoxy and yet stand in tension with it. The new stance would be expressed in art. In *Naive and Sentimental Poetry* Friedrich Schiller wrote that the goal of the poet and artist is to ascend personally to a redemptive dramatic abstraction of an ascent to freedom and to communicate that redemptive vision to others. The quality of the inner life of the wanderer was to become the cornerstone of the new society. And the quality of that inner life depended in part upon the mythology that expresses it. Schiller created a redemptive mythology in his plays. He thought that the great artist of the new age should be an awakener of society to the importance of the wisdom of the wanderer.

> *To promote and nourish freedom of temperament is the fair task of comedy just as tragedy is destined to restore by aesthetic means the freedom of temperament that has been violently disrupted by emotion.*

Schiller was eloquent in recognizing the importance of the wanderer's wisdom and the freedom that is its condition. The freedom to think, assess, and create was essential as a condition for life in the new age. Only a free man or woman could address concrete value conflicts with the imagination and creativity necessary to resolve them in higher syntheses. He contrasted this higher consciousness of the wanderer with the slavery of the fundamentalist.

> *Freedom, for all its moral contradictions and physical evils, is an infinitely more interesting spectacle than prosperity and order without freedom, when the sheep patiently follow the shepherd, and the autonomous will reduces itself to an obedient cog in a machine. The latter makes of man a mere product of nature's ingenuity and her fortunate subject; but freedom makes him a citizen and co-regent of a higher system in which it is incomparably more honorable to occupy the lowest rank than to lead the procession of the physical order.*
>
> *Naive and Sentimental Poetry*

Within the wanderer there are different levels of consciousness, different worlds and hidden possibilities. The full beauty of the separate worlds is accessible only when they are bathed in a higher harmony. The illuminated wanderer seeks this harmony in the spiritual ascent. When this harmony is possible Schiller calls the experience "beautiful". This is the painless ideal. But this ideal is often denied to us by powers out of our control. Then the wanderer must suffer and even die in fidelity to the higher harmony. Schiller called peace in the face of this tragedy "sublime". When beauty is denied because circumstance opposes divine harmony a muted but real inner harmony can still be realized. The experience of life in which the divine harmony is dominant is called a "sublime disposition". Schiller's sublime is wisdom's victory over insuperable circumstance. It is the wanderer's experience of the *mysterium magnum*. Such a victory in the face of impossible circumstance is at once a noble triumph and a crucifixion.

> *The experience of the sublime is a mixed feeling. It is a composition of melancholy, which at its utmost is manifested in a shudder, and of joyousness which can mount to rapture, and even if it is not actually pleasure is far preferred by refined souls to all pleasure.*
>
> *On the Sublime*

Schiller is here defining most of Schubert's work following his illness in 1823. This higher consciousness, this sublime disposition of the awakened wanderer, would be for the composer the tie that unites society in the dawning new age. It arises from the interplay of divine and human worlds. And it takes place in the inner life of the suffering wanderer. Although circumstances might seem to proclaim a defeat of the higher consciousness there can be a heroic victory. Schiller makes it clear that the sublime disposition which is a necessary part of the ascent is intensely spiritual and can co-exist with physical circumstances, contradictions, which seem to deny the possibility of joy. Thus it is that the wanderer, involved in painful conflict, facing even death, can enjoy this taste of heaven.

Schiller wrote:

> *A man should, I suppose, possess all the virtues that in unison make for a beautiful character. He should find delight in the practice of righteousness, beneficence, moderation, perseverance, and loyalty...But let us suppose this same man suddenly to suffer a great misfortune...Under these circumstances let us seek him out, and demand of the unhappy wretch that he practice the same virtues to which the happy man was formerly so inclined. If under these circumstances one should find him altogether the same. If poverty has not diminished his beneficence, ingratitude his readiness to be of service, pain his equanimity, his own misfortune his satisfaction in the happiness of others, if we notice the change of fortune in his outward appearance but not in his behavior...we must abandon completely the derivation of his behavior from circumstances, and locate the reason for the behavior not in the physical world order, but in quite another to which the ideas of reason for the behavior not in the physical world order, but in quite another to which the ideas of reason can indeed soar, but which understanding cannot apprehend by its empirical concepts...Thus the sublime affords us an egress from the sensuous world in which the beautiful would gladly hold us forever and captivate. Not gradually (for there is no gradual transition from dependency to freedom), but suddenly, and with a shock it tears that independent spirit out of the net in which a refined sensuousness has enmeshed it.*
>
> *On the Sublime*

The sublime disposition would be the mark of the higher consciousness of the awakened wanderer in the new age. Schubert would celebrate it as a victory over fear and death. For Schiller the ascent to the higher consciousness involved resignation to the necessary descent into suffering and death. Death is the narrow fissure through which love, no matter how beautiful in life, must pass as it ascends to the universal harmony.

> *Oh Love, who but you has mounted heroically*
> *The steep pathway to the stars, to the very throne of God?*
> *Love, you initiate us into the mystery!*
> *Had you not led us, would we dream of eternal life?*
> *Has a single soul had this dream without being led by you?*
> *You find a better world by passing through the narrow fissure of death!*
> *Love and love alone leads us to the Father, the Font of Nature!*
>
> *Triumph of Love*

This higher consciousness of the rose cross mystery that embraces both the "beautiful" and the "sublime" in the ascent towards the new age is what society should seek for all its members. It should be the goal of religion and politics. Education must reflect a commitment to the elevation of society through an awakening to the mysterious interplay of heaven and earth.

> *The ability to feel the sublime is therefore one of the most glorious pre-dispositions in the nature of man. From its origins in the independent capacity of thinking and in the will it deserves our attention. Because of its influence upon moral man it deserves the most perfect development.*
>
> *On the Sublime*

Schiller analyzed the higher consciousness of the mystery and led Europe towards it through essays and dramas. According to him the greatest art celebrates this wisdom. It aspires to love's triumph in life's great drama yet recognizes that the triumph will cost the wanderer his life. Wisdom means reaching beyond the self towards the other, indeed towards the Ultimate Other. We yearn for something that is beyond our power to reach or control, both in this life and beyond it. Tragedy and failure are unavoidable parts of the great romance. Hope must co-exist with disappointment. Life must co-exist with death in immersion in the rose cross mystery.

The greatest artists seek creative ways to share this thrilling, terrifying, paradoxical mystery with its commitment to a ceaseless ascent in both experience and ideas. The spiritual impact of this mystery can be experienced in the great masses of Bach, Mozart, Beethoven, and Schubert. At the core of these masses is the hidden, transcendental *Truth* of the rose cross mystery cloaked in the form of a myth, ritual, and liturgy celebrating the transfiguration of earthly life by heavenly invitation. The composers had to discover in personal experience the inspiration for their liturgical music. Their masses are no mere emotional eruptions inspired by dogma. At their best they are expressions of experiences, personal to each composer, of the great romance between heaven and earth.

The artistic genius (be he poet, composer, or painter) is no mere chronicler of what exists. Nor is he simply an educator, a philosopher, or a theologian charged with conveying ideas about *the Truth*. He or she is a Magus, the archetypal wanderer, ascending to a sublime understanding of new experience. Ideas are not foreign to the process. Indeed they are essential to it. But ideas condition it; they do not define it. The microcosm created by the artist is a thing of magic, a myth, a play, a painting, a symphony, a song which alchemically suggests the drama of the spiritual ascent. The artistic genius stands astride heaven and earth and attempts to capture the ascent in the art. The genius is not merely a revealer of a mood, an emotion, a state of feeling. He is a prophet of a higher world and thus cannot be content with revealing merely actual harmonies and dissonances. The composer- genius must somehow suggest the invitation of the eternal. He is a celebrant of Everyman's spiritual ascent, committed to reaching for the unreachable star through concrete life experience. He is universal in celebrating what lies more or less hidden in everyone. He is an elitist in that not everyone is aware of what he feels in his bones. Most are asleep; he is awake. This elitism can make him a stranger to society, which feels uncomfortable in the presence of this strange and demanding consciousness Thus he is never completely at home in his own time. In his commitment to enrich his world with his inner vision he is inevitably a warrior, brazenly challenging the established order, yet wed profoundly to its traditions. Schiller thought that such artists...

> *appear sometimes more as strangers at which one wonders and as uneducated sons of nature at whom one is angered...Little do they thrive upon their century. The seal of the ruler rests upon their brow...They are hated by the critics as disturbers of limits.*
>
> *On Naive and Sentimental Poetry*

Indeed there was a strong movement of European composers, artists, and poets at the end of the eighteenth and beginning of the nineteenth centuries to give expression to this elitist consciousness that challenged society. Participation in the movement was not limited to Germany. It found expression in the dramas of Victor Hugo in France, in the operas of Donnizetti, Bellini, and Verdi in Italy, and in the genius of the American founders, especially Thomas Jefferson. Moved by the Roscrucian movement within Freemasonry many artistic and intellectual leaders could almost taste the better world. As we saw in the words of Novalis the new messiah would be a light-bearer, the speaker of a world-awakening challenge to contradictions, inviting a split society to transform itself in unity. The bride of this messiah would be a world illuminated by the wisdom of the wanderer. The romance of the messiah and his beloved would transfigure the world. Sacred symbols from the past such as the life, death, and resurrection of Jesus are awakeners to the great romance that defines the "now". Awakening to the "now", truly experiencing life, would be empowering, life-giving. Anticipated was the gradual illumination of the world, transfiguring men, women, sun, moon, and stars. Anticipated was the dawn of a new age.

War over the Mystery

The elevation of the wanderer into an immersion in the *mysterium magnum*, a romance with God mediated through Sophia, had influenced leading figures in religion and politics from the time of Christ through the eighteenth century. The movement was always politically incorrect. It consisted in the reconciliation of an overlay of contradictions, one between God and man, the other between earthly opposites by an emancipated and independent wanderer. This immersion could be symbolized in the form of a rose cross. A rose is placed precisely at the intersection of the vertical and horizontal bars, indicating the "now" moment in the life of the wanderer. Awakening to the full meaning of the "now" is what the mystery is all about. This mystery envisions a penetration of the wall of contradictory values that separates the hidden God from the wanderer. Each value in a conflict simultaneously betrays and reveals that God. The wanderer through a discriminating embrace of both sides of the contradiction can fleetingly bring heavenly life to earth.

Eighteenth and nineteenth century Germany hosted many efforts to explore and define this metaphysical universe that underlies the rose-cross mystery. Some of these efforts produced ground-breaking insights that have born fruit in the development of religious thought over the past two hundred years. One of the most important of these Germans was Friedrich Wilhelm Josef von Schelling, While a professor at the University of Jena he recognized two metaphysical universes that must somehow be synthesized. He addressed the contradiction between the actual universe of Nature and the actual-ideal universe of the Spirit. Each universe demands its own kind of genius, its own kind of ontology and epistemology. For him the great artist properly sought to reconcile these contradictions in his art. Caspar David Friedrich was making such reconciliations incarnate in his paintings Schubert was doing the same thing in his music. Schelling gave this movement a philosophical underpinning. He underscored the nobility of the Magus whom he charged with bringing about a union of worlds in tension. Schelling insisted upon the counterbalance between the union of man and God on the one hand and the union of earthly opposites on the other in the dawning new age. He accepted the core of both the Judaic and Christian orthodoxies, namely that this Divine Other has entered history with a life-giving invitation. But this historical activity by the Divine Other does not render the creativity of the wanderer meaningless. For Schelling both the fundamentalism of the religious orthodoxies and the nihilism of the secularists were disastrous distortions of *the Truth*. He thought that the higher consciousness demands a creative encounter between reason and revelation, between Self and Other. The perfect world, the perfect image of God, needs to be both messiah and bride. This messianic romance is the key to life. It entails an interplay of opposites in the ascent to harmony with God.

Like Novalis Schelling called for magicians in the arts capable of awakening others to the beauty and joy of the higher consciousness and leading them out of the twin traps of religious fundamentalism and secular nihilism. These magicians were to be free from the prison of simplistic dogmatic absolutes. They would be attuned both to the infinite beauties of the goddess and to the divine invitation from the Ultimate Other. Such magicians can follow the ways of wisdom through imaginative drama, thus showing the way to others as they reach for the stars.

Capar David Friedrich expressed this in paintings. In works like the *Cross Beside the Baltic* earth and heaven stand in a tension resolved by the cross atop the hill. Here the retinal is handmaiden to something of a different order altogether. In the painting *Woman Before the Rising Sun* heavenly light transfigures the earth seemingly at the behest of a goddess-like woman. Two universes blend and become ever more splendid through the magic of the *mysterium magnum*. In his *Evening Landscape with Two Men* we encounter the same mystery. The universe is transfigured. Earth receives the illumination of heaven in unity with the inner lives of the two men observing it. And in the painting *On the Sailing Boat* a man and a woman in love sail towards their goal where heaven meets the earth, the symbol of which is a cathedral. In work after work Friedrich celebrates the mystery arising from a transfiguring overlay of the earthly romance upon the transcendental one. This art was judged to be politically incorrect during Friedrich's lifetime and was trashed by many.

The effort to more deeply define and implement the rose cross mystery triggered a reaction from religious fundamentalists. They sought to discredit the works of each new magus. For instance the creative German Catholic Johann Michael Sailer (1751-1832), a contemporary of Goethe, was denounced as "a mystic" by some of his rationalistic countrymen who rejected the perennial philosophy of true wisdom and the experiential romance between heaven and earth. But Sailer played an important role in maintaining the vertical relationship between the wanderer and God as an essential part of the new age. He insisted upon the overlay of vertical and horizontal bars in the rose cross mystery by pioneering the re-discovery of the great German mystics, Suso, Tauler, Eckhart, etc. with their simultaneous embrace of divine invitation and penetration of the walls of contradiction. Sailer led German Catholic visionaries in a rejection of both scholastic rationalism and of nihilism. For him art could play a special role in the nurturing of the higher consciousness of the great mystery.

> *What makes the inner life of man outward, or expresses that inner life outwardly is art in the widest sense of the word. And what makes the inner religious life outward is sacred art in the widest sense of the word.*

An eighteenth-nineteenth century awakening to the rose cross mystery was pursued by Friedrich Schlegel (1772-1829) and "Novalis" (Friedrich von Hardenburg) (1772-1801), wellsprings of the German romantic movement. Both saw in the wisdom of the wanderer the key to the new age. Both had an awareness of the paradoxical nature of the great romance and the higher consciousness it created. For both men mere ideas with their clear relationships and unassailable logic both express and betray reality and must be passed through the prism of the wanderer's experience. They insisted upon the epistemological ability of the wanderer not to ignore, but to transcend old judgments in an effort to adequately understand new experience. The artistic genius has a special and irreplaceable role to play in depicting the challenge posed by experience to old judgments. He should be the awakener to the inadequacy of old judgments and a visionary with respect to required adjustments. More than other artists the ideal composer of music would have the power to awaken society to the quest for a higher world. The composer might uniquely express mystical experience. Led by a messianic musical genius society could conceivably ascend beyond the pedantry of ideas and the triviality of raw emotion towards a new age.

Just as Palestine at the time of Christ was alive with the anticipation of a new age built upon a higher consciousness, so was Germany as the nineteenth century began. A great artist-musician-messiah was expected who could awaken Europe and lead it by way of myths clothed in music to a radically higher way of life. This anticipation had been heightened by Mozart's opera *The Magic Flute,* which leads us to the temple of wisdom from which society's redemption must come. Mozart, Schlegel, Schelling, and Novalis during those heady days lived in vibrant expectation of an imminent triumph of wisdom over the tyrannies both of fundamentalism and of nihilism. Novalis could almost taste the new age. The day star of the romance of the *mysterium magnum* was about to dawn!

Or was it? The high hopes for a new age of wisdom were conditioned by a reverence for both the vertical and horizontal bars of the cross and for the wanderer through whose genius they are brought together. This implied a reform of the orthodoxies. Largely because this reform did not take place there was a growing cynicism by many about all religion If the early nineteenth century hosted a strong hope for an ascendancy of the higher consciousness, it also hosted something more ominous, a dualism that promised unending wars, both against religion and within and between religions. Jewish and Roman Catholic fundamentalists formed an alliance with nihilists to oppose the mystery and put their distortions in its place. The enemies of all religion were empowered. Both the religious orthodoxies and the nihilists preferred eternal war to the new age.

Jewish fundamentalism attacked more liberal Jews. It wiped out as completely as possible every trace of Jacob Franck. Catholic fundamentalism was no less thorough. In the course of the nineteenth and early twentieth centuries Rome under Pius IX and Pius X undercut the rose cross mystery with the declaration of papal infallibility, the oath against modernism, and the Syllabus of Errors. The promising life among Catholic theologians in Germany, America, and France was stifled. Despite the fact that Catholics hungry for the awakening had joined with enlightened Jews in Vienna to produce some of the greatest art in history, Rome wanted none of it. The movement towards the liberation and dignity of the wanderer was suppressed by both church and state. In response many of those hungry for the new age saw religion as its enemy and declared war against it. The bars of the cross were pulled apart. The rose cross mystery was denied its dawn.

With insight Madam Blavatsky wrote of the savage effects of this perversion of wisdom by both religious and secular power. She warned:

> *The materialism today is born of the brutal yesterday. Unless its growth is arrested, it may become our master. It is the bastard progeny of the French Revolution and its reaction against ages of religious bigotry and repression. To prevent the crushing of these spiritual aspirations, the blighting of these hopes, and the deadening of that intuition which teaches us of a God and a hereafter, we must show our false theologies in their naked deformity, and distinguish between divine religion and human dogmas.*
>
> *Our voice is raised for spiritual freedom, and our plea made for enfranchisement from all tyranny, whether science or theology.*
>
> *Isis Unveiled*

Distortions of the mystery were complemented by what was going on in the universities. Bi-polar reality was reduced to a monolith. Ideology flourished. Johann Gottlieb Fichte, 1762-1814, re-defined the tension between the Self and the Other by making the Self absolute. The Other became merely a function of the Self. Divine invitation was not the entrance of a Divine Other into the life of the Self. It was self projection. The higher consciousness, subjectively and objectively a harmony of opposites, became for him monolithic. Logic would be king in the new world of idea relationships. The Self was the first principle from which everything is derived.

For more and more thinkers the "secret" of life, its *mysterium magnum*, was no longer a creative reach upwards towards a reconciliation of opposites, but rather an imposition downwards, a deduction from an arbitrary principle. There was a quarrel over the character of this arbitrary principle. New and profound insights into the nature of the mystery were mixed with crippling limitations. Johann Wolfgang von Goethe and Georg Wilhelm Friedrich Hegel called the first principle at the core of the mystery a *primary phenomenon*. A grasp of the *primary phenomenon* and its deductive application to life would be the key to the new age. Philosophers wanted to grasp in clear and explicit terms what that primary phenomenon was and scientifically apply it to the life of society.

The profundity of Fichte, Goethe, and Hegel is obvious. But they each compromised the richly paradoxical, bi-polar nature of the *mysterium magnum*. The core of the life experience was cheapened. The source of the divine invitation became an impersonal principle within the self. Goethe defined the *primary phenomenon* as Nature. Hegel defined it as historical process. Nietzsche defined it as the will to power. Schopenhauer identified it as the triumph of the ego over the will to life. For Marx it was the ascendancy of a social class. For Paul Anton de la Garde it was the ascendancy of the German race. Soon in Germany the *primary phenomenon* would be the state. In France it became equality. In America it became democracy and then free trade. The effort was to replace the overlay of the profound contradictions between self and other and between judgment and intuition at the heart of the mystery with something more "scientific", something amenable to deductive logic, something more self-aggrandizing, an absolute and arbitrary first principle.

The art world also betrayed the mystery. Turner created paintings in which the mystery is identified with Nature. French Impressionism limited the mystery by making it solely retinal or musical. The valley separating relatively superficial expressions of the mystery from the paradoxical mystery-consciousness of Novalis, Schelling, Friedrich, Mozart, and Schubert slowly grew into a chasm. So we have the anomaly that at about the same time that Novalis was anticipating a spiritually rich new age enthroning the mystery the poet Jean Paul was lamenting:

> *I lay down on a summer evening and dreamed..I awoke in a graveyard…All the dead cried: "Christ, is there no God?…He answered: There is none!…I wandered through the worlds, climbing to the sun, flying with the Milky Way…through the deserts of heaven…but there was no God.. I descended far, far into the abyss and cried: Father, where are you?…but heard only the eternal storm and a sin-less rainbow stretched over the abyss and falling into it! And when I search the distances for the divine eye…an empty eye-socket stared back at me. Eternity lay upon chaos, gnawing at it, chewing upon itself. Cold, eternal necessity! When shall you shatter the world and me? How alone each of us is in the wide tomb of the all!*

A new age was certainly dawning. But what would it look like? Would it be Novalis' triumph of the human spirit? Or would it be Jean Paul's universe of the damned? Would the leaders of society seek the paradoxical blend of faith and reason championed by Schelling and Novalis or would they seek to make incarnate the ominous metaphysics of Paul de la Garde and Karl Marx? We know the answer given by the twentieth century. The same question looms above us in the twenty-first century. Will some arbitrary selection of a "little absolute" determine problem solving and make war inescapable? Or will we bring the rose cross mystery to new life?

Music and the Mystery

Every spirit...is similar to colors and vocal songs, odors, and movements of the soul. For that reason it can move quickly through these things.
Marsilio Ficino

The rose cross mystery means an embrace of opposites in a movement towards ever higher harmony. The greatest art is a romance of the *mysterium magnum*. This makes of the practitioner of such art a kind of priest, a mediator between worlds, pursuing the hidden God indirectly through immersion in the divine, created, bi-polar image. The greatest art had always played this mediating role between transcendental and sense experience. Transfiguration was suggested by Vermeer in his priceless counterbalances of light and darkness. Caspar David Friedrich explored the tension between Nature and Spirit on his thrilling canvases. Van Gogh paintings suggest the triumph of inner light, for example in eruptions of light out of a wheat field.

But music was thought to have supreme power to inspire an ascent beyond Nature to a higher consciousness. In classical mythology Orpheus had turned men from slaughter, moved giant rocks, and built Thebes through the power of his poetry and music. His power derived from combinations of poetry and music. Orphic hymns and incantations sought to harness this power and place it at man's disposal. The Pythagoreans utilized songs to induce desired dispositions. And the Greeks at the time of Aristotle were already looking to the past to rediscover the art of uniting music and religious wisdom. Plato recognized that poetry and harmony enter into the innermost part of the soul with momentous effect. The combination has the ability to either harm or elevate the listener. For this reason Plato wanted laws enforcing good music, recalling the earlier practice of the Egyptians in which combinations of drama and music were used to educate and radically empower the young. The Greek historian Plutarch held that ideas expressed in poetry and harmony expressed in music were destined to be united. Cicero thought that every movement of the soul has its image in music. Music had long been seen as an alternative language that complements words by expanding and intensifying their meaning. While words can point to objective relationships between things music can identify the knower with the dramatic thrust in being of the known.

Recapturing this respect for the power of music Marsilio Ficino demonstrated in the fifteenth century that a wedding of poetry and music in song could be a magical tool for spiritual awakening in the hands of a master magician. Such a wedding could make wisdom incarnate. Ficino, developing the thought of Plotinus, Synesius, Iamblichus, Proclus, and Thomas Aquinas, made this movement towards harmony central to his life-view. A world soul pervades all things and insures sympathies between them. There is an underlying drive in things that accounts for their evolutionary thrust towards imaging the hidden and transcendental God in a divine harmony. Ficino thought that song, uniting the opposites of music and poetry, is an analogue of that thrust and can stimulate a powerful movement of the spirit towards harmony. Ficino in the fifteenth century laid the foundations for Schubert's art in the nineteenth century.

Ficino was a powerful figure in fifteenth century Florence. In his profound grasp of the rose cross mystery the interplay between intuition and judgment was the path to wisdom. He gave the heart with its sensitivity to value equal importance with the intellect with its power of judgment. The movement towards value sensitivity was for him the necessary counterbalance to reason in the wanderer's ascent to truth. Music which can unite the intellect with the heart has priority over philosophy. Ficino set out the principle of complementarity, essential to the rose cross mystery.

His thought was soon developed with respect to art. The eye, focused upon truth, needs the ear, focused upon harmony, to ascend to the better world. Giuseppi Betussi, a follower of Ficino, expressed this:

> *The first things that cause us to consider beauty are the eyes, to which because of the acute vision that they have, the corporeal forms of things are first imaged; then, immediately following, are the ears, which give us hope as they hear harmonies which quickly penetrate deep into the soul. Yes, hearing is far more spiritual. As the eyes and the ears unite the mind becomes active.*

The way this ascent to harmony worked was through what Ficino called "furors". As Gary Tomlinson shows in *Music in Renaissance Magic*, these were forces that could invade the soul and raise it to the harmonies of higher worlds. They did this in two ways: first by possession, a kind of soul surrender to the higher (divine) harmonies; second by a kind of Shamanism in which there was first a soul loss followed by an association with the higher harmonies. The wanderer could be a kind of magician capable of unleashing powerful forces in one world by uniting it with another. The harmony of the universe, indeed the oneness of God, could be progressively and dramatically imaged in the reconciliation of tensions between opposing worlds and the imaging could unleash unsuspected forces. The ascent of the wanderer towards the harmony and power of divine life can be imitated uniquely through the ascent through the opposites of music and poetry to the higher consciousness. Such music can be a link to divinity, it can raise the soul into a higher world.

The great Arabian philosopher al Kindi had an impact upon Ficino. He had held that a song is demonic, a kind of organism with a spiritual composition. Music for him was the spiritual art par excellence, a magical art through which man creates an image of the mystery at the core of the life experience, an image that has unique power to awaken the wanderer to the hidden beauty of life.

Words and music together convey the dramatic thrust of Becoming towards Being better than separately. In the Renaissance the counterbalance of music and poetry was recognized as a powerful force. Marsilio Ficino with never-failing instincts claimed that music united with poetry imitates the harmonies of the universe, harmonies based upon the spirit of the living God which fills that universe. Such music then can be a link to divinity, a pathway to God with magical power to penetrate the wall of contradiction. It could be a life-giving microcosm of the universe, a hieroglyph that points beyond separation to a divine, harmonizing power of the soul. For the composer and his listeners the music/poetry combination could be a communication in the higher consciousness.

There was a body of thought in the seventeenth and eighteenth centuries which insisted upon the role of poetry in the creation of great music and refused to respect their separation. Poetry with its more precise suggestion of meaning was thought to be the necessary companion to music, the more feeling-focused art. While trivial music makes no such self-transcending demands, great music does. According to Frances Yates in her book The *French Academics of the Seventeeth Century* the goal of the Florentine Academy and Baif's *Academie de Poesie et de Musique* was a restoration of what they saw as a golden age of music and culture in which musicians, poets, and philosophers were in harmony, a time when people could be aided in their spiritual ascent by listening to heavenly wisdom sung by a bard. Plutarch had thought that music and poetry were inseparable. Some seventeenth century French composers attempted to re-create that close relationship by translating ideas into music by way of modes. This was a realization of Cicero's axiom that every movement of the soul has by nature its own look, sound, and gesture. The translator of Plutarch, Jacques Amyot, decried the tendency of the polyphony of his day to separate meaning from sound.

In late eighteenth century France, Jean Jacques Barthelemy recognized that ideas conditioned the musical hieroglyph and were therefore necessary for the inspiration of great music. He reflected upon the aptness of poetry for the task. "Poetry is a great teacher of courage, prudence, and honor, for it is more philosophical and instructive than history, selecting as it does finer models and delineating nobler characters." Therefore Barthelemy demanded that the art of music maintain a close alliance with poetry. Apart from the enriching ideas contained in the poem, music, according to Barthelemy, could only be a frivolous exercise in self promotion on the part of musicians.

Therefore commentators like the translator of Plutarch, Jaques Amyot, decried the tendency of the polyphony of his day to separate meaning from sound, words from harmonies. In late eighteenth century France Jean Jaques Bartholemy thought that ideas were necessary for the inspiration of great music. "Poetry is a great teacher". Philosophers at the University of Berlin sought to unite the intuitions of the human drama, suggested by music, to ideas about that drama expressed in poetry. Georg Wilhelm Friedrich Hegel thought that music which does not express a spiritual content that can be more concisely yet less sensitively stated in poetry is unworthy of the name of art. Music for him was linked firmly to its inspiring spiritual vision through poetry. Music rises to the level of true art only when the sensuous element of sound in its innumerable combinations expresses some meaningful realization of the spiritual ascent. Music at its best is no mere stimulant for the subjective imagination, but rather an alternative and complementary way of communing in *the Truth*. Music needed a close alliance with poetry. And the great composers of the late eighteenth and early nineteenth centuries experimented with this alliance.

The counterbalances of the *magnum mysterium* can be appropriately celebrated through a counterbalance of music and poetry. Such celebrations reached their highest point in Beethoven, Schubert, Verdi, and Wagner in the nineteenth century. In the eighteenth and nineteenth centuries Bellini, Donizetti, Verdi, Mozart, and Beethoven created revolutionary celebrations of the thrust of Becoming towards Being in which ideas and dramatic experiences in tension with one another touch and produce something new. Their music cannot be properly understood outside of its celebration of the life-giving wisdom of the new age. Artists and especially composers of music in search of this paradoxical wisdom were to be knight-magicians whose weapon was a sword of mystical might. Mozart, Beethoven, Schubert, and later Wagner saw themselves as messianic, sometimes even Shamanistic figures who had entered a higher world and lived to bring its secret mystery back to earth. In the face of fundamentalist opposition they celebrated an ascent to a new age in which divine harmony was symbolized in combinations of music and poetry. They thought that they had both the divine call and the quasi-magtical power to celebrate a higher life through their unique and imaginative weddings of poetry and music. Vienna is where much of this magic took place.

In late eighteenth century Vienna this emergence of a language to express the great mystery through combinations of words and music was accompanied by conflict over its content. Freemasonry played an important part in the conflict. The lodge *Zur wahren Eintracht* was a prestigious academy of intellectual and scientific inquiry matching the famous Royal Society in London. It was dominated by the Illuminati and sought to define true wisdom as science. Christian mysticism in all its forms was seen as the enemy. For this lodge the *mysterium magnum* was clearly Nature. Its secrets would be laid bare through the application of the scientific method. But this "wisdom" was not unopposed. In spite of the prominence of this lodge and an invitation to join it, Schubert's great predecessor, Wolfgang Amadeus Mozart, joined a lesser lodge *Zur Wohltatigkeit* because its sense of the mystery was more inclusive, more transcendental, an embrace of both what can be measured and what can't. *Zur Wohltatigkeit* included men with Rosicrucian backgrounds and linkages to Judaic and Franciscan mysticism. Former *Asiatic Brethren* lodge members like Baron Otto von Gemmingen and Count Franz Josef Thun assured an interplay of Jewish and Catholic mystical visions as well as a respect for science and reason. The lodge had hopes for a new synthesis between religion and the Enlightenment. Mozart placed his art at the service of this lodge and created masterworks in service to the Rosicrucian-flavored Masonic vision of a new age.

Some of Mozart's music saluted the dawning of a revolutionary new age in which reason and religion could unite in a higher consciousness. In the opera *The Magic Flute* he created a myth in which a naïve children's tale is told against the backdrop of Mozart's own Rosicrucian abstraction of life. One world is superimposed upon another. It is left to the audience to see and experience the spiritual ascent that the art celebrates. Mozart presented this invitation to wisdom with wit and consummate skill. Kant had challenged: "Dare to know!" In his last opera Mozart dramatized a living realization of Schiller's deeper challenge: "Dare to be wise!" Mozart was saying in effect:"Dare an immersion in the rose cross mystery!" "Dare to enter the new age!" "Dare to romance the Divine Sophia!"

In an earlier opera, *Der Stein der Weisen (The Philosopher's Stone)*, composed by Mozart in collaboration with four friends in 1790, the invitation to an illuminated inner life is incarnate in a woman. She offers the hero access to a higher life of wisdom and love in exchange for his willingness to forsake the sword. Here is the Rosicrucian invitation to transcend myopic materialism and the eternal war that mere manifestations of the divine guarantee. Through a higher consciousness Mozart is giving us a key to the new age through the superimposition of divine and human dramas.

Mozart's Catholicism was real but esoteric. In his eyes the mysteries of his religion celebrated in his masses and works like *Ave Verum* and *Panis Angelicus* were priceless expressions of divine invitation. But the authoritarianism and power orientation of Rome was for him and many other Viennese a distortion of what the church should be. For Mozart both Rome and the Enlightenment needed an awakening to the transcendental mystery underlying beliefs and rules. The awakening reached the late eighteenth century composer-genius by way of an offshoot of the Berlin-based *Brothers of the Gold and Rose Cross*, a conservative Masonic fraternity. In 1781 Hans Heinrich von Ecker und Eckhoven, whose mystical roots were a combination of Franciscan spirituality and the Jewish Cabala, led a Viennese re-incarnation of the group under the name of the *Knights of Light* or the *Asiatic Brethren*. The intent was to unite the clashing religious visions of the time. This reformation had the special goal of reconciling Jews and Catholics. As indicated above after the disbanding of this group some of its former members introduced Mozart to a Masonic lodge that they found sympathetic with their values. The lodge posed a distinct challenge to that portion of Enlightenment philosophy that recognized only the measurement of matter as *the Truth*. Thus Mozart took sides in a momentous dispute within freemasonry on the side of a fast-dwindling group who sought the reform of religion and not its annihilation. At issue was an understanding of the life-giving mystery that we are calling the *mysterium magnum*. During the course of the nineteenth century wars between religion's reformers and religion's annihilators were fought all over Europe. Both sides were opposed by the Catholic Church. The annihilators used money and political power. The reformers used art.

In Italy Gaitano Donizetti and Giuseppi Verdi created operas celebrating the sublime in which the romance between heaven and earth leads the wanderer through death to transcendental fulfillment. The interplay between life's painful contradictions and the spiritual ascent underlies operas like *Lucia di Lammamoor, Aida, La Traviata,* and *Il Trovatore*. The greatest composers celebrated a higher consciousness in which the ascent to God is realized in the harmonious reconciliation of earthly contradiction, a reconciliation symbolized in sexual love, pointing the wanderer through and beyond death. Their visions of conflict resolution suggested higher unities between man and woman, science and religion, Jew and Christian, Protestant and Catholic, between races and nations. Their art was ultimately transcendental, a bitter-sweet invitation to others to ascend to the sublime disposition of the artist or composer, an ascent tragically realized through death and transfiguration.

In the nineteenth century two composers above all others united poetry and music in celebrations of the mystery. They were Franz Schubert and Richard Wagner. Like Caspar David Friedrich, Wilhelm Grimm, Novalis, and Friedrich Schlegel both Schubert and Wagner fashioned their myths out of a paradox. For the composers one element was an insightful grasp of both poetry and music, the other element was intense personal experience. Both composers thought music coupled with poetry appropriate because each venue contributed something essential to a transcendence of nature. Their art was an ascent to a divine harmony that emanated out of contradiction, both in the materials used in the art (music and poetry) and in the life experiences that had to be reconciled. They both thought that words devoid of music were lacking in spirit, while music devoid of poetic inspiration and idea content was trivial. For both composers some combination of art forms was necessary if their art was to be a vehicle for reaching the stars and expressing the higher consciousness. And both composers found their inspiration in the concrete value conflicts that their personal lives and their age presented. They were magicians whose vision of art necessitated an imaginative penetration of the walls of contradiction. They had to stand firm against the tendencies in both religious orthodoxy and the secular state to worship idols.

In the eyes of Wagner, the gods of organized religion have feet of clay. They betray the mystery. Their destruction is assured. The need for a revolutionary new age is crucial. The older Wagner of *Parsifal* and the essay *Religion and Art* celebrated a Manichaean kind of Christian wisdom as the goal of the revolution. He spoke prophetically through Hans Sachs in *Die Meistersinger* of the power of great art and especially of music to capture the life-giving mystery and by it elevate the consciousness of an age and keep it alive.

> *Respect art! You enjoy your dignity not due to birth nor weapons, but by virtue of the poet's wisdom!... How can you despise such art that enriches a people so lavishly?*
> *But times are coming when false foreign wisdom will reign...*
> *So honor the great German masters if you want to survive.*
> *Even if holy Rome should disappear there remains sacred German art!*

According to Wagner, the musical art of the great German masters is vibrant with the spirit of wisdom and does what science, theology, and philosophy can not do. It prepares society for the new age by transfiguring the consciousness of its citizens through a world-transcending, harmony-seeking abstraction of life. Wagner thought that such music can redeem religion from its betrayal of the mystery. He wrote in *Religion and Art*:

> *Where religion becomes artificial it is up to art to save its spirit...Religion has in fact sunk to an artificiality, multiplying dogmatic symbols, concealing the divinely true beneath its unbelievable theology...In such cases she has always turned to art for redemption.*

Wagner saw the task of art to be identifying and celebrating the very soul of all religion, the *mysterium magnum*. But how can man ascend to a consciousness of this mystery when paralyzed by a fear of dying? How can the new age dawn upon a people controlled by fear? For Wagner as for Arthur Schopenhauer the ascent to a higher consciousness of the mystery is conditioned upon coming to grips with death. For both thinkers this meant a renunciation of the will to live. Both were convinced that renouncing life is the key that unlocks the wanderer's prison and opens the gate to the *mysterium magnum*..

> *The deepest root of every true religion is the frailty of this world and our need to escape its chains... the reversal of the Will to Live in defiance of all nature is the greatest miracle of all. It implies an abrogation of the laws of nature; it must consequently be above nature, a superhuman power. It is longed for as the only object worth our effort. It is this Other that Jesus spoke of as the "Kingdom of God" as opposed to the kingdom of this world.*
>
> *Religion and Art*

As an expression of the higher consciousness of the mystery Wagner coupled cosmic empathy with a renunciation of the will to live. In 1880 he wrote that an acceptance of the invitation to cosmic redemption must express itself in profound sympathy with the pain of every living thing, even animals. Cosmic suffering must not be ignored; it must be shared and eased. This sharing, he thought, was at the heart of the Christian religion. It explains the death of Jesus Christ and his victory over the grave. The illumination of the higher consciousness is a lightning flash into the darkness of sorrow and death.

> *Nature surrounds us with the violence of the elements, the unchanged emanations of the Will to Live. In the world beneath us, in sea and desert, in the insect, the world that we unheedingly walk on do we experience the awful tragedy of this world-being and daily lift our eyes to the redeemer on the cross as last and loftiest refuge.*
>
> *Religion and Art*

The iron will committed to greed and self-preservation was seen by this composer as the implacable enemy of the new age and the mystery at its core. Not the living but the dying Christ, not the resurrected but the crucified Christ, is the perfect, the complete symbol of gnosis, the Absolute:

> *The very shape of the divine presented itself in anthropomorphic guise. It was the body of the quintessence of all-pitying love, stretched out upon the cross of pain and suffering...a symbol...beckoning to the highest pity, to esteem for suffering, to an ethic of the breaking of the self-seeking will.*
>
> *Religion and Art*

The dying Christ for Wagner was the liberating secret that sets man free in the new age that is dawning. And Wagner hoped for that dawn. The artist sings of the ascent to the higher consciousness:

> *The Redeemer himself has commanded us to sing our longing, faith, and hope. The song passes beyond the walls of the church and fills all of nature with new life*
>
> *Religion and Art*

The singer of this song, the artist, is to be a poet-priest, a Christ-figure, bringing a reconciliation of the contradiction between love and death. This is the ultimate dignity of the composer/genius who sees this union of opposites in the vision of Christ crucified.

> *Well for us then that we keep our senses open to the mediator of the crushingly sublime and let ourselves be gently led to reconciliation with this mortal life by the artistic teller of the great world tragedy. This poet-priest, the only one who never lied, was ever sent to mankind at epochs of direst error;*

as a mediating friend; us too will he lead over to that reborn life, to set before us in ideal truth the likeness of this passing show.

Religion and Art

The older Wagner saw art as an allegorical celebration of the harmony of opposites through love. It is the artists' task to reclaim by allegory the corrosions of the mystery effected by the replacement of love with belief and obedience. It is the artist's task to rescue society from the shallow legalism encouraged by an authoritarian orthodoxy. Thus the artist must be a high priest, celebrating the higher consciousness of the mystery that lies above and beyond every articulation of it.

Allegorical accessories overlay the noblest kernel of religion to such a point that they have lost credibility and the kernel itself is corroded. So it is the role of Art's greatest genius to save for us the ancient, exalted meaning of the allegories, molding them to the ideal.

Religion and Art

Wagner anticipated a coming transfiguration of life on earth by a higher consciousness transmitted by art. This would be possible only when enough people shared a redemptive experience of that consciousness. The people must be awakened to liberating dramatic abstractions of that consciousness, that unique fruit of head and heart which promotes freedomWagner, like Novalis, thought that the German people were ready for such an art. And indeed he expected that his operas would play their part in preparing them for it. They would, he hoped, lead to a new world of peace.

We have a new people,... capable of redeeming itself to new life.

We can bring about the great regeneration that can spring from nothing save the deep soil of true religion.

It dawned on me that another, better state of future man might well arise if religion and art were not merely retained, but for the first time were rightly understood and employed. From this path all violence is eliminated. The seeds of peace must flower, seeds which are taking root everywhere.

Religion and Art

In his later dualistic but priceless operas Richard Wagner enthroned a unique kind of wisdom that he believed could unlock the true beauty of the life experience. His wisdom had both power and beauty. For example in *Parsifal* he addressed the reform of religion by turning to Manichean-like incarnations of gnosticism, the Cathars, who were a religious group living in southern France and northern Spain in the Middle Ages and viewed as heretical by Rome. They had a monastery at Montsalvat which was the inspiration for the opera. The higher consciousness of the Cathars consisted in the sublimation of the Will to Live with its passions, drives, loves, enthusiasms into an anticipation of "heavenly", i.e. non-material, life. This was expressed in their vow of chastity, their fasting (three days a week), their avoidance of meat, their refusal to kill animals, ideals that Wagner respected. The vision, like Wagner's operas, was often enough sublime. But like all visions it was limited. The limitation meant an unhealthy rejection of matter, especially the flesh. The flesh, the body, and sexuality were for the Cathars as for the composer associated with evil. Women in their sexual allure were temptations with demonic power, symbols of matter that must be set aside in the spiritual ascent. The ideal man or woman for them was an angel walking, a being only partially incarnate. Wagner in *Parsifal* gave dramatic new life to Montsalvat and its dualistic version of Christianity. Baptism for both the Cathars and the opera was the point at which the redeeming spirit entered and annihilated the body. This spirit brought peace not by transfiguring but by destroying Eros. The Cathars called Baptism *Consolamentum,* a term used by Wagner in the Third Act of the opera. The dualism is simultaneously elevating and poisonous, a thrilling grasp of the divine invitation to a higher life coupled with an ominous rejection of major portions of creation.

Beside the Cathars an additional mystical source for the opera *Parsifal* was the Grail legend. The Grail contained the hidden secret of Sophia that unlocks the life experience and sets one free. But what was that secret? In *Parsifal* it was the blood of the dying Christ. But to the medieval poet Wolfram von Eschenbach the Grail was oblong and luminous, a be-jeweled stone upon which is served a feast, a banquet of earthly delights, a symbol perhaps inspired by the Jewish Shekhinah. The contradiction seems glaring. In the first case the secret of life is union in renouncing the will to live with the dying Christ. In the second case the secret is the erotic joy of living, a secret that gave birth to the Venusberg legend. Wagner was absolutely honest in operas (e.g. *Tannhäuser*) in setting before us the contradiction just as he experienced it. Who is not speechless before the glorious music of the *Good Friday Spell* in *Parsifa*l? There life is transfigured as a consequence of a sublimation of sexuality, the illumination of the body by the spirit. And who can remain unmoved by the glorious music of the night scene in *Tristan* when the cosmos is transfigured by love. Wagner presents icons of conflicting Gnostic and/or Cabalistic traditions and perhaps of his own inner conflict and sweeps us up musically into that conflict. But the dualism the opera is unhealthy despite its lop-sided honesty and beauty. The higher consciousness calls us beyond contradiction to a love experience of divine harmony that extends beyond tonal impressions and deserves mythical expression.

Earlier in the nineteenth century another poet-priest had already created a mythical expression of the romance of the *mysterium magnum* through a unique union of poetry and music. His musical mythology expresses a creative, imaginative movement out of chaotic contradiction towards the divine harmony of a sublime higher consciousness. The goal of Schubert was a celebration of that ascent. His art, because of both its authenticity and beauty, can awaken others to life's fearsome and mysterious beauty. Because of its power to do this this the art is a treasure beyond calculation.

Who was this man in whose art immersion in the rose cross mystery, the lost soul of the new age, is such an awakening presence. Franz Peter Schubert lived in Vienna from 1797 to 1828, the first quarter of the nineteenth century. It is unclear when his serious composing actually began, but by the time he was sixteen, two decades after Mozart died and while Beethoven was still alive, he was composing majestic symphonies, masses, and chamber works. He stands with Beethoven as one of the most influential musical figures of the nineteenth century. Benjamin Brittin characterized the eighteen months after Beethoven died, the unbelievably creative last months of Schubert's life, as the most important year and a half in the history of music. As we shall see the inspiration for Schubert's art was the rose cross mystery as it was expressed in poetry.

Schubert was born 16 years before Wagner and died when Wagner was 15. Like Beethoven and Wagner, he saw himself as a messianic figure, a light-bringer from a better world, a celebrant of the mystery that is the soul of life. In those thirty-one years he created sublime celebrations of the great romance between heaven and earth realized through a romance of earthly opposites. He did this by musically telling tales of a wanderer's romance of a dream maiden. His Lieder, operas, liturgical, and instrumental works, all inspired by poetry, are expressions of an ascent to a higher world, a new age. Even today these tales are grasped only superficially.

Schubert was Catholic and sympathetic with the thought of Friedrich Schlegel, Novalis, and Schelling. His art suggests a familiarity with both Jewish mysticism, German pietism, and the Great German (Protestant)Awakening. The artistic expression of his spirituality was neither philosophical nor theological. But he created in piano sonatas, symphonies, quartets, operas, liturgical music, and Lieder musical expressions of life's drama from birth through death. In that art the yearning wanderer ascends through the darkness of value conflicts and death towards the hidden source of divine invitation. This art both embraces and challenges the orthodoxy of Roman Catholicism. It celebrates the core of the life experience of the wanderer, whether Jewish or Christian, Muslim or Buddhist.

Schubert was a mystic. In his book *The World and the Individual* (published by Peter Smith, 1976) Josiah Royce dealt with the subject of mysticism with its search for the higher consciousness and might as well have been defining the composer:

> *The mystic is a very abstract sort of person, I will admit. But he is usually a keen thinker. He gets his reality not by his thinking, but by consulting the data of his experience. He is not stupid. And he is trying very skillfully to be a pure empiricist. Indeed I should maintain that the mystics are the only thorough-going empiricists in the history of philosophy.*

What does the mystic seek? Royce responds:

> *Look deeper, but not deeper into illusory ideas. Look deeper into the interior of experience itself. There you shall find a fact, an immediate and ineffable fact, such that satisfies every longing, answers every inquiry, and fulfills the aim of every thought.*

The meaningful and satisfying "fact" in Schubert's art is often the reconciliation of the wanderer's yearning for peace with the sorrows and concerns of his life. This reconciliation is realized through an awakening to transcendental invitation. The acceptance of sorrow and death as parts of the spiritual ascent is a key to his embrace of the mystery. It is his liberating "fact".

Schubert's challenge was to express an ascent to this liberating "fact" in music. The composer again and again penetrated the walls of contradiction that sprang up in the life of his wanderer with a discovery of his "fact". The "fact" was an awareness growing from the indirect, mysterious experience of divine invitation. The invitation, if it does not eliminate the wanderer's pain, at least gives it meaning. It transfigures the wanderer's life. After his illness in 1822 Schubert's instrumental works enter deeply into the experience of pain and the mystery of death where the darkness seemed absolute. But in the face of the darkness he found the invitation to ascend. Thus most of his masterworks are a surprising and paradoxical stairway to the stars that leads first deep into life's sorrow and despair only to ascend to the hope-filled experience of divine invitation. The profoundly Catholic theme of passing through death to new life appears often in Schubert's art. It is the uniquely Catholic approach to the *magnum mysterium.*

Magical Immersion in the Mystery

At Schubert's music the eye first begins to tear without first asking the soul, so image-less and real is its entrance. We weep without knowing why...because we are not yet what the music promises, and because we need only that promise to assure us that one day we shall be so.

Theodor W. Adorno

Schubert's art is always lyrical but combines lyricism with intense drama after his illness in 1823. The drama is that of a man romancing the *mysterium magnum* in the face of death. Understanding the drama of his art requires, like the paintings of Caspar David Friedrich, insight into the inspiration of the art, insight provided always by the poems that inspire the music. The dramatic movement of the art is an ascent to true wisdom. Only the music lover who is also a romancer of the mystery can truly appreciate the art.

In May of 1819 Schubert set to music a hymn by Novalis (*Hymn IV* D.662) which two years later he would use to inspire the fourth movement of *the Seventh Symphony D.729.* The wanderer imagines a new age of light dawning in the face of human suffering and death. Heaven is touching the earth. The messiah has come and his bride is being prepared. Our earth is being transfigured by the touch of a better world, a world of divine harmony. The cosmic Christ lives! The wanderer is ecstatic.

I tell the world that he lives,
Is risen to new life!
He is among us and will not abandon us!
......

The world is radiant with a new light...
Now at last it is home!
New life comes as a glorious gift from his hand!

Down to the bottom of the sea
The fear of death is gone!
Everyone looks to his future in freedom and joy!

The wanderer in the above poetry experiences earth trasnsfigured by a higher life. This heaven dawns with the wanderer's emergence from sorrow. In the fourth movement of the *Seventh Symphony* it follows upon a first movement inspired by Schiller's poem *Sehnsucht*, which begins with an intensely human experience of alienation and the hope for a better world, a new age.

This mountain valley is cold, enshrouded in fog!
If only I could leave it I would be happy.

Johann Mayrhofer wrote a poem celebrating Schubert's amazing ability to capture the dramatic ascent to a better world.

Tell us who taught you to sing so sweetly, so gently,
Transforming what is earthly into heaven!

First the land lies in mist before our eyes.
Then you sing, and suns are shining!
Springtime is nigh!

If an old man slakes his thirst,
You see in the water life of a richer kind.

As he sings his songs one simply marvels!
What such divine genius composes astounds us and him as well!

Schubert was acutely aware of his mystical and mysterious power to musically express life's transfiguration with its experiential and intellectual components. This power could transform pain, even dying, into a moment of the great romance. In setting a poem by his friend Franz von Bruchmann he celebrated this strange power of his music. His wanderer declares:

D.785
Come here, all of you, if you dare!
In the dark mystery of the mountain
Did I find this lyre!

I myself split the wood out of an aged oak,
Under which our fathers paid tribute to Wotan.

The strings were snatched from the mellow rays of the dying sun,
As once, in sacred content it sank over the valley's lush meadows.

You, oh lyre, are made of sacred oak!
Made of the crimson glow of the setting sun!
You will be mine as long as the gods smile upon me.

The composer simply reveled in the power that came from his unique experience of the *mysterium magnum*. He experienced the call to celebrate the divine harmony and spread its joy. Is the wanderer a Pagan Magus or a Christ-figure? Is he an initiate into the deep meaning of the human experience or is he an inspired believer in revelation. Surely all of these as he celebrates an inner harmony that can transfigure all of life. In the following poem of Goethe the wanderer is an incarnation of the Logos, romancing and giving new life to an incarnation of Sophia while awaiting transcendental union with her.

Wandering through field and woods, I pipe my little song,
Going from place to place.
As I play the whole world steps to my time,
And moves with me.

I can hardly wait for the first spring flowers,
The first buds on the tree.
My songs greet them.
And when winter returns
I continue to sing of that same dream!

I sing it far and wide over the frozen land...
And winter is transformed into spring!
Yet winter's bloom will also fade,
Only to have new joy aborning
On the mountain pastures.

When by the linden tree I find young people gathered,
I capture them by the music.
The slow peasant lad looks alive;
The awkward girl begins to dance...
To the magic of my melodies!

You lend wings to my feet.
You drive the young heart out of its home
To wander the mountains and valleys.
Dear, wondrous Muse,
When will I come to final rest at your bosom?

A counterbalance of pagan, Jewish, and Christian mysticism was the condition for this immersion in the *mysterium magnum*. Awarness of the mystery could come and go. When it faded he had to bring it back. Otherwise he was miserable and could not create his art. We have a record of this in the fourth movement of the *Piano Sonata in C Minor* D.958 and in the Lied inspired by the following poem:

> ***Lebensmut***
> *Ernst Schulze D.883*
> *Oh, how the forces of youthful life*
> *Flow through mind and heart!*
> *I feel everything within me come alive..*
> *Doubly sensitive to joy and pain.*
> *It is impossible to hold*
> *The spirits within me!*
> *Be my rulers for suffering or for joy!*
>
> *This delaying, this yearning*
> *Which vainly pulses within me,*
> *These sighs, these tears*
> *Which only pride can stifle,*
>
> *This pointless struggle,*
> *This fight without strength,*
> *Without hope, without fulfillment*
> *Have stolen my youth.*
>
> *Let now awaken my speed and courage.*
> *Sound the battle horn for my sleeping spirit!*
> *I dreamed and rested long enough.*
> *Far too long was I in prison.*
>
> *Here is neither hell nor heaven,*
> *Neither frost nor desert heat.*
> *So up and go into battle!*
> *With renewed strength brave the floods!*

Poetry is the stepping stone by which we can share Schubert's vibrant and profound experience of the mystery. So with Schubert's instrumental compositions it is important to identify the inspiring poems. And this is not impossible to do. His composing was a transfiguration of poetry. Music for Schubert was his first language and the translation from German into music was easy. So just as there was a pathway that he followed from the inspiring poem to the music, so there is a pathway back from the music to the inspiring poem. Our ability to recognize the inspiring poem in his instrumental compositions is made easier by the fact that each poem inspiring a movement of an instrumental work was set first as a Lied by this composer, often at the very same time.

Let us look more closely at the poetry-music linkage. What was it in a poem that inspired the composer? Schubert set poems to music that were written by other people but which are intimately expressive of his own romance of the mystery. There are several graphic accounts of his creative process. It was a rare phenomenon of nature. His friends marveled at the self-revelation triggered by the appropriate poem. The movement from poem to music flowed so easily, so naturally for the composer that Grove speaks of an:

> *inspiration of dictation, as much so as in the utterance of any Hebrew prophet.*

Baron Schonstein wrote:

> *One morning in September, 1824, in which year I once again spent some weeks in Zseliz with my friends, Countess Esterhazy invited Meister Schubert during breakfast, which we all took together, to set to music for our four voices a poem of which she was particularly fond; it was the above-mentioned "Gebet". Schubert read it, smiled with inward joy as he usually did when something appealed to him, took the book and retired forthwith, in order to compose. In the evening of the same day we were already trying though the finished song at the piano from the manuscript.*
>
> *Memoirs*

The music erupted as a rare and priceless natural process out of the poetry. There is a natural connection between the ascent into the mystery expressed in the poem and that expressed in the music. It should be possible then to recognize the movement from poem to music when you can hear the music and see the poem. The dramatic movement in the music and in the poem are closely linked and can be recognized. This connection between music and poetry is mentioned by Anton Steinbuchel:

> *...in Vogl's delivery of poems each one presented an articulate whole, in which each individual part occupied its allotted space, without encroaching on that of another. A few introductory words created the appropriate atmosphere. Whether chance friends, Vogl, or Schubert himself had made the choice he (Schubert) listened and did not always respond to the effects. But should a chord of his feelings be touched, there began in his innermost soul the musical storm; the slumbering sea of harmonies was stirred to its depths, until the pearl in the form of a song broke loose and came to the surface. After which Vogl would give a performance of Schubert songs as a boat glides, now on smooth, now on ruffled water; and Schubert would delight in his creations.*
>
> *Memoirs*

Albert Stadler, a friend from Schubert's early school days, underscored the special nature of this composer's compositional process. Fidelity to an inner directive that takes shape in response to a poem was an ethical imperative. The process always began with an experience of the mystery in a poem and proceeded, almost organically, to the expression of that experience in music.

> *It was interesting to see him compose. He very seldom made use of the pianoforte while doing it. He often used to say it would make him lose his train of thought. Quite quietly and hardly disturbed by the unavoidable clatter and din of his friends around him, he would sit at the little writing table, bent over the music paper and the book of poems (he was shortsighted), bite his pen, drum his fingers at the same time, trying things out, and continue to write easily and fluently without any corrections, as if it had to be like that and not otherwise.*
>
> *Memoirs*

Schubert described the process this way:

> *When you have a good poem, immediately you get a good idea; melodies pour in so that it is a real joy. With a bad poem you can't make any headway; one torments oneself over it, and nothing comes of it but trash. I have already refused many poems which have been pressed on me.*
>
> *Memoirs*

Josef Hüttenbrenner, one of the composer's friends, spoke of this state of inspiration as a kind of rare phenomenon of nature: ???

> *When composing Schubert looked to me like a somnambulist. His eyes shone, standing out as if they were made of glass.*
>
> *Memoirs*

These descriptions of the passage from poem to music call to mind divination. The practitioner gazes at some object (a crystal ball or, in Schubert's case, a poem) and falls into a light trance. He must set aside for a while the critical, analytic function of the mind while not disabling it for it will soon be used. He focuses upon what Hermetic thought calls the astral aspect of the thing. It is this astral aspect that Schubert expressed musically in his songs and other creations. It is clear that what he saw was the content of the poem...but a content illuminated and enriched by the diviner. The process to this point is intuitive and non-purposeful.

This natural process of utilizing a poem as inspiration for an ascent to a higher consciousness and expressing that consciousness musically was essential to Schubert's composing. He was unable to compose successfully any other way. His close friend, Josef Spaun, underscores the irreplaceable character of this process for creations:

> *The suggestions made to him so often, especially by art dealers (i.e. music publishers)...he had to ignore...because he wrote, as it were, in a state of inspiration and consequently had to compose exactly as in fact he did. If on rare occasions he did actually try to comply with such requests, constraint of this kind was quite certain to have a detrimental effect on the work.*
>
> *Memoirs*

From these observations it can scarcely be doubted that the inspirational process for Schubert involved a surrender to a phenomenon in which the higher consciousness of the composer was brought to life through a poem and then expressed in music. The poem was the trigger for the inspirational process. It was the condition of the musical creation. This composer was not free to interfere with the process, only to expand upon it, exploiting it for purposes of his own. Interference with the integrity of the process destroyed the art. If a truly inspired composition was to occur absolute respect for the poem was one of its conditions. Never is Schubert's creative process described independently of this symbiotic relationship to inspiring poetry. The great singer and friend of Schubert, Michael Vogl, speaks of the results of the symbiosis:

> *What a tremendous and universal effect these truly divine inspirations, these products of musical clairvoyance, would have made in a world able to understand the German language. How many might have understood for the first time the meaning of things like poetry expressed in music, words in terms of harmony, thoughts clothed in music. They might have learned how the finest poems of our greatest poets, translated into a musical language such as this, could be further enhanced, no, even surpassed.*
>
> *Memoirs*

The above process was Schubert's key to composing. Without it he could not compose. He used this key in composing his Lieder and also in the composition of his instrumental works. Knowledgeable commentators have no doubt that Schubert's instrumental compositions are indebted to poetry for inspiration. Dietrich Ficher-Dieskau recognized that Schubert the Lieder composer "fertilizes" Schubert the instrumental composer. John Reed wrote about the linkage between Schubert's instrumental compositions and his Lieder settings of poetry:

> *The great instrumental works of his middle and late years...are dependent upon his earlier success as a songwriter, not merely in the obvious sense that most of them openly exploit the popularity of individual songs...but also because they adapt the expressive freedom and inwardness of Romantic song to the formal patterns of instrumental music in such a way that, as Schwind put it, these instrumental works stay in the mind, as songs do, fully sensuous and expressive.*
>
> *The Schubert Song Companion*

The "fertilization" of the instrumental works by poetry settings was recognized by the Schubert biographer, Alfred Einstein. He wrote:

> *What he (Schubert) was trying to do (in his instrumental works) was to expand and develop in a less constricted form what he had expressed in musical terms in the song, and to intensify this expression by means of musical as opposed to poetical contrasts.*
>
> *Schubert, A Musical Portrait*

Einstein was suggesting that Schubert's instrumental works are expansions upon the Lieder. The instrumental works are able to do more personally, more vibrantly what many of the Lieder did, namely express the sorrows and joys in the romance of the *mysterium magnum*. The process was for this composer necessarily conditioned by the appropriate poems. Einstein gives as instances of this bond between instrumental works and poem settings the fourth movement of the *Piano Trio In* B *Flat* and the Lied *Skolie*, the second movement of the *Piano Trio in E Flat* D.927 and a Swedish folksong, the second movement of the posthumous *Piano Sonata in A Major* and the Lied *Pilgerweise,* the fourth movement of the same sonata and the Lied *Im Frühling*, the first movement of the *Piano Sonata in B Flat* and the Lied *So lasst mich scheinen*, and in general to the piano sonatas composed before 1825 and unspecified songs set by this composer.

The fact is that all of Schubert's major instrumental works were inspired by poetry that he had set previously as songs. And these inspiring poems can be recognized and the correlations experienced. (They are computer accessible with this book.)

Just as no one in the case of Lieder composition could responsibly deny a linkage, primary and dominant, between the purely literary meaning of the poem and its musical expression, no one should doubt a similar linkage between the meaning of the inspiring poem and its musical expression in the instrumental work. Once the inspiring poem has been identified, one can observe the fidelity of the musical composition to the inspiring poem.

But there was more to Schubert's inspiration. Josef Spaun, Schubert's longtime friend, spoke of the "state of inspiration", also wrote that:

> *...anyone inclined to believe that Schubert was only an excellent natural composer, a belief into which several intimations in the biography could mislead one, would make a great mistake. He possessed the most thorough musical knowledge and had studied the works of the great masters, both old and new, in the greatest detail. Bach and Handel he worked through thoroughly and held in very high esteem; all Gluck's operas he could play almost from memory and there was probably not a note by Mozart, Beethoven and Haydn that he did not know. With such knowledge one is no mere natural composer.*
>
> *Memoirs*

Eduard von Bauernfeld spoke of the remarkable breadth and depth of Schubert's profundity, intelligence, and sensitivity:

> *In his own subject he knew the masters and the masterworks fairly thoroughly and under Salieri's guidance, had also given adequate attention to the theory of his art. Moreover in literature too, he was anything but unversed; and how he understood how to interpret, with inventiveness and vitality, the different poetic individualities, like Goethe, Schiller, Wilhelm Müller. J.G.Seidl, Mayrhofer, Walter Scott, and Heine, how to transform them into new flesh and blood, and how to render faithfully the nature of each one by beautiful and noble musical characterization! These recreations in song should alone be sufficient to demonstrate merely by their own existence and without any further proof from how deep a nature, from how sensitive a soul these creations sprang."*
>
> *Memoirs*

It is precisely the qualities of this "sensitive soul" that is of interest here. Schubert's goal of an ascent to the transcendental harmony of the *mysterium magnum* was not reached simply by translating poems into music. Just as he violated the sacred borders of the opposites of poetry and music, he sought to break the barrier between heaven and earth by expressing in classical sonata form the experience of the spiritual ascent awakened by the poetry. He wanted mysticism in music. He worked hard as his sketches and revisions reveal. Important among these are sketches of the posthumous piano sonatas and the revisions of the *Symphony in C Major*. What appears is a labored ascent to the mastery of the sonata form, not as Beethoven realized it, but rather in his very personal and paradoxical way of uniting poetry and music. For the magic to work as he wanted it to the music had to be true to the inner dynamic of the poem, to his own experience., and true to the accepted sonata form in music. The ultimate challenge was for the art to be an authentic expression of his own romance, of the *mysterium magnum* and simultaneously faithful to the clasical form. And he considered himself successful in what he set out to do. According to Bauernfeld Schubert said of himself:

> *I am Schubert, Franz Schubert...who has written things great and beautiful that you do not begin to understand. I will compose still more beautiful things...the most beautiful things! Cantatas, quartets, operas, symphonies! I am not merely a composer of Ländler as the foolish journalists say and as the foolish public repeats. I am Schubert, Franz Schubert! Do not forget it!"*

Once the fact of the poetry connection in the instrumental works is recognized, the other, far more interesting realities appear. The poems inspiring a sonata type instrumental work occur in a certain order. And the order amounts to a drama. The juxtaposition of poems within individual works and in larger thematic grouping of works like the posthumous piano sonatas and the two piano trios is for the mature Schubert an exposition of the wanderer's life as death approaches. It even seems evident that there is a kind of organic unity of all the major works so that they express the dramatic development of the composer's life from youth to death. It becomes obvious from the inspiring poetry that we are listening to an autobiographical ascent into the *mysterium magnum* at various points in the composer's life. The art is authentic because it emanates out of the personal experience of the composer. It is universal in that Schubert's experience and that of the listener can overlap. Adrift in the turbulence of horrible contradictions, the wanderer (the composer and the alert listener) ascends to the peace and harmony of a better world.

Of considerable help for the listener in uniting with the composer in his ascent to the higher consciousness is the identification of the poems that inspired the instrumental works. Since Schubert did not often speak of these connections, the task might seem impossible. It is not. The correlation between the inspiring poem and the inspired movement is frequently so close, so transparent, that it can hardly be doubted. All that is necessary is to become very familiar with a movement of the instrumental piece and then review the texts previously set as Lieder. Almost always, one leaps out as matching the music. Each idea finds its musical expression with at least as much fidelity as found in a Lied or a part song. And there is a predictable chronology governing the settings of the poem first as a Lied or part song and then as an instrumental movement. In his early years and at times throughout his short life, Schubert set poems almost simultaneously as Lieder or part songs and as movements in an instrumental work. Later the composer tended to set groups of poems as Lieder or part songs and then reach back for a year or two and use them as inspiration for instrumental works. As he grew older the effort to musically express the vision contained in the poem with utter fidelity became more, not less, evident. Thus, the masterworks of this composer are often the ones in which the correlation can most easily be identified and affirmed with the most security. The correlation was quite obviously a consistent principle of his art, one scrupulously followed. It was not an artistic crutch he might have wished to discard.

The reader can experience the "fit" between the instrumental music and the inspiring poem. That poem is usually "set", almost line by line, idea by idea, dramatic moment by dramatic moment in the instrumental work. Important ideas like a birdsong, a star, or transfiguration have their unmistakable musical expression. The correspondence between poem and instrumental composition is sometimes but not always musicological. It is primarily and always idea-centered. The composer is saying through the music what the poetic idea inspires him to say. The music is launched from the idea, faithful to it but transcending it. The fidelity of music to the inspiring poetic ideas is often even more compelling than in the case of the songs. The fact that a given poem, set already by the composer as a song, actually served him a second time as the inspiration for a movement in an instrumental composition is clear when the poem and the music are experienced together. To make experience easily accessible, the author is preparing an number of computer-playable "movies," files which, when viewed with any standard media player program, show the words on the screen while the music plays on the computer's speakers. As the correlation of movements in the instrumental works to poems that inspired some of the Lieder becomes clear, the source of inspiration of this composer becomes evident. That inspiration is nothing less than a celebration of the rose cross mystery.

The above statements about the inspiring nature of poetry and its effects upon the art of Schubert will perhaps seem incompatible with the classical development of a work in the sonata form. Indeed there is a contradiction. Yet, through Schubert's unique genius, the contradictory poles of musical form and of poetic mysticism are reconciled to an unprecedented degree.

The Goddess and the Mystery

The one I love is so distant, so far away!
I so yearn for her over there…on the other side!
Shepherd on the Rock D.965

Schubert expressed the ascent to the *magnum mysterium* through stories of a wanderer. The wanderer is awakened to the mystery by a woman. In her and through her he finds it. Then in and through her it disappears. Once a blissful presence, but now a sublime memory, this woman hovers like a distant star above the wanderer's journey, an unattainable figure of divine allure. In and through her God invites. In and through her God is unattainable. This intermingling of joyful hope and catastrophic sorrow is the hallmark of Schubert's art. It follows in the great tradition of the Troubadours, of Petrarch, Dante, and Giordano Bruno. A real woman makes incarnate the feminine face of God. Divine wholeness can be realized by the wanderer only in and through her incarnations and, paradoxically, by transcending her incarnations to rediscover her transcendentally.

She is the eternal feminine, incarnate in many forms. They include the moon, a brook, a starry night, a silent forest, etc. But above all she is a concrete person. She can be the Blessed Virgin. She can be Theresa Grob, or Karoline Esterhazy, women he loved. She is the symbol of all the thrilling beauty of creation.. And she is sacred, holy, alight with a divine radiance. She leads the wanderer to God. For example:

Die Tauschung
Ludwig Kosegarten D.230
I have a vision!
I see it among the alders and in the pines;
I see it in sunshine and moonlight,

And amid the glistening stars!
It rustles in the evening sunset;
It flies with the dawn breeze,
And dances in the meadows,
It sings with the quail,
And sparkles in the quiet brook;
Its shimmer is in the dew!

Oh beautiful spirit, who are you?
You with gentle charm bring me such joy!
Do you come to announce a better world?
Do you lead me through this life of sorrow
To my true home?

But why a goddess? Is not the God of revelation enough? Underlying the recognition of a goddess is an axiom: Every human grasp of the hidden God is a betrayal as well as a revelation. The masculine deity of revelation limits as it reveals the hidden God who transcends both masculinity and femininity. The truth lies beyond the contradiction. And revelation never can transcend the dualistic world of contradiction in which we live. Therefore a goddess is the necessary counterpoint to the God of revelation. Only by recognizing her as the necessary counterpoint to the masculine God of revelation is it possible to ascend to the hidden God who is the unity that we crave.

This goddess is an imagined incarnation of the Divine Sophia in the tradition of the Wisdom literature of the Old Testament. She is a star above the wanderer, divine yet gentle and human, a presence yet absent, an alluring, beguiling, frustrating assurance that one day he will be what as yet he is not. She is the image of Being that is both present and absent in all Becoming. Out of a chaotic ocean of value conflicts she calls the wanderer to love's fulfillment. She is the "other" without which the self is destitute. She invites and empowers, yet paradoxically is hidden and distant. She is a powerful symbolic figure. And she is sometimes an actual person. For Schubert she was Theresa Grob or Karoline Esterhazy.

For Schubert then there was a goddess who led him to God.. What importance does this goddess have? She provides the counterpoint, the contradiction to a facile masculine vision of God and reality. In recognizing her the wanderer opens to the larger universe of fragmented values which must be reconciled. She represents for him the kingdom of love that must counterbalance and control the kingdom of power. If the Greeks developed for us the power universe of ideas, she is the pagan remnant which was suppressed. The peaceful way of earlier societies, the way of the Goddess, is indicated by the cults of Dionysus and Demeter. The fruits of the earth and sensuality, the domain of the Goddess, provided a pagan highway into the mystery. Schubert's art suggests that she be restored to her rightful queenship. The hidden God is neither a masculine reality nor a feminine one but touched in the loving and creative union between the opposites.

Schubert's art sings of the queenship of Sophia, the beloved of God, the beloved of the wanderer. She is both of this world and yet is alive with a higher life. Through her two worlds touch and the composer makes the romance real for us. And as we noted above she has many faces, not all of them human. But always she is luminous with the *mysterium magnum*. In the following poem she is the wanderer's dream::

Nacht und Träume
Matthäus Kasimir von Collin D.827
Holy Night, descend upon us;
With you comes the Dream,
Like moonlight into the room,
Into the quiet hearts of the sleepers.

They recognize the dream with joy,
And lament when dawn awakens them.
Return oh Holy Night;
Sweet Dream come back to us!

She is radiant in nature's beauty and so is the gateway to a higher world.

Die Erde
Friedrich von Matthisson, D.989
How enraptured my eyes and my heart
When our Mother Earth blossoms in the spring!
When all her children draw sacred life from her full breasts!
Ah, how she loves each of them,
How anxious to share her life, impart her strength,
Spark and nourish health and growth!
My intoxicated heart is drawn to sing the praises
Of the Creator of this wondrous world!

She is the incarnation of the *magnum mysterium*, and is found where outer and inner worlds meet. That meeting may occur in music.

An die Musik D.547
Franz Schober
You precious art! How often in distress,
When life seemed too oppressive to bear,
Did you warm my heart with love,
And lead me into a better world.

Often has your harp's whisper
Breathed a gentle, holy peace,
Opening to me a higher and better world.
Oh precious art, I thank you.

In July of 1822 Schubert wrote an allegory focusing upon the role of this goddess of many faces who makes incarnate the *magnum mysterium*. She brings heaven to earth:

One day my father took me once more into his pleasure garden. He asked me if it pleased me. But the garden was hateful to me and I did not dare reply. Then he asked me a second time and more impatiently if I liked the garden. Trembling I told him no. At that my father struck me and I fled. For the second time I turned away, and my heart filled with infinite love for those who scorned it. I wandered once more into distant lands. Through long, long years I sang my songs. But when I wished to sing of love it turned to sorrow, and when I wanted to sing of sorrow it was transformed for me into love.........so was I torn between love and sorrow.

But once a pious maiden who had just died appeared to me. A circle had formed around her tomb in which many youths and old men wandered as though in eternal bliss. They spoke softly so as not to awaken her. Heavenly thoughts like bright sparks seemed to flicker unceasingly out of the virgin's tomb and to fall in a silent and gentle shower on the young men. I longed to walk there too. But only by a miracle, so people said, could one enter the circle. I went forward however, slowly and devoutly, with my eyes lowered towards the gravestone, and before I knew it I was in the circle from which the loveliest melody sounded, And I felt pressed as it were into a moment's space, the whole measure of eternal bliss. I saw my father too, loving and reconciled. He folded me in his arms and wept. And I still more.

Franz Schubert

The "pious maiden", an incarnation of Sophia, manifests divine life in light sparks that illuminate the circle. She transfigures life. She transfigures art. She is the spouse of God.

Was there a "pious maiden" in Schubert's life who lifted him into a higher world, a light-bringing creativity? Were there women who were for the composer incarnations of the Shekhinah? Surely such a thing was "in the air" of Vienna at the time. For many Jews Eva Franck, the daughter of Jacob, was such a figure. She died in 1816. To her was ascribed nobility and radiant holiness. Gershom Sholem wrote that:

Many Franckist families kept a miniature of Eva Franck which used to be sent to the most prominent households and to this day some families honor her as a saintly woman who was falsely reviled.

Some of those Franckist families were located right in Vienna. Jewish Cabalism of Jacob Franck's type probably affected the composer and inspired him. While it is improbable that Eva Franck played such a symbolic role in Schubert's mythical life it is beyond doubt that he experienced an aura of the sacred in special women, "stars" who led him "home". Each star in her erotic allure was divine invitation. "Heaven", the better world to which he felt called, was inconceivable for him apart from such stars.

Final union with the dream maiden or goddess is a necessity for Schubert's wanderer, inseparable from his commitment to God. She is the divine spirit without whom creation is devoid of life and beauty. Her ascendancy to queenship is needed to usher in a new age. Schubert describes her at length and often through the words of his inspiring poets. Examples abound. One is a poem set both as the Lied *Blondel zu Marien (D.626)* and as the opening movement of the *Piano Sonata in F Minor (D.625)*. Here as elsewhere Schubert's dream maiden appears in an overlay of three worlds, one outer, one inner, the third mythological.

Schubert's wanderer sings:

Blondel zu Marien
Anon. (Used in Grétry's opera, *Richard Coeur de Lion*) D.626
In the midst of the dark night,
When sorrow overwhelms me,
And my happiness has vanished,
I see in the distance a glow,
A wondrous shining light
A bright witness to love,
A mystical beautiful star.

Eternally pure,
It shines through joys and sorrows,
And deep within my heart
That light is reflected,
So lovely, so gentle
Is that faithful reflection,
That I am wondrously consoled
Though you are still so far away.

This goddess, this dream maiden, is hidden in both the outer world and the wanderer's imagination.

Das Bild
Anon. D.155
Day and night a young girl is my dream maiden,
A heavenly vision, but still flesh and blood!

When the morning sun shines through my window I see her;
And when the Evening Star sparkles gently she is there.
Her image is faithful, a true friend in relaxation or struggle.
She is in heaven; she is here on earth!.........

Does she exist only in my dream?
No! However glorious the dream,
It is but a shadow of the radiant girl I love!

This girl, radiant with divine life, invites the wanderer to a higher and better world:

Der Morgenstern
by Theodore Körner D.172
Star of Love, radiant Bride of Heaven!
You wander through the light fields, proclaiming the coming dawn!
You come as a friend, aloft in the sky,
Sparkling above the billowing clouds,
Beaming hope into our hearts.

The composer devoted a piano sonata for four hands to celebrating the multifaceted, paradoxical nature of the dream maiden/goddess. She is a real woman who awakens the wanderer to a new and higher life. She is the moon, a part of one world but transfigured in light by anhother. And finally she is the apex of creation, its perfection, a loving mother who powerfully protects her children and calls them "home". The *Piano Sonata in B Flat Major D.617* is a celebration of these three aspects of the dream maiden, following closely upon the charming *Piano Sonata in C Major D.613* that uses the same poems with the same purpose but in an inverted order. In the third movement of the *Piano Sonata in B Flat* and the first movement of the *Piano Sonata in C Major* the dream maiden is earthly, seductive, alluring, identified closely with her incarnation. She is the awakener of the wanderer, who first alerts him to the possibilities of a better world, a new age to be realized through the reconciliation of opposites, that means concretely the romance between the wanderer and the girl.

Der Blumenbrief
Aloys Wilhelm Schreiber D.622
I send flowers to a beautiful girl.
I beg her to end my suffering with one kind word.

Rose, tell her how love has ravaged me,
How painfully I(yearn for her!
Marigold, reveal to her my despair;
Tell her, "Without your love he will die!"

In the first movement of the *Piano Sonata in B Flat* and the third movement of the *Piano Sonata in C Major* this Goddess is the moon, a mystical presence in nature, mythically overseeing the interplay of vastly different universes.

An der Mond in einer Herbstnacht
Aloys Wilhelm Schreiber D.614
Your face is that of a friend, oh Daughter of the Heavens,
With softest step you wander through the skies, dear friend of the Night...
In your soft light a mysterious yearning seized me...

In the Second Movements of both sonatas this goddess is heavenly, the Divine Sophia, the Blessed Virgin. She stands atop the human race as its summation, its perfection. She is the loving mother who assists the wanderer in his ascent.

Das Marienbild
Aloys Wilhelm Schreiber D.623
Hail to you, Lady of Grace,
Full of pure, radiant love...
Gladly will I erect a small hut here in this quiet forest,
That your star may shine for me always,
And that here I might touch the better world.

The divine Sophia, the eternal feminine is the missing and utterly necessary counterbalance to the masculine God. She is the symbol for the reconciliation of contradictions. In her are both an embrace of this world of contradictions and the experience of a higher one. Jewish mysticism had used a similar symbolism in the creation of its Wisdom literature, portions of the *Book of Genesis*, and portions of the *Zohar*. Christian mysticism had used something similar to condition portions of John and Paul, the *Book of Revelation*, and the Gnostic Gospels of Phillip and Thomas. The counterbalance underlies the devotion to the Virgin Mary in Roman Catholicism. Such imaginative projections are not infantile. They are not unnecssary and excessive accretions to religion, but rather archetypal eruptions suggesting a hidden truth of immense power.

Schubert's fascination with this feminine side of the hidden God must be made clear. For his wanderer her ascendancy is the key to the transfiguration of life.

Abendstänchen: An Lina
Gabriele von Baumberg D.265
Dear Twilight, like her soul be gentle,
Like her eyes be full of joy,
That my faithfulness be rewarded!

She is Nature which acts as the wanderer's guide, giving him strength for his ascent.

An die Natur
Friedrich Leopold, Graf zu Stolberg-Stolberg D.372
Nature, so precious, so sacred,
Let me follow your ways,
Lead me like a child by the hand.
When I tire I find refreshment at your breast,
And there like a suckling child I experience the joys of heaven.

She is the divine spirit of joy that fills the heavens and transforms the earth:

An die Freude
Friedrich von Schiller D.189
Oh Joy, divine flame, Daughter of Heaven!
With hearts afire, oh Goddess, we draw near your throne.
Your magic can unite what man's tyrannical laws split asunder.
All men can be brothers under your mighty wings!

This goddess of many faces is the mediator between heaven and earth. Schubert's wanderer romances her as a Lover romances his Beloved. He is her servant, her knight. His task is to bring her enrichment, to ensure her ascendancy. In return she will bring his yearning to an end and lead him to final joy.

Romanze des Richard Löwenherz
Sir Walter Scott D.907
Joy to the fair!...my name unknown;
Each deed and all its praise thine own;
Then oh, unbar this churlish gate,
The night dew falls, the hour is late...
Let grateful love quell maiden shame,
And grant him bliss who brings thee fame!

The goddess is captured in memory and illuminates the inner life:

Adelaide
Friedrich von Matthisson D. 95
All alone wanders your lover,
Walking slowly through the Spring garden,
Aglow in mystic light that suffuses the trembling blossoms,
Adelaide!
Your image appears in the lake's mirror
And upon the glittering alpine snow,
In the golden sunset,
And the far-flung stars of heaven,
Adelaide!

She is the vibrant invitation of a higher world, both an inviting presence and an often painful, physical absence. She comes and goes. When she is present everything, all of life, is transfigured in love. Love is her sacrament, bringing a better world to earth.

> ***Das Madchen aus der Fremde***
> Friedrich Schiller D.117
> *In a mountain vale in early spring when the first larks come,*
> *A maiden, beautiful and enchanting, would visit the shepherds.*
> *She wasn't born there; no one knew whence she came.*
> *But when she would leave even her footprints disappeared!*
> *There was something holy about her...*
> *The folk would open their hearts to her.*
> *But there could be no crude familiarity.*
> *She brought flowers and fruits from distant lands,*
> *Nurtured by a different sun, wondrous, otherworldly!*
> *She gave gifts to everyone, fruits here, flowers there,*
> *To young and old, a blessing to all!*
> *Everyone was welcome, but when she saw a couple in love*
> *She gave them the most glorious flowers of all!*

This goddess who leads the wanderer to heaven through a transfigured earth calls the wanderer to the fullness of the human experience. She is present in hope-filled dreams and premonitions, alluring him, enticing him irresistibly to a higher life.

> **Widerschein**
> Franz Xaver von Schlechta D.639 and D.949 and in Drei Klavierstücke D.946, No. 2.
> *The fisherman stands on the bridge...His beloved is late.*
> *Impatiently he looks into the brook and daydreams.*
> *She is hiding in the lilac.*
> *Clearly he sees her reflection there in the water...*
> *More clearly even than in life!*
> *He recognizes her ribbons and sweet smile...*
> *And grabs the railing lest he dive in!*

Yet this Goddess, the glory of nature and the joy of mankind, is often absent or hidden from the world. Can her absence be explained by the jealousy of Zeus, the male distortion of the true but hidden God?

> ***Klage der Ceres***
> Friedrich Schiller D.323
> *How long have I been a wanderer, searching far and wide.*
> *Titan, Sun in the heavens,*

I have sent all your light to find her…to no avail!
Zeus, have you stolen her away?
Has Pluto, enchanted by her beauty,
Taken her to the black rivers of Orcus!

If now the dream maiden, the luminous incarnation of the *mysterium magnum*, is dead and gone, she will return bringing new life to a world locked in winter's death.

Klage der Ceres ***continued from above***
And is there nothing of her left to me?
Is there no sweet memory that I still can love?
Is there nothing here from her own dear hand,
Nothing of the bond that tied us together?
Is there no union between the living and the dead?
Could it be that she is not entirely gone?
That we are not completely separated?……
Seeds that seemed dead to us, lying cold in the winter's ground,
Now erupt joyfully in colors bright and beautiful.
Even when a plant reaches up towards the heavens
Its roots drive downwards into the darkness…
When all seems locked up in the darkness of winter,
Remember the blossoms of spring.
However far from golden light is the kingdom of the shadow,
The blossoms of love survive!…
So happily I greet you, children of nature's new life!
Your cup is filled with life's wonder.
I would bathe you in sunlight and the moonbeam,
Painting your leaves like the dawn.
In the dried leaves of fall I see every yearning heart.
I see both my suffering and my joy!

Despite the wanderer's hope for the mysterious and presumably transcendental return of the goddess, her absence is painful. At times she is alive for him only in the inner life, and that is not enough. She must become incarnate.

Sie in jedem Liede
Karl Gottfried von Leitner D.896a
In the rose-tinted land of dreams and poetry, you my love are close.
But in life, so tragic, so bitter,
We are separated by the cruel hand of savage fate!

Thus the wanderer's ethic is to search for the goddess, the joy of creation, the perfect spouse of the messiah, the higher consciousness of the *mysterium mag-*

num, until he finds her, in this life or, mysteriously, in some transcendence of it.

Alind
Johann Friedrich Rochlitz D.904
The sun sinks into the ocean depths. She said she would come. ...
Reaper, have you seen my love?.........
Dark night steals over the woods,
Still she does not come.
I am all alone, fearful and concerned.
You Echo, I will tell of my love.
The Echo answers, "Alinde".
And suddenly she is standing beside me.
She whispers, "You were faithful. Now I am yours."

Again and again the theme of the disappearance of the goddess is sounded along with an intimation of the occasional mystical presence.

Romanze
Friedrich von Matthisson D.114
Rose of Montanvert was praised in song by Troubadours,
And esteemed by many a knight as the loveliest flower of creation...
Her uncle, a knight named Manfry, was her guardian
Who wanted only her gold......
Her uncle held her in a dank prison,
But pretended to bury her in the vault of her fathers.
She heard the litanies of the priests...
And shuddering, understood her fate!...
And death closed her eyes...
And many a shepherd will say
That often at night they see in the air,
High like a cloud of silver, that beautiful girl.

This goddess controls the wanderer's destiny.

Atys
Johann Mayrhofer D.585
I am in love! I am frantic! I have seen her!
She sails through the turbulent clouds in a lion drawn carriage.
I call to her: Wait for me! take me!
My life is over! Don't deny me!

She looks upon him, smiling sweetly
And her chariot brings him to Thrace.
There he serves as her priest,
And his joy is sublime!

The mystical romance between the wanderer and the ephemeral goddess who can elude him and who must be re-captured, a goddess incarnate for him in certain women, is a central theme of Schubert's life's work. Inner and outer worlds touch. Fidelity to this romance is his abiding ethic. It was a matter of great pride that he remained true to this romance as he saw it until death. That fidelity gave meaning to his life and substance to his art.

Sei mir gegrüßt
Friedrich Rückert D.741
You are torn from me, from my embrace.
Accept my love! Accept my kiss!
You can be reached only in my dreams.
Accept my love! Accept my kiss!

The goddess awaits the wanderer at the end of his journey as his surest joy, the answer to his erotic longing.

Das war Ich
Theodore Körner D.174
When I finally awakened...
Your sweet face was near me.
I saw you responding to my warm kiss,
And your happiness in my embrace!

While the wanderer is faithful to the Goddess and to the God who sends her and to whom she leads, many in the world are not. The Goddess has been persecuted and rejected by society, replaced by idols. The perfection of creation in love has been replaced by the primacy of power. Her ultimate return and triumph aqre assured.

Uraniens Flucht
Johann Mayrhofer, D.554
Jupiter stared at her. Can you be Urania? Yes. The gods were thunderstruck. How can this be?.........Said Zeus: When you left here to visit the earth you were full of beauty and grace. You had one task, to give to the people of earth the good news and lead them to my dwelling place.

Unania: The mission which I with all my heart desired to accomplish failed...

Earth's people mix good with evil and are slaves to foolish pleasures.

...

But Zeus asked Urania to look down upon the earth. There she saw two lovers in a grassy meadow, beside a brook. And there was a small alter dedicated to her.

> *The couple knelt before her statue, praying to the absent Goddess. And the prayer like music encompassed her like an ocean. Her eyes filled with tears and she was shaken. Her anger, like a moistened bowstring, lost its edge...*
>
> *Give me permission to descend once more to earth, to tell them of your invitation and introduce to their dreams the better world where perfection flowers.*
>
> *Zeus replied: Let it be as you say... You, the goddess of patience, will have more honor even than we. Our power is limited and we will fall, victims of the coming storm. Your star, however, will shine ever more brightly in the darkness of the night.*

For Schubert the Goddess of the higher consciousness is tantalizing and alluring. But she is also quiet, gentle, and wise. She becomes incarnate in everyone, but uniquely and symbolically in the Virgin Mary. Schubert wrote exquisite works in her honor, including several "Salve Reginas" and the following.

> ***Das Marienbild***
> Aloys Wilhelm Schreiber D.623
> *Hail to you, Lady of Grace,*
> *Full of pure and radiant love,*
> *Without fault or guilt...*
> *Small birds sing their praise of your child from every branch.*
> *Angelic spirits ascend and descend the golden beams of sunlight.*

and:

> ***Marie***
> Novalis D.658
> *I see you in a thousand pictures, Mary, so lovely.*
> *Yet no picture can describe you as I see you in my heart.*
> *I only know that the worldly madness has vanished like a dream,*
> *While an unspeakably sweet heaven lives on in my heart.*

and:

> ***Ellens Dritter Gesang (The Ave Maria)***
> Walter Scott D.839
> *Ave Maria, undefiled!*
> *When we upon this rock lie down,*
> *Thy protection shelters us and hard stone seems soft;*
> *If you smile the scent of roses floats through life's murky cavern.*
> *Oh mother, hear a child's prayer!...*

Indicative of the heavenly status of this supreme symbolic incarnation of the Divine Sophia, the perfect image of God, are two works completed in September and October of 1816. In the following setting, created for no specific liturgical purpose, the sophianic Mary draws to herself and to us all divine love and the invitation to ascend to our rich destiny.

> ***Auguste iam coelestium*** in G Major D.488
> *May you, already received in heavenly majesty,*
> *Enter the loving hearts of those who honor you!*
> *Symbols of your glorious beauty are everywhere!*
> *Signs of divine love for you fill the earth!*

In a thrilling *Magnificat*, Mary, the incarnation of the higher consciousness, sings of her elevation out of earth's chaos, hatred, and greed to the transfigured state of heavenly perfection. Here she is both a single person and a symbol of the divine beauty of creation. She is its perfection, the complete image of God, the worthy recipient of his love. And importantly she is each of us in our higher consciousness which like her must receive a messianic awakening.

> ***Magnificat*** in C Major D486
> *My soul magnifies the Lord,*
> *And my spirit rejoices in God my savior.*
> *For he has regarded the lowliness of his handmaid,*
> *And behold, from this day forward, all shall call me blessed!*
>
> *He has put down the powerful from their thrones,*
> *And has exalted the humble, the powerless.*
> *He has fed the hungry with fine food,*
> *But the powerful he has sent away.*
> *Remembering his mercy he has helped Israel,*
> *As he promised to Abraham and his seed.*
>
> *Glory be to the Father, the Son, and the Holy Spirit,*
> *As it was in the beginning, is now,*
> *And ever shall be; world without end.*

The place of Mary in Roman Catholicism is analogous to the place of the Shekhinah.in Judaism. According to the Cabala, the Shekhinah will ascend to her queenship. Having completed her task of re-uniting the light fragments, after reconciling the contradictions that make of the Qelippah a kingdom of darkness and sorrow, she will ascend in glory to reign over her kingdom of love.

The goddess will be the Queen of the New Age. Inspired by a German translation of William Shakespeare Schubert sings the praises of this perfect and triumphant queen in whom transcendental life reigns:

Ständchen
William Shakespeare D.882 and the third movement of the Piano Sonata in A Major, D.959
Hark, hark the lark at heaven's gate sings!...
......
Winking Marybuds ope their golden eyes;
With everything that pretty is,
My lady sweet arise! Arise! Arise!

And:

An Sylvia
William Shakespeare D.891 and the Variations based upon a theme from Herold's "Marie" D.908
Then to Sylvia let us sing.
That Sylvia is excelling;
She excels each mortal thing
Upon the dull earth dwelling;
To her let us garlands bring.

In her radiant beauty shines the promise of a higher and better world, the new age.

Die Erscheinung
Ludwig Kosegarten D.229
Then from the woods, radiant in sunlight, a young girl appeared,
A white veil falling softly from her dark brown hair.
Her eyes sparkled like drops of dew;
Her lashes glistened with tears of sadness...
I tried to embrace her but she turned aside...

Farewell dear vision.
I understand the meaning of your apparition.
For a short time a mystical bond unites us.
But love's kingdom is not here;
But rather high above in a better world.

Union with her means a new and higher existence in the transcendental new age.

Memnon
Johann Mayrhofer D.541
How I long to be one with you, oh Goddess of the Morning,
Far removed from all this empty striving!
In a realm of noble freedom and pure love
I will peacefully shine, a golden star.

The beloved goddess is a distant star. Yet she seems to draw the wanderer mystically to herself. Finally, beyond death, they will be one with the goddess and through her one with the hidden God.. The wedding will take place in the new age, paradise.

Trost
Johann Mayrhofer D.671
......My beloved lies in her grave.
But when the horns sound in the forest night
I feel that she is here, drawing me to herself.
One day, radiantly she will shine before me!
What a joy that will be!
The grave holds no terror for me.

The higher consciousness has enriched the wanderer's life in the distant past. Now again she is to lead him to his true home, to the hidden God.

Iphigenia
Johann Mayrhofer D.573
Goddess, once you brought me to this land which is now a prison.
Help me once more! Let me re-unite with my own people!
Grant that I may re-enter the halls of the Great King!

Death is the pathway that leads to love's final triumph. The new age cannot be fully realized short of death. The goddess and we ourselves must pass through death to ascend to the new age. Like the Messiah the goddess must first die before being reborn in consummate union with the Other. The acceptance of death is part of the fidelity that the wanderer and the goddess owe to God. The faithful Sophia endures rejection and even persecution by worldly powers for her fidelity to a higher power, that of "the King".

Der Zwerg
Matthäus Kasimir von Collin D.771
...the queen sails with her dwarf. She gazes up at the vault of the heavens, woven of strands of light and the pale Milky Way. ...Soon I must go. Stars, you tell me so. In truth I die gladly...The dwarf speaks: "You yourself are to blame for you have forsaken me for the King. Now only your death can make me happy......Bemused by death the dwarf looks upon the queen and commits her to the waters.

The effect of this life-giving yet distant goddess upon the wanderer is the Eros-driven transfiguration of his life in the face of every sorrow. That effect is so overwhelming that the acceptance of his own death is possible.

Der Zürnenden Diana
Johann Mayrhofer D.707
Yes! Ply your mighty bow to send me death, heavenly Goddess!
The flush of wrath makes you yet lovelier.
I shall never regret that I saw you in the flowery meadows
Among the Nymphs whom you surpassed in beauty!
The rays of your loveliness spread all over the land!
Even in death the vision of that loveliness will strengthen me. …
The failing senses are atremble with your vision at this last, sweet hour!

In Schubert's mythology the wanderer, his imaginary hero, seeks to unite with Sophia, seeks to be illuminated with the higher consciousness. In the process he is at times naïve, muddling, vulnerable, sometimes a Christ figure, a Logos incarnate, a light-bringer, sometimes an incarnation of the Shekhinah, yearning for redemption, a divine spark in exile, always searching for the beloved "other". The wanderer's probing, diffident romance of the higher consciousness through the reconciliation of opposites is an ever-present backdrop for the art. The song cycles, *Die Schöne Müllerin* and *Die Winterreise*, and the operas, *Alfonso und Estrella* and *Fierabras,* celebrate this romance of the mystery. The romance is so frustrating and painful at times that it leads the wanderer to the brink of despair. The betrayals take place in the context of an overarching invitation that calls the wanderer to a transcendental triumph that begins on this side of the grave but leads inevitably and mysteriously through it.

WHO WAS SCHUBERT'S GODDESS?

Laura Am Klavier
Friedrich Schiller D.388
Laura, tell me the truth,
Do you not bring heaven itself to earth?
Do not conceal it! It is your playing
That is the language spoken in paradise!

The *mysterium magnum* implies a wedding of God and Goddess, of Messiah and Shekhinah, of the Lamb and the Bride. It implies a reconciliation of opposites in ever higher harmonies in the transfiguration of the human by the divine. This reconciliation must become incarnate. The symbol of the incarnation is a dream, not a reality. Its symbol id the dream maiden. For the wanderer she betrays the divine image even as she expresses it.The dream maiden in both song cycles awakens the wanderer to a better world but disappears. This incarnate spark of God, this elusive higher consciousness, is, paradoxically, the unattainable Other. Her symbol is a distant star.

Schubert's musical mythology tells the tale of a kaleidoscopic interplay between religious life, daily life, and nature in the romance of this dream maiden. The woman appears for a time, enchanting him and enriching his life. Then she disappears, forcing him to change his focus from the merely earthly to a mystical and mysterious transfiguration of the romance that beckons from afar. He has only memories of her sacred beauty and wispy premonitions of the transcendental reunion. And this feminine symbol was at times a real person in his life.

This sensual, sexual mysticism was a life-transfiguring force that inspired Schubert's works from the time he first fell in love with Theresa Grob. The attachment began when both were in their teens. She was one year younger than he and was the daughter of a widow who ran a small silk mill near the Leichtental church in Vienna.. Her father had been an immigrant from Switzerland. Schubert courted Theresa and apparently wanted marriage, only to lose her partly because of the Viennese marriage laws of the time which required a higher income than he was able to provide. According to Anslem Hüttenbrunner, Schubert reminisced later in his life:

> *"There was one girl I loved very much, and she loved me too. She was a little younger than I was and sang the soprano solo in my Mass very beautifully and with deep emotion. She was not really very pretty, and had a pockmarked y face...but she was an angel. For three years she hoped I would marry her, but I could not find a post that would support us both. So she married another man at the wish of parent(s)...and I was deeply hurt. I still love her. Since that time I have never met anyone who meant so much to me..." (Memoirs).*

Anton Holzapfel wrote that Schubert told him of his love for Theresa in a long, passionate letter. Holzapfel treated it as an inordinately powerful infatuation, saying that he knew little about the love other than that "Schubert's feelings were violent and kept locked within himself, and were certainly not without influence upon his first works!" (Memoirs). The implication here is that the prolific composer who astounds us even today with his amazing output in 1814, 1815, and 1816 was inspired through these years by this young woman. The poetry selected for his songs and instrumental works provides a window to his personal experience. Although it was written by others, it had to meet conditions set by that experience. In songs Schubert celebrated a Beloved sparkling with transcendental beauty. His wanderer, his alter-ego, sings:

> **Die Erste Liebe**
> *Johann Georg Fellinger D.182*
> *The first love fills the heart with yearning*
> *For an unknown land of the spirit...*
> *One sees the goddess in her radiance!*
> *In her are united all the glories of religion!*

He is bound to her with a sacred commitment:

> **An die Apfelbäume**
> *Ludwig Heinrich Christoph Hölty D.197*
> *My heart reaches out to you*
> *With a mystical kiss.*
> *I pledge to you here in this flower-decked woods*
> *My true, my eternal love!*

She leads him beyond this world to a better one:

Erinnerung
Ludwig Kosegarten D.229
From the woods, radiant in the sun,
A young girl appears, a white veil falling softly
Over her dark brown hair…
I understand the meaning of her appearance.
For a short time a mystical bond unites us.
But love's kingdom is not here,
But rather far beyond this world!

She is alive with divine life, and never more so than when she makes music:

Laura Am Klavier
Friedrich Schiller D.388
Laura, tell me the truth,
Do you not bring heaven itself to earth?
Do not conceal it! It is your playing
That is the language spoken in paradise!

For songwriters of the twentieth century such emotionally charged ideas were usually intended as sentimental flourishes. But sentimentality was not a characteristic of Schubert. His feelings were always proportioned to ideas. The ideas in the poems he selected had a profound meaning for him. Not only as a youth but throughout his life Theresa Grob made incarnate the divine invitation that inspired his art. She, perhaps more than anyone else, was his earthly dream maiden, the girl in whom divine beauty and the allure of the divine Sophia came into his world. She gave character to his vision of his transcendental goal. She gave shape to his romance with God. This is evident in Lieder settings such as that of Hölty's poem *Der Traum.* The girl who brings the Goddess to earth for the composer was both as sensuous as the dream maiden in Hölty's poem and as unattainable. The sensual and blatantly sexual power of Theresa, Schubert's goddess, over the composer erupts in a song and then, far more suggestively, in the fourth movement of the *Third Symphony D.200* based upon this poem:

Der Traum
Ludwig Heinrich Christoph Hölty D.213
In my dream I was a little bird!
I flew onto her lap,
And to stay busy I toyed with the bow of her blouse.
Then in joy I flew on to her white hand,
And from there to her blouse,
And pulled at the red ribbon tying it.

I flew over her blond head, singing with joy,
And when I got tired I nestled against her white breast.
No heavenly bed of roses could compare to that place of rest!
How wondrous my peace on that flowered throne!

The time that intervened between falling in love with Theresa Grob (probably 1814) and the decision to go their own separate ways (1816) was full of erotic musical celebrations. Some are expressed religiously; others are secular and sublimely human. But whether composed for the Catholic liturgy or for the drawing room it is Eros that takes flight and leads to the stars. *Gretchen am Spinnrade,* the Offertory hymn *Totus in corde langueo,* the Lied *Rastlöse Liebe,* two superb Masses, all are instances of the erotic spiritual ascent in which the composer's romance with a higher world and his love of a girl intermingle, one illuminating, enhancing, or threatening the other. In a hymn, **Totus in corde langueo,** written for the voice of Theresa, Schubert celebrated an experience of the *mysterium magnum* that was at once sublimely divine and intensely human:

Filling my heart is the burning fire of divine love.
Never has the sacred flame faltered,
But always has it lived in my heart.
Hellish terror has not swayed me,
Nor separated me from heaven,
Through the loving power of Christ.

The intermingling of sexuality and the spiritual ascent in the higher consciousness was no easy mix for the composer. There was a tension and sometimes a conflict between them. Thus their union could be difficult and costly.

Gretchen am Spinnrade
Johhann Wolfgang von Goethe D.118
My peace is gone! My heart is in agony!
Never, never will I find that peace again!

But the prize seemed to the young composer to be worth every bit of the agony. Schubert set the love song by Goethe in which Eros is decidedly earthy and no less sublime. It drives the wanderer into life and all the harrowing sorrow and thrilling joy that that entails.

Rastlose Liebe
Johann Wolfgang von Goethe D.138
Through blizzard and rain-storm,
Battling wind and hail...
Through the mist of mountain chasm,

Steaming in its depths…
Ever forward, ever forward,
With no rest! No peace!

It would be easier to live with pain
Than to suffer so much joy!
All this longing from heart to heart…
Ah! How much suffering it brings!
So what then? Should I escape?
Should I run to the forests?
That is useless!
Glorious crown of life!
Bliss without peace!
Love, oh love, this is you!

Cynics might see this union of religion and sexuality as a lack of seriousness. If so, the immaturity persisted until his death and played a central role in every masterwork. But perhaps the opposite is indicated. Perhaps it is the cynic who is guilty of myopia in his inability to comprehend the majestic beauty of this uneasy tension between opposites, a tension so pregnant with beauty and life, a tension more Islamic than Christian. Even as a teenager, heaven and earth were united in the uneasy tension that was the womb of his creativity.

The poetry inspiring Schubert's early instrumental music follows faithfully the events of his romance of Theresa. In late spring of 1816, before the separation from Theresa which occurred at the beginning of autumn, Schubert composed a *Piece for Violin and Strings, D.438*, that radiates the joy of love. The five inspiring poems by Ludwig Hölty, surely selected with Theresa in mind, were set as Lieder at the same time that he was composing the instrumental work. The love commitment seems sacred and sacramental. With respect to the dream maiden it was prophetic.

Widerhall
Friedrich von Matthisson D.428
I am forever yours..even when mountain and lake disappear…
Whether the breeze is gentle or the desert burns…
I am yours forever!

Three months later, shortly after the decision to separate, Schubert finished a second fantasy, an *Adagio and Rondo Concertante, D.487* inspired by poems by Johann Georg Jacobi This exciting work adds to a celebration of the heavenly beauty of love and marriage a note of profound sadness. The wanderer must look beyond this earth for a transcendental crowning of his love.

Orpheus
Johann Georg Jacobi D.473
Away from this earth of bright sun and silent moon,
Of be-dewed moss and singing meadows,
Away from man's earth and smiling skies
I am drawn by gentle ties of love.

There is also an insistence upon secrecy, obvious in the music as well as the poem, hiding the pain lest it create a burden for the beloved. Clearly Schubert seems to be protecting Theresa, with whom marriage was then impossible.

In der Mitternacht
Johann Georg Jacobi D464 and Adagio and Rondo Concertante D.487
I must not name my beloved;
Must not by tears betray her;
One day she will be laid to rest in a grave beside me.

In the years between the separation from Theresa in 1816 and her marriage to someone else there is not a note of bitterness, but rather stoic acceptance of a painful trial period that ends in a mysterious triumph only beyond this life. For example in 1818 in the *Grazer Fantasy,* we find the next chapter in this romance. Three sonnets by Petrarch, set as D.628, D.629, and D.630, are put together to form a dramatic whole just as were the Hölty and Jacobi poems in the earlier works just mentioned. They give fresh insight into the improbable Platonic romance that inspired Schubert's creativity for several years and, perhaps, until he died. Here the wanderer has only dreams and memories of the beloved, who now is gone. He is tortured and tantalized by thoughts in which she is a continuing mystical presence.

I lie awake, distraught by bittersweet thoughts of her…
My tormenting, intoxicating dream maiden!

But through all the pain there is the expectation of erotic future fulfillment.

Then to our astonished joy the beloved will appear,
Reclining in the meadow, shaded by her own upraised arms.

As always the poetry selected by the composer reveals an intimate bond between the art and his love for Theresa. Even later when the real life identity of the dream maiden seems to be shared by at least one other woman, Theresa should be considered a lingering presence. The singing of love songs to this unnamed absent beloved continued throughout his life. The wanderer myth gives no indication that the dream maiden or goddess of the later art differs at all from the dream maiden or goddess of 1816.

Lied der Annie Lyle

The original, given below, is by Andrew MacDonald and was included in Walter Scott's novel *A Legend of Montrose*. Deutsch says the German translation used by Schubert was by Sophie May, but this translation is not traceable. The poem was used as the text of D.830 in early 1825 and may have inspired the second movement of the Piano Sonata in C major, D.840

Wert thou, like me, in life's low vale,
With thee how blest, that lot I'd share;
With thee I'd fly wherever gale
Could waft, or bounding galley bear.
But parted by severe decree,
Far different must our fortunes prove;
May thine be joy - enough for me
To weep and pray for him I love.
The pangs this foolish heart must feel,
When hope shall be forever flown,
No sullen murmur shall reveal,
No selfish murmurs ever own.
Nor will I through life's weary years,
Like a pale drooping mourner move,
While I can think my secret tears
May wound the heart of him I love.

or:

Fülle der Liebe

Friedrich Schlegel D.854 August 1825 (inspiring the First and Second Movements of the Piano Sonata in D Major, D.850)

At our separation my heart was crushed by pain.
But your image dwells in the depths of my soul...

......A star appears in the heavens where surely we will be together.
...
The magic of the vision overcomes me, ordering all in my life,
Uniting soul to soul in the mystical power of the spirit.

or in 1826:

Im Frühling

Ernst Schulze, D.882 (inspiring the second movement of the Piano Trio in B Flat D.898 and the fourth movement of the Piano Sonata in A Major D.959 in 1828)

A gentle breeze plays in the green valley where once I was so happy.
I walked by her side, so close, so much in love!

...
But will and desire change,
Happiness gives way to conflict,
Now love's bliss is gone,
And only the love remains,
The love and alas the pain!

Or (contemplating a world where the wanderer's love for his Beloved is not compromised by her marriage to someone else):

Lied der Mignon
Johann Wolfgang von Goethe D.877 1826 inspiring the first movement of the *Piano Sonata in B Flat* D.960 1828
......Then a new world will appear......
The spirits of the heavenly world do not limit love to man and wife.

or (in avid anticipation of reunion beyond the grave):

Auf der Bruck
Ernst Schulze, D.853 1825 inspiring the fourth movement of the posthumous *Piano Sonata in B Flat* D.960, 1828
All over the land birds seek a warmer home;
Is it possible that true love not do the same?
And though the way is dark and mysterious,,
My longing is awake and watchful,
And I race ahead in sweet anticipation!

We get hints of Schubert's passionate but hidden love life, a life lived mostly inwardly, through the poems of his wanderer as Lieder, part songs, and instrumental works. The poems describe a mysterious romance with a semi-divine figure that for several years at least and perhaps throughout his life was Theresa Grob. The girl is idealized. There is something inescapably sacred about the romance. She raises the wanderer to a better world. Real experiences of agonies and ecstasies seem to account for the authenticity and the sublimity of the music. Can we legitimately surmise anything about the composer's life from the drama depicted in the art? With some hesitancy the answer is yes. The poems set in the years immediately following the separation in 1816 are not bitter. They suggest that Theresa was still the beloved and a willing partner in a continuing but Platonic love.

For example:

Abschied
Franz Schubert D.578 (inspiring the second movement of the Piano Sonata in B Flat Major D.575) and dedicated to Franz Schober, but perhaps with Theresa in mind.

Farewell, my dear friend, you go to a distant land.
Take with you my love.
Hold it in hands that are faithful. Farewell!
As you remember this song my spirit will be close to you,
Like a breeze passing over the strings of your heart!

Was Schubert's surrender of Theresa affected by outside influences, ones promoting the art of the composer? In October of 1816 Schubert set a poem by Johann Mayrhofer that provokes that suspicion. For Goethe the "Tower" was a Masonic group that guided affairs from behind the scenes and sought the betterment of society through their secret control. Schubert was a member of a similar group. Could the separation from Theresa have been a kind of trial in preparation for his life's work, a trial influenced by a secret society?

Der Hirt
Johann Baptist Mayrhofer D.490
Tower, you reach to the heavens;
To my sorrow you heartlessly show me what I have lost!
In her lovely eyes there was nothing but fidelity.
I saw nothing but heavenly love!
They were mirrors of her soul!
Now, wherever I turn
I see that tower.
It is that tower, not old age, that is destroying me!

Whatever was its cause, the separation from Theresa was to prove a crushing burden for the composer, one against which he rebelled again and again. In November of 1817 he set the following poem as a Lied giving voice to these feelings:

Der Kampf
Friedrich Schiller D.594
No, I cannot fight anymore
This battle of commitment!
Virtue, if you will not cool the fire in my heart,
Do not demand this sacrifice!

I have committed myself
To deny my own satisfaction.
Virtue, I return your crown!
Take it back. Let me betray my vow!

Virtue, let us destroy our agreement!
She loves me…and your crown I renounce!

He is blessed who is so intoxicated by love's joy
That he can forget how far he has fallen.

The girl watches the worm destroying my youth,
Sees the springtime of my life disappear.
She marvels at my heroic fidelity
And with full heart offers her reward.

But beware, o noble soul, of this good angel!
Her pity will turn me into a traitor.
In all of the wondrous panoply of life
Is there a higher reward than one's own virtue?

It is indeed more noble than the betrayal
Which I have so long battled.
Oh tyrannical fate!
The only reward I can realize for my virtue
Is contained in that last eternal moment!

If the suspicion is correct that Schubert and Theresa made a joint commitment to "Platonize" their love in a kind of Tamino-Pamina moral trial and Theresa "betrayed" the relationship in 1820 to marry, it would at least make understandable the strong feelings that the wanderer expresses in works following the marriage. In 1823 the wanderer in *Die Schöne Müllerin* is betrayed by a fickle girl. And in 1822 Schubert had lamented in several songs the shocking truth that the wanderer is not loved.

Die Liebe hat gelogen
August von Platen-Hallermünde D.751......
Hot tears run down my cheeks,
Heart, if you could but stop beating!

Love has lied. My burden is heavy.
Deception! Ah, all in my life is deception!

How do we evaluate Schubert's decision, if that indeed is what it was, to forego marriage presumably for the sake of a commitment to art? Was it fair to Theresa to expect her partnership in the commitment? Evidently she thought not because in 1820 she married someone else. Did it help his art? He surrendered the physical possession of his love at least for a time in exchange for the freedom to compose. And the result is some of the world's most sublime art. But he lost his love completely, something he had not intended nor wanted, and his art was not understood by the society he wanted to enrich. Ultimately the exchange cost him his life at the age of thirty-one. There are indications that Schubert wrestled until the end of his life with the wisdom of what he had done and was continuing to do. For example:

> ***Der Atlas***
> Heinrich Heine, D.957 Schwanengesang No. 8 (1828) inspiring the first movement of the Piano Sonata in C Minor, D.958
> *I am Atlas doomed, carrying the world upon my shoulders!*
> *I stagger under what I cannot bear, my heart strained to breaking!*
> *Proud heart, you did this!*
> *You gambled for heavenly joy against the agony of the damned,*
> *......And now you have lost!*

Yet despite frustration and afterthoughts the composer never surrendered his artistic goal. And most telling of all, his wanderer, in spite of the bitter resentment at what he perhaps thought was love's betrayal (Theresa's marriage), never faltered in his commitment to the beloved. That Platonic romance was the thematic core of his art until his death. The separation from Theresa was the price he paid for his ascent to the higher consciousness. The exchange cost him his life and much pain. It also enabled him to create the definitive liturgy for a new age that is yet to dawn.

Despite the close link between the painful separation from Theresa and his wanderer myth, there is a limit to our ability to see the facts of Schubert's life in that myth. Romance for this nineteenth century troubadour was what it had been for Petrarch and Dante. It was love for a goddess that was made possible by love for a real woman who was not to be his. His love of that real woman was powerful. He chanced a Platonic relationship with the woman whose presence in his art seems luminous with divinity...and he lost. She did not wait. She would not be celibate with him for the sake of his art. His adjustment following her marriage gives a fuller understanding of the sublime and thrilling beauty of the compositions of the last several years of hius life.

Two years after the breakup with Theresa, Schubert went to Zseliz in Hungary as a music instructor for the two daughters of Count Johann Esterhazy. Here again we find the contradiction between the physical and the metaphysical worlds resolved in a romance of his dream maiden. "I live and compose like a god." "I am alone with my beloved, and have to hide her in my room, in my piano, and in my heart...Although this often makes me sad, it also helps inspire me the more." At the same time he speaks of a "very pretty housemaid" who was "often his companion." Alfred Einstein speculated that it was from her that he contracted venereal disease. The separation from Theresa had opened the door to the sublimation of his Sophia and to other things besides.

Theresa married someone else in 1820. Four years later in 1824 Schubert returned to Zseliz. One of the countesses was Karoline Esterhazy, then eighteen years old and an accomplished musician. Schubert fell in love with her. He wrote of "a certain attractive star" in the castle. Karl Freiherr von Schonstein expands upon this "star" and her meaning to Schubert.

A love affair with a maid servant which Schubert started soon after he entered the house subsequently gave way to a more poetic flame which sprang up in his heart for the younger daughter of the house, Countess Karoline. The flame continued to burn until his death. Karoline had the greatest regard for him and for his talent but she did not return his love. Perhaps she had no idea of the degree to which it existed. I say the degree, for that he loved her must surely have been clear to her from a remark of Schubert's—his only declaration in words. Once when she reproached Schubert in fun for having dedicated no composition to her, he replied, "What is the point? Everything is dedicated to you anyway." (Memoirs).

The intensity of Schubert's feelings for Karoline is confirmed by others. Leopold von Sonnleithner wrote that Schubert "languished greatly for a lady of superior social position." Eduard von Bauernfeld wrote insightfully about the meaning of Schubert's love for Karoline to his art.

(Schubert) was head over ears in love with one of his pupils, a young Countess Esterhazy, to whom he also dedicated one of his most beautiful piano pieces, the Fantasy in F Minor for pianoforte duet. In addition to his piano lessons there he also visited the Count's home from time to time...On such occasions Schubert was quite content to take a back seat, to remain quietly by the side of his adored pupil, and to thrust love's arrow ever deeper into his heart. For the lyric poet as well as for the composer an unhappy love affair may have its advantages, provided it is not altogether too unhappy, as it enhances his subjective feelings and stamps the poems and songs which spring from it with the color and tone of purest reality. Works like the two "Suleika" songs, "Die Zürnende Diana," much of the "Müllerleider" and the "Winterreise," all of them musical self confessions, bathed in the fire of a true and deep passion, emerged purified and refined, as genuine works of art, from the tender heart of the lover (Memoirs, 233).

Bauernfeld goes on:

In Schubert there slumbered a dual nature. The Austrian element, uncouth and sensual, revealed itself both in his life and in his art. New and original melodies as well as harmonies, welled forth abundantly from the bosom of a richly gifted nature and not infrequently their features displayed the character of the soil, rich in song from time immemorial, from which their creator sprang...If there were times both in his social relationships and in art, when the Austrian character appeared all too violently in the vigorous and pleasure loving Schubert, there were also times when a black-winged demon of sorrow and melancholy forced its way into his vicinity-not altogether an evil spirit, it is true, since in the dark, consecrated hours, it often brought out songs of the most agonizing beauty. But the conflict between unrestrained enjoyment of living and the restless activity of spiritual

> *creation is always exhausting if no balance exists in the soul. Fortunately in our friend's case an idealized love was at work, mediating, reconciling, compensating, and Countess Karoline may be looked upon as his visible, beneficent Muse, as the Lenore of this musical Tasso (Memoirs, 234).*

This memoir indicates that from at least 1824 until his death in 1828 Karoline was a "star" and perhaps *the* star in Schubert's life. Through her the divine world became incarnate. She personified for him the Divine Sophia. She awakened anew his higher consciousness. His platonic love for her was the contradiction-reconciling inspiration for the masterworks of the last few years. She (and/or Theresa) was the real life incarnation of his dream maiden, the transcendentally inviting star in his dramatic abstraction of life. There was never the prospect of marriage with Karoline. She was an aristocrat and he was not. Still according to Bauernfeld she played an essential and irreplaceable role in his most important and creative years, a role analogous to that played earlier by Theresa Grob. With Karoline the love was more Platonic, more sublimated. Based upon the poetry inspiring the late masterworks we can surmise that one or both of these women were part of the inspiration. Schubert dedicated the *Fantasy for Piano D.940* to Karoline. The late Franciscan, Reinhard van Hoorickx, a well-respected Schubert scholar, suggested that the fantasy was inspired by the poem *Sie in Jedem Liede (D896)*, set in the autumn of 1827 as a Lied. In the poem as in the music we sense both the beauty and the tragedy of an impoverished music teacher making music with a beautiful but unattainable woman. She transfigured his life experience, inspiring a highly idealized romance of an untouchable goddess who was both a real person and a symbol of divine invitation. She made incarnate for him the *mysterium magnum*.

> ***Fröhliches Scheiden***
> Karl Gottfried von Leitner D.896
> *I take up my harp…*
> *And following the deepest longing…*
> *I dream of you.*
> *Beloved, you must know it…*
> *Without these songs*
> *I would be indeed lost!*
>
> *As I sing*
> *I think of hermit's cells,*
> *Of castles and tournaments…*
> *And there among the great ladies,*
>
> *With their hats and furs,*
> *High upon the balcony I see you!*

As I sing of the high mountains and the winds
Playing far above the town's tumult,
It is you who fill the mountains with your singing,
And the small wooden hut with your laugh!

If I sing of the beautiful water maidens
Playing alone in the moonlight,
Swimming in the sea,
You are there among them,

Gliding through the blue waters,
Stretching your snow white arms out to me!

How close you are to me, my beloved,
In the rose-tinted land of dreams and poetry!
But, ah, in life, so bitter, so tragic,
We are separated by the cruel hand o f savage fate!

Schubert's higher consciousness of the sacred mystery was certainly inspired by his yearning for both Karoline and Theresa. Each masterwork gives us fresh insight into the life-transfiguring power that came to the composer through these women. The poetry reveals the interplay between his life and his art. In March of 1826 Schubert set as a Lied the poem *Richard the Lionheart's Song* by Sir Walter Scott, D.907. This setting occurs within the time frame indicated by Bauernfeld when he says that Schubert's works were inspired by the unattainable Karoline. The *Rondo for Piano and Violin D.895* is clearly an alternative and far more personal and revealing setting of Scott's poem. Perhaps it was intended to be presented coupled with a dramatic reading of the poem. In the poem the wanderer is a heroic knight returning to his lady-love from his crusade. His beloved has inspired him to feats of might. She it is to whom the wanderer brings his trophies. She has the power to reward him. She is the beginning and end of his life's adventure.

Romanze des Richard Löwenherz,
Karl Ludwig Müller after Walter Scott, D.907
High deeds achieved of knightly fame.
From Palestine the champion came;
The cross upon his shoulders borne,
Battle and blast had dimm'd and torn.
Each dint upon his batter'd shield
Was token of a foughten field;
And thus, beneath his lady's bower,
He sang, as fell the twilight-hour:

Joy to the fair!-thy knight behold,
Return'd from yonder land of gold:
No wealth he brings, nor wealth can need,
Save his good arms and battle-steed;
His spurs, to dash against a foe,
His lance and sword to lay him low;
Such all the trophies of his toil,
Such-and the hope of Tekla's smile!

Joy to the fair! Whose constant knight
Her favour fired to feats of might;
Unnoted shall she not remain,
Where meet the bright and noble train,
Minstrel shall sing and herald tell-
Mark yonder maid of beauty well,
'Tis she for whose bright eyes was won
The listed field of Askalon!

Note well her smile!-it edged the blade
Which fifty wives to widows made,
When, vain his strength and Mahound's spell,
Iconium's turban'd Soldan fell.
Seest thou her locks, whose sunny glow
Half shows, half shades, her neck of snow?
Twines not of them one golden thread,
But for its sake a Paynim bled.

Joy to the fair!-my name unknown.
Each deed and all its praise thine own;
Then, oh unbar this churlish gate,
The night dew falls, the hour is late.
Inured to Syria's glowing breath,
I feel the north breeze chill as death;
Let grateful love quell maiden shame,
And grant him bliss who brings thee fame.

The Wanderer and the Mystery

Oh precious art! How often in times of distress …
Did you warm my heart with love
And lead me into a better world!
Franz Schober **An die Musik D.547**

From time to time Schubert selected a poem for a musical setting that seems especially revealing of his understanding of his unique realization of a romance with the *mysterium magnum*. In this awareness he seems a kind of neo-Renaissance, messianic magician. For example the very first song of which we have any record is an incomplete sketch of the poem *Lebenstraum* by Gabriele von Baumberg. John Reed recognized the importance of this poem for the very young composer. As an extended allegory the poem presents a wisdom perspective on life and paints a fairly accurate picture of the dramatic unfolding of both the inner and outer life of the composer. The poem is quite long and Schubert's settings of it, D.2 and D. 39, are unfinished. In it the wanderer is called out of a lower into a higher world by a messianic figure, an awakener. This wanderer is a woman, a singer of songs, who experiences a divine call to compose. Her life is transfigured by a divine infusion of light. Her illumination makes her messianic. She becomes an awakener for others through her musical creations. In true Gnostic fashion her songs lament the sadness of life on earth and yearn for a higher life, a better world, a new age. Her compositions reveal a romance between heaven and earth. Finally she is allowed to leave the lower world of the spiritually blind which is perceived as a place of exile, and come to her true home, the transfigured world of love.

This poem is archetypal in its expression of Schubert's understanding of life's drama. It is strangely prophetic with respect to Schubert's own life. Before he was fifteen years old he was obviously immersed in the wisdom tradition with its romance of the mystery and drawn to the poem as a kind of ideal self portrait. There is a parallel between the poetess and the young composer in their spiritual awakenings, their artistic commitments, their creative lives, and their anticipation of an ascent to a higher world. Both wanted to share their higher life with others, yet despite honest intentions their art alienated them. In the end they both are ready and even anxious to move definitively from this world where they are strangers to a better one that is their true home. Obviously both composer and poetess share a living but decidedly esoteric tradition. Because the parallels between poet and composer are so striking and the allegory so illuminating concerning Schubert's understanding of himself and his art I present the complete poem which twice he started to set, though never completing either setting:

Lebenstraum
Gabriele von Baumberg, D. 39
I sat before the temple courtyard in a sacred grove.
A waterfall splashed beside me in the soft twilight.
No breeze stirred.
The setting sun glazed the weeping willow in its mellow gold.
Quiet and bemused I sat there a long while, head in hand,
Thinking of things past and yet to be.
I saw on the mountain, high, near the god's own dwelling,
A divine singer whose songs of times past and future enraptured unnumbered generations.
Ancient idols of forgotten gods lay in the deep recesses of the valley,
Shades of days long gone.
Slowly, out of the dank hero's grave in the valley,
A shadowy figure emerged, a vision of death and decay…
And from the very waters of Lethe it offered me a flowered chalice,
A magic potion which promised…oblivion!
Shocked, I wanted to ask the apparition what the drink would do to me.
But it had already vanished…and I looked about impatiently.
But my infatuation with the drink I could not suppress.
Suddenly a godly youth appeared with lightly dancing step.
He winked and called, Come along!
Leave behind the fearsome shadows! They hide the truth of the sunlight!
Come with me. I will lead you to a grove of laurel,
Into which only consecrated souls can enter!
A poet's wreathe awaits you. Its freshness is spring-like,
Crowned with myrtle."
He spoke and quickly led the way.
I followed, full of trust in the handsome boy,
Entranced by the sweet illusion.
A sacred stillness reigned over the grove.
The object of my life's desire I saw glistening
Amid the shading leaves of the distant hill.

I stood there, lost in my rapture.
Again the youth spoke:
It is Apollo's will that you take with you this golden lyre
In the worst of times it has the power
To transcend time and space with its haunting melodies,
And through its music to heal your wounds, transfigure your life!
Be proud of the music you make with it.
Of all godly gifts this is the most sublime.
You will use it worthily.

Now I breathed a higher freedom.
The golden lyre, Apollo's gift was by me night and day.
At first I was unmindful of its true power and sang only short songs.
They echoed joyfully in young hearts,
Which recognized in them their deepest dreams.
But my songs displeased my friends.
Silence, they thought, was their duty,
And shyly they retreated behind their veils.
Perhaps, just perhaps, they felt guilty
Because they misinterpreted the true meaning of the music.
Foolishly they thought themselves betrayed,
Their youthful flirtations mocked by their own sister.
But I was innocent of their suspicions.
Their concern had no ground at all.
My only thought, my driving desire, my supreme life value
Became clear in those sacred hours.
In my innocent sincerity I realized it was my yearning for a better world!
A world where the human spirit is pure and free, full known and knowing.
This sublime rapture, which no fate could destroy,
After which every noble soul strives,
Divides man from beast,
And raises him to life everlasting!
This most noble, this purest of human experiences
Is one of guiltless and true love.

By this time, feeling comfortable with heavenly beings,
I decided that love was the only subject worthy of my music.
I lamented the sad lot of women, a lot of suffering,
Due so often to men's cruelty.
Gradually I found it necessary to withdraw from my happy friends,
Keeping more to myself.
My solitude gave me a quiet joy and a fuller vision of life.
So I sang my songs with an open spirit, sometimes in joy, sometimes in sorrow,
Singing away the springtime of my life!

Often I planted roses around the weeping willows,
I planted forget-me-nots and evergreens.
In that dry grove I created a little heaven on earth.
In life's ebb and flow I was safe in my peaceful retreat.
The world's rush could be easily forgotten.
My small boat, gently rocking, was safe from life's storms;
My bemused heart cried out: if this joy is but a dream, may I never awaken!

But alas, my peace was suddenly cut short.
The experience of life's inner conflicts,
Like a storm, rocked my ship,
And the magic of the lyre seem exhausted.
All around me the waves threatened, the thunder rolled, the lightning blazed,
Menacing through the clouds of the dark night!
Beware little flowers! You have so enriched my life.
I have tended you so carefully, so lovingly............!
And suddenly, in this chaotic rebellion of nature's forces,
A new day dawned!
The menacing storm, the agitated waves,
Instead of splintering my boat on the rocky cliffs,
Raised it up ever higher to the very starry pathway celebrated in my songs.
How quickly the dark storm clouds disappeared!
A lovely rainbow breathed its friendly greeting from the newly-bright heaven!
Two flowers, spared the terrible wrath of the storm,
Raised their moistened heads, joy-filled in the dew.
In trusting friendship they glistened softly, radiant in color.
They seemed to say: Now again the gods make peace with us.
Tiny forget-me-nots appeared, symbols of friendship and love,
Modestly hiding themselves in the dark and cool moss.
The many-petaled rose, surrounded by its protecting thorns,
Reminded of love's sweet caress.
Charmed by the westwind it bloomed in the quiet security,
So trusting, so childlike and, amid all the flowers,
So naive, so unmindfull of its destiny,
Hardly noticed in the bosom of nature.
And it grew to maturity, that growth being a reward for virtue,
A recompense for fidelity and integrity,
A symbolic triumph, to grace the victor's crown,
Bestowed upon only the most worthy of mortals.

Through the oppressive heat of the summer days I raised my cry.
Apollo! I am here in your temple! Take back your gift!
I thank you for the joy it has given.

How often it has taught me patience!
How often courage in trial! How often strength in adversity!
How often it has charged my tired spirit with fresh power!
How often it has awakened my tired heart to new youth and vigor!
This beautiful world avenges itself upon me by calling my songs illusory.
It calls my consecration to you a fantasy…an unpardonable crime!
Yet I ignored the criticism.
I permitted only my heart to lead.
My rule was ever to follow my youthful guide.
And I discovered freedom, inner peace.
Never was I in need. Never did I have an excess.
Only to your voice did I listen, Oh Apollo!
I was true only to truth and to you!
I have dedicated my life, my every joy to you, and you alone,
Oh regal god of the sun!
Now, in return, give me everlasting life.
With a kindly smile Apollo listened to my request.
Then he told me that, although my request was rash,
He would grant it!
"I caution you,
Swear to face wisely every danger as you finish your course."
Next to me the poet's winged steed pranced impatiently,
Proud in his mighty pinions
When he heard Apollo's pronouncement, so totally unexpected,
He was stunned by the demand that he obey me, a woman.
He could scarcely accept that he, who served men with such joy,
Must now obey the guiding hand of a woman!
He found it repulsive to fly from one sacred spot to another under my control.
Yet I sprang to the saddle to encounter my destiny……
Sometimes in fear, sometimes in joy.
Swiftly, with reins firmly in hand, I flew over valleys and hills.
Through this time of testing I encountered thousands of illusionary dancing shapes.
All along my daunting course were sirens,
Pretending friendship, but glancing aside in envy, filled with hate.
Jealousy whispered and spit amongst them.
Out of the swamp a specter emerged to lead me astray!
But never did I leave my guiding youth.
For this strength I thank Apollo with heartfelt gratitude.
In the face of the fearsome trials
He led me directly, unerringly, towards my goal.
Through a thousand impenetrable and thorn-filled obstacles
He brought me at last to that most final of all bridges
Under which the centuries disappear!

A muffled noise brought me to consciousness
Awakening me from my long dream.

Schubert's poet tells the tale of the spiritual awakening of a wanderer to the dramatic journey of life. This awakening is to an interplay between higher and lower worlds. Heaven can touch and transfigure the earth and does so through the wanderer. The drama is that of a journey in the inner life that affects the outer world. First a messianic figure leads the wanderer out of darkness and into the light. Then the wanderer herself becomes a messiah who gives illumination to the world. In this messianic-sophianic romance between higher and lower worlds there are sacraments, music being one, that can enhance this world through contact with a higher one. Fidelity to the romance will mean a separation, an alienation from friends who cannot understand it. Yet the recipient of the gift accepts the responsibility and sacrifices that go with it. So the dreamer withdraws even from friends and alone creates a sublime art (flowers) that celebrates the better world and the higher wisdom. Demonic dangers from enemies of the awakening and its wisdom threaten. But then comes an elevation to sublime peace. The heavenly art is spared, and new art, even more beautiful, more revealing of the higher world, is produced. After repeated attacks by the lower world upon the higher one the wanderer calls out to Apollo: "Bring me home to where love is triumphant!" In fidelity to her guide the dreamer arrives finally at the bridge that leads to transcendence, to eternal life.

The heroine of the poem is an alter-ego for the poetess. The self-portrait coincided closely with the very young Schubert's understanding of his own life. It prefigures not simply his mystical illuminations and their artistic expressions but even his illness and early death. The drama of the poem was in fact the drama of Schubert's wanderer, the omni-present hero of his art.

At the very end of Schubert's life he expressed his understanding of what was happening in his art.His wanderer is at the doorway to final transcendence. In the magnificent *Shepherd on the Rock* Lied the inspiration comes from three distinct poems that say exactly what Schubert wanted to say. They express anticipation of death. The wanderer greets death with a song. The divine, messianic creation goes forth as music that penetrates to the very depths of earth's darkness, reflecting back as light and life. The more "materialized" the song becomes the clearer is its echo out of the depths. So the Shekhinah voices her plaintive cry of loneliness and yearning for her lover "over there, on the other side" and is answered with hope. Finally there is the anticipation of the divine wedding. Death faces the wanderer yet in its darkness he finds life.

Der Hirt Auf Dem Felsen

A composite text: the first four stanzas are by Wilhelm Müller, the next two by Wilhelmina Christiane von Chézy, née Klencke, and the last from another work by Wilhelm Müller. D.965

When I stand upon the mountain peak
I look out over the valley so deep, so dark...
And I sing!

Up from the distant blackness
The echo rises...
From out of the depth of the earth.

The further my cry reaches
The clearer is the echo from the depths.

My beloved is so distant, so far away,
And I so yearn for Her...
Over there...on the other side!

In deep grief am I torn.
I have no more joy in life...
No hope left upon earth.
I am so alone here.

So plaintive is the cry in the woods,
So tortured is the voice in the night,
That the heart speeds the prayer to heaven...
With divine power.

Spring is coming! Spring, my joy!
Even now do I make myself ready...
Ready to wander away!

Here clearly is a triumph of the sublime disposition in the face of death. Schubert's work is inspired by a collage of poems by different poets, selected by the composer to sing a swansong and to celebrate the higher consciousness in dying. Verses one through four and verse seven are written by Wilhelm Müller (two poems). Verses five and six were written by someone else, perhaps by Schubert himself. He obviously arranged this poetry to say exactly what he wanted to say at this climactic time of his life, continuing and deepening the themes that we saw in *Lebenstraum*. This wanderer now stands at a point of ascent from one world to another. He has completed his course, has been obedient to his Muse, and looks forward to going to his true homeland and to final union with his absent beloved. Below him the valley is lost in darkness. His song is a symbol of creative power penetrating the darkness ever deeper and reflecting back ever clearer. The great romance of the *mysterium magnum* in which opposites are united in a divine harmony is coming to its triumphant conclusion. The wanderer, separated from his beloved, cries out to heaven for mercy. He pleads to be released from his exile...and his prayer is heard. Spring, eternal May, the triumph of love is coming and he must make himself ready to rejoin his beloved. Sorrow has been transfigured into joy.

Schubert used this prophetic poetry as the inspiration for a series of swan songs: his last symphony, the unfinished *Symphony in D Major D.936* in its entirety, the third movement of the *String Quintet,* as well as the Lied *The Shepherd on the Rock.* In each case the composer was expressing his personal premonitions concerning the death-transfiguration passage. And not only an inner transfiguration is in question. The adventure takes place in the inner life, yes. But for both poets and composer it embraces also the mysterious and frightening reality of death and transfiguration.

This reflection of his actual life experience in the songs of his wanderer can be seen in the first movement of the *String Quintet in C Major,* inspired by the poem *Hymn to the Holy Spirit* by A. Schmidl, D.948. The wanderer sings his acceptance of the divine invitation that leads him beyond this life.

Oh Lord, my God, hear my prayer
Which longingly reaches up to you in your goodness.
Gaze down upon me, oh Comforter,
And give your heavenly peace to my heart.

By 1825 when he was twenty-eight Schubert's compositions were consistently intense self revelations of his personal awakening to the dramatic journey that centers the rose cross mystery. By 1827 the mystical sublimity of the art astounds us. In the *Fantasy for Piano and Violin, D.934* the wanderer describes the ascent tó the better world of his Beloved who is obviously a mythical Sophia and just as obviously a concrete person in his life. A poem by Franz Bruchmann, *Schwestergrüss, D.762*, is paired with other poems including a poem by Friedrich Ruckert, *Sei mir gegrüsst D.741* to inspire an instrumental work. *Schwestergrüss* focuses upon the triumphant ascent of the Beloved to her transcendental coronation and wedding. *Sei mir gegrüsst* focuses upon the tragic dimension of this incarnation, the earthly imprisonment. But the triumphant conclusion of the journey is evident in the settings of *Gott in der Natur* by Kleist D.757 and *Des Tages Weihe* Anon D.763. The composer is acting as a mystic, using poems and music, myth, and memory to illuminate the great drama of life, so rich in paradox, so multi-layered, so tragic and so sublime. A brief taste of one of the poems gives an indication of this. The complete poetry can be found in the last section of this book.

Schwestergrüss
Franz Bruchmann D.762
I am wafted now in pure light.
I see the sun and moon at my feet...
As pure flame she rises
Without pain or sorrow to the angelic choir.

Sei mir gegrüsst
Friedrich Ruckert D.741

You are now torn from me, from my kisses!
But accept my love! Accept my kiss!

Schober and the Mystery

Man's spirit, free of daily concerns,
Is enveloped in a cloud of sweet yearning.
In peaceful joy it drinks in
The sacred life of the higher world.
Franz Schober, Mondenschein *D.875*

The rose cross mystery, the *mysterium magnum*, demands an embrace of opposites. The incarnation of the rose cross mystery was the intensification and wedding of opposites. This paradoxical development in different directions found expression in attempts to reconcile religious and social life. In the early years of the nineteenth century. Vienna was host for dynamic youth movements that focused upon an integration of citizenship and mysticism. According to both Josef Kenner and his son Friedrich there was a circle of young men at Vienna University who between 1811 and 1816 made organized efforts to promote humanitarian activities and a noble development of mind and heart. Josef Kenner wrote a book on the moral development of youth. A multi-faceted *Bildung (*development of personality) was envisioned. Schubert grew up in this pietistic atmosphere and was a central part of it. His friends from this formative period numbered Josef Spaun and Anton Ottenwalt, both well-respected and decent. Along with them the young composer intended his art as a celebration of all that is best in a citizen of the new age.

Josef Kenner a childhood acquaintance of the composer, claimed in his Memoirs that Schubert was harmfully dominated in his life by Schober. Kenner suggested strongly that Schober led Schubert to a spiritual collapse from which he later recovered. Kenner wrote:

Schubert's genius subsequently attracted, among other friends, the heart of a seductive, amiable and brilliant young man, endowed with the noblest talents, whose extraordinary gifts were so sorely in need of a moral foundation and would have richly repaid a stricter schooling than the one he unfortunately had. But shunning so much effort as unworthy of genius and summarily rejecting such fetters as a form of prejudice and restriction, while at the same time arguing with brilliant and ingratiatingly persuasive power, the scintillating individuality, as I was told later, won a lasting and pernicious influence over Schubert's honest susceptibility. If this was not apparent in his work it was all the more so in his life. Anyone who knew Schubert knows he was made of two natures, foreign to each other... how powerfully the craving for pleasure dragged his soul down to the slough of moral degradation, and how highly he valued the utterances of his friends he respected... and so will find his surrender to the false prophet, who embellished sensuality in such a flattering manner, all the more understandable. But more hardened characters than he by the devilish attraction of association with the apparently warm but inwardly merely vain being were seduced into worshiping him as an idol. This intimation seemed to me indispensable for the biographer's grasp of the subject, for it concerns an episode in Schubert's life which only too probably caused his premature death and certainly hastened it.

Memoirs, 85-86

Kenner believed that Schober himself:

devised a philosophical system for his own reassurance and to justify himself in the eyes of the world as well as to provide a basis for his aesthetic oracle, about which he was probably as hazy as any of his disciples; nevertheless he found the mysticism of sensuality sufficiently elastic for his own freedom of movement; and so did his pupils. The need for love and friendship emerged with such egotism and jealousy that to these adherents he alone was all, not only a prophet, but God himself and apart from his oracles he was willing to tolerate no other religion, no morals, no restraint. Anyone who did not worship him exclusively, follow him blindly, was unfit for elevation to his intellectual heights; and anyone who eventually turned away from him dissatisfied, could no longer be held by his phrases and tears, such a one, he persuaded himself, he had allowed to fall away as unworthy. He had no respect for marriage, no respect for property. For Schober there were two kinds of women, worthy ones who accepted him, and unworthy ones who did not!

Memoirs, 87

In the quotation Kenner suggests that Schubert was a weak victim of Schober, led helpless as a lamb into an acceptance of what Kenner calls a hedonistic philosophy that glorified sensuality. And while Kenner never tells us much about that philosophy, he leaves no doubt as to what he thought of it. Was Kenner right, or was he a voice of a simplistic fundamentalism, unwilling to recognize the need for an integration of sensuality into the higher consciousness, a radical change for traditional morality and religion? There is room for more insight than Kenner provides. Some friends of Schubert did not completely agree with Kenner. According to Franz von Hartmann, Schober had a reputation for being a "dangerous leader of young people." He was well read and had "a dignified, bombastic manner of speaking, assumed an air of superiority." But Hartmann adds:

> *on the whole he seemed to be an upright and honest man. On us he had no demoralizing effect Memoirs*

The respected Josef Spaun, a friend of Kenner, Schubert, and Schober, saw in Schober a very important positive influence with respect to Schubert:

> *One must not disparage the great services rendered by the extremely talented Schober with his burning enthusiasm for art. Schober, with his mother's permission, repeatedly received Schubert into his home and gave him many proofs of his friendship and his care. In particular, Schober is deserving of the greatest credit in regard to Schubert for having brought about the latter's association with Vogl, which was only achieved after great difficulties. The society of a young man so enthusiastic about art and of such refined culture as Schober, himself a successful poet, could clearly only have the most stimulating and favorable effect on Schubert. Schober's friends also became Schubert's friends, and I am convinced that living among his circle of people was far more advantageous to Schubert than if he had lived among a circle of musicians and professional colleagues, though he did not neglect these either.*
>
> *Memoirs*

Certainly Schubert agreed with Spaun, finding in Schober and his friends a spirit in whom the hunger for truth and beauty burned. Outside of this circle Schubert felt intellectually starved:

> *Now I sit here alone in the depth of the Hungarian countryside, where I have unfortunately allowed myself to be enticed a second time, without having a single person around with whom I could exchange a sensible word.*

There was an intellectual timbre to Schober that was important in the development of the young composer. But Schubert's attraction to it did not rob him of intellectual independence. Bauernfeld wrote:

> *Schober surpasses us all in mind, and much more so in speech! Yet there is much in him that is artificial, and his best powers threaten to be suffocated in idleness... Schubert has the right mixture of the idealist and realist. The world seems fair to him.*
>
> *Memoirs*

Schober indisputably had an impact upon the way Schubert saw his world. Schober himself wrote:

> *It was an extraordinary pleasure for me that the chance visit of Fraulein Hermann became the occasion for bringing me into touch with such a close relative of my dear, never-to-be forgotten, boyhood friend Franz Schubert. I shall always retain the eternally uplifting feeling of having freed this immortal master from the contraint of school, and of having been united with him in true and most intimate friendship right up till his last breath*
> *Memoirs, 208*

Schober with his notion that he himself made divine life incarnate and could determine his own morality without regard to custom or law seems in this respect to be a mirror image of Shabbetai Zevi and Jacob Franck. Shabbetai in the seventeenth century and Franck in the eighteenth expressed their Jewish cabalism by assuming a messianic identity, seeing themselves as incarnations of divine life, superior to the law, capable of moral self-determination. They each thought that they had a godly task to perform, the celebrating of a radically new experience of life's central mystery. Creativity was essential. This produced activities that were considered licentious by their more traditionally inclined brothers. At the end of the eighteenth century their followers were a powerful presence in Moravia and around Vienna. Both Schubert and Schober saw themselves in a similar light. They were to be communicants in a higher life, a divine life that transfigures everything it touches. And for Schober as for Shabbetai and Jacb Franck that higher life was not necessarily antithetical to sensuality. In the new age sensuality would be recognized as a pathway to the stars.

Schubert's art reveals such a higher consciousness that creatively unites spirituality and sensuality. It is clear that Schober had something to do with that reconciliation of opposites. Schober offered the composer an inspiring and creative vision of an ascent to the new age. The poems by Schober that Schubert selected for musical setting were allegorical with an importance far beyond the seemingly superficial stories they told. Each contained a "secret" of the inner life, a unique experience of life's core mystery. They were just what Schubert wanted. Schober and Schubert were challenging in the name of the archetypal goddess the tyranny of arbitrary absolutes that reigned supreme in their society, whether in Judaism, Catholicism,, the secret societies, or the Enlightenment. Their heaven like the paradise of Nicholas of Cusa lay beyond the contradiction. These celebrants of the great romance between heaven and earth provided a ready target for powerful opposition. They were attacked both for their ideas and their behavior. Neither were invulnerable. Schober's "mysticism of sensuality" had led them both into sexual adventures that brought about Schubert's sickness and early death. But the adventurous view of sexuality that they shared did not include a note of nihilism if we can judge the matter by the poems that Schubert selected for his songs. That poetry addressed the sufferings of a wanderer pursuing a painful spiritual ascent in a world of fundamentalists. In this world he is a stranger, far from his true home and surrounded by others whose ways differ and who mistrust him. Schober speaks eloquently of this wanderer and Schubert sings in settings of this poem:

Pilgerweise
Franz Schober D.789
I am a wanderer upon this earth.
Quietly I go from house to house.
Please, in friendliness and good spirits,
Give me your gift of love!

With open sympathy
And a handshake
You could refresh my spirit
And ease its pain, so long endured.

Do not think that in return
I will do you a service.
Rather with wreaths of blue flowers
I will shower your doorway.

I will play my zither,
And sing you a heartfelt song.
Perhaps this seems silly to you,
Of not much value at all

But its important to me,
I can't do without it!
How valuable it is to a Pilgrim!
You can barely imagine its meaning
To one who longs for home.

You have a great deal of wealth,
And can easily replace your offering
Each day adds to your treasure.

But I, in my wandering,
Stick in hand,
See my fortune disappear…
As thread parts from thread in my mortal vesture!

So I live on handouts
From moment to moment.
Won't you, without anger, give me some food?

For you it will be pleasant,
And truly bliss for me!

I am a wanderer on the earth.
I go from house to house.
Please, in friendliness and good spirit,
Give me your gift of love!

This wanderer is a Gnostic hero, a pilgrim driven by a higher consciousness in a world alien to it. He is wisdom's celebrant whose allegiance is to a far distant, better world where love reigns supreme. Schubert turned to the above poem in the Second Movements of the *Ninth Symphony* and the *Piano Sonata in A Major, D.959.* to inspire his lament of the human condition before proceeding to an anticipation of redemptive triumph. The expression of the disappearance of the wanderer's fortune is in each instrumental work quite dramatic, in the case of the piano sonata constituting what Alfred Brendel called one of the most terrifying passages in music. Schubert and Schober were expressing the root drama of the life, the paradox of ascending into heaven by descending into the earth, romancing God by romancing the goddess. Judging from the poetry this is how they both apparently understood the new age.

For Schober the ascent to a better world through a romance of the goddess can sometimes be anticipated in a mystical experience. In another Schober poem set first as a Lied, *Mondenschein*, and then as the first movement of the *Piano Sonata in G Major, D.894*, we find a magic moment of a conscious awakening to a higher world of love and peace. The reign of love dawns, but then disappears.

Mondenschein
Franz Schober D.875
The magic flower of the moon smiles
And soulfully invites
Our dusky night world
To a paradise of love.

Vanquished by sleep's power
Worry, guilt and pain are gone.
Only gentle beauty reigns,
In spiritual freedom,

Look there! The fields are new!
The old earth is gone.
I see a garden of silver, with perfumed scents,
Bathed in golden mist and magical light.

Man's spirit, free of daily concerns,
Is enveloped in a cloud of sweet yearning.
In peaceful joy it drinks in the sacred life of the higher world.

But the song of the nightingale
Reminds our dream-filled hearts of the lower world of daily concerns;
In the midst of that heaven,
Her call brings to life the deepest pain, the pain of love.

This vision is of a romance of the *mysterium magnum*. Perhaps it owes something to the messianic expectations of Shabbetai Zevi and Jacob Franck. The vision is that life is lived in the anticipation of the midday glory, the fullness of the dawn that has already begun but which comes in fits and starts. This seminal life and hope hope is the key to the illuminating quality of Schubert's wisdom, and can be felt in music like the first movement of the *Piano Sonata in G Major* that it inspires.

Schober's new age is an age of transcendental peace. The following poem of Schober was set as a Lied by Schubert and celebrates the peace of the higher consciousness that follows upon the good news of divine invitation realized in Jesus Christ.

Pax Vobiscum
Franz Schober, D.551
"Peace be with you."
This was your parting gift.
You were radiant in glorious divinity,
As you left the earth for the Eternal Home!
And indeed peace came to the faithful hearts…
A gift of peace in the midst of sorrow and pain!
This gave them strength to face their own death.
I believe in you, oh mighty God!

The Lied was composed in 1817. Two years later Schubert used that same poem to inspire the triumphant last movement of the *Trout Quintet*. Here the threat of death has been swallowed up in the victory of the higher consciousness. The Shekhinah has become the Divine Sophia. Schober celebrates poetically the resolution of the contradiction between death and life. Schubert celebrates the same mystery musically.

Schober's vision of an ascent to a kingdom of love and peace and the final union with the Beloved are alternative symbols of the Gnostic, Cabalistic, Hermetic, and Christian homecoming. That ascent paradoxically means a descent into death. Schober celebrated in the poem *Todesmusik*, the transfiguration of life that beckons through death. In 1822 Schubert was inspired by this poem in the celebration of what he knew to be the core of *gnosis*, an acceptance of the divine invitation that begins with a responsible embrace of the "now", with its joys and sorrows, its hopes and fears, and leads through light and darkness into eternal light. The key to joy for the wanderer is awakening to the invitation that beckons in every "now".The poem.*Todesmusik* expresses this mystery perfectly. The poem inspired not only a Lied but also both movements of the *Unfinished Symphony*, part of the *Wanderer Fantasy,* and, in 1827, the first movement of the *Piano Trio in B Flat.* It focuses upon the mystery as the ultimate transfiguration of the life experience. The new age with its higher life cannot be won simply by science and technology. It exists only where love transfigures everything, even dying. The sublime beauty of Schubert's musical creations indicates the inspirational power that Schober's poem had for him. Here is the poem:

Todesmusik
Franz Schober D.758-1822
At the sacred hour of death,
When I shall leave this earth,
And in pain fight my last battle,
Holy spirits, bless me
A final time with your peaceful melody,
Your pure harmony;
Ease the pain in my heart,
Torn by its fatal wound.

Free my simple and tortured spirit in its last battle!
Sweep it aloft! Upon your wings carry it into eternal light!
Then will the sweet, heavenly harmonies envelop me,
And my chains will become light, and drop away!

I will see all the wonders of life,
Which brought me such joy.
All the beauty which bloomed in my life
Will stand transfigured before me!
Every star that sparkled for me
In the sultry darkness of my winter's journey,
Every flower that graced my path will be there!

And those fearful minutes when I am in agony
Will be accompanied by joy-filled anticipation!
And I will see all things transfigured!
So I will surrender my life in joy!

In February of 1827, less that two years before his death, when Schubert was embarking upon the period of his most monumental creativity, the period called the most important in the history of music by Benjamin Brittin, he again turned to Schober for meaningful inspiration. Both poet and composer apparently anticipated the coming eruption of genius, seeing it as a bold and terminal voyage into the unknown. They tell a tale of a man ready to embark upon an adventure demanding creativity and daring. It will take him to "distant shores". All other concerns must be put aside. Once again the tale appears both as a Lied and as an instrumental work, *Lebensturm D.947.* It proclaims the composer's readiness to celebrate the ascent to the new age even while dying in the process.

Schiffers Scheidelied
Franz Schober D.910
The waves thunder upon the shore;
The wind billows the sails
And sings in the foam-flecked waves.
I hear its wild song.
The boat beckons me to leave..
Inviting to distant shores.
Tossing impatiently at anchor.

And out there so endlessly far;
You, my beloved, must not venture.
How quickly my stars can vanish!
How fast does the breeze turn into a storm.
Were you with me, threatened by a thousand-headed death,
How could I fight my battles?

Better let me go! Better free even your heart of me!
I know not if I will survive and return victorious.
These very waves which now sound so benign
May indeed draw me into their depths.

Yes, let me sail knowing that in this world I am alone.
Then, before all terrifying danger and unspeakable peril
I shall stand in courage.
Perhaps in my game with terror I can be victorious.
As long as I know what I am doing all will be well.
I do not wish to die…
How could I wish to leave a world that holds such heaven as you!

Through Schober's poem Schubert's wanderer sees himself as a manly, courageous incarnation of the Logos. But certainly for Schubert and presumably for Schober a mystical feminine figure plays a central role in the ascent. She is his immortal Beloved. She is Sophia. She is a concrete woman. She is a transcendental ideal. She is sometimes present, more often absent, yet somehow mystically inviting. She calls the wanderer through life and death. Outside of her sensual invitation there is no higher consciousness. Schober writes and Schubert sings:

Jägers Liebeslied,
Franz Schober D.909
I hunt the deer in the green woods,
The doe in the quiet valley,
The eagle in its mountain nest,
The duck upon the lake;
There is no safety anywhere from my gun!
...

Yet when she looks down upon me,
When her glance sets me afire,
Then I understand the inner torment
Of the fleeing beasts I hunt.
Yet the torment unites with
All the happiness of earth...
As when my closest friend embraces me!

For Schober here the incarnation of Sophia is the Beloved of the Logos. Romance defines reality. It defines the *mysterium magnum*. The romance between Sophia and the messianic Christ figure is the prototypical ascent to the higher consciousness. The love between men and women, indeed all love, shares in this romance. The sophianic Shekhinah needs the messianic Logos to ascend out of her lower-world prison. When she is sufficiently prepared she will enjoy the divine wedding to the Lamb through which she will become her full and true self. In a priceless Lied inspired by a yet another poem by Schober Schubert's wanderer sings of the Shekhinah's avid anticipation of a wedding. She is incarnate in the many flowers of Spring, separated shards of divine light, and she yearns for the coming of her lover, the Christ, who will bring about the divine harmony she seeks. She is especially incarnate in Viola who must die before the great feast of divine harmony can take place.

Viola
Franz Schober D.786
Snowdrop, little Snowdrop,
You sing in the fields,
You sing in the quiet of the forest,
Ring and sing merrily on!

You announce a time of joy!
Spring, the Bridegroom, is coming!
Victorious in battle with Winter;
He has no need for weapons.

So hold aloft the golden rod!
Let the silver bells ring out!
And let your perfume send out its invitation.

Flowers everywhere, rise up out of the dark earth!
Be worthy of the Bridegroom!
Be arrayed gloriously for the wedding feast!

An Ascent into the Mystery in the Opera "Alfonso und Estrella"

In praise of the radiance of God's grace, the heart is seized!
Love draws the reign of peace over all the world!
Alfonso und Estrella

Schubert and Schober created a unique, profound, and thrilling cabalistic allegory celebrating the dawning of the higher consciousness of the rose cross mystery in a war-torn, hate-filled world. The allegory was probably inspired by events in the brief but beautiful eruption of the mystery in Northern Spain and Southern France in the 12th century, a celebration of the necessary counterbalance between the masculine and feminine, expressed in music and poetry by the Troubadours and finally suppressed brutally by Pope Innocent III. The outer story is of two kingdoms split apart but returned to an original unity through the love and courage of a young prince and princess. The metaphysical theme hidden within the opera is the pursuit of the reconciliation of opposites, first with respect to the hero and heroine, and then throughout their worlds. The opera treats of the archetypal triumph of love. One by one the characters in the opera become messianic and sophianic figures who are luminous in union with one another. Through repentance and forgiveness love triumphs in a world torn apart by hatred. In a Rosicrucian allegory realizing symbolically the religious hopes of Novalis, the opera celebrates the dawning of the new age. At the beginning of the opera value conflicts are everywhere in a male-dominated, polarized society. Woman is prey to man's lust. Frustration, fear, and hatred characterize a power-driven, warring world. The divine light has been shattered and dispersed. Redemption is symbolized in a love union of partially divine beings, masculine and feminine light fragments on both sides of the contradiction, who when unified are luminous in godliness, but when separated are helpless prisoners. The pathway to illuminated freedom leads through the necessary forgiveness of past wrongs.

The opera *Alfonso und Estrella* depicts first the state of the world as it is now, torn apart in value conflicts, and then its electrifying redemption by embracing the "Lord's grace". This grace is a wedding of opposites. The Manichean dualism of "good" and "evil" worlds dissolves through the miracles of repentance and love into illuminated harmony. There are two worlds locked in conflict. In one of them the messianic symbol, Alfonso, impatiently waits for the time when he can unleash war upon his enemies. In the other world the Shekhinah symbol, Estrella, is alone and threatened in a society alien to love. Both worlds are confused but await a misunderstood dawn. Estrella has an inner fire, a higher life, but is faced with a terrifying threat in the form of Adolfo. Neither Alfonso nor Estrella alone have the power to face their enemies. But then Estrella, an incarnation of the Shekhinah, and Alfonso, a Christ figure, meet. Empowered by this romance Estrella addresses the task of uniting the scattered sparks of her suffering people. The love of the light-bringer, the semi-divine, messianic Alfonso, has given life to her which she in turn shares with others who depend upon her. The dualistic forces under Adolfo are defeated. A world of separation and mutual fear and hatred, of meaningless obedience and shallow beliefs, is replaced by immersion in the rose cross mystery. Wisdom is triumphant in a kingdom of love. In the romance of Alfonso and Estrella Sophia, true wisdom. ascends to her throne. Man and woman transfigure one another and their world in love. Opposites are reconciled through the forgiveness of past offences and the acceptance of all creation into the new unity. Slowly what had been savagely separated becomes radiantly one. Love, the higher consciousness, is triumphant. Here is cabalistic redemption in ravishing musical splendor!

The opera is in three acts. The First Act presents a symbolic reflection upon the world as it is: split apart into a maze of contradictions and value conflicts. The opera tells us quickly that something important is in preparation. As the opera begins it is night and a mighty adventure of love, a mystical dawn, is being prepared. A splintered world is about to be put back together. By the conclusion of the opera we will be in the light of midday. Divine love will radiate throughout the earth. But first, into world darkened by hatred and ignorance and ruled by force love, the higher consciousness of the rose cross mystery must enter and transfigure everything.

The main characters are:

Troila, the dethroned king, the embodiment of wisdom in times past, who once ruled over all, but who was betrayed by the ignorance and greed of his subjects, and now has fled them to preserve his life;

Alfonso, a Christ-figure, the messianic light-bringer, Troila's son, who will bring true wisdom back to the world, but must wait to do so until the time is right;

Mauragato, the usurper king who betrayed true wisdom and who now reigns over the world;

Adolfo, the military and political power figure who made Mauragato's betrayal possible. He has been used by Mauragato but now rebels against him. He has no understanding of true wisdom nor of love except that he somehow recognizes their value in Estrella and his need for her.

Estrella, the Shekhinah, a Sophia-figure, the alienated star of love in a love-starved world. She refuses to abandon her fallen world and together with Alfonso transfigures it into a kingdom of love. She and Alfonso are the holy pair who are to reign together over the new age.

The darkness at the beginning of the opera awaits a new dawn. The expectation is shared by all. Yet no one knows what the "dawn" really means. We don't know it yet but that dawn will come with an apparently chance meeting of god and goddess that foreshadows the triumph of "God's grace. This romance initiates a world transformation restoring the primordial unity and transfiguring the world in love.

Troila is the symbol of primordial unity, the heaven that was lost. He is now in exile and his power is limited. He awakens before dawn to greet the sun, the symbol of divine wisdom. He sings of the redemptive interplay between sun and earth, creator and creation, reminiscent of the interplay between God and Wisdom, the divine Lover and his Beloved, Sophia. When the sun warms the earth new life erupts, reaching heavenwards. This suggests that soon wisdom, the interplay between higher and lower worlds, will heal the savage pain that now exists:

> *"Greetings oh Sun; each day you pour new joy into my heart. Your rays draw the pain from each side and heal my suffering."*

Troila finds in the sun, the empowerer of the earth and a symbol of God, the inspiration to prophesy that Alfonso, his son, will set aright the unseemly separations of our world and re-establish a unified kingdom purified of its flaws. In this prediction he is right but incomplete. Alfonso will be a redeemer, but he will need a co-redemptrix, Estrella.

Alfonso is so much a reflection of the Logos and a messianic Christ-figure that the words of *The Book of Wisdom* seem apt:

> *But to your saints there was a very great light…For when quiet silence kept all things, and the night was in the midst of her course, your almighty word leapt down from heaven from your royal throne, as a fierce conqueror into the land of destruction.*

Later in the opera Estrella will describe this conquering hero, Alfonso, in a more erotic yet otherworldly vein:

> *Magnificent he shone on the mountain, his golden hair flying, his cheeks ruby red, courage radiant in his face, confidence in his eyes, his mouth expressing love's sweetest enchantments. When he sang his heavenly songs the forest listened, transfixed, the highest peaks echoing the sound. Once smitten by this joy I have still the memory, ever seeing his face, luminous and inviting, before me.*

Yet as divinely elevated as is the messianic Alfonso, the Christ or Logos figure, he exists to first find, then romance and ascend with his divine "other", his Shekhinah, his earthly Sophia. She is Estrella, who not only changes his life but is at the heart of the redemptive action. Without her there is no myth. Without her there is no contact with the archetype. There is no magic, no power. The divine invitation comes to him through her. She is every bit as intriguing as Alfonso. She is the symbol of wisdom, a star of promise that sparkles in the vast night of her fallen world. She is Sophia incarnate, wise, erotically alluring, maternally protecting, the Eternal Feminine. Like Beatrice, like Laura, like Pamina she leads Alfonso on the pathway to redemption. She is his Goddess, appearing to him as a

> *sweet vision from heaven,*

repeated three times for emphasis. He promises to be her knight and calls upon her to command him. She awakens his erotic desire and inspires him to undertake his redemptive mission. She plays a critical role in that mission, becoming a life-giving Goddess for her father and his kingdom.

The Second Act is a symbolic enactment of the drama of the preparation of the Shekhinah for her joint apotheosis with Alfonso. It begins with the presentation of a legend from the past depicting the disappearance of the Goddess and the catastrophic effect this has. Her disappearance means that the experience of divine harmony through the reconciliation of opposites has been replaced by a lower form of life. Here is the mysterious "Original Sin", the disappearance of the feminine and effectively of the romance between opposites and the consequent concretizing of insuperable contradictions. In the story of the Cloud Maiden we encounter the Goddess in the form of a beautiful girl who once led a young hunter to the summit of earthly bliss. But suddenly, inexplicably, she disappears leaving him to fall to his death. Wisdom, the Divine Sophia, has vanished from the world. Problem solving has become a matter of mere logic and not a blending of ideas and intuition.

The separation of worlds, symbolized in Alfonso and Estrella, begins to be altered in their first meeting as they fall in love. Alfonso's awakening to the magical empowerment bestowed by love is brought on by meeting Estrella. After the meeting her he sings:

When I see you I can imagine no pain!
You enrapture my heart!
My sorrows disappear!
A thousand suns shine in the heavens on joy-filled nature
And new forces intoxicate my heart!

They sing together:

What a mysterious power fills me!
I am alive with new strength!
With a joy never felt before!

Estrella, symbol of the Shekhinah, will prepare her world for the messiah. Before the redemptive meeting with Estrella Alfonso is powerless, complaining to his father, Troila: "Save me from this dismal place." Estrella, lost in the woods, asks "Who will show me the way home?" But after Eros touches them and love dawns everything changes. Each is divinely empowered by the other. Alfonso suspects the momentous nature of the event, calling the girl a "sweet vision from heaven". Both sing of a "strange stirring", a joy they have never felt before. Alfonso recognizes the immense power that Estrella has to transform his life. Refusing to see her as a suppliant, he insists upon placing his power at her service. This subordination of power to wisdom and love brings with it a harvest of joy. "Suddenly, from the heights of heaven, happiness appears." Both man and woman sing of their awareness that life has been radically altered, even though they must separate and live apart for a time. This separation is necessary because Estrella has a job to do. She, the Shekhinah figure, must gather into one the scattered sparks, unite her people, and save them in their moment of danger. This she does by courageously facing death. This is a kind of Rosicrucian trial, analogous to the trial of Tamino and Pamina in *The Magic Flute*. Conditioned by a readiness for the ultimate sacrifice a world is transfigured little by little as contradictions are reconciled. The leader of the rebellion against Troila was Estrella's father, Mauragato. Symbolically he lost the Goddess when he lost Estrella. But faced with the dissolution of his kingdom, he gains a sobering understanding of the tragedy.

Only Estrella's love gave me joy!
She scattered love's roses over my path.
But now the roses have vanished like my happiness.
My wounds will never heal.
Oh Estrella, come back!

In the face of threatening tyranny the drama reaches a highpoint when Estrella, after meeting Alfonso and being empowered by his love, returns to her homeland and to her father. This return, an essential chapter of the great romance, inspires some of the most thrilling music of the opera (music that is amazingly eliminated in most modern productions of the opera which follow Franz Liszt's tragic adaptation). Estrella's return and love union with her father sets in motion the action that leads to world redemption. By the end of the Second Act Estrella has done her work of preparation. The stage is set for the definitive apotheosis of the young couple from whom heavenly light radiates throughout the land.

In the Third Act Alfonso, who has been Estrella's inspiration in her preparations, now enters into her world to effect a final triumph over the disruptive powers that have torn it apart. Estrella inspires Alfonso, empowering him to assume his role as redeemer. He responds by becoming her knight and servant, placing his masculine power at her service. Through their partnership the savage value conflicts that split society are resolved. Repentance and forgiveness, essential to the kingdom of love, unite what male domination has torn apart. Mauragato, who treacherously betrayed King Troila, expresses his guilt and is forgiven. Troila accepts the repentance:

> *I come to forgive. Hatred is no more.*

The opera ends in a triumph of the rose cross mystery. The storms of war are set aside. Opposites are reconciled. Wisdom triumphs. Love, the life of the new age, reigns supreme. Society is bathed in "the Lord's grace". A new age is born.

> *After the savage fury of the storm follows the warm sunshine!*
> *...To praise the Lord's grace makes all men joyful!*
> *...Love has drawn the bow of peace over this world.*
> *All grief is compensated when the heart runs high.*
> *Hail, hail to the young couple!*
> *On the throne of the gentle king shines the golden sun of grace.*
> *Life, glory, and joy radiate through the entire world.*
> *Hail, hail to the loving couple, hail!*

In this profoundly symbolic tale of an ascent to a new age opposites creatively embrace one another in a triumph of love. Fear-driven dualism is vanquished by the higher consciousness. Even Adolfo, the symbol of pure power and the one most distant from the divine light of wisdom's true religion, repents and is forgiven by Mauragato. He becomes part of the new age. Radiant in the sun of divine love a new society is born, one reigned over by the "holy pair". Yet even here the kingdom of love is not completely secure. Unlike the Finale of Beethoven's *Fidelio* Schubert's Finale questions the grasp by society of what has been achieved. While the women's chorus chant the praises of the "holy pair", the men's chorus praise only the "young king". Is this intended by the composer as an awareness that the triumph of love is always short-lived. Indeed in the Troubadour stronghold of Languedoc in southern France it soon fell victim to the deadening savagery of religious fundamentalism.

The opera has Gnostic roots. Redemption occurs on three levels just as it does in Valentinian (Christian) Gnosticism. After the divine prototype of the romance is celebrated by Troila in his greeting to the Sun the story of the redemption of the lower world begins. First, redemption comes to the most "spiritual" of the dramatic figures. Alfonso and Estrella are aware of the heavenly light in one another and the divine invitation to unite in love. Then that light spreads from Estrella to the morally-confused Mauragato and his followers. Finally it comes even to those most distant from the light of grace, Adolfo and his conspirators, who have little if any sense of the divine call to the spiritual ascent. Wisdom's triumph is complete. The new age begins.

Yearning for the new age where contradictions are reconciled is a constant theme of German mystics. Nicholas of Cusa defined the new age as the penetration of the walls of contradiction. Friedrich Schiller defined it as the triumph of love. That new age suggests here a radically new relationship between the orthodoxies. It suggests a problem solving that re-creates the world in love. The symbol for this new age with its alternative metaphysical universe is the love relationship between a man and a woman.

It is clear that cabalism, Catholicism, and freemasonry all were inspirations for this opera, both in their prodigious strengths and in their glaring weaknesses. It is precisely in its gnostic embrace and transcendence of these orthodoxies that the opera creates its own enemies and is fated to exist in lonely isolation. It resolves the tension between groups not by the destruction of one group by the other but through a new and higher unity made possible by mutual recognition of guilt and repentance.

The cabalistic overtones are evident. It is interesting that the hero is Alfonso of Leon (or Lion). The great patriarch of Jewish cabalism was Moses de Leon. Isaac Luria, the great sixteenth century cabalist, was known as the Lion of Safed. Sabbetai Zevi's name, Zevi, means Lion. Both in such accidentals and in substance there are indications that both Schober and Schubert profited deeply from whatever contact they had with the Jewish Cabala. The most powerful theme of their art is the cabalistic romance between opposites, a romance that unites earth to heaven by uniting earthly opposites.

Schubert's cabalism, evident in so many works, probably owes much to his friendship with Schober. Because of the obvious influence of Jewish thought in this opera it may help the reader to review the Jewish myth of redemption. Estrella is clearly an incarnation of the Shekhinah in her ascent towards union with the Divine Sophia. The Divine Sophia, the higher consciousness, the perfect image of God, the ideal of Creation, is understood in Jewish wisdom through the following romance. Kether, the messianic light-bringer, brings divine light into the infinite void. The Shekhinah must collect and unite this light in becoming what she is eternally destined to be. Until awakened and empowered by the Messiah, the Shekhinah is split asunder and utterly lost. But once touched by the Messiah she enters confidently upon her destiny, preparing herself for a divine wedding as conflicts are reconciled and love triumphs. Before the redemptive meeting between Kether and the Shekhinah there is the darkness of separation between man and woman and indeed throughout all created things which are locked in violent value conflicts. But after the meeting there begins a long and difficult re-weaving of creation, a progressive re-imaging of God through small triumphs of cosmic love and unity. This preparation of the bride for her final wedding with the Messiah and the final love triumph is the cosmic drama. The pathway to the Shekhinah's restoration leads through Hell before coming to Heaven. Tempting voices call the wanderer back to an ethic of fear and hatred of the "other". Resentment, revenge, hatred and fear motivate more quickly than does love. Power can be more readily accessible through them. Yet those endowed with sophianic wisdom trust that the wedding day will come. The Shekhinah, perfected in unity, will be wed to her messianic spouse. The Estrella story images the ascent of the earthly Sophia or Shekhinah in becoming the Divine Sophia. Variations on this myth have bathed the lives of many, many Jews in wisdom and love.

Christianity inherited from Judaism a similar vision. Love, not mere power, fuels the spiritual ascent. And love means a special kind of resolution of conflicts, conflicts between the self and the other, between man and woman, between opposites throughout the universe. Reality at every level is a triumph of love. Love defines a Trinitarian God and the relationship between this God and the world. Whereas fundamentalism defines God as a distinct being, wisdom finds the transcendental source of life's invitation in a divine romance. Whereas fundamentalism defines redemption as a top-down imposition from a lawgiver wisdom defines it as a creative emanation out of love. The Book of Revelation anticipates the coming of the wedding day when the earthly Sophia will identify with the Divine Sophia and re-union with the Father is possible:

> *Let us rejoice, be glad, and give him glory,*
> *For this is the wedding day of the Lamb;*
> *His bride has prepared herself for the wedding;*
> *She has been given a dress to wear…*
> *Made of finest linen, radiantly white!*

The opera *Alfonso und Estrella* is a life-transfiguring abstraction of this archetypal ascent to a better world. The wedding of the Messiah and the Shekhinah, or in Christian terms, the Lamb and his Bride, can take place when the Shekhinah is crowned queen of her earthly kingdom, now transfigured by love. This ascent of Sophia to her kingdom is celebrated by Schubert in several major works including the *Fantasy for Piano and Violin D.934,* the *Rondo for Four Hands in A major, D.951,* and the *Piano Sonata in A Major, D.959*. But the celebration is uniquely developed in *Alfonso und Estrella*. The opera celebrates a transcendence of dualism and proclaims an era of unity, based upon the triumph of love. A Christ figure, the messianic Alfonso, has come, not as a lawgiver but as an awakener to a new age of divine harmony. The opera seems to shout: the time for waiting is done! Let a new era of creative freedom begin!

Love must triumph now! Now is the time for repentance and the forgiveness of past offences so that love may reign everywhere. Now is the time to accept death as the passage to fullness of life. This is the vision that inspired seventeenth and eighteenth century Jewish Cabalism. This is the vision with which the Catholics and Jews associated with Rosicrucian Freemasonry awakened portions of the western world. This is the vision that inspired Pope John XXIII and the Second Vatican Council in declaring an "aggiornamento".

Schubert and Schober wanted what was not allowed. They challenged the religious orthodoxies and the secret societies to transcend themselves, to become something higher and better than they were, to recognize their inescapable fallibility, to repent amnd forgive. *Alfonso und Estrella* was intended as a life-giving elixir for a war-weary world. It suggested that the true wisdom underlying Judaism, Christianity, and the Enlightenment, once purified, might still unite religion and reason in the creation of a truly illuminated society. Despite the allegorical profundity of its libretto, the brilliance of its music, and the sublimity and spirituality of its vision that message could not be staged then. It is almost never staged today. And when it is presented there are usually changes effected, including a disastrous curtailment of the scene depicting the return of Estrella to her homeland, changes that betray either a fatally flawed recognition of its spiritual depth or perhaps a deliberate intent to conceal it.

The opera was dismissed as a failed effort, the failure often attributed to Schober's libretto. Yet, wonder of wonders, Franz Schubert, called the "most poetic of composers" by Franz Liszt, with an unerring intuition regarding the inner meaning and artistic potential of poetry in his Lieder composition, considered the opera one of his finest works.

Leopold von Sonnleithner raised the specter of "ill-will" when he wrote:

> *Among all his operas Schubert regarded "Alfonso und Estrella" and, after that, "Fierabras"as the best and most suited to presentation. The fact that so few of these works have so far reached performance can be attributed only to the ill-will of certain persons, and in the last resort to the changing conditions of our opera.*
>
> *Memoirs*

Do we have here what in the opinion of many musicologists today is a strange lapse of judgment by the composer, a few of his friends, and this commentator ? Or do we have exactly what Sonnleithner suggested it was: monumental ill-will towards the wisdom component of the opera? Twenty-five years after Schubert's death Franz Liszt tried to get *Alfonso und Estrella* staged. He wrote to Louise Kohler March 2, 1854:

> *I think we shall still produce Schubert's opera, "Alfonso und Estrella", so long as the same theater influences which asserted themselves over the 'Indra' performance, while you were in Weimar, do not oppose too resolutely*

> *this quite interesting musical work, fully endowed as it is with inherent natural charm*
>
> *Memoirs*

In a letter written six months later to music publishers, Breitkoph and Hartel, Liszt concluded that many changes had to be made in this work, once thought to be fully endowed and charming, if ever it might be produced. A "large number of cuts" were "clearly necessary." But why? Even the author of the libretto, Schober himself, surrendered to the opposition. Writing to Ferdinand, Schubert's brother, he hinted at the inappropriateness of the opera to the times, suggesting that its staging would require destructive changes. He marveled at the fact that the opera had been in existence for twenty-eight years *"without a performance being attainable."*

> *I made fruitless endeavors to get it staged, and offered it in vain to the opera houses in Vienna, Dresden, Berlin, Prague, Pesth, Graz…now it is a hundred times more difficult than it was then…How much the musical world has changed. Only half a miracle can bring this belated child of the past into the light of day without destroying it.*
>
> *Memoirs*

Why did it have to be destroyed? Ferdinand wrote to Schober in 1848, indirectly revealing what many were saying about the opera, namely that there was something "spiritual" that was unacceptable:

> *The fact that the opera "Alfonso und Estrella" has remained so long unperformed should not give cause for concern that, on this account, the undertaking might meet with suspicion regarding the spiritual value of the work, since most of the blame for this can be traced to the following circumstance, an admirer of Schubert's in Graz, out of conscientiousness, stored away this opera so carefully in a chest, that he only found it again fourteen years later.*
>
> *Memoirs*

Here Schubert's brother explicitly denies any problem of spirituality. But why bring it up? In doing so he implicitly contradicts Schober concerning the effort to stage the opera and reveals that some people thought that spirituality was indeed its problem. As any salesman would Ferdinand attempted to weaken the case against the opera by saying that the impossibility of getting it staged was really due only to a lack of effort. But one cannot avoid entertaining the thought that Schubert was saying something that should not, could not be said on the stage in the years following the composition of the opera, years when religious and secular fundamentalisms vied for the control of Europe.

Schubert was affirming the sublime beauty of a symbiosis of German Christianity and Judaism, a higher synthesis of the Enlightenment and the orthodoxies sparked by seventeenth and eighteenth century movements within Cabalism, developed and channeled through the secret societies. The symbiosis transcends now as it transcended then the narrow sectarianism of many Jews and Catholics. It offends the myopia of both fundamentalists and nihilists. Jewish and Christian fundamentalists must reconcile themselves to the redemption, not the destruction, of the *Qelippah*. They must recognize their religion as a unique, irreplaceable, redemptive, but limited and often-distorting light on the world rather than its enemy. Assumptions that outside our church there is no salvation, the pretense of infallibility, claims to political power based upon scriptural promises, all must be rejected as leading to eternal war. Judaism, Christianity, Islam, and the Enlightenment are all starting points for a journey that must transcend them in a unity that can be common to all.

Schubert was bridging the chasm between ideas and value, between science and religion, between heaven and earth. In creating artistic reconciliations of contradictory visions he had things to say that were politically incorrect in a very serious way. It did not take long for Schubert and Schober to discover the price they would pay for this daring. After becoming aware of the opposition to the opera they united in creating this song:

> ***Schatzgräbers Begehr***
> Franz Schober D.761
> *Down in the earth is an ancient law.*
> *I am driven to discover it, distracted by nothing from my task!*
> *Powerfully the world spins its golden web to seduce me!*
> *Powerfully its siren voices preach their false wisdom!*
> *"You waste your life away!"*
>
> *But still I continue, digging relentlessly for the treasure.*
> *And even if I fail in my search,*
> *Even if I succeed only in digging my own grave,*
> *Gladly will I lie in it and my longing will be satisfied.*
> *So leave me alone! You must allow everyone at least a grave;*
> *Do not deny me mine, dear friends!*

Alfonso und Estrella, like *Zauberflote (*Mozart), *Poliuto,* and *Dom Sebastien (*Donizetti), expressed a spirituality that was not wanted by the reigning powers of religion, politics, or art. The composers of these operas, all influenced by Rosicrucian freemasonry with its blend of the Jewish Cabala and Christian wisdom, thought that the great war was between the rose cross wisdom and its religious and secular distortions. Schubert and Schober celebrated the many-layered wisdom of love's kingdom in their opera. Like Mozart and Donizetti, they paid a high price for their politically incorrect vision. Their opera was trashed as being fluff, the product of incompetence. Nonetheless it was remembered by the composer as one of his fairest flowers, one perhaps commemorated in the Lied *Die Rose* with its Rosicrucian intimations:

Die Rose
Friedrich Schlegel D.745
The lovely warmth attracted me to venture out into the light.
There I was burned in the great heat; I now lament it.
I might have bloomed long through the mild days of autumn,
But now I must wither early and surrender my young life.
When the day dawned I forgot to be cautious,
And opened my blossom and exposed my beauty.
I spread my sweet scent. I wore my crown,
But then…the sun became more painful…
I so regret it!
And of what use to me now is the cool evening, I ask you sadly.
It can no longer ease my pain.
The rose-color is whitened.
Soon I will feel the bite of the cold.
The story of my short life I would tell you before I die!

Die Treue, Fierabras, and the Mystery

In 1823 Schubert composed his second grand opera, *Fierabras*. And once again he set to music a drama of the spiritual ascent of a society to the *mysterium magnum*. Schubert's masterworks are almost always influenced by Jewish Cabalism with its emergence out of contradiction. The wanderer is a divine emanation charged with the re-uniting of a world split apart. This leads to tension both between the soul and aridly secular forces (suggesting nihilism)and between the soul and aridly "spiritual" forces (suggesting religious fundamentalism). The soul, a victim of this polarizing contradiction, becomes the fallen daughter and unfaithful bride of God. She must first suffer the effects of this polarization and then arise from degradation and be restored to her rightful dignity as the Divine Sophia, the all-encompassing unity of the wisdom of God.

The problems brought about by the ascent take a strong form in Fierabras, where the blending of the human and the divine poses a practical problem. The hero cannot marry his beloved. She belongs to someone else. He is alone and must live out his life deprived of the one who makes life worthwhile. Seemingly heaven disappears for him. He must live in agonized fidelity to the higher life that he has experienced only through his absent and forbidden love. This theme is prominent in Schubert's works and will be expressed with special poignancy in the two song cycles.

Whereas the ascent to a higher life in *Alfonso und Estrella* was a direct march towards the new age, in Fierabras that march is interrupted. Tragedy replaces triumph as the hero's lot. The transfiguration of this decidedly unwelcome life experience in the new age through the interplay of higher and lower worlds brings with it a new ethic, *die Treue*. The birth of the new age through a higher consciousness is a long-term and painful event. It requires heroes and heroines ready to suffer and die to bring it about. It requires fidelity in love. Schubert's second grand opera celebrates the raw courage needed by the soul in its reconciliation of contradictions.It sets the tone for the masterworks that will follow his near fatal illness in 1822-23. Suffering and death are to be fully incorporated into the ascent to the kingdom of love.

Die Treue had been necessary in the composer's personal life. In Schubert's love for Theresa Grob and Katherine Esterhazy divine invitation had a price tag. These women were for him alive with divine light, but he had to face a life without them. The effect of this renunciation is evident in Fierabras, which celebrates love's triumph achieved in the context of heroic self-sacrifice. Schubert raised the experience to a higher level by associating it with the mythical romance of Christ and Sophia. In the allegory there is a suggestion of Holy Week. The challenge before the protagonists in the opera is to live according to the ethic implied by love, even when the joys of love are denied. This theme was surely influenced by what Schubert was experiencing when he composed the opera. In 1823 he had been faced with death. By 1824 the terror had not disappeared. Theresa Grob, his first love, had married someone else. As always he reflected his inner struggle in his stories of the wanderer, or in the case of this opera, several wanderers.

The libretto by Leopold Kupelweiser focuses upon the responsibility of the individual to wrestle with the painful contradictions of his or her life and translate the higher synthesis into the immersion of society into the rose cross mystery. The libretto is an elaboration of Bildung, the German-romantic conviction that each wanderer must tame the warring beasts in his or her own life, wedding them in ever higher unities, and projecting that harmony into society. Wisdom in Fierabras means courageous fidelity in fashioning the painful contradictions of life into steps of the spiritual ascent. There are five protagonists who are challenged by wisdom's demands. Each re-incarnates the passion and death of Christ, bringing heaven to earth and ascending personally to a higher life. Heaven comes to earth, not as a top-down messianic thrust, but rather as a romance between a life-bringer and a light attracter, i.e. between a Christ-figure and a Sophianic one. The focus is directly upon the heroism that the higher consciousness demands in her messiahs. While the challenge varies from person to person the one constant is that the romance leads the wanderer home to the light only after by plunging the lovers into the darkness of death.

The First Act begins with a sublime meditation on life viewed as a love mystery that begins at birth, continues into adult life when the wanderer makes his love commitment, then strangely leads to "something less attractive, but sadly true", namely a struggle to remain faithful to love and friendship in the face of terror and death. This struggle to remain faithful to the love dynamic of the new age is *die Treue*. The individual dramas are suggestively related to the life, death, and resurrection of Christ. There is a kind of Palm Sunday, a Good Friday, and an Easter. For example Palm Sunday is suggested as the Frankish knights anticipate a final triumph:

Let peace advance into the halls of the Prince!
If songs of rejoicing ring out
The palms also must blossom.
Heaven's might sends peace to this land,
Granting the highest of gifts.

The pathway to this higher peace leads through the courageous acceptance of an honorable death. One of the young couples, Emma and Eginhard, sing:

Our souls, so truly united, will soon soar aloft.
When we are reconciled to death our pain will end.
We need to break its mighty reign of terror over us.

For Florinda and Roland, the second couple, *die Treue* means union between messianic and sophianic figures even in dying:

With my beloved's life mine too departs.

For the knights who have accompanied Roland in his mission of peace to the Moors *die Treue* means dying with their heroic leader:

Let us be led with our friend to public death in the flames!

But death in Schubert's wisdom is always paired with the Christian vision of transfiguration. In the midst of the tragedy, at the very darkest hour hope dawns. The maidens sing:

Soon songs will resound and joy will fill our hearts.

And indeed all pass through the trial to the higher consciousness of peace and joy:

Horror and pain have vanished like the mist.
Happiness has been vouchsafed through "die Treue".
Pure joy awakens and songs of jubilation sound from every heart!

One of the heroic knights, Fierabras, is acutely aware of the mixture of horror and splendor that constitutes his initiation into love's kingdom. That kingdom for him means painful sacrifice. He calls his fate "damnable"; yet he never retreats from it. He is falsely accused of betraying the king and sent to prison. Emma, the girl he loves, loves the Frankish knight Eginhard and is a party to the betrayal of Fierabras. Yet Fierabras, a Schubert alter-ego, remains true to her, repressing his pain, keeping it secret, making her happiness possible. He groans: "Hush, deluded heart! Be silent, futile lament!" The hero, although powerful, chooses to subordinate his power to love for Emma. Her tragic betrayal of Fierabras is a foretaste of the wanderer's betrayal by the fickle dream maiden in the great song cycles. Everything earthly, even love, is both an expression of the transcendental and its earthly betrayal. While Schubert recognizes the transcendental in the love between Eginhard and Emma and between Roland and Florinda he recognizes also that allegiance to the divine Sophia sometimes comes with a high price in terms of earthly joy.

In Fierabras the core of the drama is a commitment to the higher world in which contradiction is reconciled through fidelity in love. This demands courage in a world alien to love. The dawning world has love as its queen and the erotic experience of transcendental invitation at its core. The dull wit of fundamentalist orthodoxies symbolized both in the Moorish enemy and in a decent but uncomprehending King of the Franks must be transcended in the love that unites the men and women, Christian and pagan, and brings them new life. As in Beethoven's *Fidelio* Schubert's Florinda descends like Isis into the darkness of death's prison to bring new life to her beloved and open the pathway to freedom. The heroine, here a messianic figure, opens the door to transfiguration. Tradition and law are transcended in a romance of spirits. The old fundamentalist order gives way to wisdom. This is an alternative expression of *Novo cedat ritui* from the *Tantum Ergo,* so prized by Schubert and set to music powerfully in 1828. The higher law of a loving romance must supplant the old law of belief and obedience as *gnosis* must supplant a belief in ideas. This *gnosis* must be realized in an infinitude of ways, each conditioned by the state of chaos from which it must be woven. Schubert was celebrating one of life's core mysteries, the thrilling, chilling nature of the cosmic romance that ultimately weds heaven to earth but at the cost of death. *Die Treue* is necessary for the incarnation of divine harmony and the birth of the new age.

Lazarus and the Mystery

The hidden mystery, Jesus,, the Christ...enlightened them; he showed them a way...

- *The Gospel of Truth*

The new age of immersion in the rose cross mystery, the *mysterium magnum*, demands the reconciliation of the contradiction between life and death. The higher consciousness means a paradoxical act of love for the earth and a radical transcendence of that same earth. Opposites unite in mutual enrichment. This penetration of the wall of contradiction in a rite of passage assures a constant tension with any ideology. The powerful secular fundamentalisms, secular and religious, that opposed whatever "spiritual" there was in *Alfonso und Estrella* overflowed in opposition to at least one of his oratorios in which the ascent to a higher life is realized in the very shadow of death. The lower world of fear and pain is simply transfigured by the wanderer's apprehension of the higher world.

But this mystical effusion upon the stage was politically incorrect in a Europe dominated by nihilism and religious fundamentalism. In an unsigned letter published in the *Donau Zeitung* on March 29, 1863, thirty-five years after Schubert's death we read that the oratorio *Lazarus,* to a text written by August Hermann Niemeyer, was:

> *"set to music by a young Viennese musician who...was nothing less than a genius. He lived to see it but not to hear it. In this Niemeyer shares Vienna's fate and that of the whole musical world, for it became known only yesterday, when it was performed for the first time, that Franz Schubert wrote this Easter Cantata. A distressing fact and a new contribution to the unheard of martyrdom Schubert still suffers, even after his death. In February 1820 as a young man of twenty-three Schubert sang this moving*

> *song of death and resurrection, and not until fully forty-three years later does a favorable wind waft his voice over us......It shocks one to think of such a destiny, and feelings of exasperation have to be consciously stifled to prevent curses from breaking out against the callousness of Viennese publishers, and against the faithlessness of his numerous comrades, who indeed every minute boast of their friendship with Schubert but who have looked on with equanimity whilst whole works of the great master were plucked to pieces and then vanished without a trace. Where for example is his great cantata "Prometheus", the score of which has been seen by many of his friends? No one knows. Ah, if chance were not more merciful and more generous than these people, we should be without some of the most important Schubert works, and not even be in a position to judge in its full range the genius of the greatest artist Vienna has produced. Memoirs*

In 1820 Schubert had set to music a celebration of paradoxical, sublime peace in the face of death. The work addressed the ultimate challenge: the transfiguration of dying by the higher consciousness of the rose cross mystery. The text by the Halle theologian August Hermann Niemeyer calls for three acts focusing first on the death of Lazarus, then his burial, and finally his return to earthly life. Schubert set in music the dying at some length, the burial more briefly, and the return to earthly life not at all. The composer saw in the death of Lazarus not the miracle of a return to life, but rather the ultimate ascent to a btetter world. It is clear from its beauty that *Lazarus* meant something special to Schubert. He did with it what he wanted to do. *Lazarus* celebrates an illumination so powerful that it completely transfigures life at a point when pain and fear are most intense. In the face of death, life's ultimate contradiction, Lazarus has an inner peace that does not leave him. His dying is an act of love, both for the God who calls him and for the friends, especially the women, who love him. The inner illumination, the heart of wisdom, is discussed and shared with some of his friends for our benefit. Some do not share this luminous wisdom. Their lack of *gnosis* permits them to experience the moment only as an approach to eternal darkness. Thus Martha sees only the blackness of the grave while Mary counsels her not to "oppress his soul with laments" lest "sublime peace" "forsake him." She encourages Martha to "stand by the weary man that his soul may be filled with sublime, sweet peace".

Lazarus sings of the transfiguring effect of transcendental illumination with moving beauty:

> *Never again to see these fields, these flowers, never again, alas, to see you, dearest ones! How troubled my soul once was......*
> *But now... all is bright around me,...like the light of morning!*

Another friend, Nathanael, becomes part of the mystical event:

> *Receive me, peace of the grave, receive me when I have fought enough…as gently as you receive my friend!*

Lazarus finds empowerment for his elevated state in Jesus Christ, "who took our sickness upon himself, who guides our way to the Father." Mary, Lazarus' friend, is wisdom incarnate and experiences a higher world than does her sister Martha. In Schubert's mind she is perhaps Mary Magdalene, the beloved of Christ, and a semi-divine figure in the Johannine tradition that reached Europe when the Knights Templar and the Teutonic Knights returned from the Crusades. Through her we hear of the progress of the suffering, the burning cheeks, the unrest, the struggle, and the continued presence of illumination. She respects that illumination and protects it:

> *"God holds you and does not waver."* …… *"In God's love he trusts."*

Another friend, Jemina, has had a similar illumination experience. Lazarus asks her to sing him a "song of death and resurrection" that "he might sink gently down in soft starlight," and that with the song his soul might "rise to God for whom it thirsts." Jemina then sings of her awakening to the radiance of the divine invitation at a time when she herself seemed to be dieing. The gnosis she shares with Lazarus and with us is peace in the mystery of love that aids the wanderer in the great romance that inevitably leads to the passage through death to transfiguration.

In Schubert's eyes the new age of immersion in the rose cross mystery had already begun in Lazarus' higher consciousness. However, it had not yet dawned upon the outer world. Each wanderer was called to live that new age in the inner life while seeking a life commitment to making it real in the outer world.

The Song Cycles and the Mystery

Die Schöne Müllerin

> *I shall preserve my pearl for paradise, until you lay aside your earthliness. Then I will give it to you as a possession. But I will eagerly give you my presence and the sweet beams of the pearl during the time of this earthly life!*
>
> *- Jacob Boehme*

The new age of light, the kingdom of love, the incarnation of the rose cross mystery, is a transcendental dream, completely and mysteriously achievable only beyond this life, in a "better world". The meaning of this is not clear. Certainly it means in this life...in a higher consciousness". Certainly too it means transcendentally, somehow beyond death. Thus the wanderer is first awakened to a higher life of love, and then commits to it, only to find that it lies in important ways beyond his reach. The beautiful miller's daughter awakens him. But immersion in the rose cross mystery will lead him to his goal through an acceptance of death.

Franz Schubert's first great cycle painfully longs for the coming of the new age. It tells the story of a romance between a wanderer and a girl. All hope for his happiness rests in the success of that romance. The girl is all that is splendid in the world.. She is his only escape from the drudgery of the lower world. And that romance has an auspicious start, awakening the wanderer to powers both within himself and in the outer world of which he never dreamed. Today we can recognize this awakening in the science and technology, the democracy and rule of law, that promises so much to our hungering world. But the romance falters. The miller's daughter is not ready to play her part. She has a sublime destiny but does not know it. She like the wanderer must be awakened to a higher consciousness. That has not yet happened and the results are tragic.

Die Schöne Müllerin is riveting. The wanderer at first is unaware of what life is about, but does understand that he must wander out and seek whatever fate has in store. He imagines that he can capture heaven on earth. His Eros-blessed meeting with the miller's daughter awakens in him a growing awareness of a new and expanded inner life that reaches out towards the infinite. His awareness of this mysterious invitation develops as he falls in love with the girl. She is angelic, an incarnation of divine harmony. All of nature shares in the mystery. Stars, flowers, the brook all sparkle with heavenly beauty. But it is the magic of the girl above all else that reveals just how divinely beautiful is his dream. In her he experiences the beauty of life's mysterious invitation that shines in the stars and sings in the brook.

And deep in that brook I saw the heavens.
They reached out to draw me into their sacred depths;
And all the while the brook running above the clouds and stars
Called joyfully to me, playing and singing,
Friend, friend follow me!

Slowly it becomes clear that this invitation to transfigure the outer world by the inner one must lead to sorrow, pain, and death. The outer world into which the wanderer is inexorably driven to find his beloved is strangely resistant to life's romance. The great romance that he has begun is completed only with a transcendence of this life. True gnosis means awakening to the transcendental nature of the dream.

Before his illness in 1822-23 Schubert could not have composed this cycle. But in 1824 Theresa Grob had married. Death was threatening. His work was not understood. Life seemed to be a waste. The heaven he wanted to make incarnate was a sour memory. Yet it is just here that Schubert discovers the key to the rose cross mystery and to his most sublime art. The songs tell in a series of lyrical chapters of life as an ascent through tragedy, suffering, and death. The wanderer paradoxically must be immersed in the *Qelippah* with its agonizing contradictions before ascending to a "better world". This paradox is wisdom's "secret".

Die Schöne Müllerin tells a tale in which the wanderer is paradoxically invited both into an immersion in this world and to world-transcendence. Sophia's kingdom, the kingdom of the higher consciousness, is not always welcome in this world. It must fight at times against orthodoxies of every sort. After being awakened to the higher consciousness by the miller's daughter the wanderer awakens also to the mysterious fact that the treasure he has discovered is not simply the girl as she is. It is the divine invitation that is incarnate in and through her to a transcendental goal. She awakens him, empowers him, and leads him. But she leads him into a puzzling mystery. Ultimately she betrays him. She in fact gives herself to someone else. Only after drinking the cup of sorrow with resignation does gnosis dawn mystically in the Lied *Trockne Blumen*. In the literal meaning of the poetry the new age is as dead as the flowers on his grave. In its mystical intimations *Trockne Blumen* expresses a radiant invitation to the fulfillment of dreams. This cycle is a challenging paradox containing the mystery of life.

The cabalistic influence is clear. The wanderer's invitation to the spiritual ascent is first experienced in the feminine allure of the miller's daughter, an earth-bound goddess, who transfigures the wanderer's world but then leaves him for a rival. Thus the awakening has ominous overtones. The hope it inspires is for something beyond what life actually will give. The initiation of the wanderer leads him through a severe trial in which he experiences what on one level is the definitive loss of his beloved. Gnosis is achieved when in the Lied *Trockne Blumen* a *conjuntio divina* is subtly suggested and love's triumph is experienced. The song cycle recognizes the need to ascend to divine life through a parting from its limiting earthly incarnations.

Die Schöne Müllerin masterfully plays with the paradoxical relationship between divine invitation and the incarnations that channel it to the wanderer. While the miller's daughter totally transforms the wanderer's life and possesses majestic power, in the end she betrays the wanderer. If she is a symbol of divine beauty and attracts the wanderer to a higher life, she is simultaneously the symbol of the limitation of all incarnations of the divine, including the world's religions. "All beauty must die." is a constantly recurring theme for this composer. Inevitably the earthly Sophia's weakness is exposed. And inevitably the wanderer is faced with a new challenge that occurs in the life of everyone. Does life have meaning in the face of this betrayal? In the allegorical Lied *Trockne Blumen* the answer is "Yes"! The earthly Sophia will one day ascend to her own higher consciousness and recognize the wanderer's love. In the meantime life can be unbearably painful.

On the surface the story is simple to the point of being childish: an overly sentimental young man cannot handle rejection and commits suicide. But in counterpoint to this is a sensitive and profound handling of an explosive issue. The religious orthodoxies, Roman Catholicism, Judaism, Protestantism, Islam, and the political orthodoxies are simultaneously awakeners to divine invitation and betrayers of it. It is only by virtue of the higher consciousness of the rose cross mystery that the wanderer can navigate these perplexing and troubled waters.

Is the song cycle tragedy or comedy? Life is alive with divine invitation, and the world sparkles with heavenly beauty. Yet all its beauty dies. In the perspective of false wisdom the "heaven" of human dreams is simply a mirage. Better to ignore it. But from the perspective of the rose cross mystery heaven is destiny. Even in the face of death the invitation lives. This wanderer's life, apparently a waste, is not a tragedy at all, but an ascent, begun in joyful hope, yet pursued in sadness and great suffering. It ends with the transcendental hope awakened early in the cycle and superimposed upon a dying wanderer. The importance of Trockne Blumen is underscored by Schubert's instrumental setting of the poem soon after completing the cycle. The instrumental work gives us the composer's personal understanding of the poem. More than the Lied setting it reveals his own interpretation of the drama in question. In the

Variations for Flute and Piano D.802 we find the theme of new life and resurrection expressed variously in section after section, freely expanding upon the meaning that this poem had for the composer in the context of the whole cycle. These variations sing of hope in the face of death! Spring with her divine harmonies will come again! For Schubert these ideas are not sentimental flourishes, nor are they meant to be cynical. Mysteriously the dream maiden will appreciate the wanderer's love. The new age will dawn.

But spring will come again, and winter will go,
And little flowers will bloom in the grass...
Little flowers will bloom upon my grave...
All the little flowers that she gave me!

And when she walks along this hillside,
She will think: his love is true!
Then little flowers, spring forth, spring forth,
May has come! Winter is over at last!

The cycle ends with the brook singing the wanderer to his final rest. Earth has failed him. The earthly Sophia has betrayed him. He must await the final chapter of the romance which lies mystically beyond them all.

Good night, good night, until all comes to life!
Sleep away your sorrow; sleep away your joy;
The full moon is rising, the fog disappears,
And above are the heavens...how vast they are!

Die Winterreise

My God, my God, why hast thou forsaken me?
- Matthew 27

In the great song cycle *Die Winterreise* the kingdom of the goddess, the new age, is invisible in the cold winter sky. The joy in the rose cross mystery is gone, absent like the Beloved. While *Die Schöne Müllerin* gives a broad overview, from cradle to grave, of the great romance, *Die Winterreise* zeroes in upon the pain, "the dark night of the soul", that afflicts the abandoned wanderer and that paradoxically conditions Sophia's triumph. In *Die Winterreise* the girl who is the symbol of all earthly beauty, the very beauty that awakened the wanderer to divine invitation, has long ago disappeared. In the face of every hope for a new world and a triumph of love in his life there is only the bleakness of shattered hopes. One need only reflect upon the present state of the world today to find resonances. Do shattered dreams of earthly love have artistic value?

The thought patterns are Hermetic. Each heavenly body can affect human experience in a unique way. Mercury, for instance, leads upwards in the spiritual ascent. Venus reflects the allure of a union of opposites. The Moon is a bridge linking the inner and outer worlds. All influences have their proper time and place in the cosmic drama of becoming whole. This Hermetic vision was recognized by Carl Jung as a guide to the archetypal experiences of the wanderer. There is one planet whose influence is ominously meaningful for the spiritual ascent. It is by virtue of a descent into the agony of Saturn that the stage is set for transcendental rebirth and the transfiguration of life through the higher consciousness. Between February and October 1827 Schubert set to music Saturnine poetry that seems to be the antithesis of the love ascent. It addresses experiences like alienation, depression, madness, despair, and thoughts of suicide, experiences that might seem completely foreign to the wanderer in the great romance. Marsilio Ficino in his three books of life, *De Vita Triplici,* attributes such experiences to the influence of the planet Saturn. Ficino saw malevolence in Saturn. There is sickness and sadness. Saturn's children are grave diggers and latrine cleaners. His scythe cuts apart the opposites of father and mother, sky and earth. His influence is generally to be avoided. His metal is lead, weighting us down, cutting us off from others, alienating, isolating. He makes action all but impossible, inhibiting thought, memory and introspection. Because of Saturn energy dissipates and one becomes externally inactive. And to this inactivity there seems to be no ending, only a frozen state of icy death, a state that brings to mind *Die Winterreise.* Hidden within Saturn's frozen and isolated world of death lie treasures of deep religious contemplation and artistic genius. Like the earth in winter when the spirit turns away from earthly joys, the wanderer suffering through these times is prepared for new and richer life. In mystical terms the Saturnine experience is the Dark Night of the Soul preceding the illumination that is the new age. Thus an experience full of both dark danger and an almost completely hidden promise is presented by an immersion in the tragic spirit of Saturn. It is this immersion with all its horrors and with all its potential life-resuscitation that Schubert brings to us in this song cycle. *Die Winterreise* plunges us into despair, yet, strangely, also prepares us for a spiritual ascent to the higher consciousness.

Earlier in his creative life Schubert had given many indications of a Saturnine dimension to his thought and to his art. There is reference to Saturn in the poetry inspiring the *First, Second* and *Sixth Symphonies.* In both cases the reference to pain is followed by a vision of transcendence. The Lied *Gruppe aus dem Tartarus* is an immersion into a sea of black melancholy, followed immediately by the luminous joy of *Elysium.* Schubert's mythological adventures of the wanderer's encounter with the black-winged demon are always controlled, never a spiritual collapse. And they are inevitably followed by miraculous eruptions of life and joy that seem to be measured by the antecedent descent. In the posthumous *Piano Sonata in A Major* after the Saturnine agonies of the First and Second Movements there is no earthly reason why the joyful wanderer should awaken at Heaven's Gate in the third movement or experience the divine invitation so erotically in the Fourth; but he does. And the ascent to newfound joy measures itself to the descent into despair in the first two movements, both poetically and musically. Can we say this about *Die Winterreise?*

Die Winterreise ends in alienation and pain. There is no *Trockne Blumen* to suggest experientially a positive outcome. There is only a sorrow that reminds us of the lament of the exiles in *Gruppe aus dem Tartarus*, "Will this never end?" This suggests to some that Schubert in the end was a nihilist. But he was not. While composing the songs (or shortly thereafter), Schubert composed two piano trios which begin in darkness and then mount to sublime light and joy. Readers should refer to my analyses of these trios. One of them, the *Piano Trio in E Flat* D.927, begins deeply immersed in the Saturnine mode of *Winterreise*. But the light from a higher world simply transfigures the darkness. The other work, the *Piano Trio in B Flat*, is a celebration of the transfiguration that affects "every star, every flower" in the wanderer's life, transforming darkness into light. The first movement looks upon death as the point of definitive transfiguration. The Second, Third, and Fourth Movements are variations upon that transfiguration, recapturing the joy of an earlier spring when love was triumphant. Yet a third instrumental work, the *Fantasy for Piano and Violin in C Major, D.934,* followed closely upon the heels of the song cycle. In it the wanderer joyfully and thankfully unites earthly sorrow with transcendental expectation. Here again we have a celebration of the ascent to a higher consciousness made possible by an immersion in Saturnine melancholy. And finally the String Quintet is a prayer in the face of death, asking for peace, courage, and to be "led home". Saturn in the hands of this composer is inseparable from sublime freedom and the rose cross wisdom in which contradictions are reconciled.

The deeper this composer plunged into the sorrows of life's betrayal of the divine the more intense and elevated were his victories over it. It seems quite likely that the miracles of Schubert's last eighteen months were made possible only by his intense immersion in the saturnalian depths of *Winterreise* and later *Schwanengesang*. *Die Winterreise* develops the archetypal story told in *Die Schöne Müllerin* by focusing upon a single part of it, ther end time, the time of winter, the time for withdrawal from the world and its dreams.

Schubert received his vision of death resurrection directly from Catholic mysticism. The Christ of the gospels experienced utter alienation and death before resurrection. *My God, my God, why have you abandoned me?* Christ asks others to be one with him in death and the ascent to new life. Many mystics describe a dark night of the soul before illumination. So Schubert's wanderer suffers a complete absence of light before the new day dawns.

In Schubert's mythology the Shekhinah is the light of the world, all the world, the religious and political orthodoxies, men, women, all scattered light fragments. She is to be transfigured by passing through death. Her imaging of the divine Messiah in the higher consciousness does not permit a cheap ascent. She, like the Logos, must become the victim of fundamentalist idolatry. The composer expressed this mystery in the Lied setting of the following poem by Matthäus von Collin. Speaking to the incarnation of the Divine Sophia …

Der Zwerg
Matthäus Kasimir von Collin D.771
The dwarf said,
You yourself are to blame for this
Because you renounced me for the King;
Now only your death will make me happy.

We live in sunshine and shadow. Divine unity appears and invites, but also disappears. Sometimes the contradictions facing this wanderer are so blatant and irreconcilable that sanity is threatened and death is assured. In the twenty-four songs of *Die Winterreise* the wanderer is faced with experience he finds backbreaking. He must reject as his lodestar the illusion that merely earthly loves in their separateness, in their tragic limitations of the divine, can satisfy him. He is a citizen of a higher world, and is not at home until that world definitively transfigures this one, a transfiguration that seems very remote indeed.

Beyond the village stands the organ grinder;
With numbed fingers he plays what he can;
Barefoot on the ice he staggers around,
His little plate always empty.
No one listens; no one notices him;
Dogs snarl at him.
But he lets it all happen, turning the handle, never stopping.
Mysterious old man, can I go with you?
Will you accompany my songs?

....

PART TWO
THE INSTRUMENTAL WORKS AND THE ASCENT OF THE WANDERER

We have seen how able musicologists differ in their opinions of what this composer was trying to do. We have developed our own unique perspective based chiefly upon poetry that Schubert selected for his inspiration. It is time at last to take the final step in this development. We will analyze the poems that inspired the instrumental works along with the composer's arrangement of them. In doing so we are opening a door to a new age. A unique and profound entrance into the universe of Schubert's instrumental compositions lies ahead. I do not exaggerate the value of the treasure that is hidden here. A daunting yet promising stairway to the stars beckons. With Goethe we sing:

Have you seen the mountain with its steep, misty path?
The mule feeds his way through the clouds,
While in the chasm lives the monster serpent's brood.
The cliffs are sheer; the water cascades…
Do you understand?
There, there our road lies!
Oh Father, let us go!
……

The goal of this analysis of Schubert's instrumental compositions is to make more accessible to the reader an experience of the life-giving mystery that is everywhere present in these works. The instrumental works of Franz Schubert are intensely personalized celebrations of the spiritual ascent through a harmonies of opposites. These works can of course be evaluated merely in terms of emotions or musical technique. But this is like evaluating a new car merely in terms of its color or its weight. The instrumental works are experiential emanations out of musical and mystical ideas. The linkage, for Schubert necessary and universal, of the musical experiences to the mystical ideas found in poetry gives us sure insight into the inspiration of the art.

The poetry that inspires Schubert's art often expresses a stage in the romance of the *magnum mysterium*. The romance is never idea-independent. The art is never poetry-independent. To ignore or distort the ideas expressed in the music and contained in seminal form in the inspiring poetry is to trivialize the art, a crime committed often against this composer.

That art expresses uniquely in each masterwork a dramatic emergence from a lower to a higher world. These dramas are celebrated on many levels. Sometimes the setting is Christian. Sometimes it is pagan. Sometimes it involves death. Sometimes it involves a girl. Sometimes it involves nature. Always however it is the harrowing romance of a transcendental-imminent goal that inspires the work. And always that drama is evident in the inspiring poetry as well as graphically expressed in the music. The true Schubert experience means accompanying the composer in the spiritual drama expressed in the music. For most of us that drama is so towering that help from the inspiring poems is a necessary part of the preparation.

We will follow the Schubertian dramas from his mid teenage years to his death through the poetry that inspired them. Each inspiring poem is one first set by the composer as a Lied and then used to inspire a portion of the instrumental work. The Lied title and number are given. This poetry will prepare the reader for a richer understanding and a more rewarding experience of the music. Why? Because it was just this poem that the composer used, most often line by line, always thought by thought, to inspire the instrumental work. An awareness of the thought progression and intimations of the poem will enable the reader to first understand and then experience the spiritual ascent that is germane to each work.

Symphony No. 1 in D major, D.82

October 1813

Schubert began his symphonic output with an explosive bang, not a whimper. It is fitting that his first symphony celebrates the ascent to a better world culminating in the unveiling of Isis. Pagan wisdom is celebrated in a thrilling ascent to wisdom. Here is a musical experience of the journey of the soul through Becoming towards Being. Here is the archetypal ascent out of sleep and prison to a higher consciousness of the mystery and to freedom. This ascent is through the triumph of love. The composer is celebrating life as he sees it. And that life includes a transcendental dimension that has pagan, Cabalistic, and Christian roots. The *First Symphony* reveals to us that the rose cross mystery, the paradoxical passage to a better world, the realization of Being through Becoming, the touching of God through the World, was a conscious presence from the time Schubert began to compose.

For the young composer life is beautiful. In the face of suffering and death there is life-transfiguring hope. This hope will be sorely tested later, but it will weather its storms. In fact there is a remarkable consistency between the composer's world view at the age of sixteen and that expressed throughout his life. At the age of sixteen however the challenges to his optimism are more imaginary than real. Against the backdrop of the passage through death to eternal life there is projected the awakening of the soul to the mystery of divine invitation and to the divine spark of the wanderer. The exploration is carried out through myth. Drawing upon the most ancient pagan traditions as well as upon his Catholicism Schubert used the Schiller poetry to inspire musical evocations of the spiritual ascent, thus celebrating the divine fullness that invites us all to a mysterious passage through life and death to a mysterious fulfillment, a new age, here described as a kingdom of love. This joy-filled imaginative celebration of life's central mystery, the mystery that underlies the Egyptian and Greek mystery religions as well as Christianity, emanated from a spiritual awakening to the invitational experience of a better world, an awakening that breathes the spirit both of pagan and Christian wisdom. Before the awakening the wanderer in anguish observes the apparently endless agonies of mankind. But the cry for release is answered. The higher consciousness of divine invitation dawns. The poetry of Schiller inspires this early and revealing symphonic expression of Schubert's redemptive understanding of the life experience.

In the first movement who are the agonized mourners? The wisdom tradition suggests to us that they are the un-awakened masses who must toil and suffer through this life without hope, without a higher consciousness, without the illuminative experience of divine invitation. Yet within the prison of this ignorance Saturn's scythe with which he cuts down every effort to escape is shattered by divine power. This movement sets before us the contrast between the sorrows of a life without true wisdom and the presence of a life-transforming power that towers above the present pain.

In the second movement we encounter an imaginative, non-literal exploration of the higher and better new age, the triumph of love, that invites us. Elysium is depicted as a love triumph. The divine life that towers above our life can transform it. And the name of this life is love. Life is a direct romance between the soul and others and an indirect romance between the soul and God. Here the lovers relish the peace of love's fulfillment.

In the third movement the young Schubert continues a playful, musical exploration of the wealth of the higher consciousness mythically contained in Schiller's poem. A Schubert alter-ego, the messianic warrior-knight, is introduced. This self portrait as a knight will continue throughout the composer's life. The knight is granted his transcendental reward, a peaceful paradise. Next a second and even more important self portrait as the Wanderer, appears, also enjoying transcendental peace. With the wanderer lies Death, the Erlkonig...who is no longer a threat. Death's repose is charmed, full of the gentle beauty of the Better World.

Finally, in the splendid fourth movement, the wisdom-inspired illumination is celebrated. The new age has arrived! It is a triumph of freedom! It is sometimes playful, sometimes joyful, always triumphant. Here is the scintillating life of the higher consciousness. Religion, philosophy, and politics reach their apex as the veil is ripped away and Truth is revealed. Becoming has at last imaged Being.The goddess is ready for her God.

This same theme of anticipated bliss will re-occur often in the composer's life. For instance eternal May triumphs in the posthumous *Piano Sonata in A Major.* Eternal Youth is met again in the posthumous *Piano Sonata in B Flat.* The golden dreams are seen in the *Grand Duo*. This security in the final triumph of love is characteristic of the wisdom tradition and is a dominant theme in Schubert's art. The veil that has for so long concealed wisdom is wrenched away... revealing Sophia in her naked beauty.

FIRST MOVEMENT:

Ignorance of the Father brought about anguish and terror; and anguish grew solid like a fog, so that no one was able to see.

Gospel of Truth

The work begins with a glimpse of human suffering in a land that contradicts all hope. From the yearning, searching wanderer comes the repeated question, "Will this never end?", a question raised in a different form and with far greater intensity at the end of Die Winterreise. Here it is asked in the shadow of eternal wisdom which rises triumphantly in the background like a mountain peak that will shatter the cruel cycle of birth, death, and re-birth.

Elysium
Friedrich Schiller D.584

Listen! Like the rumbling of a mighty ocean,
Like the whine rising from a cascading river,
Comes a groan out of the depths,
Impassioned and anguished!
Their faces are twisted in pain,
Despair and curses their cry,
Vacant their staring eyes,
As they look in terror upon the bridge over Cocytus.
Mournful their sorrowful journey,
As anxiously they whisper:
"Will this never end?
Will this never end?"

Eternity towers above their journey…
Shattering the scythe of Saturn!

SECOND MOVEMENT:

Through this gospel…he enlightened them and showed them the way; and the way is the truth which he taught them.

Gospel of Truth

The higher consciousness answers the question "Will this never end?" with a poetic vision of triumphant love. Here a new world appears; hushed, joy-filled peace reigns. The agony of the wanderer is over. Love is everywhere queen.

Elysium
Friedrich Schiller, D.584

Faithful spouses here embrace
And make love in the sweet green of the meadow,

Gently caressed by westerly breezes.
Here love is queen.

Lovers, safe for ever from death,
Enjoy an eternal wedding feast.

THIRD MOVEMENT:

Oh such great teaching! He draws himself down to death...He put on imperishability which no one can possibly take from him!

Gospel of Truth

The imagined scene is still paradise. But the focus changes to first the warrior, then the wanderer. The warrior sleeps by the running brook, his battles but memories. The wanderer too is freed from the agonies of his long journey. Death, once an enemy, is now a friend.

Elysium
Friedrich Schiller, D.584 and D. 57, D. 58
The mighty warrior,
Used to the raucous sounds of death,
Under whose boot even mountains trembled,
Sleeps quietly by the running brook, which
Tumbles over silver stones,
The clash of swords is now only a dim memory.

Here the wanderer rests his body
In the cool shade.
He surrenders forever his life-long burden.
The scythe drops away from the hand of Death...
And Death sleeps to the soft music of a harp,
Dreaming of gathering hay.

FOURTH MOVEMENT:

He gave them thought and understanding, mercy and salvation, and the powerful spirit from the infinity and sweetness of the Father.

Gospel of Truth

Schiller's poem, *Elysium,* inspires Schubert to this gloriously triumphant music. It will do so in many instrumental works later in his life. Eternal joy and freedom sparkle and shine here as we experience a foretaste of the transcendental goal that invites the wanderer throughout his life. The golden dream, the freedom, the joy are all here, triumphant!

Elysium

Friedrich Schiller, D.584 and D. 51, D. 53

The time for sorrow is done.
The joys of heaven
Drown every pain.
Heavens' life is eternal joy, eternal freedom,
By the gentle brook in the lush meadows of Elysium.
The world is young and joyful,
And bedecking every field is eternal May.
The hours pass by in golden dreams.
The spirit reaches into endless space,
Truth rips aside every veil.

Unending joy inflames the heart.
Anguish and pain do not exist.
Mild delight is called sorrow.

SYMPHONY NO. 2 IN B FLAT MAJOR, D.125

1814-1815

There is a remarkable consistency to this composer's world view. In this second symphony the love that in the earlier symphony transfigured the life of the wanderer now transfigures nature and friendship. This theme of a cosmic transfiguration by love will continue throughout Schubert's life. In the last symphony, the unfinished *Tenth Symphony in D Major*, it will be love that inspires and nourishes the wanderer at death's doorstep. In this symphony we are invited to enjoy the eruption of sacred beauty in nature. Schubert is a Hermetic Magus who musically expresses the ascent realized both in nature and in the human adventure. The music reveals an inspired young composer who elevates his appreciative audiences with mystical power.

In the first movement dawn is breaking. The sunrise is a sacred experience for the wanderer. He senses in the sun's invitation to the earth the divine invitation of the wanderer to triumphant life and love. Life on one level unites with life on a different one. What follows is a mystical and powerful suggestion through Nature of the divine invitation to the human spirit, similar to the suggestion found in the allegorical landscape paintings of Caspar David Friedrich. Dawn is sacramental, leading the illuminated wanderer to an anticipation of a higher world. The spiritual ascent celebrated here occurs through a wedding, not a separation, of nature and the sublime.

The Second and Third Movements are inspired by Schiller poems that are set as part songs by Schubert. The second movement focuses upon love as the pathway to the stars. The third movement is an experience of the higher consciousness as it rejoices in nature. The fourth movement, a Herder inspiration, relishes joy in a life in which man and nature are in harmony. For the higher consciousness this harmony transfigures sexual love and nature. Schiller's poetry celebrates love's triumph, uniting nature's harmonies with harmonies of the spirit, This poetry served the young Schubert well. The composer often turned to Schiller for inspiration not only in early Lieder and symphonies but also in later works (e.g. the Seventh and the Ninth Symphonies). Schiller's poetry could sometimes be musically expressed better in the expanded freedom of instrumental compositions than in the songs.

FIRST MOVEMENT:

To the Sun:Harken, oh blessed one, whose eternal eye sees all. Radiant as gold, celestial light, sweet sight to living creatures, yours are the golden lyre and harmony of the cosmos. Hear my words and show us life's sweetness!

Orphic Hymn

The dawning of wisdom is like the rising of the sun. It is majestic in both cases. Symbolically the Alpine peaks, their pine trees, and the birds slowly come to life. With true wisdom all of the life experience is gradually transfigured. As the sun rises the activity in the valley increases. We hear the horses, the careening wagons, and experience nature's reach towards its deity in the swooping, soaring hawks and eagles. The higher consciousness here brings to these experiences a radical transformation, indeed a transfiguration in new life and joy, similar to the eagle's triumph, depicted with graphic lucidity in this music.

Der Fluchtling
Friedrich von Schiller, D. 67
Fresh is the breath of morning.
Crimson sun-flakes seep through the pines.
Radiant beams of dawn fall upon the leaves…
Golden sheets of flame
Illumine the cloud-laced peaks.
Joyous song erupts from the awakening larks
And salutes the sun.
That sun, in transfigured joy
Already radiates the warmth of love's embrace.

Oh glorious light, I salute you!
Your inviting warmth spreads
Over field and meadow.
How the pastures glisten!
How in silver dew-drops sparkle
A thousand suns!

In the soft, cool breeze
Nature plays its morning games.
Soft zephyrs caress the roses,
Their perfume filling the enchanted world.
High over the cities the smoke billows,

The horses neigh and snort, shuffle and stamp.
Wagons and screech and careen into the valley.
The woods come to life, eagles, falcons, and hawks swooping, soaring,...
Triumphant in the dazzling rays of morning.

SECOND MOVEMENT:

Amour, le vray moyen...
Que l'homme est homme et sans lequel n'est rien!...
Marguerite

In a series of variations the wanderer relishes the higher consciousness which transfigures one world through its union with another. This is love's triumph.

Selig durch die Liebe
Friedrich von Schiller, D. 55
Here is love's kingdom!
Man is a god by virtue of love!
Man is divine!
Heaven is love.
The earth transfigured by love
Is truly the kingdom of heaven!

THIRD MOVEMENT:

Kronion Zeus, whose sceptre is the thunderbolt, earth-shaker,
Grant me divine peace, riches and glory without blame!
Orphic Hymn

The celebration of love's triumph continues. Earth is transfigured by heaven:

Thronend auf erhab'nem Sitz
Friedrich Schiller, D. 55
Kronion sits in splendor,
Brandishing his thunderbolt!
When his long hair flies in the wind
Olympus reels in fear!

Ein Jugendlicher Maienschwung
Friedrich Schiller, D. 61
Hovering over all is the spring-like joy of May.
It breathes through the air, sky, sea, and earth
Like the enchanted half-light of early dawn.

FOURTH MOVEMENT:

> *I call upon Bacchos...he slumbers...When he stirs up again the revel he sings a hymn; he puts to sleep and awakens the years! May he show us life's sweetness!*
>
> *Orphic Hymn*

Continuing in this vein of a wedding of worlds that transforms all it touches the wanderer celebrates friendship that relishes such life-transfiguring beauty. In a room surrounded by happy friends and sparkling glasses all are invited to enjoy the friendship in which Nature is illuminated by divine invitation. We sense the companionship and are enlivened by the glistening goblets that are alive in the music. Here Nature's treasures are symbols of true wisdom, and we are invited to make them our own.

Trinklied
Johann Gottfried Herder D. 75
Gather together in a circle, dear friends,
And enjoy life as your fathers did!
Join together in song!
Friendship offers the cup of joy
To the happy drinker.
The golden wine invites us.
So in this hour of celebration
Join hand to hand,
And dear friends, be merry!
Let us all be truly brothers!
Look, friends, the glasses are sparkling!
Now a boy drinks water,
But a man drinks good wine!
Our lives should ever be
Like the grapes' golden juices...
Strong, noble, gentle and pure.
Let us empty our glasses
In honor of our friendship.
Strong, noble, gentle and pure:
Such is our life! Such is our wine!

Piano Sonata in E major, D.157

1815

Man is split between spirit and flesh, between something eternal; and something mortal. At the heart of the mystery is a cosmic invitation to return from a primordial "fall" of separation to a yet more primordial divine unity. Peace and joy are found through accepting death as the definitive passage to this "true home" of harmony and peace. Franz Schubert celebrated this paradox of finding life through death and finding joy through sorrow in musical tales of a wanderer. This wanderer is both Schubert and a kind of Everyman.

The poetry inspiring many of Schubert's earliest works is sometimes difficult to determine, perhaps because the inspiring poem is missing. This is perhaps the case with the first movement of this piano sonata. But the inspiration for the Second and Third Movements is clear. And I include this poetry because of what it reveals about the composer.

Franz Schubert in 1815 at the age of eighteen is proclaiming his intent to let his art sing of the beauty and sweetness of the mystery of life, especially at his dying. He sings of his music ascending "like radiant beams of light in the evening". That this literally will be the case is clear from the miracle of Schubert's last eighteen months, months Benjamin Brittin has called the most important in the history of music. It is strongly suggested here that this was this composer's intent from his early years of composing. In the words of *Auf einen Kirchhof* Schubert sang as if illuminated by divine spirits, celebrating a redemptive life vision that is Gnostic-Christian with Hermetic and Platonic overtones. Here life is an ascent of the soul out of darkness into eternal light. The composer does not merely accept this, he responds with a commitment to celebrate the fearsome yet hope-inspired ascent in his music.

Schubert selected the poem of Franz Zaver von Schlechta to inspire the second and Third Movements because of the central place that death plays in the poetry. The poem is intensely transcendental. From these early creative efforts until his own death the passage through death to a higher existence was the archetypal mystery at the heart of his art.

FIRST MOVEMENT:

The inspirational poem for this movement is unknown to me.

SECOND MOVEMENT:

Natural contemplation…takes possession of the soul,
raises it, and makes it divine !

Giordano Bruno

The life of the wanderer fits into the order and clock-like pattern of the universe. The vast stillness of nature, sensed in the churchyard, invites thoughts of one's own destiny, a destiny which leads inevitably to dying and the grave.

Auf einen Kirchhof
Franz Xaver von Schlechta, D.151
I salute you, sacred stillness!
You awaken in me a gentle sadness
Through the color and beauty
That adorns the graves with love.

The clouds pass by; a light breeze blows;
The sun is finishing its daily round.
Out of the darkening earth the blazing
Sunset reaches upwards in its crimson glow.

And you, my lifeless brothers,
Have finished your journey…
Did you not sink like the sun splendidly
Into the darkness of the grave?

Slumber now softly, dear hearts, so cold
In your dark and long, long sleep.
All your wounds, all your pains
Are now gently cradled in the earth.

Our world destroys and creates anew
In its driving, clock-like way…
Forcing what was buried in rocks
Into new blossoms in the meadows!

You too, mortal shell,
Will one day, quivering, expire...
Only to blossom anew,
Like a flower upon the grave.

THIRD MOVEMENT:

I have burned for thy peace!
Saint Augustine

The wanderer asks the question: Is this life with its hopes and dreams in the face of death meaningless? The answer rings out that no, this hope is God's own doing, a personal invitation requiring a personal response, a commitment. The wanderer commits himself in dying to shine like a flame in praise of his creator-inviter.

Auf einen Kirchhof
Franz Xaver von Schlechta, D.151
And you, life within me,
Are you a mere prey to worms?
And you that uplifts and delights me,
Are you too but empty dust?
No. What I sense in my own experience,
What in joy raises me to the stars
Is God's own doing!
It is the divine spirit that lives in me!

Like a flame will you shine in your dying,
Giving light like a sunset,
Like radiant beams of light in the evening,
Reaching like music towards the heavens.

SYMPHONY NO. 3 IN D MAJOR, D.200

July 1815

According to ancient Hermetic thought one analogy for the relationship between God and creation is a divine light source refracted in an infinitude of reflections. The reflections are so true that the very creativity of the source is replicated, though at a lower level. Thus each emanation becomes itself a source for other emanations. The earth for instance, receiving its light and life from the sun, passes on that illumination to her children. Yet the multitude of light emanations must ultimately return to the source through a re-uniting process. This reunion is their apotheosis. The stars, the moon, people in love have this cosmic drama of bi-polarity between self and other in common. When differing light reflections unite something new can be generated. Sexuality is the prime analogue for this mystery. Men and women are divine sparks, alive with godly beauty, each in their own way taking part in the paradoxical romance that unites infinite differentiation with infinite harmony to generate infinite creation.

Heaven and earth intertwine in a celebration of the ascent from a lower to a higher world, an ascent inspired by a girl. She is alive with divine life. She is a spark of God. In the *Third Symphony* composed in 1815 this mystery of love is in focus. Springtime and May are illuminated by the sun becoming fruitfully maternal, imaging the divine Mother in the Hermetic Trinity who unites with the Father and produces a divine child. This is the archetype for other union/generation adventures, the romance between men and women and the invitational romance between the soul and God. The composer's enraptured intoxication at the wonder of the romantic adventures is at once sublime, sensual, and melancholy. The union of the opposites rather than their confl;ict is rare.

The wanderer sings about the great romance between an inviting divine unity and an invited differentiated cosmos. The source of the drama and the goal of the longing is the divine light, a light that becomes incarnate in "stars" like Theresa Grob and Karoline Esterhazy as well as in nature, but which is never completely at home here on earth. The wanderer's plight puts us in mind of the *Fourth Gospel* which tells us that this world, though created through the light, is now a stranger to that light and does not welcome it. Still the invitation to the fullness of the life experience burns like a flame within us all.

This *Third Symphony* is a celebration of the beginning of the spiritual ascent in young love. The spiritual ascent and sexuality are often uneasy partners. Here the thrilling power of young sexuality gives a hint of the spiritual miracles that will come later in the life of this wanderer. Through the setting of *Mailied* we experience the drama of earth's sensual response to life-giving light. The slow but inevitable triumph of love in spring is sounded. But there is a second poem, *Seufzer*, with a different mood recognizing that the triumph of the divine in the wanderer's life is a different matter. The search for that triumph begins in life but leads ultimately beyond it.

In the Second and Third Movements the sensuality of nature introduces us to the sensuality of young love. The primary focus is upon the wanderer and the otherworldly beauty of his girl. The better world is an experience here. Precisely through her feminine charm she makes heaven come to earth.

The fourth movement is at first sensual and then blatantly sexual in its suggestion of the better world in the girl. The joy of the movement is everywhere. Heaven is right here in the music inspired by her youthful beauty. The dream-adventure is thrilling. It foreshadows the spiritual energies that will come to play even sooner than this wanderer expects.

FIRST MOVEMENT:

Eros set them aflame;
As from a single lamp many lamps are lit.
On the Origin of the World

Slowly light, life, and love emerge from the sleeping earth in response to the gradual ascent of the spring sun. The rhythmic pulsing of this newly birthed expression of divine life introduces this movement, which soon enough erupts into the vibrant beauty of a May morning. The life is blatantly, gloriously erotic. The wanderer immerses himself deeply in nature's rich life, one with the birds in joy and desire for love. His drama is that of the doves. He searches for love, for the divine, but earthly love is but a taste, a dream, a promise of what he seeks.

Mailied
Ludwig Christoph Heinrich Hölty, D.199
By the brook the grass comes to life; the sky turns a rich blue;
The robins return, and the first chirps of their new-born bring the woods to life!

The blossoming shrubs perfume the air!
Spring reigns everywhere, and love is triumphant!
The flowers are painted rich red, as are the lips of the young girls.
Brothers, the years go too quickly, kiss those lips!
There is nothing evil in that! Who could condemn it?
Enjoy those lips while the invitation is there!
Watch the dove as it makes fluttering love to its mate.
Like that dove find your love,
And let joy fill your heart!

Seufzer
Ludwig Christoph Heinrich Hölty, D.198
All through the woods and on every branch
Nightingales sing their magical songs…
And all of nature becomes a symphony.
Young couples walk along the clear brook,
And, enchanted, pause to hear the music.
But the music of the nightingales
Brings only pain into my dark life.
As I wander I am all alone.

SECOND MOVEMENT:

Love… the gracious force which mortal minds from earth to heaven draws.
Benivieni

In breathless rapture the wanderer sings of his beloved, this girl who in her beauty and charm makes divine invitation incarnate on earth. She is flesh and blood, a real woman. She is also an incarnation of the divine Sophia, inviting to a transcendental fulfillment of yearning.

An die Apfelbaume
Ludwig Christoph Heinrich Hölty, D.197
Enchanted woods, your sacred murmur, your whispered music
Breathes through the treetops.
Here the quivering longing of first love disturbed my heart!
The sunset would bathe the crimson flowers in gold…
And that gold illuminated the silver veil at her breast…
And I melted in rapture!

Now, after our long separation,
My faithful heart reaches out to her with a mystic kiss.
I pledge to her, here in this flower-decked woods,
My true, eternal love!

After we die flowers will bloom where she has walked…
And each flower will sing of the woman I love!

THIRD MOVEMENT:

How beautiful you are, how pleasing, my love, my delight!
Song of Songs

The wanderer sings of his happiness, his delight in this entrancing beloved. She is heaven, divinely transfiguring his world. She is a goddess, full of divine power, and when she touches his world it becomes paradise.

Der Liebende
Ludwig Christoph Heinrich Hölty,D.207
How blessed is anyone
Who looks upon you…
Who tastes the heaven in your beauty,
Sees the angelic radiance of your eyes!

One glance, one wink, one nod
Brighten the world for me like the sun on a spring day!
I think of it all through the day,
And I am swept up into heavenly joy.

Your vision is ever with me,
Drawing me gently
Through a magical world of flowers.
That vision warms my arms.
And fills my dreams at night.

FOURTH MOVEMENT:

Plato…the father of Philosophie, which to his Critias, shaded oft from sunne, of love full manie lessons did apply, the which these Stoic censours cannot well deny.
Spenser

Heaven comes to earth for this young wanderer in the thrilling, sensual beauty of a girl. Sexuality here is joyously sacramental, thrillingly sacred. Here is the wanderer's dream of love, focused upon a girl who is divine allure and beauty incarnate. This attractiveness simultaneously calls the wanderer to the sexual, sensual delights of the girl, and beyond to the higher world that radiantly appears through such incarnations. This is a celebration of Eros in young life and sensuality. It is full of transcendental promise.

Der Traum

Ludwig Christoph Heinrich Hölty, D.213

In my dream I was a little bird!
I flew on to her lap,
And to stay busy I toyed with the bow of her blouse.
Then in joy I flew to her white hand,
And from there to her blouse,
And pulled at the red ribbon tying it.
I flew over her blond head,
Singing with joy,
And when I got tired I restested on that breat…
No heavenly bed of roses
Could compare to that place of rest!
How wonderful was my sleep,
On that flowered breast!

String Quartet No. 11 in E major, D.353

1816

At the heart of the mystery, reconciling all contradiction in an ascent towards the divine, is love. Love invites the wanderer to the higher consciousness. Opposing worlds intertwine through the medium of love. Young love is a great sacrament in Schubert's wisdom. Through it divine light and love come to earth. From 1815 through 1818 Schubert's love of Theresa Grob inspired an enormous output of music. He seems at times to anticipate marrying her. Yet the love to which he gives expression in these instrumental works extends upwards, beyond this earth, uniting the divine and the human, fusing his love for a woman with the great romance between the human and the divine.

The transfiguration of the love experience grows out of Schubert's unique wedding of pagan wisdom and Christianity, a wedding which both expresses and develops the visions of Novalis, Friedrich Schlegel, and Josef Schelling. These visions owe much to the Rosicrucian-tinged Freemasonry of eighteenth century Berlin. They break out of the prisons of both narrow Christianity and paganism in a higher union that brings those ancient enemies to a higher perfection. The higher consciousness is reached not by running away from human love, but by relishing it. That love of love is all the more poignant when the Beloved cannot be reached. The art of finding divine beauty and, above all, personal invitation in tragic love is Schubert's greatest treasure. He seeks to share it through such music as this magical quartet.

FIRST MOVEMENT:

Heavenly, smiling Aphrodite, everything comes from you. You have harnessed the world!

Orphic Hymn

Out of the depths the wanderer reaches upwards towards the land of his dreams. It is love's triumph that he craves, a world that is one with the beauty of the starry skies. This wanderer senses something happening, senses that the dark mists are dissolving, that soon the clarity of the heavens will transform his conflicted world. Yet that time has not yet come, and his yearning is agony.

> ***Licht und Liebe***
> Heinrich Josef Colin D.352
> *Love is a precious light!*
> *As the earth yearns for the sun and the beautiful stars*
> *In the blue fields of heaven,*
> *So does my heart yearn for the joy of love.*
> *Love is a precious light!*
>
> *Look how the bright stars sparkle festively in the heavens above!*
> *And the sadness that darkly enshrouds the earth is vanishing!*
> *Yet deep in my heart I am despondent.*
> *Once I lived in joy,*
> *Now I am without my love… and am in agony.*
>
> *Love is a precious light!*
> *As the earth yearns for the sun and for the beautiful stars*
> *In the blue fields of heaven,*
> *So does my heart yearn for the joy of love.*
> *Love is a precious light!*

SECOND MOVEMENT: *inspiring poem unknown*

THIRD MOVEMENT:

> *For you must know, my love,*
> *That by wine we become divine!*
> — *Rabelais*

The dream of love becomes real in the delights of nature, and specifically here in the joys of friendship and wine. Nature gives body and strength to the life of the spirit. The scintillating beauty of this experience derives from the higher consciousness that unites the mystery of divine invitation with sensuality and thus transfigures life.

> ***Trinklied***
> Anon. D.356
> *The sweet gold nectar*
> *Of precious grapes,*
> *So dear, so delightful,*

So bright and alive,
Shines in the glass.

Likewise shines
This beautiful life of ours,
So rich in friendship,
So lavish in beauty,
As clear as the golden
Fruit of the wine.

So happy celebrants of life,
Lift those glasses!
The wine is
So friendly, so delightful!
And our lives
Sparkle like gold!
Drink! Drink!

FOURTH MOVEMENT:

Reason and love have never yet been twain;
They are by kind of such contrary mould
As one mislikes the other's lewd device;
What reason will, Cupido never would.
— George Turberville

Woman in general and this girl in particular are radiant with divine beauty. Precisely in her feminine allure she is an incarnation of the higher world of celestial love. Sexuality in this sublime sense fits awkwardly into our world.

Die Nacht
Johann Peter Uz D.358
You do not disturb us, oh night,
As we drink our wine beneath the trees.
A cool wind stirs
And brings freshness to our drink.

Mother darkness, so dear,
Night, trusted confidant in our sweetest concerns,
How often have you cheated the guardians of propriety?
How many kisses have you hidden from them?

You alone can understand
What profound joy enlivens me,
When I rest lovingly upon her breast...
Beneath dew and flowers...

THE SONATINAS

Schubert is nineteen years old. He creates here an assemblage of works for the violin and piano which depicts outer and inner worlds in their romance of God.. The profundity of this teenager is impressive. In his Hermetic world the life of the wanderer and nature constitute two separate emanations, each of which is divine. They interact and re-enforce one another. Nature brings death and through death new life, a passage that is eternally repeated. Nature goes upon its way of eternal re-incarnation in peace and joy, singing hymns of praise to its creator. But nature alone cannot satisfy the wanderer who can never be content with such a destiny. His inner life cries out for a consummate triumph of the very love experience that begins on earth and in nature, a triumph realized in the wanderer's love of a woman. That love is the great sacrament of the interplay between heaven and earth.

These sonatinas focus first upon the passage through death to new life. The last of these splendid works leaps high above nature into the realm of personal love. Thus the composer celebrates both the unity of the wanderer with nature and also the love that places him in a realm yet more sublime.

Sonatina Number One D.384 1816

In this first of the three works the wanderer relishes his higher consciousness of the spiritual ascent inspired by a sunset. The musical setting is of the poem *Abendlied,* written perhaps by Schubert himself. In the first stanza of the poem the sun quietly sets casting a magical spell over the countryside and charming the wanderer.

FIRST MOVEMENT:

Abendlied

Anon D.382

The evening sun casts its soft glow upon this quiet field,
Beaming everywhere its peace and love;
Dewdrops sparkle in the lush grass.
Light and shadow play in the flowery meadow;

SECOND MOVEMENT

In the second stanza of the poem, the sunset is sacred, a special time, a mystical portent. The wanderer shares in the mystery. His spirit awakens to it.

Abendlied

Anon D.382 (continued)

My noblest spirits awaken to the soft breeze and the song of the birds;
I breathe in the joy of this sanctuary of nature;
All pain dissolves in the warm glow of the setting sun.

THIRD MOVEMENT

In the third stanza of the poem the night song of the day's end reaches beyond itself to a divine architect and the wanderer's spirit opens to the divine inviter. The movement through life and through death to its glorious conclusion is one of peace and beauty, both in nature and in the life of the wanderer. Just as nature must endure the night in order to reach the dawn so must the wanderer pass through death in order to reach eternal life.

Abendlied

Anon D.382 (continued)

You are the divine Architect of this evening paradise!
You are the composer of this glorious night song!
In thanksgiving I dedicate my heart to you.
Joyfully it will beat 'til the day that life departs!

Sonatina Number Two D.385 1816

Once again the world of Nature is united with the world of the inner life. Night is crowned by the dawn. The wanderer sings his morning song. Associated are the call of nature to rise to the new day and the divine call to the wanderer to pass through death to eternal life. This theme of passage remains with Schubert throughout his life as the backbone of his creativity. The invitation to the wanderer is to a higher and better life, a new dawn of the spirit.

Dawn is the incarnation of an awakening to divine life and joy. The focus is first upon nature but then changes to the divine invitation to eternal life.

FIRST MOVEMENT:

Morgenlied

Anon. D.381 2-1816

The freshly blooming fields sing their thanks to God;
Oh Father of Nature let my spirit be one with theirs!
You give joy to the wise;
This wisdom is my goal!
I sing your praise with delight!
When I am called to the better world
A new dawn will break
And I will rise to eternal life!

SECOND MOVEMENT

Nature is the wanderer's guide. Both Nature and the wanderer are called. Although the invitations differ, Nature is the wanderer's faithful instructor, leading him to thoughts of transience and eternity.

An Die Natur

Freidrich Leopold zu Stolberg-Stolberg D.372 1-1816

Nature, so precious and sacred! I will follow you!
Lead me like a child!
When I tire I am refreshed at your breast;
Like a suckling child I experience there the joy of heaven!

I am one with you, faithful in love;
Take me with you, oh sacred nature!

THIRD MOVEMENT

The wanderer is aware of the call to ascend and he is eager to respond. Life is an exile. He is far from home, an alien in a strange land. He longs for the new age and deliverance.

Klage

Anon. D.371 1-1816

Sadness enshrouds my life;
My efforts come to nothing;
Slowly, laboriously, fearfully my life goes on.
I can bear it no longer!

Pain and guilt tear at my heart.
No soft breezes soften my dread of what is coming,
I can bear it no longer!

FOURTH MOVEMENT

The wanderer's despair is relieved by the dawning of all his hopes in the awareness of divine invitation. The sun will rise upon his life. He will pass through the night of death to the definitive new dawn. His soul, so tragically separated from its true homeland, will be healed. Eternal life will crown his long journey.

Klage
Anon D.371 1-1816
Only through death will I find my joy.
On that day the gates will open
And I shall be healed!

Sonatina Number Three D.408 1816

In the sweet mystery of love the wanderer finds his joy. Heaven calls him through his Beloved. How different is his destiny from that of the swan, yet how much the same!

FIRST MOVEMENT

Nature moves in peace through life towards the grave. All beauty must die.

Abschied von der Harfe
Johann Gaudenz von Salis-Seewis D.406 3-1816
Sing, oh Harp, again in the language of the heart;
Sweetly become mellow singing the song of the swan,
Peaceful as life moves relentlessly towards death.

How brightly you sang when life was young;
But such music cannot last;
As we labor and struggle that brightness must slowly fade.

SECOND MOVEMENT

Suddenly we ascend into a higher world, a world of love. The death and resurrection of nature is but a shadow of the death and resurrection of the wanderer. For him life is a romance. And the Beloved is not made incarnate through a field or a flower but through a woman.

Sprache der Liebe
August Wilhelm von Schlegel D.410 4-1816
Sweet Lute, gently I touch you;
Dewdrops form as we whisper our love;
Your song grows, sighs, and laments...
As my heart seeks its beloved,
Telling her soulfully of its longing.
Love speaks through the song.

THIRD MOVEMENT

The Beloved makes heaven incarnate. Nothing compares to her. The wanderer knows that this love is triumphant.

Stimme der Liebe
Freidrich Leopold zu Stolberg-Stolberg D.412 4-1816
My Selinda! The voice of your love is angelic!
You are mine! You are mine!
Heaven and earth are no more!
Tears of love quiver on pale cheeks,
Falling as tears of joy!
Heaven proclaims: she is mine!

FOURTH MOVEMENT

In the drama of life, the great romance, love is triumphant. The wanderer celebrates the victory. In this girl heaven transfigures the earth!

Entzuckung
Friedrich von Matthisson D413 4-1816
Oh day of heavenly joy!
The sacred rapture of love dazes my soul
In the mystery of Laura's eyes!
Her magic intoxicates me;
I fall to her trembling breast
With passionate kisses!

Every cloud is lines with gold;
Every leaf whispers: she is yours forever!
So blessed on earth I could not be happier in paradise.

Oh day of heavenly joy!
The sacred rapture of love dazes my soul
In the mystery of Laura's eyes!

Symphony No. 4, in C minor, D.417

April 1816

The impatient sensuality of the *Third Symphony* is now challenged. It is still here, but for some reason this wanderer questions its future with more obvious concern. The spiritual ascent is governed by a dream maiden in whom are all the splendors of divine life. She is Theresa Grob. She is nature. She is the girl whose eyes beguile the wanderer so graphically in the second movement. For him she is the image of God. And she is beyond his reach. The contradiction underlying this symphony is between the yearning for the dream maiden and the impossibility of having her. The *Fourth Symphony* grapples with the perplexing impact of the mystery upon the life of this wanderer. The mystery takes the form of the eternal feminine, the immortal beloved. Yet it must become incarnate. Without the incarnation the wanderer is lost. This poses a question that will haunt the wanderer throughout his life. Can he be true to the transcendental dream maiden and still enjoy her incarnation? The answer for him will be no. He will not always be satisfied with his answer. This wanderer's higher consciousness will be a paradoxical harmony of love's painful yearning and a fate that separates the lover from the beloved, perhaps through his own free choice. The beloved will shine only as a distant star above the wanderer's life.

Here the wanderer is enraptured, fascinated, beguiled, bewitched by a girl who brings heaven to earth. She is a goddess precisely in her feminine allure, making divine invitation incarnate. In the magic of her eyes is his eternal destiny. Yet strangely, ominously, mysteriously this heaven on earth is threatened. The yearning for celestial joy in this life is to be painfully frustrated yet somehow remain as the stepping-stone to eternal joy. The transcendental dream maiden is betrayed by the transience of her incarnations. The wanderer knows that, even as the pain starts.

What in Schubert's own life occasioned these thoughts and fears we can only guess. 1816 was a fateful year. In September he was rejected for a music post and the income necessary for marriage. Did he anticipate this rejection, or were there other reasons for his inner turmoil? Certainly in earlier works throughout 1815 and 1816 the themes of the separation between the dream maiden and the wanderer was sounded. Schubert's rejection for the music post perhaps confirmed a dread that this separation from the dream maiden was to be his painful lot. That theme is pursued relentlessly later in his life, as, for example, in the song cycle *Die Winterreise*. Now in the summer of 1816, as marriage seems like a possibility, this Wanderer fears that this joy, so ardently desired, will not be his. Whatever the reason, it was not that he did not love Theresa. It is precisely his love for the woman who made incarnate the dream maiden that guarantees his misery. The *Fourth Symphony* is a celebration of earthly love that makes divine love incarnate, but with shattering transience and the promise of tragedy.

FIRST MOVEMENT:

Onward, dear heart, into the endless abyss of all charming things!
— *Henry Suso*

The wanderer has been set afire by love, entering a new and higher existence, enjoying a new and higher consciousness. His "enchantress" makes present a better world. Her magic brings him to a pinnacle from which he plunges into an abyss of pain. Her beauty, her innocence, her charm are strangely threatening. She is an angel, a heavenly presence in his life, and it is precisely this heaven that causes agony. Will she be his?

Julius an Theone
Friedrich von Matthisson, D.419
I must conceal from you, enchantress,
The mystical rapture that filled my heart
Since that first gentle touch of your hand.
My sighs of love are for naught!
My tears go unnoticed…
Though they will fall for you
Until I go to my grave!

You had the innocence of an angel
As you looked into my eyes.
You knew nothing of the power of your own beauty!
Oh Theone!
In that moment could you not detect the anxiety in my eyes?
Did my flushed cheeks not betray my lost peace, my despair?
If only an ocean had separated us after that first touch of your hand!

But I now stand dazed above an abyss...
In that dark valley is a bed of thorns, an unmercifully hopeless love,
Arrayed in diamond-spangled beauty waiting to seize me!
Sweet enemy of my peace, give me the chalice of oblivion!

SECOND MOVEMENT

You disclose in nature as in art the Font from which flows everything desirable!

— *Nicholas of Cusa*

The spirit of love leads the wanderer in his spiritual ascent. He senses this spirit in the magic of the night, the peace of the sea, the loveliness of spring, but, above all, in the girl he loves, especially in the mystery and the magic of her eyes. He is a brother to nature, entranced by its beauty. But the girl speaks directly to his yearning heart and calls him home.

Geist der Liebe
Friedrich von Matthisson, D.414
Evening shrouds flowers and fields
With its gentle, loving veil of dusk.
High above the star, the Queen of Love,
Shines through the gold-laced clouds.

The waves sing their slumber song.
The trees chant their vespers.
The grass in the meadow is brushed
With the kiss of the Spring breeze.

Spirit of Love! Lead me to my beloved.
One inviting look from her eyes
Makes heavenly radiance incarnate!

THIRD MOVEMENT:

You inspire holy yearning!

— *Nicholas of Cusa*

Having met the girl the wanderer finds no peace in nature nor in his inner life. The sun of the outer world gives a light that is necessary to satisfy him. The night lights, suggesting his inner life, no longer satisfy. And without this girl they are incapable of ever doing so.

Klage
Friedrich von Matthisson, D.415
The sun rises and sets;
The moon sends its beams to earth
Amid the pale sparkle of dancing stars.
Ah! The sun is too bright!
The moon's peace, the star's glory,
So quiet, so clean,
Cannot satisfy my longing!

The lush meadow, the green bushes,
Echo with songs of spring;
The brook rushes on at sunset,
Ever downwards towards the valley.
But the treetop serenade,
The flowered fields,
The running brook at sunset
Cannot make me happy, as once they could.

FOURTH MOVEMENT:

I am life, whole and entire, not struck from stones!
— *Hildegard of Bingen*

The coach of life is too slow for the eager wanderer. He is living a drama. By panting and pulling he will do it successfully. He takes time out for a romantic dalliance, but awaits impatiently the time when his carriage will plunge finally through the gateway to the afterworld, his final destiny. Life invites somehow through death. Freedom is conditioned upon a relishing of the whole adventure.

An Schwager Kronos
Johann Wolfgang von Goethe, D.369
Get a move on you, Time!
Draw my coach at a faster pace!
The road is hilly.
I am sick and tired
Of your laziness!
Smooth road or rough, get on,
Over rocks and stones...
Rush headlong into life!

Don't delay! Go ahead! Ever upwards!
Work your way towards the peak!
Striving, hoping, go on!

Wide, high and noble is the vision
Of life here at the peak.
From mountain to mountain
Hovers the spirit of the gods,
Foreshadowing eternal life!

There to one side is a little cottage.
Its roof draws you toward it.
At the door is a young girl
With saucy look, offering refreshment.
Enjoy it! Give me some of that delight, my girl!
Your sparkling wine,
Your fresh and buxom glance!

Away now, down the hill yet faster!
Look, the sun is already sinking!
And before it does, before old age
Steals me into the fog of the moor;
Before my gums are toothless,
Before my limbs begin to shake
Draw me, drunk from the last beauty of the setting sun,
With crimson fire still in my eyes,
Staggering and dazed,
Down through the dark door to the other world!
Coachman, sound your horn!
Let the pounding hooves thunder!
Let Orkus know it: I am coming!
And let him prepare to make me welcome!

Piece for Violin and Strings, D.438

May or June 1816

In this magical work the romance between the wanderer and his dream maiden is given a unique setting in the form of a fantasy. Each of Schubert's major instrumental works can be thought of as a tone poem celebrating the mystery of divine invitation in a concrete earthly setting. But one of his most personalized expressions of this mystery occurs in the form of fantasies. In them the link between the inspiring poem and the music is immediate, direct. There is little or no effort to respect the sonata form. There is the effort to musically tell a love story, a story that is invariably linked closely to events in the composer's life that find expression in the inspiring poetry.

In the month of May, 1816, Schubert set several poems by Ludwig Hölty expressive of the wanderer's commitment to his beloved. She is at once a dream maiden and obviously someone quite concrete for the composer. There is no trace of melancholy, little suggestion that the love is threatened, simply a joyful, profound, "eternal" commitment. Five poems are set in the key of E Major. At about the same time Schubert composed an instrumental work which seems to spring directly from these same poems. Both the poems and their musical settings present us with an uncomplicated, straightforward celebration of love in its radiant sensual joy, its eternal perspective, clearly inspired by Schubert's love for Theresa Grob. The permanency of the commitment is significant. Setting aside all hesitation the composer here anticipates an eternal bond.

In April, 1816 Schubert had applied for the post of music master in Laibach on the recommendation of his teacher, Antonio Salieri. He was hopeful of getting the position. But on the 7th of September the Civic Guard in Vienna notified him that the position had been assigned to Franz Sokol. This was effectively a denial of the financial conditions requisite for marriage in Austria, because in January of 1815 new laws passed by Metternich's regime made it impossible for young men of Schubert's class to marry without proof of sufficient income to provide for a family.

This work is interesting, not simply because of the joyful music, reflecting the composer's anticipation of both the job and the marriage, but because of the commitment it proclaims. "Forever yours" meant something to this composer, and will continue to do so in future works, even after separation from Theresa. The love will remain throughout Schubert's life and have significance for his art. For at least a time and in certain ways throughout his life Theresa was Schubert's stairway to the stars, his awakening to the higher consciousness. Even after the girl leaves him the wanderer finds in her his dream maiden. His love for her and what she makes incarnate, is his lodestar, the core of his higher wisdom. There are few important instrumental works that do not refer to her in some fashion. She initiates his experience of divine invitation and leads him upwards in its pursuit.

If I might just see my dear one! What must she look like if she has so many delightful things hidden within? Is she divine or human?

Henry Suso

Widerhall
Ludwig Hölty May 1816 ???
Friedrich von Matthisson D.428

I am forever yours…
Even when mountain and lake divide! ??? seas
Even when storms come!
Whether the breeze is gentle or the dessert burns,
I am forever yours.

I am forever yours…
By candle glow,
In the silver moonlight,
In the quiet Alpine valley.

When some day
My life is done,
When I am finally set free,
Even then will these words arise from my dying heart,
I am yours forever!

Minnelied
Ludwig Hölty D.429 May 1816

The birds sing more sweetly
When the girl who conquered me,
Walks like an angel
Through the woods.

The valley and the mountain meadows have redder blossoms,
The woods are still greener
Whenever she picked
The many-colored flowers.

Without her there is no life!
Every blossom wilts!
the spring sunset
Fails to cheer!

Dearest, most loving woman,
Never leave me!
Only with you can my spirit
Blossom like this meadow.

Erntelied
Ludwig Hölty D.434 May 1816
Sickles whine!
The corn falls to the ground,
Prey to their stroke!
Blue ribbons blow
Atop the girls hats…
Joy is everywhere!

Sickles whine!
The girls are singing
To their stroke.
They work til in the moonlight
There is only stubble on the ground.
And songs of harvest are sung!

Everyone jokes;
Everyone caresses
His favorite girl.
Finally, when the wine is gone,
They go home
Full of music and joy!

Seligkeit
Ludwig Hölty D.433 May 1816
Joys beyond counting
Blossom in heaven's halls.
Angels and spirits abound there
As we are taught.

And Oh! That I were there
In eternal happiness!

For each man there smiles
A celestial bride.
Music and prayer resound,
Singing and dancing too.
Oh! I wish I could be there,
Eternally happy!

But if Laura would only look at me,
I'd stay right here!
She'd smile and say,
You have suffered enough!
And I will be happy
Staying right here with her!

Blumenlied
Ludwig Hölty D.431 May 1816
It is half of heaven's treasure
When like the flowers of Eden
May flowers rise from the earth,
And birds sing sweetly…
Here in the garden, there at the spring,
And all through the blossoming woods!

Even more glorious is a noble woman,
Of high spirit and fair!
To the blossoming of her spring
No flower can compare!
Look at that lovely woman!
Does her gentle beauty not enchant you!

Die Frűhe Liebe
Ludwig Hölty D.430 1816
Even when I was a boy I would look at the girls;
I forgot balls and birds and toys
When a special one sat by me;
She thrilled me with her rosy cheeks, her face, her blond hair…
I would look at her clothes…
At her figure as she leaned against a tree,
And I'd lie close to the hem of her dress.

Symphony No. 5 in B flat major, D.485

September and October, 1816

You who live in Darkness, listen to my song!
fourth movement

Franz Schubert is aware that he is a man with something to say, something to do. He exists to celebrate in art the *magnum mysterium* that gives life its meaning. He proclaims the coming of a new age, the dawning of a higher life. He celebrates this good news again and again. That good news co-exists with his own death and with the sorrow of separation from the one he loves. The "wild fire" of sexual yearning that has been prominent in the Third and Fourth Symphonies must be controlled. In this *Fifth Symphony* the sensual girl who inspired this wanderer is a pain-tinged memory, only a Platonic companion now. The tension between the yearning for what he cannot have and the spiritual ascent is a central theme for Schubert. They can contradict one another. Or, as here, they can be united in paradoxical harmony. Springtime, love, and life first are celebrated, then contradicted in the life of the wanderer. Here the contradiction is resolved in transcendental hope. Love is not rejected; it becomes radically expanded in its expectations. The divine spark in nature foreshadows the divine spark in human life, the higher consciousness.

The invitation to ascend to a higher life, a new age, underlies the human experience. And yet that experience leads to tragedy. Paradoxically it is only through death that we definitively become what we are meant to be. The Divine Light-Source illuminates diverse emanations, each one reflecting the Source in its own unique fashion. The universe is a cosmic drama consisting of an infinite number of mini-dramas, each a light pursuit, each an emergence in its own way from darkness.

In this symphony, Schubert celebrates the life-giving touch between the well-spring of life and the wanderer. The effect is electrifying. Worlds are grasped at the point that becoming is most meaningful. They touch one another and share the meaning and beauty of their separate dramas. Something new and more wonderful is born. Schubert here is the master magician, carrying on consciously, deliberately, brilliantly the emanation process that fills the universe with divine light and beauty.

With this symphony, composed just five months after the *Fourth Symphony*, Orpheus, the incarnation of Spring, is a life-bringer, a redeemer, a Christ-figure. Divine light pours into the world through this hero, bringing radiant new life to all of nature. In response tthe earth rises up, becoming itself an incarnation of divine light, sparkling in beauty, singing the praises of the source of this wonder, the font of its life and joy.

Christian and Jewish mysteries unite as the second movement moves from nature's romance with life to that of the wanderer's very personal divine invitation. Just as the sun brings divine life to the earth, so does divine invitation bring life to this wanderer. The earth is brought to its perfection each year but the wanderer walks a longer path. His adventure leads him quite personally through death before finally resolving in a triumph of light and life. But there is security for the wanderer in this harrowing ascent. This psalm setting creates a wisdom-inspired, Sophia-like prayer in which the wanderer faces his task with peace and trust.

In the third movement, *Die Liebesgötter* is a poetic vision of transcendental triumph. The music is shaded with mystery, alive with joy, imaginatively anticipating the satisfaction of the wanderer' longing.

In the final movement the wanderer makes a heroic commitment to the trek. The "wild fire" that has been consuming him must be controlled. He realizes that his call leads beyond every earthly dream and through the fearsome mystery of death. The inspiring poem is *Orpheus*. Our wanderer must counterbalance sensuality with something that at first seems incompatible: the divine invitation to sing a life song celebrating the ascent to a better world. The fire that must be controlled is earth's power both to inspire the spiritual ascent and to entrap the soul.

FIRST MOVEMENT:

Hark! My beloved! Here he comes!
— Song of Songs

The wanderer finds in Spring an analogue of the mystery, a divine force that brings nature to its long-awaited triumph of love. Here in terms of flower and bush, of woods and birds is the archetypical drama of redemption. We begin this symphony with a celebration of earth's transfiguration through the touch of divine life.

Gott im Frühling
Johann Peter Uz, D.448
In shimmering beauty, oh Lord,
You give us the gift of Spring!
You garland his head with roses!
And here he comes in joy!
He sits upon his throne of flowers attended by his subjects.

He visits the bushes and they sprout flowers;
Green returns to the meadows.
Shadows once again invade the woods,
And the west wind spreads its dewy wings
In whispered love!
Birds everywhere sing their joyous melodies!

Little birds, my song together with yours
Will fly sweetly up to the Father of nature.
My heart is full of joy!
I must sing the praise of the Lord
Though whose power, I exist!

SECOND MOVEMENT:

He walks ahead of them, and the sheep follow him because they recognize his voice.

Gospel of John

At the root of the mystery is divine invitation. The wanderer, awakened to his own inner life, reflects upon the constant presence of the divine inviter in the "great romance" of life. This invitation gives direction, strength, and comfort. The wanderer responds with praise and thanks.

Der gute Hirt
Johann Peter Uz, D.449
Soul of mine, why are you troubled?
The Lord is indeed a good shepherd.
He loves me as I am;
And denies me nothing.

He nourishes me in flowered meadows,
And leads me to clear waters!
In the dew-cooled twilight
He gives me peace and rest.

He lovingly protects me from the day's heat,
Sheltering me from storms and the black fury of the human heart;
And whether we enter the dark valley or parched desert,
I fear nothing for beside me is the true shepherd.

I praise him and thank him,
And will be faithful forever;
Trusting him though others turn away!

THIRD MOVEMENT:

Heavenly Aphrodite, you control all in heaven and on earth!
— *Orphic Hymn*

With fanciful anticipation the wanderer looks forward to the completion of his dramatic romance, the goal of his every erotic desire, when his beloved will grace a higher existence and love will reign.

Die Liebesgotter
Johann Peter Uz, D.446
Venus, looking like my Phyllis,
Reclines in the company of the Graces!
I saw that godly kingdom!
There was a grove of Myrtle,
Mysterious and holy in its dark shadows,
Where the goddess lay and the cupids played.
In that dark green grove,
Under a roof of leaves and twigs,
The nymphs rejoiced in freedom.
They gathered in goodly number,
Guiltless, without care,
Flying here and there
Between blonds and brunettes.

FOURTH MOVEMENT:

It is necessary for the All to ascend to Him and for each one to receive what is his own!
— *Gospel of Truth*

The tendency to imprison dreams and to narrowly define the absolute is a hungry fire that must be controlled. This fire is idolatry, replacing the mystery with an idea. The wanderer must break free of earths chains to experience the freedom of the higher consciousness. He must mount the pathway to the stars. The Wanderer has no doubt that he is the master of this fire, and that his divinely ordained task of bringing divine light to earth and realizing it within his own life will be accomplished. The call is bitter-sweet. Breaking the chains is painful, demanding sacrifices and leading to death. Here is the invitation to transcend this earth, to come home to the love that has illuminated his life in the past and promises more in the future. There is urgency, the taste of future victory. The homecoming has already begun, yet its consummation lies beyond the grave.

Orpheus
Johann Georg Jacobi, D.474
Get back, hungry fire!
The strings of my lute were made by God himself…
The very one who judges the monsters of the deep and Hell itself!
These strings were tuned by his right hand.
So begone, spirit of evil, begone!
And you, pitiable ones who live in darkness,
Listen as I sing!
I am called away from this earth
Of bright sun and silent moon,
Of freshly bedewed meadows,
Of song-filled pastures.
I am called away from the land of man,
Where the skies once smiled down upon you…
Ah, I am drawn by sweet threads of love…back to you!

My pain is one with your own.
Life's bloom is gone, but memory remains…
Think back to that time of joy!
If ever you reached to one in pain,
Do it now, again!
Your compassion can transform this long agony.
You weep, bringing hope to this darkness!
The gods who are good will not punish for ever.
They created this earth for you,
And out of your dark night of pain
Will call you into the sacred fields of heaven
Where beauty smiles amid the roses.

ADAGIO AND RONDO CONCERTANTE, D.487

October 1816

The wanderer and his dream maiden are wed...but tragically separated. In another fantasy Schubert celebrates in an intensely personal way the ascent to a consciousness of the mystery made possible by transcendental hope. Just as in the *Piece for Violin and Strings* composed in May, 1816 there is an assemblage of inspiring poems, all set as Lieder at about the same time, and all obviously inspired by Schubert's love for Theresa Grob. In each there is a lead instrument that sings the song of the Wanderer. Yet there is a difference. In May there was no separation; now in October separation is inevitable. This second fantasy finds the peace and joy of the mystery by rising above the agony caused by the absence of the Beloved.

The poems inspiring this later love fantasy are all by Jacobi. With one exception, they were set by Schubert as Lieder in August, before the shattering news that the composer was refused the job he sought, and thus denied the possibility for a legal marriage. The exception, *Orpheus*, was set in September. Like the Hölty settings, there is a counterbalance between transcendence and imminence, between heaven and earth. Yet Jacobi's *Orpheus* radically changes the principle focus from earth to heaven. Tragedy is an inescapable presence. While there is a spirit of joyful hope, that hope relates not to prospects for an earthly union, but to an eventual transcendence of earthly pain, a hope that is apparently shared by the lovers.

Here is a clear instance of what Schiller called the sublime disposition, the ability to be at peace in the face of tragic loss. At its core is the paradoxical nature of the human experience, consisting of two interpenetrating worlds which affect one another in ways that transcend and often defy logic. This is inexplicable except by reference to a vision of reality that includes but transcends this earth. This triumph of the sublime disposition over the logical implications of events in the lower world will remain a principle characteristic of Schubert's art.

Since this work was intended for presentation at the Grob home it was especially important to Schubert that he conceal the intensity of his love and pain. He does this not by falsifying experience, but by transfiguring it through its incorporation in the larger romance between the soul and God. The poem *Orpheus* suggests that the decision to separate is somehow related to a mutual commitment by the lovers to the composer's music. The inspiring poems are:

***Hochzeitlied* D.463 Johann Georg Jacobi August 1816**
***In der Mitternacht* D.464 Johann Georg Jacobi August 1816**
***An Chloen* D.462 Johann Georg Jacobi August 1816**
***Trauer der Liebe* D.465 Johann Georg Jacobi August 1816**
***Die Perle* D.466 Johann Georg Jacobi August 1816**
***Orpheus* D.473b Johann Georg Jacobi September 1816**

Still more sweetly he plays, still more beauty he reveals,
That his pain might be cloaked in gentle melodies.
Johann Mayrhofer D.473 (September 1816)

Hochzeitlied

I will sing you an old song,
One of love and fidelity.
One our ancestors sang,
But, like love, is ever fresh!
Its message in good times gives joy,
Comforts when times are evil:
Nothing, nothing can separate loving hearts,
Nothing 'til death!

In der Mitternacht

The valley is deathly still,
Shrouded in the weak light of the moon!
The shuddering winds sing their sad night song.
A softer song echoes in my anxious heart,
Stealing my hope as the cloud steals the moonbeams.
I must not name my beloved,
Must not by tears betray!

One day that beloved will be laid to rest,
Deep in a grave beside me!

An Chloen

With the pure flame of love
The small cottage shines!
beloved! Forever one!
Dreaming! Awake!
We share every experience,
Sun, moon, stars,
Joy, suffering,
Work, prayer, celebration!
Yes, in the radiance of love,
The Wanderer's course is complete!
Peacefully we ascend together,
Beloved, the pathway beyond the stars.

Trauer der Liebe

Where the doves in still branches unite;
Where nightingales find their love;
Where grapevines join and brooks meet,
I sometimes wander with a happy heart;
Yet at times with tears of longing,
I seek my own beloved.
Ah, what comfort in the dark woods
At the golden hour of sunset!

…

I hear the invitation in the whisper of the wind,
I must seek until I find you, Beloved!
But love, where on earth can you be?
True love is heavenly, angelic!
On earth I find pain,
As I seek for what betrays me.
Peace for lovers lies beyond the grave!

Die Perle

A wanderer set out on the glory of Spring,
Through forest and field, far and wide,
Past birch and bush and alders,
All glowing green in the light of May,
All with flowers beneath them,
Yet none did he see,
For he sought a pearl!
How sad for this wanderer!
I, like him, make my journey through Spring,

Past birch and bush and alders.
The wonders of May I cannot see;
Yet what I crave is more than just a pearl!

Orpheus

Roll back, wild fire!
My music is divine!
A spark of One with whom every monster,
And even Hell itself must be reconciled!
These strings were tuned by his hand,
So, Evil Ones, away!
And you, prisoners of the night,
Awaken to my song!

Away from this earth of bright sun and silent moon,
Of dewed moss and singing meadows,
Away from man's earth and smiling skies,
I am drawn by gentle ties of love.
My song and yours commingle;
Not on this earth is our joy!
Remember then what we have known!
As before you embraced this poor wanderer,
Do it now again!
In the magic moment my long Hell will be eased!
Yes, you are weeping. In the tears is my hope!
The gods do not demand eternal suffering!
They created the earth for us,
And, out of the darkest night,
Call us to the Elysian fields,
Where eternal love blooms amidst the roses!

Piano Sonata in E flat major, D.568

After June 1817

The higher consciousness of the mystery is realized through a layering of experiences, each making the other more intense. Here the wanderer discovers heavenly beauty both in nature and in a woman who sadly must depart. Nature is transfigured as is his love for "Laura" (yet another incarnation of Sophia). And everything is elevated through music. This sonata starts with nature in its beauty. The fresh May day is reflected in the opening movement, so captivating and faithful to the experience. Then the attention is expanded to embrace human love. In this case the love is mystical but potent. The beloved is a spiritual presence leading the wanderer towards his final goal. In "real life" the lover has departed. In mystical life she lives as a spiritual shadow that from time to time seems a presence. The sonata concludes with a rhapsodic tribute to Laura, (probably an idealized Theresa Grob), the wanderer's guide to the homeland where love reigns triumphant.

FIRST MOVEMENT:

Wisdom penetrates and pervades all things by reason of her purity.
Book of Wisdom

The wanderer sings of his intoxication with nature where the mystery finds unique expression. There is Sophia's providence for her children and the ascent towards the creator. The spontaneous response is a rhapsody of praise for this wondrous deity from whom proceeds such beauty and life.

Lied im Freien
Johann Gaudenz von Salis-Seewis, D.572

How beautiful is nature
In the freshness of May!
How beautiful are the woods!
It is a joy to drink in the sun,
Away from the town,
Here on this fragrant hillside.

There under the hedge
Golden sunbeams play
With the shadows.
And here a man can relax,
Refreshed by the perfume
Of hazel and elderberry.

Walk a little further…
Pick up a twig, a flower,
Or perhaps a strawberry along the way.
If you are warm after the climb
Use the leaves
As a fan.

In the brook
The ripplets rise and fall,
Sparkling in the sun.
You can watch them disappear,
Nodding and drowsy,
In peaceful reverie.

Der Strom
Franz Schubert ? D.565

The quiet valley, the green meadows are alive in quiet peace;
They sigh for perfect tranquility and exult in life's beauty!

But I never find what I seek, driving beyond every achievement,
Angry, turbulent, never satisfied, never at peace.

My life fiercely rushes ahead, rising and falling in waves,
Now joyful, now despairing in high arches and wild excitement.

SECOND MOVEMENT:

Heavenly stars, you determine the divine path!
— Orphic Hymn

The wanderer turns from nature to the woman who transforms his life. Through her the mystery has become real. In her eyes is the incarnation of heavenly power. There he finds his destiny and his guide. Those eyes reveal a goddess. They are divine invitation.

Augenlied
Johann Mayrhofer, D.297
Gentle eyes, pure springs,
My pain and my joy are truly in you!
Where I stop, Where I go
Your loving smile brightens my way
Bedewing it with tears.

Faithful stars, shine on!
Lead me to Achereon,
And with your last light
Let my life depart!

THIRD MOVEMENT:

My desire, wherein you shine forth, leads me to you.
Nicholas of Cusa

Life in this exile often betrays the mystery. It does so here. "Farewell" is the lamentation that the wanderer sings. The one he loves leaves, yet the friendship remains; the love continues. The bond between the wanderer and the one who is so loved is mystical, painful yet beautiful. That beloved is at once the meaning of the wanderer's life yet absent from it.

Abscheid
Franz Schubert, D.578
Farewell, my dear friend!
You go to a distant land.
Take with you my true friendship.
Hold it in hands that are faithful.
Farewell, my dear friend!

Farewell, my dear friend!
As you remember this song
My spirit will be close to you,
Like a breeze passing over the strings of your heart.
Now, farewell my dear friend!

FOURTH MOVEMENT:

She is a pure effusion of the glory of God!

Book of Wisdom

Laura was the inspiration for Petrarch's art and yet an absent beloved, a Platonic love, a goal unavailable in this life. Schubert's wanderer has been elevated to a higher life by his beloved, suggesting that the composer's life was similarly enhanced by Theresa Grob. She too was removed, a Platonic love, unavailable to him in this life. Here the splendor of what she meant to him is apparent in music. Here her image liberates the wanderer from the prison of earth and nature. May becomes eternal life and youth in her eyes. Deep, deep into those eyes the wanderer looks and thereby finds a new world, his true homeland. Melodies from there enrapture him.

Die Entzuckung an Laura
Friedrich Schiller, D.577

Laura, when your shining eyes meet mine,
I rise to a better world,
Immersed in everlasting May
When I see my reflection in your blue eyes.

I seem to hear music from a distant Paradise,
Harps sounding from a better star;
The idyllic hour is at hand
When silver notes rise
From your from your sweet lips!

Cupids fly! The trees are given life by your voice!
When you dance, fluid and whirling like a brook,
The stars and galaxies spin in their own dance above my head!

Your eyes, sweetly suggesting love,
Might coax statues to speak,
And bring hard granite to hot life.
Dreams become real,
When I see love in your eyes,
Laura, my Laura!

Piano Sonata in F sharp minor, D.571

July 1817

Different life moments lead to a rich experience of the paradoxical mystery. This sonata is fantasy-like in its awkward depiction of life stages. It is more like a set of impromptus than a piano sonata. But there is unity here. Schubert tells the story of a love ascent towards the divine source of all emanations. The Gnostic-Christian myth that had meaning for him identifies man as God's emanation, sharing in divine creative powers with eternal life as his birthright. Anthropos, a noble creature-creator, leaned down through the spheres toward divinely beautiful nature and fell in love with her. To rescue her from death Anthropos voluntarily took on the burdens of sorrow and mortality. He became a wanderer, a divine spark alien to darkness and death, yet trapped in them with his beloved. His destiny is to return together with her to the original kingdom of light.

In this myth life is a love adventure between a Christ figure (Anthropos) and an image of God in creation (Sophia). Like them we first find ourselves in darkness, then awaken to the divine invitation incarnate in and through the other and, thus empowered, rise painfully, laboriously, heroically towards the light.

The *Piano Sonata in F Sharp Minor* is a celebration of this life-giving mystery that illuminates the separate stages of this great drama. In the first movement we find a cradle song, rich in the warm, maternal love celebrated in Ottenwalt's poem. Schubert's thought here is no mere depiction of mother and child, but rather of primordial bliss, the state of love, which establishes our inner demand for fulfillment, and to which we, enriched by life, shall return. The beauty here is a memory, tinged in melancholy, for the wanderer is far from his homeland of love. Yet the feminine character of its goodness dwells within the wanderer, reminding him of his true goal, the homeland that he seeks.

The second movement continues in this meditative mood. *Erlafsee* inspires the contemplation of nature with its intimations of death. Mystery fills the world around the wanderer, and the mystery suggests a movement from life through death towards that distant homeland.

The Third and Fourth Movements are settings of *Elysium*, a poem that inspires a number of Schubert's instrumental works from this period. Darkness is overcome by the divine light. In the triumph death is transformed from a horror into the passage to dream fulfillment. Just as nature integrates death into its organic wholeness, so too does the human experience not only include death, but realizes through it its transcendence of things earthly and the triumphant return to the homeland of love.

FIRST MOVEMENT:

What a great miracle is Man… He is issued from the race of heavenly spirits!

Corpus Hermeticum

A cradlesong celebrating the mystery! The wanderer's homeward journey in the inner life begins by looking back to an original Eden, where love reigned supreme. The music faithfully follows the mother, her anxious longing, her joy in her child, her protective concern, the meeting of worlds as the eyes of the mother share their inner life with the child. Here the eternal feminine is both source and goal of the infant's longing. In the touch between her inner life and his own the child-wanderer has an overpowering experience of a better world.

Der Knabe in der Wiege
Anton Ottenwalt, D.579

Peacefully the infant sleeps.
The mother follows every breath;
With anxious longing she carried the child
Beneath her own heart.

In joy she notes the glow of his cheeks,
His yellow hair;
And gently she covers the arm
Stretched out in sleep.

Still more gently she rocks the cradle
Softly singing to the sleeping child;
Contentedly he smiles, his eyes serenely closed.
When you awake, look into your mother's eyes
and revel in pure love,
Guarding you in your weakness.

SECOND MOVEMENT:

Nature…of her I am born; her I follow. She knows me, and I know her. The light which is in her I have beheld in her…

Paracelsus

The wanderer looks out upon Erlafsee, the peace of the pine trees and the blue, smooth lake. Like the lake he is brought to life by the shimmering golden spear of divine invitation. Divine invitation transfigures his life and ours.

Erlafsee
Johann Mayrhofer, D.586
My heart is so full, yet so melancholy
On peaceful Erlafsee.
Sacred silence reigns
Among the pines.
Still and smooth
Is the blue bosom of the lake.
Only cloud shadows
Pass over
The dark mirror.
Fresh breezes
Gently ruffle
The waters,
And the golden spear
Of the sun
Shimmers palely upon the waves.

THIRD MOVEMENT:

Turn to me and be safe, all you ends of the earth!

Isaiah

The invitation is to eternal life, the triumph of love.

Elysium
Friedrich Schiller, D.584
The time for sorrow is done.
The joys of heaven
Drown every pain.
Heavens' life is
Eternal joy, eternal freedom
By the gentle brook in the lush meadows.

FOURTH MOVEMENT:

We trusted your voice and joyfully entered into the new land!
Franz Grillparzer

The wanderer is intoxicated by an imaginative vision of the eternal triumph of his love.

Elysium
Friedrich Schiller, D.584
The world is young and joyful,
And bedecking every field
Is eternal may.
The hours pass by in golden dreams,
the spirit reaches into endless space,
Here truth rips aside every veil.

Unending joy
Inflames the heart.
Anguish and pain do not exist.
Mild delight is called sorrow.

Here the wanderer rests his body
In the cool shade.
He surrenders for ever his life-long burden.
The scythe drops away from the hand of Death…
And Death sleeps to the soft music of a harp,
Dreaming of gathering hay.

The mighty warrior,
Used to the raucous sounds of death,
Under whose boot even mountains trembled,
Sleeps quietly by the running brook, which
tumbles over silver stones,
The clash of swords is now only a dim memory.

Faithful spouses here embrace
And make love in the sweet green of the meadow,
Gently caressed by westerly breeze.
Here love is queen.
Lovers, safe for ever from death,
Enjoy an eternal wedding feast!

Duo for Piano and Violin in A major, D.574

August 1817

The mystery associates earthly experience with divine invitation. The anticipation of eternal life is strengthened by the wanderer's experience of spring. In this Duo we have another celebration of an ascent through nature to the throne of God. The wisdom that intensifies experience through a harmony of universes sees in nature a prefiguration of man's destiny. In the ascent out of winter darkness and death into spring's radiant new life it envisions the wanderer's passage through death to a higher life. The wanderer lives in a world where transfiguration simply sparkles......in May, in the inner life, and in love.

The first movement begins as an ambling walk through the Vienna Woods. The wanderer's reverie is interrupted briefly with a refection upon the contrast between nature's peace and his own experience of life. This counterpoint between the world of nature and the world of the wanderer, a counterpoint that is fruitful both in similarities and dissonances, will be repeated in the two quintets and in much of the instrumental work for which this composer is famous.

The second and third movements continue the focus upon nature in her luxuriant splendor. The last movement changes the focus to the triumphant completion of the wanderer's search for peace and joy.

FIRST MOVEMENT:

This is the place where you may assuage your sorrows past Here is that joy and bliss that flourished in the antique golden age. Here needs no law...

Tasso

With a slow, rocking gait the wanderer ambles through the glories of May with joy in his heart. There is playfulness in the shadows, and nourishing generosity in the brilliant life of nature. Still the wanderer is aware that his experience is unique,

Lied im Freien
Johann Gaudenz von Salis-Seewis, D.572
Beautiful is nature,
In the freshness of May!
How beautiful are the woods!
It is a joy to drink in the sun,
Away from the town,
Here on this fragrant hillside.
There under hedge
Golden sunbeams play
With the shadows,
And here a man can relax,
Refreshed by the perfume
Of hazel and elderberry.
Walk a little further…
Pick up a twig, a flower;
Or perhaps a strawberry along the way.
If you are warm after the climb
Use the leaves
As a fan.
In the brook
The ripplets rise and fall,
Sparkling in the sun.
You can watch them disappear;Nodding and drowsy,
In peaceful reverie.

Der Strom
Franz Schubert ? D.565
The quiet valley, the green meadows are alive in quiet peace;
They sigh for perfect tranquility and exult in life's beauty!

But I never find what I seek, driving beyond every achievement,
Angry, turbulent, never satisfied, never at peace.

My life fiercely rushes ahead, rising and falling in waves,
Now joyful, now despairing in high arches and wild excitement.

SECOND MOVEMENT:

What came to be through Him was life.
Gospel of John

The wanderer unites with nature in her ascent to the Divine Architect of this Spring paradise.

Die Erde
Friedrich von Matthisson, D.579
How Enraptured my eyes and my heart,
When our beautiful world blossoms in Spring!
And when all earth's children
Draw sacred life from her full breasts!
Ah, how she loves each of her offspring,
So anxious to share her life,
So ready to impart her strength,
To spark and nourish health and growth!
My intoxicated heart is drawn
To adore, to sing his praises,
Whose life and goodness
Sparkles so throughout the universe!

THIRD MOVEMENT:

The darkness is passing away and the true light is already shining!
First Epistle of John

Peace reigns in the splendor of the pure air. The darkened valley is bathed in crimson light, and birds sing their songs of life. Reconciliation in nature is realized in this gentle music. Reconciliation in the life of the wanderer, healing all wounds, is the deeper truth that sets his spirit free.

Nach einem Gewitter
Johann Mayrhofer, D.565
On the flowers pearls are aglitter,
Philomele's plaintive song ascends,
With more courage now dark alders
Shoot up into the cleansed air.
To the sun-forsaken valley
Gentle redness now returns;
Birds bathe amid fragrant blossoms.

Once the heart has ended storming
The god lays his warrior's bow aside
And his golden countenance radiates waves of peace.

FOURTH MOVEMENT:

Oh such great teaching! He draws himself down to death…He put on imperishability which no one can possibly take from him!
Gospel of Truth

The scene is paradise, the better world. The wanderer is freed from the agonies of his long journey. Death, once his fearsome enemy, is now a friend.

Elysium
Friedrich Schiller, D.584
The time for sorrow is done.
The joys of heaven
Drown every pain.
Heavens' life is
Eternal joy, eternal freedom
By the gentle brook in the lush meadows.

The world is young and joyful,
And bedecking every field is eternal May.
The hours pass by in golden dreams.
The spirit reaches into endless space,
Here truth rips aside every veil.

Unending joy
Inflames the heart.
Anguish and pain to not exist.
Mild delight is called sorrow.

The mighty warrior,
Used to the raucous sounds of death,
Under whose boot even mountains trembled,
Sleeps quietly by the running brook, which
Tumbles over silver stones,
The clash of swords is now only a dim memory.

Piano Sonata in B flat major, D.575

September 1817

The dream maiden takes many forms. Always she is love...in nature and in the life of the wanderer. She is here a loving mother. Sorrow and joy constitute a contradiction that is hard to reconcile. The reconciliation takes place through the merciful invitation of heaven. A symbol of that invitation is Mary, the mother of Jesus. She is the incarnation of the Divine Sophia, sacred wisdom. Schubert's wisdom initiates him into the romance of Sophia. She is the fullness for which he yearns. She seems to lead him into accepting a separation from the woman he loves in order to enjoy a more intense artistic commitment to his life as a Magus, bridging the chasm between heaven and earth. The immortal beloved, the eternal feminine, who is incarnate presumably in Theresa, has different faces. She guides the wanderer in his long journey and protects him. She attracts him, beguiles him, initiates him into the wonders of the better world. She is mother and lover, hovering above his life, a ready source of help and understanding, yet betraying and tantalizing him by her many absences. In this sonata we are present at the world-tragedy of the crucifixion and then are elevated to a vision of love's triumph when the long journey is over and the eternal wedding has begun.

The first movement expresses the agony of the wanderer who has been denied the joy of this world and must look to a better one. This incarnation of the Divine Sophia, is the Mother of the crucified Christ, a source of hope throughout life's trials.

Abschied inspires the second movement. It suggests the intensity, for Schubert at least, of the spiritual bond between him and Theresa. The request to hold the friendship in faithful hands suggests the composer's understanding that there is danger in that separation. In the second portion of the second movement the poem *Gruppe aus dem Tartarus* expresses the pain experienced by the composer, now separated from Theresa. Schiller's meditation upon the agonies of the group of wanderers is a meditation upon the sorrows of earthly existence. This Gnostic pessimism is counterbalanced by the possibility of emergence through gnosis.

The third and fourth movements, inspired by *Elysium*, are musical realizations of that better world into which the wanderer has been elevated.. That better world mysteriously invites from beyond this life, but simultaneously attracts us to a measure of peace and joy in this world as a function of mystical illumination.

FIRST MOVEMENT:

Woman, behold your son!
Gospel of John

The agitation of the wanderer is shared with a mother who has experienced it herself. The feelings are of fear, suffering, and alienation. The mother of divine wisdom, here, Mary, the mother of Christ, reveals that the wanderer is not alone in his pain.

Gretchens Bitte
Johann Wolfgang von Goethe, D.564
Lean down towards me in my agony,
Oh Lady of Sorrows.
You watched your own son die,
A sword in your heart,
In bitterest pain!
And you, then, looked up to the Father,
And pleaded with heaven
For your son and for yourself.

If anyone can understand the gnawing pain
That eats at my very bones,
Or the terror in my heart,
Its trembling, its yearning,
It is you! Only you!

Wherever I go
My very bosom is torn
In suffering,
I am alone,
I weep bitter tears.
The heart within me is broken!

SECOND MOVEMENT:

Though I walk in the valley of darkness…

Psalm 23

The wanderer bids farewell to the one who brought heaven to earth for him. The parting does not mean the end of the friendship which continues, and mystically unites the lovers. Yet the spirit is sad.

Schubert then musically interprets Schiller's poem describing the seemingly endless journey of the damned as they ask "Will this never end?"

Abschied
Franz Schubert, D.578
Farewell, my dear friend!
You go to a distant land.
Take with you my true friendship.
Hold it in hands that are faithful.
Farewell, my dear friend!

Farewell, my dear friend!
As you remember this song
My spirit will be close to you,
Like a breeze passing over the strings of your heart.
Now, farewell, my dear friend!

Gruppe aus dem Tartarus
Friedrich Schiller, D.583
Listen! Like the rumbling of the mighty ocean,
Like the whine rising from the cascading river,
Comes a low groan out of the depths,
An impassioned, anguished wail!

Their faces are twisted in pain,
Despair and curses their cry,
Vacant their staring eyes,
As they look in terror upon the bridge over Cocytus.
Mournfully they observe their sorrowful journey.
Anxiously they whisper,
Will this never end?
Will this never end?

Eternity towers above their journey…
It shatters the scythe of Saturn.

THIRD MOVEMENT:

... I shall dwell in the house of the Lord!

Psalm 23

As always after Schubert's meditation upon the sorrows of life, sorrows that seem without end, he turns to the experience of new life that transforms his life. The time for sorrow is done. For this composer death is part of living and demands its artistic and mystical space. But death is not thought of as separate from its accompanying vision of transfiguration.

Elysium
Friedrich Schiller, D.584
The time for sorrow is done.
The joys of heaven drown every pain.
Heavens' life is eternal joy, eternal freedom
By the gentle brook in the lush meadows.

The world is young and joyful,
And bedecking every field
Is eternal May.
The hours pass by in golden dreams,

The spirit reaches into endless space,
Here truth rips aside every veil.

FOURTH MOVEMENT:

Beloved, we are God's children now. What we shall be has not yet been revealed!

First Epistle of John

Intoxicating joy inflames the heart of the wanderer. His sufferings are transfigured by his overall vision of life's sublime invitation. The goal of that invitation is here presented in rollicking excitement. The wanderer celebrates his illumination.

Elysium
Friedrich Schiller, D.584
Unending joy
Inflames the heart.
Anguish and pain do not exist.
Mild delight is called sorrow.

Here the wanderer rests his body
In the cool shade.

He surrenders for ever his life-long burden.
The scythe drops away from the hand of Death…
And Death sleeps to the soft music of a harp,
Dreaming of gathering hay.

The mighty warrior,
Used to the raucous sounds of death,
Under whose boot even mountains trembled,
Sleeps quietly by the running brook, which
Tumbles over silver stones,
The clash of swords is now only a dim memory.

Faithful spouses here embrace
And make love in the sweet green of the meadow,
Gently caressed by westerly breezes.
Here love is queen.
Lovers, safe for ever from death,
Enjoy an eternal wedding feast!

Symphony No. 6 in C major, D.589

October-1817 to February-1818

A new age is dawning! A triumph of love! Participation in the mystery is the spiritual ascent that leads from a lower to a higher world. The goal of the ascent is the new age. Getting there demands a journey. The *Sixth Symphony* celebrates wisdom's ascent out of chaos to the triumph of love. Schubert here is in love with life. For him life is transfigured by divine invitation. The price as he saw it was at least a temporary separation from Theresa Grob. Here there are no regrets. In yet another setting of Schiller's *Elysium* Schubert celebrates this new life. The slow introduction to this movement seems inspired by ideas in Schiller's *Gruppe aus dem Tartarus*. But there is little of the intensity found in the realization of these same verses in the *First Symphony*. Unlike the opening movement of the earlier symphony the composer seems already suffused in the light of the better world. Within the first movement he moves from the yearning of the wanderer to a celebration of the triumphant conclusion of the journey.. And here that conclusion is a triumph of love. Contradictions are reconciled in the love ascent from a lower to a higher world.

The Schiller poetry that inspires this symphony and several other works as well had been set to music as part songs by this composer in 1813. Again in 1817 he set the poetry in anticipation of settings in a series of the instrumental works. In work after work Schubert used this Schiller poetry to inspire celebrations of the journey of the wanderer. The vision of this journey is the central mystery of both ancient and Christian wisdom. It unlocks the prison of life. Life is lived against the backdrop of life, death, and transfiguration.*Elysium* is the poetic symbol of the ultimate transfiguration that redeems life.

FIRST MOVEMENT:

Lo, the great kingdom of salvation waits on high, ready for those who have gnosis, so that they may find peace there.

Manichaean Hymn

"Listen" is the command. Attend to the long life of sorrow, to the pain of the pilgrims. They ask "will this never end?" The response comes quickly. We are already in the better world. There is little time for sorrow. The wanderer awakens to a world of bliss. Eternal May hovers over all. Here is the wanderer's vision of his own journey.

Gruppe aus dem Tartarus
Friedrich Schiller, D.583

Listen! Like the rumbling of the mighty ocean,
Like the whine rising from the cascading river,
Comes the low groan out of the depths,
An impassioned, anguished wail!

Their faces are twisted in pain,
Despair and curses their cry,
Vacant their staring eyes,
As they look in terror upon the bridge over Cocytus.
Mournfully they observe their sorrowful journey.
Anxiously they whisper,
Will this never end?
Will this never end?

Eternity towers above their journey…
It shatters the scythe of Saturn.

Elysium
Friedrich Schiller, D.584

The time for sorrow is done.
The joys of heaven
Drown every pain.
Heavens' life is
Eternal joy, eternal freedom
By the gentle brook in lush meadows.

The world is young and joyful,
And bedecking every field
Is eternal May.
The hours pass by in golden dreams,
The spirit reaches into endless space,
Here truth rips aside every veil.

Divine joy reigns;
There is no more guilt;
Peaceful is the gentle triumph!

SECOND MOVEMENT:

As I have loved you, so you should love one another.
Gospel of John

In the new age of the higher consciousness of the mystery love is queen and death is no longer feared. Love is not betrayed. Nature and human love are in harmony, their gentle beauty reigning over all.

Elysium
Friedrich Schiller, D.584
Faithful spouses here embrace
And make love in the sweet green of the meadow,
Gently caressed by westerly breeze.
Here love is queen.
Lovers, safe for ever from death,
Enjoy an eternal wedding feast!

THIRD MOVEMENT:

In my Father's house are many mansions…
Gospel of John

In the new age the warrior and the wanderer are at peace. War is done. Peace and joy everywhere abound. Even death has sweet dreams.

Elysium
Friedrich Schiller, D.584
The mighty warrior,
Used to the raucous sounds of death,
Under whose boot even mountains trembled,
Sleeps quietly by the running brook, which
Tumbles over silver stones.
The clash of swords is now only a dim memory.

Here the wanderer rests his body
In the cool shade.
He surrenders for ever his life-long burden.

The scythe drops away from the hand of Death…
And Death sleeps to the soft music of a harp,
Dreaming of gathering hay.

FOURTH MOVEMENT:

If we love one another God remains in us and his love is brought to perfection!

First Epistle of John

Love is victorious in this world of the higher consciousness. It is a world of magical enchantment, of peace. It reigns secure against all challenge. The tone is not martial but joyful, playful. Love is the elixir that suffuses the human with the divine spirit. It not only conquers death; it transforms it, making of it the pathway to the stars.

Triumph der Liebe
Friedrich Schiller, D. 61, D.62, and D.63
May joyfully hovers over all,
Breathing through air, earth, sea, and sky,
Magical, like the half-light of early dawn!
...
Kronion sits in splendor,
Brandishing his thunderbolt!
When his long hair flies
In the wind
Olympus reels in fear!
...
Oh love, who has mounted
As a hero the steep path to the stars,
To the very throne of God, but you?
Who has been initiated into the mystery,
Finding a better land by going through the narrow fissure of death but you?
Had you not led us
Would we ever dream of eternal life?
Has ever a single spirit had this dream
Without being led by you?
Love and love alone leads us
Towards the Father, the Font of Nature!

Piano Sonata in B Flat Major for Four Hands, D.617

1818

At the center of the rose cross mystery is the ascension of the goddess to queenship in the new age. The dream maiden appears kaleidoscopically to the wanderer, always to draw him into the mystery. The mystery that Schubert celebrates in his art demands that this feminine symbol of the perfection of creation be raised to queenship. Her divine beauty must be recognized. Wisdom, the higher consciousness, is feminine. She is Sophia. The *Piano Sonata in B Flat Major* is a celebration of her many-layered beauty. This sonata for four hands follows closely upon a sonata for two hands, the *Piano Sonata in C Major D.613*. The inspiring poems are the same, but used in reverse order. A woman mediates the transfiguration of earth by heaven. That woman is incarnate in three ways, each an idealization of one of the wanderer's worlds.

The first of these incarnations is the feminine presence in nature, the moon. She is a lady of airy grace, a semi-mystical presence above the world, empathizing with those who suffer, encouraging those who love. Yet she cannot enter the tomb of the wanderer with an understanding of what death means for him. She is, after all, of the earth.

The second of these incarnations, the lady of heavenly grace, reigns above the stars, yet looks with maternal love upon the struggling wanderer, giving him new life as he pursues his arduous ascent. She is the woman to whom the earth sings and in whom earth finds its joy. So the wanderer cherishes her, builds and protects her shrine.

The third incarnation seizes the soul of this wanderer and with cosmic electricity raises him into the higher universe of love. This new world is one of otherworldly beauty, of searing pain, of eternal triumph, of catastrophic loss.

The new age dawns only with the ascension of this goddess to queenship. In the romance between heaven and earth it is a woman (the moon, a blessed mother, and a lover) who makes the better world incarnate for the wanderer. Without her the wanderer and his world are trapped in absurdity. Embracing her is essential.

FIRST MOVEMENT:

Harken, oh divine queen, waxing and waning, brooding, shining in the night, all-seeing, vigilant, surrounded by stars... grant fulfillment and favor.

Orphic Hymn

Delicate as moonlight the daughter of the heavens is introduced. She is a moving, dynamic presence, a background for love, a comforter, a recorder of memories, an observer of a strange yearning in the heart of the wanderer. But that yearning she cannot understand. While she cannot enter the tomb the wanderer knows that he soon will. The beautiful earth must be left behind.

An den Mond in Einer Herbstnacht
Alois Schreiber, D.614
Your face is that of a friend,
Daughter of the heavens.
With softest step
You wander through the skies,
Dear friend of the night.
Your light is gentle and refreshing,
Like words of comfort
From the lops of a loved one.
When the spirit sags
Under some heavy weight.
You see many tears;
You see much joy;
You hear often the whispers of lovers.
May your light help them!
Hope rides your beams,
Helping the one who patiently endures life's torments...
As he trods alone
His thorny path.
You look down upon my loved ones,
Living in distant lands.
You pour your light out
Upon that pleasant hillside
Where I played as a child.
It was there in your soft light

That a strange longing
Seized my young heart.
You look down upon the graves
Of my loved ones.
The dew falls upon them.
The grass sways above them
In the evening breeze.
But your light cannot enter
Into that dark room
Where they rest from life's troubles,
Where I soon shall end!
You will go
And return.
Many smiles
You will see.
But I shall smile no more!
I shall weep no more!
I shall no longer be even a memory
On this beautiful earth.

SECOND MOVEMENT:

The Begetter of all things... His female name is All-begetting Sophia.
The Sophia of Jesus Christ

The lady of grace, the spiritual woman is addressed. She deserves and receives the love of the wanderer. The life of the spirit, receiving and sending love messages to the better world, is in her provenance. In her the heart finds the peace that was so threatened by thoughts of death. The wanderer commits himself to building to this exalted woman a cathedral of his own, a cathedral in which he can touch the better world.

Das Marienbild
Aloys Wilhelm Schreiber, D.623
Hail to you, lady of grace,
Full of pure, radiant love.
Without fault, without guilt,
So humble of spirit.
Simple piety built this little chapel
In this oaken tree trunk.
It has no walls, no door.

Small birds sing songs
To your child from every branch.
Angelic spirits ascend and descend

Through the golden beams of sunlight.
The heart finds peace
Even though buried in sorrow.
The wanderer is given water
From grace's clear spring.
Gladly will I erect a small hut
Here in the quiet forest,
That this sailor's star
Might shine for me always;
And that in this little room
I can touch the better world,
And no fearsome specter
Might disturb my final rest.

THIRD MOVEMENT:
By one and the same ladder nature descends to the production of things and the intellect ascends to the knowledge of them.
Giordano Bruno

The third face of Eve awakens the wanderer to the awesome mystery of love and to the new age accessible only through her allure. Through her eternal love has set his life aflame. He sends her three flowers. The rose tells her of the painful yearning that she awakens in him. The myrtle expresses the hope for eternal union. The marigold reveals the thrilling heights and the terrifying depths of the great romance that now transfigures his life.

Der Blumenbrief
Aloys Wilhelm Schreiber, D.622
I send flowers
To a beautiful girl.
I beg her to end my suffering
With one word of kindness..
Rose, won't you tell her
How love has ravaged me,
How I sorely yearn for her;
And weep night and day.
And you, myrtle, whisper softly
Of my hopes.
Tell her: In his life
The only star is you.
You marigold, reveal to her
The pain of my despair.
Say: Without your love
He will die of a broken heart.

Piano Sonata in F minor, D.625

1818

The Divine Sophia unites heaven and earth as the bride of God. She is a divinely beautiful beloved for the wanderer, with the power to transfigure his life. That life in the rich tradition of Valentinian Gnosticism is a spiritual ascent out of the darkness of earth's exile into the light of divine love and beauty. This ascent is a ladder of love, mounted through the transcendence of contradictions.

In this priceless piano sonata Schubert presents a painful moment in the life of the wanderer. The beloved, goddess in whom the wanderer experienced the beauty of God, has disappeared. All that remains is a distant star, a promise of radiant light to come, a reminder that eventually his love yearning will be satisfied. This star of transcendental hope is a wondrous consolation. In the language of poetry rather than of theology the composer affirms the meaning of hope in the face of tragedy and death.

Schubert continues this theme with a sublime meditation upon sunset and death. Not only is the acceptance of death not meaningless, it is praised as a hero's act, an act of love through which all that is noble in the human heart can achieve definitive realization.

The sonata ends with a visionary, mystical insight into the wanderer's life. Although often painful that life is transfigured by divine invitation.

FIRST MOVEMENT:

Oh guiding Night! Oh Night, more lovely than the dawn!
John of the Cross

Oppressive darkness and sorrow engulf the wanderer. Earth is far removed from the better world. High above its darkness a lone star shines, witness to the dream. There love is queen. Down through space that light beams hope to the wanderer. Here is a keen sense of the sorrow that is the wanderer's life, but, even more, of the radiant hope and rhapsodic joy that comes to one who experiences the invitation to love's banquet.

Blondel zu Marien
Anon., D.626
In the midst of the dark night,
When sorrow overwhelms me,
When happiness has vanished
From all I do,
I see in the distance a glow,
A wondrous new and shining light,
A bright witness to love,
A mystical, beautiful star.
Eternally pure
It shines through joys and sorrows
And deep within my heart
That light is reflected.
So lovely, so gentle
Is that faithful reflection
That Iam wondrously consoled,
Though you are still so far away.

SECOND MOVEMENT:

Silent music, sounding solitude, the supper that refreshes and deepens love!
John of the Cross

The hour of sunset, the hour of death, the hour of beauty… are all one. The worlds of nature, the self and divine invitation coalesce in the thoughts of the wanderer. As heavens dissolve in radiant beauty and nature is illuminated, the wanderer prays that life's ending be bathed in mystical radiance.

Das Abendrot
Aloys Wilhelm Schreiber, D.627
Holy hour of sunset! The heavens dissolve in beauty.
So do martyrs die, at peace in their triumph of love.
At dawn the mountains stand in gray silence;
Now at the ending of the day they are alight.
The swan sails in crimson waters;
The grass in silver crystal is asparkle.

Oh sun, light of God, never are you more splendid
Than when you are sinking;
Ah, that you might take us with you,
That together we might come to the source of your glory!

THIRD MOVEMENT:

Redeem us from all these sufferings that have come now upon us.
Manichaean Text

The wanderer's thoughts turn to the present. Caught up in the long winter's journey and vulnerable physically and spiritually, he is sustained by divine invitation.

Sonnet II
Petrarch, D.629

Alone, reminiscing, almost lame, as from a cramp,
I walk the field, with faltering step,
Watching here, looking there to avoid
Any path where men might walk.
I find I am vulnerable, apt to be hurt
By people who pry into my life.
They see at a glance that I am joyless,
That inside I am burning.
I think that by now even the mountains and fields,
The river and forest know
Of my troubles, troubles I have hidden from others.
But in these troubles, as rough and wild as they have been,
There has never been a time when the God of love did not stand by me.
Speak with me and I with him.

Fantasy for Piano in C major "Grazer"

If you make love to the divine now, in the better world your longing will be satisfied. Kabir

The dream maiden is a constant presence in the life of the wanderer. She governs all that he does. Transcendental union with her defines his future. This splendid fantasy is another hymn to this mediator between heaven and earth. The hidden God is real for the wanderer only through her. And she has disappeared! She is now only a mystical presence. Schubert used three sonnets by Petrarch to express his tormenting love for this phantom who was all he had left of Theresa Grob. Both the erotic excitement and the frustration of the love are everywhere apparent. In this bittersweet romance we find the supreme enticement and frustrating transience of his divine invitation in a savage, pain-filled, intoxicating, thrilling romance of a dream maiden. In the words of the poet, surely applicable to the composer, the suffering is incurable.

Three Sonnets
Petrarch, set as D.630, 629, and 628, December, 1818
Now heaven and earth are silent;
The wind, birds, beasts are asleep;
Night sets the stars in place,
And the sea sinks in repose.
But I lie awake, distraught by bittersweet thoughts of her...
My tormenting, intoxicating dream maiden!

My inner chaos finds its solace in her!
My inner life, its joy, its anguish, depends upon her!
A single hand heals and wounds me!
In these endless agonies I die and rise a thousand times daily,

So incurable is my suffering!
……

Fretfully alone, limping, cramped, I walk the barren fields,
Seeking paths where no one walks.
I guard myself, for others can see my inner chaos.
The mountains, meadows, rivers, and forests know of my longing.
From others, from everyone else, I hide it.
Yet there is no path so savage that the god of love does not meet me,
And speak with me, and I with him.
……
Oh Apollo! If the longing that blond beauty once awakened is not dead,
If you are not too old,
Preserve this tender green plant from winter's ice,
Which appears when you look away!
By the power of a lover's hope,
A power that saved you from death,
Return warmth to the air! Banish winter!
Then to our astonished joy will the beloved appear,
Reclining in the meadow,
Shaded by her own upraised arms!

Piano Sonata in A major, D.664

1819

In the midst of life's troubles the wanderer is called to a profound peace and joy. Schubert's wisdom is at once rooted in ancient Hermetic tradition and profoundly Christian. His triumphant reconciliation of that contradiction can be seen in this sonata. His romance of the Divine Sophia culminates in unity with Christ, the ultimate incarnation of the Divine Sophia, and a conviction of immortality. He rejoices in a deep and pervasive peace.

The price paid by the composer for his exclusive commitment to his art was a sorrow that encompassed his entire life and left him at the end hungry for death. In return he got a surprise. He had hoped to make his mark in the musical world and be celebrated as the rightful heir to Beethoven. The celebration of his art during his short life bore little resemblance to what he had hoped to achieve. The door to public understanding and acceptance of his art never opened and probably never will Thus did Schubert wrestle with two great sorrows. First, he had to live without Theresa Grob. Second, he had to live with the realization that his sublime art would not have the impact that he had hoped for it. His music was understood only superficially and, when understood, was found to be politically incorrect. These frustrations did indeed make of his life a "sorrow", and made of his art a very private redemptive exercise. It was an apparently hopeless investment in the future. Peace in the face of these "sorrows" was a precious commodity. Yet his art celebrates the ascent of the wanderer to this peace. An instance of this is the *Piano Sonata in A Major*, D.664.

In the first movement the wanderer seeks the peace of the mystery in the face of life's troubles. Sorrows grow and threaten; yet again and again the higher consciousness is triumphant. In the commerce between heaven and earth this higher consciousness gives him ever new power to walk his path.

The second movement captures the heavenly peace of the mystery in music. It settles upon the wanderer with overwhelming beauty. The experience is inspired by Grillparzer's poem, the night, and the inner life of the composer.

In the Finale the composer has Novalis as inspiration. Conceptual concerns are evident. It is not simply a feeling he seeks, but the fuller truth of redemptive gnosis. That is found in his Gnostic-Christian life view. All of creation is redeemed. Peace is justified even in the sea's depths. Joy is the result of awakening to the most fundamental truth of the life experience: the Divine Other touches and transfigures the life of the wanderer.

FIRST MOVEMENT:

Oh Night, your gentle peace takes away our cares and gives us new life.
Orphic Hymn

Sleep is nature's gift.. In this earthly blessing the wanderer sees a symbol of eternal peace,. Two worlds are held side by side. The wanderer seeks earthly rest in the face of inner agonies that often make that rest impossible. His prayer is for both the peace that allows sleep and the peace of the inner life that comes only from above.

Ruhe, schönstes Gluck der Erde
Anon., D657
Rest, greatest earthly blessing
Descend upon us,
So that we are tranquil
As a grave reposing among flowers.
Let the storms of the heart be still.
Rock vain and idle dreams to sleep.
As they grow and multiply,
So grows and increases the soul's torment.
Give your peace to the earth.
Pour out your balsam
To heal the wounded soul,
That once again it may rise from its grave!

SECOND MOVEMENT:

Oh Night, Mother of Dreams,…come, disperse my fears !
Orphic Hymn

The prayer is answered. Peace descends upon the wanderer. Earthly peace and the foretaste of eternal peace are one in a momentary realization of the better world in this one.

Berthas Lied in der Nacht
Franz Grillparzer, D.653
Can you not sense the mystic presence of peace?
Slumber holds sway in its kingdom. So, you too, peacefully go to sleep.

Night enfolds, in fluttering wings,
Valleys and hills, calling them to rest.

Softly, gently she whispers
Her invitation to the lovely child, come and sleep.
If fear stirs to wakening,
Loving slumber, bring your peace.

THIRD MOVEMENT:

The light-bringing sun has come…Its light shines in all lands! Reverence it that it may give us joy and life eternal!

Manichaean Book of Prayer

The transcendental focus of the composer is made clear. Peace is transformed into joy and celebration. Love and life triumph in this strong affirmation of the central Christian mystery. The wanderer is not only filled with joy, he feels a need to share this joy with others. This is not an empty wish, it is the underlying motivation for his creativity. Inviting love radiates throughout creation and throughout this glorious music.

Hymn IV
Novalis, D.662
I tell the world that he lives,
That he has risen to new life,
That he is among us,
And will not abandon us!

I tell everyone. And they
Tell their friends.
Soon everywhere
The new kingdom of heaven appears!

Down even to the seas' depths
The fear of death is gone.
Everyone can in freedom and joy
Face his future.

The world is radiant with a new light.
Now, at last, it is home!
This new life comes
As a glorious gift from his hand.

Piano Quintet in A major "The Trout", D.667

1819

The *Trout Quintet* is alive and vibrant with the rose cross mystery of an ascent to a higher world that underlies and transforms experiences of nature and sorrow. The mystery is suggested by nature and made explicit by divine revelation. Hidden within the depths of this music is the secret of Sophia. This work, like all major instrumental works of Schubert, is an ascent out of one world into another. On its surface the work appears simply as exultation in the beauties of nature; it is much more. While the composer focuses upon the freedom and beauty in a swimming trout, in his peripheral vision is a bigger prize, the higher consciousness of the mystery. The magic here makes that prize available to others.

In 1819 Schubert looked back to a series of poems set in 1816 and 1817 for inspiration. The instrumental work he produced is an ascent to the sublime that is unusually accessible and immensely popular. The ascent begins in the first movement with the contrast between heavenly joy and death. This "contradiction" is posed conceptually by the poetry and experientially in the music. It is recalled in the Second and Third Movements in different ways. The challenge is to resolve the tension between nature's joy and death. The resolution is suggested in the First, Fourth, and Fifth Movements.

The *"Trout" Quintet* begins with a lush and exciting musical rendition of the story told in *Die Forelle*. There is first a focus upon the fish, then upon the contentment of the wanderer. The life portrayed is that of a higher world where freedom, beauty and love flourish. Tension builds with the coming of the fisherman who introduces a lower world and death. The incarnation of otherworldly beauty (the trout) is killed. But then Schubert turns to another poem, *Das Grab,* that suggests the resolution of the contradiction. Set as a song in the same year as *Die Forelle*, *Das Grab* suggests that in the depths of the grave the wanderer will find the beauty of life, fresh and transfigured.

In the second movement the composer simply relishes the heavenly beauty of nature, unmarked by any challenges to its all-pervasive peace. The third movement returns to the contrast between the love and joy in nature and the death of everything beautiful.

Before presenting the resolution of the tension between beauty and death Schubert turns once more to *Die Forelle*. In a series of variations transcendental freedom is savored. This rhapsodic meditation makes us the more ready for the Finale.

Schober's poem, *Pax Vobiscum,* reconciles peace and death in the classical way known to Western man. Christ accepted death as a part of his own loving invitation from the Father. Mysteriously the contradiction between beauty and death find their higher level reconciliation in the dramatic ascent through death to resurrection. This is the good news, the awakening, the illumination that simply transfigures the life experience for this composer. It is the subject of Schubert's art from the beginning, from Lebenstraum D2. It remains so until his death.

Thus the *"Trout" Quintet* is nothing less than a musical redemption experience, a hidden introduction to "gnosis". We are invited to share a lofty vision of life, a vision free to delight in nature's beauty, not by denying the fact of death, but by transfiguring it in a spiritual ascent.

FIRST MOVEMENT:

> *Oh God, I could be bounded in a nutshell and count myself a king of infinite space, were it not that I have bad dreams.*
>
> — *Shakespeare*

Here is vibrant, scintillating life; here is death; and here is the anticipation of the after-life...... all in this marvelous movement. In the joyful freedom of the fish the wanderer experiences freedom. In the assault on the trout the wanderer sees his own mortality and the tyranny that is our constant companion. And in the mystical and fearsome look into the grave the wanderer unexpectedly finds hope.

Die Forelle
Christian Friedrich Daniel Schubart, D.550

In a clear brook
In joyful freedom
A playful trout
Swam quick as an arrow.

I stood on the bank
And watched in sweet content,

As the brilliant fish
Rejoiced in the limpid water.

A fisherman with his rod
Came to the brook.
Coldly he watched
The wondrous fish.
I thought, "As long
As the water is clear
He'll never catch that fish
With his rod and hook."

But finally, he became angry,
Would wait no longer.
He stirred up the brook,
And before I knew it,
His line was taut
With the quivering fish,
While I in rage
Looked down upon the victim.
...

Das Grab
Johan Gaudenz von Salis-Seewis, D.643
The grave is deep and quiet,
Yet its shaft strikes fear into the heart.
Its darkness conceals a land
Which is simply unknown.

The poor heart, here on earth
Is beset by storms.
It can reach final peace
Only when it beats no more.

SECOND MOVEMENT:

Let us rejoice, beloved, let us go forth...to the mountain and to the hill...There you will show me what my soul has been seeking.
John of the Cross

The wanderer, freed by his vision, relaxes into nature's beauty. A day in the country, musically realized, breathes transcendental peace. Heaven and earth are for a time one.

Lied im Freien
Johann Gaudenz von Salis-Seewis, D.572
How beautiful is nature,
In the freshness of May!
How beautiful are the woods!
It is a joy to drink in the sun,
Away from the town,
Here on this fragrant hillside.

There under the hedge
Golden sunbeams play
With the shadows,
And here a man can relax,
Refreshed by the perfume
Of hazel and elderberry.

Walk a little further…
Pick up a twig, a flower,
Or perhaps a strawberry along the way.
If you are warm after the climb
Use the leaves
As a fan.

In the brook
The ripplets rise and fall,
Sparkling in the sun.
You can watch them disappear,
Nodding and drowsy,
In peaceful reverie.

THIRD MOVEMENT:

Where have you hidden, beloved?…I went out calling you.. and you were gone!

John of the Cross

Love and death, can they be reconciled? The contradiction disturbs the wanderer.

Hänflings Liebesverbung
Johann Friedrich Kind, D.552
My darling, I am in love!
The sun sparkles brightly,
The west wind is soft;
The brook bubbles quietly;

The flowers perfume the air!
And my darling, I am in love!

Darling, I am love!
I love you, gentle one!
In your feathery robe,
With your sparkling eyes,
The most beautiful of all!
Darling, I am in love!
...

Auf der Donau
Johann Mayrhofer, D.553
Over the watery mirror the boat glides.
Old castles reach towards the skies.
The woods groan like ghosts,
And our hearts are burdened.

All man does must die.
Where are the towers, the gate, the wall of the castle?
Where are the strong, courageous knights
Who once fought and hunted here?

Now ragged, thorny bushes cover the spot;
And the majesty of what once was is gone.
And we in this small boat are saddened,
For the rush of the river, like time, presages death.

FOURTH MOVEMENT

Those who love well will be elevated to what they love!
Saint Augustine

Nature and the inner life are one here in this celebration of freedom. The wanderer relishes an experience of Nature that has been transfigured through its incorporation into the mystery of divine invitation.

Die Forelle
Christian Friedrich Daniel Schubart, D.550
(for poem see first movement above)

FIFTH MOVEMENT:

You will draw water joyfully from the springs of salvation!
Isaiah 12

The wanderer contemplates the ultimate ground for all freedom, divine invitation. Here is the foundation for the higher consciousness. Here is the heart of the mystery.

Pax Vobiscum
Franz Schober, D.551
"Peace be with you."
This was your parting gift.
You were encircled by those who believed in you.
You were radiant in glorious divinity,
As you left the earth for the Eternal Home!
And indeed peace came to the faithful hearts…
A gift of peace in the midst of sorrow and pain!
This gave them strength to face their own death.
I believe in you, oh mighty God.

String Quartet No. 12 in C minor, D.703

1820

The bitter absence of the dream maiden brings the wanderer to new depths of pain. This single movement sounds an important theme that will be developed in later chamber music. The goddess has disappeared. Now the wanderer's ascent to the new age is to be measured by his descent into sorrow. Here the wanderer is in distress because the dream maiden, Rose, has died. Rose here is symbolic of the point where contradiction is reconciled, the still point of creation. She is the hope for a new dawn for society, an age of peace. Simultaneously she is the real girl that the composer has lost. She has died just as the maiden will die in the *Death and the Maiden Quartet*. The fair hopes for a life of joy and peace are gone. The wanderer must turn to the pale promise of the night sky for life's meaning. The stars are words of divine invitation calling him beyond this world of conflict to a mystical love fulfillment. This movement is an introduction to the night songs of the last three quartets, the later piano sonatas and symphonies, and the String Quintet.

Schubert's wanderer must awaken to divine invitation. Before that awakening the world is a place of exile. But the chains fall away when death is accepted as the pathway to that fullness. In this single movement that wisdom is given eloquent expression. This world is incurably blind to the mystery of love in which contradictions can be reconciled and not set in stone. In the face of the world's continuing betrayal of the heart's desire for joy and peace these are still possible through immersion in the rose cross mystery. This is the artistic, the mystical truth that the composer celebrates in this unfinished quartet.

Probably the marriage of Theresa Grob to someone else had something to do with the depression experienced by the wanderer here. It is possible that the parting of the composer and Theresa in 1816 was understood by them both as a step in a kind of Platonic marriage. Their parting, at first, might not have meant a cessation of commitment but rather its continuance in a "spiritual" form. Thus could Schubert gain the freedom to focus upon his work and remove pressure from Theresa. But the temporary accommodation, if indeed it existed, came to a jolting halt with Teresa's marriage.

Schubert's works between 1816 and 1820 celebrate his love for a woman, an "immortal beloved," who waits for him faithfully, who loves him, but who is physically absent. But now, at the end of 1820, there is a more intense sense of tragedy. Earth betrays heaven. Yet the tragedy does not stop the spiritual ascent, which achieves new beauty in this shadow-land of sorrow.

THE SINGLE MOVEMENT:

But the while the youth is not by her side, yet she is ever with him, his Bride.
Mechthild of Magdeburg

Here is inner turmoil. The lambs playing in the mountain meadow and the lush nature are contradictions to the tortured life of the wanderer. The beloved has gone, died. The coffin is lowered into the earth. The dream is dead. Heaven can no longer be at home on this wanderer's earth. His eyes turn towards the heavens, the stars. Only there is his hope, a vision of final triumph.

Der Jungling auf dem Hugel
Heinrich Hüttenbrenner, D.702
A youth sat on the side of the hill
In deep distress
His eyes were sad,
Clouded by tears.

He saw the lambs at play
On the mountain meadow,
And the sprightly brook
Running through the flowered valley.

The butterflies sampled
The pink lips of the flowers,
While the clouds like morning daydreams
Sailed high above.

Everything was so peaceful
Everything was so full of joy.
But none of this joy
Was in the heart of that youth.

The grumbling of the church bells
Rolled out of the village, and
With them as well sounded in the distance
A sad song of death.

He saw the candles
And the black garments of the funeral,
And wept bitterly…
The body of his beloved Rose was being carried to its burial!

They lowered the coffin into the earth.
The gravedigger returned
Finally to the earth
What God had drawn forth from it.

But the youth stopped his weeping,
And his expression changed to one of devotion.
He stood in anticipation of the joy of reunion,
Of a day in a brighter future.

The stars came out,
And the moon reappeared!
He read in the heavens
A sign of sublime hope.

Symphony No. 7 in E major, D.729

1821

The wanderer is called out of a lower to a higher world. Here is a divine invitation to a new age. This is the underlying theme in all of Schubert's art. In this symphony the call is messianic and cosmic. All of nature and all mankind are ascending in response to this invitation. Trust in the invitation inspires a joyful celebration. With Novalis Schubert feels that the new age is dawning. Yet within two years that new age will seem terribly remote from the composer. In 1824, faced with political tyranny, failure in love, artistic failure, and death, the composer's hopes will fasten not upon an imminent new age, but upon a distant star. But in 1821 the wanderer looks forward to a new age that seems about to transfigure his world. Although the time parameters will change Schubert's wanderer will never lose this hope. It will control his life.

The journey from a lower to a higher world is in focus in this magnificent torso of an unfinished symphony. Wisdom is concerned with a drama, not a fact. And the drama is one of transfiguration. The lower world becomes simply radiant with the light of the higher one. The poetry suggests that Schubert saw in Jesus Christ the realization of the divine in the human. In him heaven comes to earth. This for Schubert is not simply "belief" in a "fact".. It is a nebulous experience of divine invitation that finds priceless expression in this marvelous symphony.

Schubert's tale is of a wanderer who is driven to leave a lower world and ascend to higher one. The adventure is undertaken in hope, peace, and joy because of divine invitation, incarnate in Christ, the symbol of a cosmic union between the divine and the human. Over the course of the next two years this optimism and joy in life will be sorely tested. While the new age will become more transcendental, the hope will never disappear. Perhaps this alteration of perspective is why the symphony was left unfinished. But thanks to Professor Brian Newbould of the University of Hull, Great Britain, we have it to enjoy.

In the first movement Schiller's wanderer is the dreamer hero who discovers his true goal and has the daring to reach for it. The cold mountains enshrouded in fog, a Gnostic description of this world, are lifeless and loveless. The distant music coming from, the land of eternal spring and sunshine, is the sound of a better world. Seeing and reaching that world are intensely individual concerns. The wanderer is on his own, choosing, charting, finding courage in the mighty effort to be worthy of his beloved Sophia.

The challenge is made less daunting in the second movement. The wanderer is not truly alone. With him always is the divine inviter. This movement is sublime in beauty, emanating from Schubert's experience, enhancing our own.

In the third movement the beloved, who now lies in her grave, is a mystical presence, drawing the wanderer through life and beyond it. She is his dream maiden, the object of all his longing, calling him to fulfillment. The horns in sounding their longing cry voice the divine inviation to a kingdom of love.

The fourth movement is radiant in the expectation of a luminous new age. The light radiates from Christ in whom the light and life sought by the wanderer are incarnate. The wanderer's sorrow is swallowed up in triumphant joy. Again and again the music repeats the good news "he lives; he is risen". This conviction will be repeated in the *Violin Fantasy D934* in the last year of the composer's life. The anticipation of a transcendental and mysterious new age is from the beginning to the end of his composing absolutely central to Schubert's world view.

In this *Seventh Symphony* the wanderer stands upon an island and looks out over the chaos of matter. From the distance he hears the invitation of heavenly music, giving him incentive and courage for the fearsome adventures ahead. Seven years later he will stand upon a high precipice and look out upon a yet more terrifying darkness. Faced with dying this wanderer will stand alert and ready...and again he will sing! The uncompleted *Tenth Symphony*, also finished by Brian Newbould, will bring our wanderer's life to its end. His trust in his own inner light and in the power of the Other who invites is never eclipsed. Time after time it will triumph.

FIRST MOVEMENT:

What you see as beauty in the midst of southern breezes is the love of the everlasting Godhead, full of exquisite splendor, rich in bountiful mystery.
Hildegard of Bingen

This wanderer's tale begins in sorrow; yet in the distance is a better world, a world of eternal sunlight. Here is the new, more mature Schubert, expressing himself through the alienated wanderer, whose inner life has never been more vibrant.

Sehnsucht
Friedrich Schiller, D.636

The mountain vale is cold,
Enshrouded in fog!
If only I could leave it,
I would be happy!

Look away in the distance and see those hills,
Always young, always green!
If I had wings, if I could fly
It is to those hills I would go!

Listen to the distant music,
Revealing heaven's own sweet peace.
The gentle winds from there
Bring me a sweet and fresh fragrance.

Golden fruits glow
In the shadow of the dark leaves,
And the flowers there
Fear no frost of winter.

What a joy it would be to walk in that garden,
So radiant in eternal sunlight!
How peaceful and restful
Must be the air on those hills!

But I am stopped by a fierce river,
Chaotic, roaring,
A torrent of whirlpools,
A terror to my very soul!

I can see a small boat bobbing,
But there is no one to sail it!
Onward into that torrent! Dare it!
All the sails are up and full!

The gods will not reward the man who
calculates too much!
Only their power can win for you
Passage to the fair wonderland.

SECOND MOVEMENT:

The divine abundance of Love gleams and shines in the sublime lightning-flash of its gifts. It surpasses every insight of human understanding.
Hildegard of Bingen

The Good Shepherd invites the wanderer. The sublime homecoming at the end of the ascent is never in doubt.

Psalm 23
D.706
The Lord is my Shepherd,
And I shall lack nothing.
He grazes me in green pastures.
He leads me to peaceful streams.
He revives my languishing soul
And guides me along the path of righteousness
To his name's renown.
And even when I walk
In the valley of death,
I shall walk without fear,
For You will protect me.
Your staff and Your support
Are ever a comfort to me.
You prepare a banquet of joy for me
In the sight of my enemy.
You anoint my head with oil,
And fill my drinking-cup.
Happiness and bliss are mine
In this life,
Until one day I come to rest
In the eternal dwelling-place above.

THIRD MOVEMENT

Oh my beautiful and sweet spouse…if you do not wish to give me the pearl now, give me your love beams and lead me through this pilgrim's path!
Jacob Boehme

Here is the hunt for eternal life. In the hunt there are mystical moments when the absent beloved seems present and inviting.

Trost
Johann Mayrhofer, D.671
The horns sound their longing cry
Through the green forest night,

Calling to a kingdom of love.
They seem inspired by divine power.
Happy indeed is the man who has found
Another who loves him.
But I have no such happiness,
My beloved lies in her grave!

When I hear the echo
Of the horns through this forest,
I can almost believe that she is here,
Drawing me towards herself!

One day she will shine radiantly before me,
As once she did when she gave me her love;
What sacred bliss that will be!
The grave holds no terror for me!

FOURTH MOVEMENT:

Our trumpet shall publicly sound loud and clear! Our wisdom shall freely and publicly proclaimed. The whole world shall be filled with the vision!

Confessio Fraternitatis

Eternal life, the triumph of wisdom and love, the goal of the spiritual ascent, the end of the hunt…all are proclaimed in the resurrection of Jesus Christ. Endlessly does the wanderer sing of this life-transfiguring reality. Here is sublime illumination. It is whispered, shouted, always victorious, always thrilling, always empowering.

Hymn IV
Novalis, D.662
I tell the world that he lives,
That he has risen to new life,
That he is among us,
And will not abandon us!

I tell everyone. And they
Tell their friends.
Soon everywhere
The new kingdom of heaven appears!

The world is radiant with a new light.
Now, at last, it is home!
This new life comes
As a glorious gift from his hand.

Down even to the seas depths
The fear of death is gone.
Everyone can in freedom and joy
Face his future.

Symphony No. 8, the "Unfinished", D.759

October 1822

To become initiated (or perfected) involves dying!
Plutarch

The new age means the reconciliation of the contradictions that compromise everything earthly. At the very heart of the mystery is the passage through death to a higher life. This is an intensely personal invitation. Acceptance of death is the pre-condition for the wanderer's experience of the mystery. An ascent to that experience is a demanding spiritual process. The soul must be at peace above its fear. It must ascend to a higher consciousness. In doing so it loses its chains and can taste freedom. The passage through death to a higher life was the heart of the Egyptian and Greek mystery religions. It was the core of Valentinian gnosis. It is the soul of true Christian mysticism. It is the key to the symbolism of the Roman Catholic mass. It is the essence of the Pauline experience of ascending out of one world into another. The *Unfinished Symphony* is a musical celebration of this core of the rose cross mystery.

The higher consciousness or *gnosis* inevitably addresses the meaning of life in the face of death. For Schubert the definitive spiritual ascent through death to a higher life is the critical point at which all of life finds meaning and is transfigured. Freedom is a function of facing and accepting death. It is this transfiguration point of the spiritual ascent that is in direct focus in the *Unfinished Symphony*. In a supreme artistic treasure Schubert's wanderer, a Christ figure, a symbol of both the composer and the listener, is transfigured in divine light after passing through ultimate darkness. Here is both the anticipation of actual death and an initiation of the living by passing through figurative death to new and higher life. Here is the ultimate reconciliation of contradiction. The poetry and the music bring us face to face with the paradox of finding life while dying.

The first movement sets the stage for the inward journey by putting us in the presence of death, first a somber reality, then an agonized conflict. But death's suffering is overcome by the peace of the better world. Each time the enemy appears he is vanquished by the heavenly harmonies. The prayer here is that at the time of dying, both figuratively and literally, the composer will be graced with the experience of the spiritual ascent along with the ability to express that ascent in music. This will constitute the governing purpose for Schubert's art from this time forward.

The second movement is a rich development of the transfiguration of consciousness. The heavenly harmonies, the liberation from chains, the presence of life's wonders are all here. The stars and flowers, the beauty that bloomed in the wanderer's life, are given dramatic and lyrical expression. Again and again the transfiguration theme is repeated, a gentle rise and descent of seven notes, persuasive in its delicate simplicity.

This work might aptly be called the "Transfiguration Symphony", a musical setting for the wanderer's liberation. The effect of the gnosis is a radical altering of the life experience. It does not deprive life of its meaning; it makes all things new.

FIRST MOVEMENT:

> *What a great miracle is man! He despises that part of his nature which is only human, and puts his hopes in the divinity of the other part!*
>
> *Corpus Hermeticum*

Out of the depths of suffering and death this wanderer ascends to the better world. The ascent takes place as nature fails. A heavenly blessing transfigures the dying with peace, comfort, and final freedom. This wanderer must leave the world to get to its transfiguration.

Todesmusik
Franz Schober, D.758

At the sacred hour of death,
When I shall leave this earth,
And in pain fight my last battle,
Holy spirits, bless me a final time
With your peaceful melodies,
Your purest harmonies;
Ease the pain in my heart,
Torn by its fatal wound.

Free my simple and tortured spirit
In this last battle of life.
Sweep it aloft, and upon your wings…
Carry it into eternal light!

Then will the sweet, heavenly harmonies envelop me,
The chains I have escaped
Will become light, and fall away!

I will see all the wonders of my life, which brought me such joy.
All the beauty which bloomed in my life
Will stand transfigured before me!
Every star that sparkled as a friend
In the sultry darkness of my winter's journey,
Every flower that graced my path…will be there!

And those fearful minutes, when I am in anguish,
Will be accompanied by joy-filled anticipation!
And I will see all things…transfigured!
So will I surrender my life in the radiance of wondrous joy!

SECOND MOVEMENT

God, like a fire, makes one with himself those who can be divinized.
Pseudo Dionysius

Sublime radiance suffuses the transfigured state of the redeemed wanderer. Chains fall like rose petals, and all is changed. The beautiful things of the wanderer's life are here, transfigured. The mystical beauty of the heavenly world reigns, queenlike, over all. Fearsome reflections upon the final sufferings in the passage are swept up into joyful anticipation of the final triumph, and death becomes peaceful surrender, the prelude to transfiguration.

Todesmusik
Franz Schober D.758
Then will the sweet, heavenly harmonies envelop me,
And the chains I have escaped will become light, and fall away!
I will see all the wonders of life,which brought me such joy.
All the beauty which bloomed in my life will stand transfigured before me!
Every star that sparkled for me as a friend
In the sultry darkness of my winter's journey,
Every flower that graced my path…will be there!

And those fearful minutes when I am in agony
Will be accompanied by joy-filled anticipation!
And I will see all things…transfigured!
So will I surrender my life in the radiance of wondrous joy!

FANTASY FOR PIANO *THE WANDERER*, D.760

January 1822

The "sorrow" of the wanderer's life is the contradiction he finds everywhere between his dream and reality. The ascent to the new age means a triumph over this contradiction. And the triumph seems impossible. If the heart of the mystery is the passage through death to life, its fullness means a passage through the frustration of the dream to its fulfillment. In the higher consciousness the world drama is a paradox, a movement out, away from the light source, the One, into multiplicity aqnd contradiction, and a movement back, a reconciliation of the contradictions, a return to unity. The *Wanderer Fantasy* celebrates the unlocking of the door to the meaning and joy of life. In the *"Unfinished" Symphony* the life before the illumination experience, the universe of contradiction, is not in focus. The symphony certainly does not ignore the painful prelude to spiritual triumph, but through it all there is the presence of a transfigured light that beckons through what Schiller called the "narrow fissure of death".

In the *Wanderer Fantasy* the wanderer actually first finds himself in a lower world, deprived of the illumination of a higher one. In the first two movements the wanderer lives without hope, on the verge of despair in the face of life's contradictions to his dreams. The world of nature is no longer springtime and flowers, but barren, cold, unfriendly, ominous. The earth, once in harmony with the invitation to the spiritual ascent, seems strangely now to contradict it. The fantasy takes us with the wanderer from this forbidding land of exile on a journey to the promised land. The prison of Nature is transformed by grace of divine invitation.

The *Wanderer Fantasy* gives eloquent expression to a life-view already politically incorrect at the time of composition. All of life, its joys, its sorrows, even death, is transfigured by divine invitation. The higher world can transfigure the experience of the wanderer. It can change his life, set him free, release his creativity, make him volcanically productive. Death and dying, the antithesis of the Enlightenment dream, are incorporated into a different dream, the dream of the wisdom tradition. For Schubert the "translation" of transcendence into merely secular terms amounts to its annihilation. The Transcendental must remain in some respects "other" if our lives are to be illuminated. All meaning, all joy, all freedom in life is in the long run the function of a vital recognition that the invitation at the heart of the life experience is transcendental in nature, calling us beyond nature, beyond the earth.

This fantasy then expresses musically an initiation into the higher consciousness of the mystery, an initiation that plunges into darkness before discovering the light. The first two movements separate the wanderer from all limited dreams of a merely earthly paradise. The paradise sought by the soul transcends what Nature offers. The last two movements move from a Saturnine focus upon barren and wintry world devoid of love to a vision of love's radiant triumph. In the process our earth is transfigured as contradictions are reconciled. All the glories of nature, the stars, the sun, and flowers, symbolic of earthly loves, are recaptured, but in a new and higher context. Finally stars and galaxies unite in their praise of radiant divinity, the source of their being and meaning.

FIRST MOVEMENT:

> *Late have I loved you, oh Beauty, so ancient and so new! Behold, you were within me and I was outside, and there I sought for you... You were with me and I was not with you..*
>
> *Saint Augustine*

Thunderously the "sorrow" of this wanderer is announced. Only with nature in its violence is he at home. May flowers and blue skies are foreign to his winter's journey; they only intensify his pain. Over and over he asks where his joy, his peace, his final freedom is. The dream of love has driven him in his wandering, yet it remains in the distance, in another world. The violence of this movement derives from the titanic strength of inner yearning for love's fulfillment...denied.

Der Wanderer
Georg Philipp Schmidt von Lubeck, D.493
I come from the mountains.
The valley steams, the sea thunders.
I wander in silence, joyless,
And always I hear the whispered
question: "where?"

The sun is cold here.
The blossoms are dry. Life is old.

Men speak but say nothing.
I am a stranger everywhere.

Where are you my beloved land?
I have searched for you, dreamed of you,
But never have I found you!
Oh land, land so green in hope!
Oh land where all my roses bloom,
Where my friends all abide,

Where my dear departed one has
risen to new life,
Where everyone speaks my language…
Oh blessed land, where are you?

I wander in silence, joyless,
And always I hear the whispered
question: "where?"

SECOND MOVEMENT:

Let your face shine upon me in your servant; save me in your kindness!
Psalm 31

The wanderer looks at his world. Nowhere does it suggest that his dream will be fulfilled. It is devoid of promise, devoid of hope. He has searched, and dreamed…in vain! Yet the dream of a better world where love is triumphant does not die.

Der Wanderer
Georg Philipp Schmidt von Lubeck, D.493
The sun is cold here.
The blossoms are dry. Life is old.
Men speak but say nothing.
I am a stranger everywhere.

Where are you my beloved land?
I have searched for you, dreamed of you,
but never have I found you!
Oh land, land so green in hope!
Oh land where all my roses bloom,
Where my friends all abide,
Where my dear departed ones have
risen to new life,
Where everyone speaks my language
Oh blessed land, where are you?

I wander in silence, joyless,
And always I hear the whispered
question: "where?"
With ghostly breath, the answer comes:
There where you are not, there is your joy!

THIRD MOVEMENT

What a great miracle is Man, Oh Asclepius; he passes into divine life as if he were a god!

Corpus Hermeticum

The transition from the emptiness of this world to the wealth of the world of gnostic illumination is not gradual. It bursts with sudden radiance upon the wanderer. Included in the victory are the stars and flowers that have been his companions in exile. The redemption means leaving the darkness and rising to a transcendental illumination of the life experience.

Todesmusik
Franz Schober, D.758
At the sacred hour of death when I shall leave this earth,
And in pain fight my last battle,
Holy spirits, bless me a final time with your peaceful melody,
Your pure harmony;
Ease the pain in my heart, torn by its fatal wound.

Free my simple and tortured spirit in this last battle;
Sweep it aloft and upon your wing carry it into eternal light!
Then will the sweet, heavenly harmonies envelop me,
And the chains I have escaped will become light, and fall away!

I will see all the wonders of life which brought me such joy!
All the beauty Iwhich bloomed in my life
Will stand transfigured before me!
Every star that sparkled for me in the sultry darkness
Of my winter's journey,
Every flower that graced my path..will be there!

And those fearful minutes when I am in agony,
Will be accompanied by joy-filled anticipation!
And I will see all things…transfigured!
So will I surrender my life in the radiance of wondrous joy!

FOURTH MOVEMENT

Let all nature listen to my hymn!
Corpus Hermeticum

There is nowhere for this celebration of spiritual victory to go but, in ancient Hermetic fashion, into a song of praise for the inviting God who brings the wanderer into the better world of his dreams. Here starry lights are ablaze in praise of the divine creator and inviter who calls all wanderers to their eternal triumph.

Gott in der Natur
Ewald Christian von Kleist D.757
Great is the Lord! Great is the Lord!
The heavens are his castle,
The storm his carriage, thunder and
lightning his royal steeds...
Great is the Lord! Great is the Lord!
Morning's red light is but a reflection
Of his brilliance.
Compared with that splendor
The setting sun is but a spark.
He looks down in love upon the earth,
And it takes on life, blossoming in joy!
He reproves it, and rocks burst aflame,
While sea and sky tremble.

Praise the Almighty Lord!
Starry lights in his castle, majesty of the sun,
Blaze triumphantly in his name,
While we on earth sing his glory!

Piano Sonata in A Minor, D.784

1823

Out of the contradiction between the wanderer's hopes and tragic disappointments emerges a hard-won reconciliation. The higher consciousness dawns. Earth without heaven is utter frustration. But this is not resolved by rejecting the earth. Rather earthly oppositions in sex, nationality, race, and religion must be transfigured. And for Schubert the transfiguration is conditioned by an acceptance of the divine invitation that calls the wanderr through sorrow and death. All limited earthly beauty vanishes in the light of a transcendental universe.

At difficult times in the spiritual ascent the transitory nature of earthly beauty is a great sorrow. So it is here. During the month that this sonata was composed Schubert was bedridden with syphilis. Thus to his frustrations in love and art there was added yet another sorrow. The disease was not cured and was perhaps incurable. Schubert's world was a wreck, proclaiming life to be a mockery of everything beautiful. This was a challenge to him as man and artist. What did he have to say about a life that was betraying him so completely? Was he different from the many twentieth and twenty-first century savants, modernists and post-modernists, who endlessly have proclaimed the hopelessness, ugliness, and meaninglessness of the life experience?

The *Piano Sonata in A Minor D.784* is a magnificent response to that challenge contained in both the unlimited optimism of the Enlightenment and the pessimism of much post-Enlightenment thought.. It is a song of the wanderer, whose joy in life is gone, and who is still far from home. He accepts the challenge to celebrate the mystery in this wasteland. Here Schubert's song of the wanderer tells a tale that plumbs the depths of sorrow. The wanderer walks his world as an alien, a stranger. Although he sees signs of his true home in the might of nature and in its beauty, he is aware that all beauty must die. The better world lies beyond him, beyond his art, beyond all human effort. His yearning is painful and unsatisfied.

Then the wanderer turns from this contemplation of mere nature to thoughts of life in a transfigured world that has already dawned for him through a woman. The super-terrestrial satisfaction of his yearning is present as illuminating promise. But the very sacrament of this promise, the beloved, Sophia, the soul-bride who has awakened him to the great romance, is sadly only a dream in the inner life. She is but a mystical presence.

FIRST MOVEMENT

A wise man's life is all one preparation for death.
Cicero

Morose and gloomy is the wanderer as he restlessly pursues his winter's journey. Everywhere he sees life, nature's life, the joys of spring. But how alien it is to his tortured spirit! The theme of death is sounded and repeated. Nowhere in nature is life freed from its threat. The contradiction is stark. Life towers towards the heavens, unbelievably beautiful, and man is capable of towering creativity. Yet, death destroys all.

Wehmut
Matthäus Kasimir von Collin D.772
As I walk through fields and forest,
My restless heart
Is at once happy and distressed.
So happy, yet so stressed, as my eye falls
Upon the fields in their glory,
In the full joy of spring.

Everything sways and sings in the breeze,
Towering to the heavens,
And man himself, all-trusting,
Together with all the beauty that he sees,
Must pass away and vanish.

SECOND MOVEMENT:

Oh Beauty... You breathed fragrance... I drew in my breath... Now I pant for you!
Saint Augustine

The wanderer turns inwards, away from the outer world where death is triumphant to the inner world where he finds the invitation and his beloved. In this inner life he discovers the strength to live and to create. It can fill his entire life with transfiguring light. Here the transfiguration is a hope, an expectation.

Du bist die Ruh
Friedrich Ruckert, D.776
You are peace, gentle, sweet peace.
You are yearning, and what stills it.
I commit to you every joy, every pain,
My eyes, my heart as your temple.

Come here to me, and close
The gate quietly behind you.
Drive every sorrow from my breast.
Fill this heart with your joy!

This whole world of mine can
Be brightened only by you.
Fill it to the full with your radiance!

THIRD MOVEMENT:

I tasted. Now I hunger and thirst.
Saint Augustine

Two worlds interact. The outer world of nature threatens the inner world. But divine invitation can redeem the life experience and reconcile the wanderer even to his suffering. Thus where there is pain there can be peace. These two strangely intertwine, one awakening the wanderer to the other.

Dass sie hier gewesen
Friedrich Ruckert, D.775
That fragrance in the air...
Ah, it is the East Wind,
Telling me
That you have been here.

Those tears falling...
Ah, you might know,
If nothing else told you,
That I have been here.

Beauty or pain of love!
Could either remain unknown?
Fragrance and tears betray to us
That both have been here!

Variations for Flute and Piano, D.802

November 1823

In a vision of transcendental triumph the dream maiden returns. With her return comes the new age. These variations are magical celebrations of the apotheosis of the demonic, gentle, forceful, rhapsodic, threatening, motherly... dream maiden. She is the missing feminine "other" in our power-mad world. In her life-giving tension with her masculine lover is found the reconciliation of the contradictions and mysteries of creation. Her return is the symbol for the redemption of our self-destroying world.

The composition of these flute variations celebrating the return of the goddess and the dawning of the new age followed closely the completion of the song cycle *Die Schöne Müllerin*. The Variations have more than a musical relationship to the Lieder cycle. They celebrate more personally, more rhapsodically, the hidden truth of that cycle: a romance between the divine Sophia, the spouse of God, the bride of the soul, and the wanderer. In the song *Trockne Blumen* this unity is anticipated. The instrumental work develops the theme of the return of Sophia. Spring, it repeats endlessly and with rapture, will come again. Love will triumph over hatred, life over death; unity over contradiction. The heroic fidelity of the wanderer to his absent beloved will be rewarded.

The song cycle tells two stories, one of the actual life experience in the lower world, the other of his ascent to a higher world. Among the songs *Trockne Blumen* suggests triumph in the spiritual ascent. But these variations on *Trockne Blumen* remove all doubt about what the composer actually thought.. The deeper reality of the spiritual ascent is celebrated again and again. Schubert's gnosticism rejects the Enlightenment expectation of heaven on earth as deceptive and insists upon the tragedy inherent in all earthly endeavor. But this is not the whole picture. In a way Schubert is the ultimate optimist. For him all experiences can be stages in the ascent to the new age. The tragedies of life as well as its joys are elevated and transfigured.

The variations are a joyful anticipation of the return of the dream maiden. The enjoyment of that triumph eludes the composer. It exists as only a hope, a vision from beyond the grave. But he is true to that vision. The ideal preparation for sharing it is clearly to be found in experiencing the song cycle with its development of the theme of the life-transforming romance between the divine Sophia and the wanderer, a romance that raises sun, moon, stars, and flowers, and all the earth to undreamed of heights of meaning. Yet the songs lament love's betrayal. Somehow that betrayal must be incorporated into the ultimate triumph of love. This is the function of the song *Trockne Blumen*, and, even more dramatically, of the *Flute Variations*. Here the mysterious experience of transcendental hope becomes the ultimate vindication of the romance, one that gives eternal consequence to all of the beauty suggested in the early songs.

As an expression of the composer's life experience this work is interesting. While hypotheses are chancy, the words of the poem invite them. If Schubert interpreted the marriage of Theresa Grob as a betrayal of a spiritual relationship, then in some way this miller's daughter is Theresa and the earthly Sophia she represents. The earthbound, death-cursed flowers, gifts from the wanderer, symbols of his musical creations, die with him in the grave. Yet someday they will bloom forth anew, in fullness of life. Schubert in 1823 perhaps regarded *Alfonso und Estrella* as his prize flower, his supreme rose. That opera had been rejected by the music world. The *Flute Variations* imaginatively anticipate new life, but sadly that experience seems to lie far in the distant future.

These variations begin with a morose but necessary insistence upon the death of earthly dreams. In the initiation into the mystery death precedes new life. The wanderer along with the flowers stares with resignation at this sad fate. Here is the utter disappearance of the prospect for a secular heaven. Then, following the poetry the focus changes. Spring will come again. One variation on the theme follows another in a many-faceted realization of the transfiguration that crowns entrance into the mystery. This magical music should be named "Easter" or "Transfiguration" Variations.

For see, the winter is past! The rains are over and gone!
Flowers appear on the earth!
Song of Songs

Trockne Blumen
Wilhelm Müller D.795 No. 17 11-1823
All you flowers which she gave me
Should lie with me in the grave!
Why do you all look so sad,
As if you had guessed what will happen to me?

Little flowers, why are you so withered, so lifeless?
Little flowers, why are you so damp?
Ah, my tears cannot bring back the green of May,
Nor can they make dead love come to new life.

But spring will again come, and winter will go,
And little flowers will bloom in the grass…
And little flowers will bloom upon by grave…
All the little flowers she gave me!

And when she walks along this hillside,
She will think, his love is true!
Then little flowers, spring forth, spring forth,
May has come! Winter is over at last!

The Octet, D.803

Early 1824

The whole world, upper and lower, is organized on this principle...all are coverings, the one to the other, brain within brain, spirit within spirit, shell within shell.

The Zohar

Mystical premonitions of the new age occur in which contradictions are reconciled in transcendental unity. These premonitions rule the wanderer's life. Through the higher consciousness of divine invitation the wanderer is empathetic with life's dramatic ascent to love's triumph. He has risen out of the dark prison of mere Nature into the divine promise of a new age. Our wanderer is the wise man of cabalistic lore. He has a foretaste of his Beloved, the Divine Sophia, in whom light has triumphed over darkness. He is aware that the world has not yet entered this new age...but he anticipates the victory. That anticipation can be more than a belief. It is from time to time an experience.

The Schubert *Octet* is a rhapsodic immersion in this sublime disposition. It simply revels in the freedom and joy won through initiation into the mystery. The experience begins on a lake. The singer is aware that he is one of a privileged elite. He is the Rosicrucian boatsman, awake in a world of sleepers. He not only wants to travel with the moon and stars, i.e. experience life on a higher plane, but has the wisdom to do so. Unfortunately, like the star of love, this wisdom is alien to this world. Still its joys are many and varied. All of life is transfigured. It is finally an invitation that, like the rays of the setting sun, portends both death and eternal life.

This is yet another Schubert fantasy, inspired by a series of poems (most of them set as Lieder in or around March of 1824) that present an adventure of the inner life, an adventure relevant both to the spiritually elite (i.e. cabalistic) hearer and to the composer. The story is of an experience of divine life that appears as love, light, and peace. The dramatic connection between these poems witnesses to the conscious intent of the composer to present to the world, or at least to those capable of it, a celebration of true wisdom. The wanderer is raised above all anxiety in a thrilling participation in the great romance.

FIRST MOVEMENT:

Search for her (wisdom) as for a hidden treasure.

Book of Proverbs

Join the poet on a lake. It is night and the experience of nature opens the wanderer to entrance into the rose cross mystery. It is the hour when according to cabalistic thought the gates of heaven are open. The poetry expresses an invitation to initiation. It is a call to awaken from sleep and be like the boatman.

Der Gondelfahrer
Johann Mayrhofer D.808 March 1824
From Saint Mark's the bells chime the midnight hour;
Everyone sleeps in heavenly peace...
Only the boatman is awake.

The moon and stars are ashimmer like dancing spirits!
Who can worry about concerns of this world?
Come into our boat! Travel with the moon and stars!
Break free of the world and be cradled in the starry bosom of the sea!

SECOND MOVEMENT

Fools despise wisdom.

Book of Proverbs

Schubert sings a night song, one of anticipation of the new age of love. The star that appears is the star of love, a higher consciousness of the mystery. It is distinctive not only for its beauty, but also for its alienation. This star, the symbol of true wisdom, is not at home in this world.

Abendstern
Johann Mayrhofer, D.806 March 1824
I am the star of true love... Others want nothing to do with me!

Oh beautiful star, you shine so softly, with such beauty!
Why are you alone in the sky? Why do your brethren avoid you?

Why not approach them?
Surely they could not deny you, sweet lonely light!

I plant no seed; I produce no fruit;
In sorrow and silence I stand alone!

THIRD MOVEMENT

The path of the just (wisdom) is like a shining light that glows in brilliance till perfect day.

Book of Proverbs

Transfiguration beckons. Divine life unites all things, resolves all contradictions. So the gods and goddesses never appear alone. Anticipated is a triumph of unity, a triumph of love, that sadly is not at home in this world.

Dithyrambe
Friedrich von Schiller D.801 ?1824
Believe me, divine spirits never appear alone.
First comes jolly Bacchus,
Then the young and happy Amor,
And Phoebe in her glory!
One by one they come until the hall is full!

What can I give in return?
They give me heavenly life!
They raise me to the peak of Olympus,
And grant joy proper to Jupiter's temple!
Pour me that nectar! Give me that chalice!

Yes! Give the poet the chalice!
Moisten his eyes with heavenly tears;
Avert his eyes from the river Styx!
Let him feel like one of us!

The drink bubbles in the cup.
His heart is at peace, his eyes bright and clear!

FOURTH MOVEMENT

The beginning of wisdom is: get wisdom!

Book of Proverbs

In a series of variations the composer relishes the transfiguring experience of the higher world. Inspired by a fantasy-like progression of poems the movement celebrates the sublime disposition that is at once triumphant and melancholy.

Der Einsame
Karl Lappe D.800 January 1825
When crickets sing in the evening by my fire…
I stare contentedly into the flame…
For a happy hour I stay and stir the coals…
And think…another day is done…

I remember the joys and sorrows of the day…
But nothing that disturbs me…
I prepare a happy dream…
And fall asleep in peace…

I love this peaceful life…
The heart that is a prisoner of the world is not at peace…

So sing away little cricket, you don't disturb me…
When I hear your song…
I know I am no longer alone.

Der Vollmond strahlt
Wilhelmina Christiane von Chézy, née Klencke D.797
The full moon shines over the mountains…'
How I long for you..
How wondrous when lovers kiss…
Of what value is May…you were my spring…
Light of my night…smile on me again in death…

Under the moon she looked at the heavens and sighed:
In life so distant, in death so close…
And gently two hearts touched.

Auflösung
Johann Mayrhofer D.807 March 1824
Sun, give way to a triumphant warmth that transfigures me!
Music, be silent before this transformation!
Springtime joy, stand in awe!
Wondrous power surges through me,
Filling me with heavenly music!
World, kneel before this divine beauty!

FIFTH MOVEMENT

Happy the man who finds wisdom.
Book of Proverbs

The spirit soars aloft in freedom, free of its chains.

Der Sieg
Johann Mayrhofer D.805 March 1824
The clouds of life are gone!
Pure, deep, powerful dreams drift
Amid the enchanting flowers.
The spirit is free of the body,
Soaring on high!

Thoughts are enlivened with heavenly food;
The body's ancient curse is gone!
Whatever pain I have suffered
Is swallowed in triumph!
My deepest yearning is stilled!

The Muse sing their lullaby,
Calling the Sphinx to final peace.
And my arm has conquered!

SIXTH MOVEMENT

The focus changes from the joy of the mystical experience to an awareness of its implications. This poet is being called to divine life...but also to his death. Like the sun he will achieve his greatest, most definitive triumph only by passing through death. He proclaims his readiness for this ordeal.

Im Abendrot
Karl Lappe D.799 1824 or 1825
How beautiful is your world, oh Father, when radiant in the light of the setting sun!
Your splendor cascades over the earth, bringing even the dust to life!
And the crimson sparkle settles upon my window pane!

O cannot complain, cannot fear, cannot refuse the invitation!
I shall carry within me the heaven now incarnate in the sunset!
Before it stops beating this heart of mine
Must drink in yet more of this divine beauty and light.

String Quartet No. 13 in A minor, D.804

March 1824

The light shines on in the darkness, a darkness that could not put it out.
Gospel of John

The spiritual journey that Schubert celebrates in his masterworks is an ascent to a higher world through the romance of opposites. But can contradictions in gender, race, nationality, and religion be reconciled? Is his wanderer's journey a tragedy or a triumph? Here it is both. In this profoundly mystical art the tragedy prepares the triumph. The First, Second, and Fourth Movements are night songs. Night holds the promise of a better world, an escape from the murderous world tyranny that prefers war to peace, hatred to love. In the classic words above from the *Fourth Gospel* wisdom sees both the divine light that is present in worldly emanations and the darkness that threatens that light at every point. The cosmic drama is the struggle of light for its transfiguration of the dark. The victories are hard-won at best and often impossible.

In this marvelous quartet an intense awareness of tragedy blends with an enraptured vision of the light. The certainty of death from syphilis combined with the tragic destruction of Schubert's hope for freedom and a new dawn for German society to occasion these reflections upon the contrast between the emptiness of his own time and the sweet mystery that invites a blind and unheeding world. There is an awareness of the growing cultural devastation that would nearly eliminate the wisdom tradition in his age and in our own. There is also an awareness of the transcendental beauty that laces the life experience at every point.

According to Gnostic Christianity, we are born into a world where hope for freedom, joy, and beauty is bound to be dashed on the shoals of mortality and limitation. Yet there are stars and the hope of ascending to them. The star of love suggests a new and different universe. It suggests an ethic of creative love in a sea of disparate and conflicting values. The birthing of this universe is painful. The rationalistic universe of power relationships cannot understand it and is threatened by it. This quartet addresses the lot of the star of love in a world in which the love-unity is unwelcome and war-power is king. This meant something specific in Schubert's day when freedom was repressed by the police state of Metternich. It means something unique in every age.

The lament of the first movement takes its inspiration from a poem of Johann Mayrhofer. The star of love is shunned by other stars. Sophia is avoided by the Archons. Only through commitment to the source of divine invitation is there hope and beauty. This movement places beauty before us, the high truth of the inner light, and then reminds us that this beauty is not at home in our world. This recognition does not debilitate the wanderer; it does not separate him from his world. Rather it is the condition for true freedom which comes from above and transforms the world, even its sorrows, in unity. A recognition that the satisfaction of one's inner longing does not reside in merely earthly dreams is for Schubert the condition for a truly heroic ethic.

The quartet continues in the second movement with an instrumental setting of the poem *Tranenregen* from the mystical wealth of the song cycle *Die Schöne Müllerin*. The poem focuses upon a mystical experience of the divine invitation in nature in which the wanderer is called to a mysterious and perhaps ominous adventure. This is experienced in a rapturous moment of young love. The wanderer in a sublime moment of damnable transience experiences the magic when earth and heaven touch.

The third movement laments the sad state of earthly life which betrays its own origins. Here the transfigured moment has passed leaving only sad signs of its radiant beauty. It also points to the need for poetry and music to witness to the higher world which has disappeared, leaving hardly a trace.

The fourth movement celebrates the higher life symbolized in the stars. There we read of love's triumphant beauty, which we make incarnate upon earth only when we recognize its transcendental source.

Each of Schubert's major instrumental compositions is a radical denial of the Enlightenment axiom that the absolute and its transcendental invitation can be reduced to an idea system with its logical applications. Each is antithetical to both the betrayal of heaven by the nihilists and the betrayal of earth by the religious fundamentalists. No earthly dream can be absolutely trusted. Only divine transcendence is worthy of that. This primary orientation towards a transcendental reality that outstrips every effort to grasp it frees the wanderer to create.

FIRST MOVEMENT

Works created through sorrow seem not to please the world.
Franz Schubert

Slowly, sadly this music introduces to us the tragic earthly fate of Sophia, divine beauty, symbolized in a star. In horror we see worldly power reject her. She is encouraged to approach her brothers and sisters; yet when she reveals herself she is spurned. Thus she must accept that this is not her kingdom. The tragedy of earthly existence, its enmity towards love, towards beauty, towards true wisdom, is placed dramatically before us. Each wanderer will have his or her unique experience of this sad truth.

Der Abendstern
Johann Mayrhofer, D.806
Why are you all by yourself in the sky,
Beautiful star? You shine so softly.
Why is it that your splendid brethren
Stay at a distance?
"I am the star of true love.
Others want nothing to do with me."

Then why not approach them?
After all you, the star of love, should not hesitate.
Which of them could deny you,
Dear sweet, lonely light?

I plant no seed...I produce no frruit...
I sorrow and silence I stand alone!

SECOND MOVEMENT

Amid the deepest shadow they shine in radiant light!
Pseudo Dionysius

The rhapsodic beauty of divine invitation is incarnate in a girl. The higher life that fills the wanderer calls him into strange new paths. The adventure is in her eyes. It unites the wanderer with the cosmos. For the moment at least heavenly forces fill his soul.

Tränenregen,
Wilhelm Müller, from *Die Schöne Müllerin* D.795
Lovingly we sat under the alder tree;
Together we looked into the slow-moving brook'
The moon came out; the stars followed;
All stared into the silvery mirror.

I saw no moon, no star;
I saw only her reflection, her eyes!

They nodded and looked up from the water...
The blue flowers looked with them...

And deep in that brook I saw the heavens...
Reaching out, drawing me into the sacred depths;

And all the while the brook ran above the clouds and stars,
Playfully calling: Friend, friend, follow me!
My tears welled up...the reflection blurred'
She said: "Its going to rain. I'm going home."

THIRD MOVEMENT

Only by shedding all and being freed from all, can you be uplifted to the ray of the divine shadow which is above all.

Pseudo Dionysius

This world, severed from love is alien to the higher world. For this wanderer the beauty that once reigned when the worlds were in harmony is gone. He touches that beauty only in recollection that like a pale shadow reminds him of the higher life for which he is made.

Die Götter Greichenlands
Friedrich Schiller, D.677
Oh world of beauty, where are you? Will you return?
Lovely, ancient blossoms of nature!
Now only in the poetry of a song
Can we know you.

Even the fields mourn your passing.
No divine spirits are alive here.
What was once fresh and warm with life
Is now but a pale shadow.

FOURTH MOVEMENT:

They completely fill our sightless minds with treasures beyond all beauty.

Pseudo Dionysius

The wanderer sees in the stars living testimonials to the higher life that exists as a shadow world within him. These star-symbols of a higher life suggest pure light. Earth can be transformed only by looking beyond itself to the transcendental source of wisdom, beauty, and love.

Die Sterne
Friedrich Schlegel, D.684

Man, do you ask why we sparkle with our holy light?
If only you could read us better,
You would understand our message of love.
Then there would be no more sorrow on the earth,
And eternal love would reign everywhere!
All would breath the clean, heavenly air!
The skies would be a sea of clear blue!
And the stars would ever grace our valley homeland!

Everything around us is godly in its origin.
Everything around us is indeed a single choir.
The gates of heaven are wide open!
Why be afraid?
Were you awakened to the height and depth of life,
You would see the stars sparkle about you,
The gentle waters comforting your heart,
And the storms of life could never disturb you.

STRING QUARTET NO. 14 IN D MINOR "DEATH AND THE MAIDEN", D.810

1824

Unless a grain of wheat falls to the earth and dies it remains just a grain of wheat.

Gospel of John

The rose cross mystery is terrifying. Earth's sultry climate chokes out the rays of the sun. Wisdom is crucified. Death seems triumphant. The wanderer must face the loss of hope for freedom and a new dawn for society in his world. That hope here takes the form of a child. In the first movement the child is a boy. In the second movement the child is a young girl. Both are innocent. Both are doomed to die. In Schubert's Austria the hope for a new dawn of problem solving in society seemed doomed by the Council of Vienna and the Metternich regime. But for true wisdom death is the shadow side of something beautiful, transfigured life. In the face of despair and death wisdom trusts in divine invitation.

The spiritual ascent to the higher consciousness of the mystery is not bought cheaply. The terror of death must be mastered. The creation of the sublime disposition in the face of this terror is the wanderer's challenge here. It will remain a challenge throughout the composer's remaining years, one that he faces in work after work. Here as always the wanderer comes to terms with death, and thereby discovers the key to life.

The *"Death and the Maiden" Quartet* places before us first the terror connected with this experiential act of faith, then the divine invitation, and finally, the exciting new life that dawns for the illuminated, initiated wanderer. This quartet, like so many of Schubert's works, is a kind of para-liturgy. In the first movement the wanderer cries out in terror at the fearsome specter of death.

Fatherly comfort is meaningless as the fearsome and relentless adversary draws near in a dance. The Erlkönig here is not a friend, but the archenemy. The child, the higher life of the wanderer, is locked in a world where that enemy reigns. The challenge laid down by this first movement is that of finding the higher consciousness in the face of this horror. The challenge will re-surface again and again during Schubert's last four years of life, each time to be tamed and overcome, obviously for only a time, by the higher consciousness.

This commitment to a celebration of the sublime disposition inh the teeth of threatening death will continue even through the posthumous piano sonatas, composed shortly before Schubert's death. The composer and his wanderer, while feeling the threat, have spiritual resources. The uncontrolled paranoia of this movement is the that of one who lacks true wisdom. Illumination is still to come.

In the second movement Death speaks and is transformed. Now, through a set of magical variations, it becomes an invitation, a joy, enticing, coaxing, forcing the beloved to come home. An awakening occurs. The girl, the incarnation of Sophia, is called out of helpless terror and strengthened to respond to the invitation, which is to neither emptiness nor evil, but rather to love.

There is a striking change in the third movement. The wanderer sings a song of childlike faith and joy, thanking the inviter who calls in and through the life experience. The theme of child-like trust in the face of terror reflects the directive of Jesus to "become like little children" in seeking the kingdom of God.

The fourth movement of this mighty quartet is a celebration of the freedom and courage of the higher consciousness experienced in the face of death's fearsome challenge. Here is the insistent pulsing of a higher life. The wanderer now is liberated, freed from his prison of fear, supremely creative.

FIRST MOVEMENT:

As a woman about to give birth writhes and cries out in her pains, so were we in your presence, oh Lord!

Isaiah

The specter of death, the Erlkönig. looms fearsomely over the life of the wanderer who at this point can only flee and plead. With death implacably, irresistibly approaching the wanderer can barely control his fear.

Erlkönig
Johann Wolfgang von Goethe D 328 10-1815
Who rides so late through night and wind? It is the father with his child!
He holds the boy close in his arms, clasps him safely, giving him warmth.

My son, why are you hiding your head in fear?
Father, can't you see the Earl King, with crown and throne?
My son it is only mist!

Dear boy, come away with me. We'll play games.
Pretty flowers grow by the river.
My mother's clothes are of gold!
Father, father! Can't you hear the Erl Kings whispers?

Be calm, be calm my son; it is only the dry leaves rustling in the wind!

Will you now come with me? My daughters will entertain you.
They will dance for you, rock you, hold you, and sing you to sleep.
Father, father, can't you see the Erlking's daughter just out of the light?

My son, I see indeed an old willow tree shining in the moonlight!

Oh I want you! I desire your youthful beauty!
And if you don't come now I will use force!
Father, oh Father, now he seizes me.
The Erl King is hurting me!

The father shudders and rides even faster,
Holding the suffering child;
When he finally arrives the child is dead!

SECOND MOVEMENT:

...The brilliant darkness of hidden silence...
Pseudo Dionysius

Death, the wanderer's destiny, responds to the plea. "I am your friend! Trust me and come!" Again and again the invitation is repeated in a series of magical variations. Here in this darkness is the invitation to ascend.

Der Tod und das Mädchen
Matthias Claudius, D 531
Give me your hand, my beautiful one...
I am your friend...I do not come to harm you...
Do not fear...I am not evil...
You will rest gently in my arms.

THIRD MOVEMENT:

The ability to believe...pertains to the things which the soul wills...
Nicholas of Cusa

Joyfully the wanderer celebrates life. He is childlike in accepting the divine invitation.

Täglich zu singen
Matthias Claudius, D 533
I thank God and am happy,
Like a child at Christmas...
That I am here now, that I have you,
That I have a fine, human face,
That I can see the sun, the mountains and sea,
The leaves and the grass,
That in the evening I can walk out
Under an army of stars and the beautiful moon.

...

Das Lied vom Reifen
Matthias Claudius, D 532
Look at these precious trees!
So noble they are!
On each branch
Is the magic of frost.

It covers the trees
From bottom to top,
Hanging so delicately, like lace.
It could hardly be more lovely!

God's own angel each night
Sprinkles frost here and there.
And by the time the farmer wakes,
He is gone.

Kind angel
We thank you! We praise you!
When Christmas comes again
Won't you make the trees white?

FOURTH MOVEMENT

If you bring forth what is within you, what you bring forth will save you.
The Gospel of Thomas

Consciousness of the mystery triumphs over fear. Paranoia is set aside. This wanderer is a free man, not a slave to fear. His freedom originates in the divine fire of his inner life, and he pursues his own destiny in strength and courage.

Der Schiffer
Johann Mayrhofer, D 536

In wind, in storm I ride the river of life,
My clothes drenched in the driving rain.
With mighty stroke I pull at the waves,
Hoping, hoping for the dawn of a clear day.

The waves beat against my creaking boat.
The whirlpool threatens, the rocks menace.
Boulders fall from the mountains above.
The tall trees whine like spirits.

This is just the way I want it!
I cannot stand a life of comfort!
If those waves suck me down
I would not regret my life.

Waves, thunder away!
In my heart is a sacred source of life,
Giving me new strength. It is indeed divine
To dare to ride the storm with the
courage of a man!

Piano Sonata for Four Hands in C major, D.812

October 1824

The man who loves his life loses it, while the man who hates his life in this world preserves it to life eternal.

Gospel of John

The paradoxical higher consciousness of the rose cross mystery is conditioned by an acceptance of death as the passage through sorrow and death in a return "home". Its perspectives embrace the transcendental reality whose invitation gives meaning to life. This great piano sonata is the fruit of Schubert's understanding of his own life. The key to the sublime disposition that is so characteristic of this composer's work is an acceptance of his own death as a defining event in the spiritual ascent. The years 1823 and 1824 were years of sickness when death threatened the composer's peace. During those years and until his death in 1828 fear was a specter that had to be exorcised, not once, but often. While the fear was a crippling and deadening contradiction to his hopes for a new age, its taming was spiritually and artistically liberating. If death posed a recurring challenge to Schubert, his victories over fear are reflected in the peace, joy, and astounding artistic creativity of the last six years of his life. This composer had to struggle with both sickness and the frustration of his hopes for the acceptance of his art. He won his struggle with despair, and just this ascent beyond fear into the higher consciousness is the experience that lies at the heart of his art.

The *Piano Sonata for Four Hands in C Major D 812* is a celebration, not an instruction. One can experience with the composer his radiant transfigurations of the life experience. Everything comes alive, enriched in luminous beauty. One of Schubert's favorite symbols for the transfiguring effect of his experience of life's mystery was a sunset. Life in the shadow of death can have bitter-sweet beauty. This beauty has been called the "sublime". Both the First and Second Movements of this sonata express rich experiences of this. First courage then beauty are found in a premonition of living in the shadow of death. The music presents a musical celebration of the wanderer's resignation and peace.

The third movement is a quasi-liturgical preparation for the artistic challenge awaiting the wanderer. He takes a godly potion that elevates him to a higher consciousness, raising him above the earth for the creative task that he has dared to make his own.

In the miracle of this fourth movement the wanderer-hero anticipates his mystical and artistic triumph. He raises his arm in a gesture of victorious celebration. Schubert guesses that demons are in his future, but never doubts that he will climb the ladder to the stars in his own art, setting in music experiences that defy words and make of man a god.

FIRST MOVEMENT

> *...a first voice rang out, crying to Mankind peacefully sleeping on the raft of earth: We are moving! We are going forward!...*
>
> *Pierre Teilhard de Chardin*

The wanderer is called to ascend to the life of the gods through a full immersion in worldly life, including dying. The acceptance of the call is proclaimed.

Gebet
Friedrich Heinrich Karl, Freiherr de La Motte-Fouqué, D.815
O Spring of Goodness!
Spring of power and might!
You breathe gently from the flowers.
You thunder forth in war.
The world is your cathedral,
Your festival banquet!
The world in its height and breadth
Is field for your invitation.
O Spring of Goodness!
Spring of power and might!
You see into my heart.
You know its joys, its sorrow.
My final and true home gently calls me.
A noble death is to be mine!
In this are united
Innocent grace
And flaming purgation
Of shame and guilt.
I feel that in battle

I might walk in the path of my fathers.
My wife and my child are safe at home…
The love that I have for them is yours.
Yours also is the courage
That swells my breast.
If you will, oh Lord,
Let peace again reign!
A decent world can be formed!
But if this is not to be, then give us light
For hard work through stormy nights.
You are eternal love and power;
Your will be done.
Whatever happens to me,
I am ready.
Whether you call to faithful love
Or to fierce warfare and sacrifice,
In battle, in pilgrimage, or in a happy home
Your will be done.
Only let me, whatever may happen,
Rest finally in heaven!
O Spring of Goodness,
O Spring of power and might,
You breath gently from the flower.
You thunder forth in war.
The world is your cathedral,
Your festival banquet.
The world in its height and breadth
Is field for your invitation.
Whatever that invitation is for me,
Lord, I am ready…
Be it for a life of faithful love,
Or for courageous battle!
Let your will be done!
And whatever may happen,
Let me rest at last in the better world!

SECOND MOVEMENT

What then is the starting point. It is to be open to the divine workings of God, to clear the spiritual ascent towards the inheritance which awaits us.
Pseudo Dionysius

The wanderer reflects upon the glory of the invitation as revealed in the beauty of a sunset. As the day is dying beauty of special radiance can be seen. The wanderer is aware that, like the day, he is being called to the sublime beauty of the spiritual ascent while descending into the darkness of the night.

Im Abendrot
Karl Lappe, D.799
Oh, how beautiful is your world,
Father, when it is radiant in the gold of the setting sun!
Then your splendor cascades
Over the earth bringing even the dust to life!
Then the crimson sparkle which glows on the clouds,
Settles upon my window pane.

I cannot complain, cannot fear,
Cannot refuse your invitation!
No. I shall carry within me
The heaven which is now incarnate in the sunset.
This heart of mine, before it stops beating,
Must drink in yet more of this divine beauty and light.

THIRD MOVEMENT

Whoever drinks the water I shall give will never thirst.
Gospel of John

The wanderer now experiences a better world. He lives the illuminated life of the heavens as he prepares for his artistic task. Death has lost its terror. His ethic is godly.

Dithyrambe
Friedrich Schiller, D.801
Believe me divine spirits never appear alone! Never!
Bacchus, jolly as ever, arrives,
Then Amor, the smiling youth is here also.
Phoebe, in her glory pays a visit.
They come, each spirit, one by one,
Until the hall is filled!

Tell me, earthlings, what can I give
To these citizens of a better world?
They give me their divine life,
What can I, a man, offer to them?
Lift me to the heights of Mt. Olympus!
Joy can be found only in Jupiter's temple,
Pour me some of that nectar!
Give me the chalice!

Hand him the chalice! Give the poor poet a drink.
Moisten his eyes with heavenly tears,
So that he never looks upon the black River Styx.
Let him think himself one of us!

The potion foams and bubbles in the heavenly cup.
His heart now is at peace...
His eyes bright and clear.

FOURTH MOVEMENT

Let the one who thirsts come forward. Let the one who wants it receive the gift of life-giving water!

Book of Revelation

Transfiguration realized in music! Here is spiritual freedom, a taste of the better world made possible through a musical experience of gnosis. This triumph is mystical, a victory of the inner life of the wanderer and the sublime art that it inspires, a foretaste of eternal triumph.

Der Sieg
Johann Mayrhofer, D.805
The clouds of life are gone!
Pure, deep, clear, powerful dreams drift amid the enchanting flowers.

The spirit breaks free from its body prison...
It soars on high!

Thoughts are enlivened by heavenly food.
The body's ancient curse is gone.

Whatever pain I have borne,now the triumph is mine.
My deepest yearning is stilled at last.

The Muse sing the sphinx to final peace,
And my own arm is raised in triumph.

The clouds of life are gone!
Pure, deep, clear, powerful dreams drift amid the enchanting flowers.

Sonata in A major for Arpeggione and Piano, D.821

1824

The mighty shall be mightily put to the test.
Book of Wisdom

The joy of life has faded away into the distant past for this wanderer. The triumph of love seems impossibly distant. Yet there is mystery in the sadness. Here he reflects upon the tragic beauty of his lost love and finds peace in the mysterious invitation to transcend this world. The dream of an ascent to transcendental fulfillment dressed in music bathes his life in hope. Heaven and earth once again touch. And for this wanderer it is music that serves this romance with mystical power.

The new age in which love is triumphant means something unique to each of us. One font of sorrow in Schubert's life was his alienation as an artist. Accepted for superficial reasons, unknown or rejected for his true value as the foremost artistic celebrant of wisdom, his dream of acceptance by musical peers and the Viennese public had to be set aside. The experience that he wanted to share through music was that of the spiritual ascent. That ascent was unorthodox and impolitic. It was not acceptable to the church, to Metternich, nor to the Enlightenment. It would not be acceptable to later modernism nor to post-modernism. Schubert did not hate or reject the orthodoxies. Like the modern Jew who is critical of Zionism or the American who opposes his country's imperialism Schubert transcended the orthodoxies of his day. He paid a high price for doing so.

Schubert found light in the shadow of contradiction. His focus upon conflicting ideas, ideologies, and art forms created the opportunity for the wanderer to transcend them in the spiritual ascent. He found truth more in poetry than in dogma because poetry captures *the Truth* through suggestive allegory and myth and does not pretend to do so through prosaic ideas. He, like many others, was forced to speak in symbols. His operas, symbolic enough to evade public understanding for one hundred and fifty years, could not escape the discerning eye of those who controlled music in Vienna. Like Donizetti's *Poliuto* in Italy, neither *Alfonso und Estrella* nor *Lazarus* could be staged. This wanderer desired to share his core life experience with others through his music. But his beloved Vienna and the larger musical world were not interested. Much of his "sorrow" consisted in knowing that his music truly expressed an ascent to the mystery, but the ascent and the mystery itself were unwanted.

In the first movement of the *Arpeggione Sonata,* he laments the failure of the wanderer as lover and artist. His "dream" is almost forgotten. One feels the spirits rise simply through the power of the music, yet redemption remains distant. The sad beauty of this movement is magical.

In the second movement the wanderer's life leads irresistibly downhill until at last the vesper bell sounds through the valley its sad tidings of death. Thus it seems that Schubert has led us to a place where no one really wants to go. But he leads us not to rebellious defeat but to sad resignation and the recognition that there is more to life than meets the eye. There redemption finds him.

The third movement celebrates a re-awakening of life. The wanderer is given life paradoxically through an invitation that transforms his life experience. He is invited to hurry outside to life and love, and in nature's freedom to fly with a freedom that is his own. One discovers the sublime in this music, in its flight out of and above the looming specter of despair and death. The flight of the birds evokes the liberation of the soul. The sunset suggests that liberation has its transcendental dimension, realized fully only beyond death.

FIRST MOVEMENT

By the waters of Babylon we sat and wept as we remembered Zion.
Psalm 137

The sublime is discovered in life's shadows. The dream is gone. No earthly hope beckons the wanderer. Only memories serve to remind him of life and joy. Torn between the sad yearning and the recollections, this wanderer looks up towards the star of love, so distant, yet real and alive with gentle hope.

Ewige Liebe
Ernst Schulze, D.825
Strings, sound in the evening stillness;
From so far away bring my dream back to me.
I hear the music in swelling harmonies,
Filling the halls with sounds of love.
My despairing heart is rocked and raised
Above its storm of fear on a flood of melody.

Never, ever have these strings sung
For power or for gold;
They joyfully display their precious treasure
For little reward.
If some resist their beauty
The songs return to their Muse.

Ah, if only in song I could realize my golden dream,
Or in Battle could fight for it and make it real!
But love grants her reward easily to neither poet nor warrior.
How gladly would I die for love;
But for me love shine only in the distance, like a friendly star!

SECOND MOVEMENT

From this valley of tears you must ascend.
Augustine

The wanderer faces the inner truth of his life. His dream has not been realized. As the vesper bell rolls out its sad but peaceful call, he knows that life leads to the grave, which paradoxically is dawn to all the wanderer's hopes.

Wehmut
Heinrich Hüttenbrenner, D.825 No. 1
The Vesper bell chimes…
Peace is poured down from the heavens.
The eye clouds with tears…
But does not close.
My youth is wasted…
I am alone and unloved.
Every flower for me has wilted…
This is my complaint!
When I was young…
My heart and my world were my joy.
Now that my youth is lost…
My very breath is a waste!
The stream flowing from the rocky spring,
And the mountains cannot love…
Only a heart can do that…
And hearts can be so easily broken by sadness.
Sound, gentle vesper bell…
Throughout this quiet valley.
As dawn crowns the day…
So does death crown a life of sorrow!

THIRD MOVEMENT

Who can understand what the afterlife shall be if our hearts make their ascent?

Augustine

The mystery of the grave leads directly to the mystery of life fulfilled. All is transfigured in the acceptance of the invitation. Life blooms everywhere. Nature in its beauty sings the life song with the wanderer. Like a bird he has been set free.

Flucht
Karl Lappe, D.825
I want to live out of doors.
Death dwells enclosed in a box!
See the sunset
Reflecting upon the hillside…
Life blooms out of doors.
Misery stays inside.
…
Hurry then, run outside
Before the heart slows.
I need the light and the space!
…
I want to live out of doors!

Dear bird, let us both fly away,
Driven aloft by nature!

Piano Sonata in E flat for Four Hands, D.823

1825

If the wanderer was reflective and sad in the *Arpeggione;* in this piano sonata he is desperate and angrily insistent upon a destiny that he knows to be his own. The published title of the first movement called the work a "divertissement". In fact we have here a magnificent work for four hands, one better called the *Sehnsucht (yearning) Sonata*. For here is Schubert's demand for a new age where Becoming is swallowed up in Being, i.e. where love is triumphant. The ascent to Being for this wanderer is painful.

The *mysterium magnum* is a paradox. It demands a courageous and creative commitment to the union of opposites symbolized in the union of lovers. The limitations of life are accepted. The limitations upon transcendental expectations are not. The poetry in this sonata for four hands is the same as the poetry inspiring the *Arpeggione Sonata*. But here the higher consciousness takes a different form. It is a strong, almost strident commitment to the freedom implied by love's transcendental triumph.

This is a disturbing work. Not peace but a fierce and almost feral fidelity in the higher life is in focus. The commitment is revolutionary. The quest for freedom becomes a demand. While three poems *Ewige Liebe, Wehmut*, and *Flucht* inspire both the *Arpeggione Sonata* and the *Piano Sonata in E Flat,* in the *Arpeggione* the sadness is gentle, the memories full of love, the vision of freedom airy and transcendental. In the *E Flat Sonata* the lament has a raw edge and the freedom that is sought seems to be both personal and political. Each work is true to the inspiring poetry. But that poetry allows for many interpretations... here by the same composer. In the *Piano Sonata in E Flat* a longer version of the poem *Ewige Liebe* is used as inspiration. The new portion of the poem proclaims a fidelity in love that leads through death. The addition brings ferocity with it. This wanderer commits himself to the dream of freedom and love with awesome power. The world's resistance to this dream only serves to intensify his determination to pursue it, a pursuit that leads to thoughts of death.

The first movement poclaims monumental love for an absent woman. Who is she? Certainly she is the idealized world, its "stars and flowers", certainly nature, certainly political freedom, certainly artistic success, certainly Theresa Grob, Schubert's immortal beloved. The woman sparkles and invites. She indeed is Sophia, the divine image in creation, finally to be won beyond death. Romancing her demands courage and commitment. A split between earthly objectives and transcendental expectations combines a strongly willed commitment with an almost breezy dismissal of any expectation that the fruits will be harvested before death.

In the sublime second movement the transcendental realization of the dream is in clear focus through variations on a musical expression of: *As dawn crowns the day, so does death crown a life of sorrow.* In the musical setting of these sad words the composer ascends to the higher consciousness in which transcendental perspectives replace earthly ones. He revels in the peace and beauty of the ascent.

In the powerful third movement, heaven and earth commingle in a fierce demand for freedom. Mysticism has political consequences. This underlying idea is made even more powerful by a fourth poem *Der Tanz* by Kolumban Schnitzer von Merrau D 826 in which the emptiness of life devoid of the higher consciousness leads to a demand for a higher life, a better world..

FIRST MOVEMENT:

> *Though the outer self is wasting away, the inner self is being renewed, day by day.*
>
> *Second Epistle to the Corinthians*

The demand is made for music to bring back the dream. With despair and anger the wanderer looks at what has happened to his dream of a kingdom of love. And with the awareness comes intense re-commitment that does not shy away from the death that the dream will demand. The wanderer uses the beauty and mystery of the dream to strengthen his commitment to its realization.

Ewige Liebe
Ernst Schulze, D.825
Strings sound in the evening stillness;
From so far away bring my dream back to me.

I hear the music in swelling harmonies,
Filling the halls with sounds of love.

My despairing heart is rocked and raised
Above its storm of fear on a flood of melody

Never, ever have these strings sung
For power or for gold;

They joyfully radiate their precious treasure
For little reward.

If some resist their beauty
The songs return to their Muse.

Ah, if only in song I could realize my golden dream,
Or in Battle could fight for it and make it real!

But love grants her reward easily to neither
Poet nor warrior.

How gladly would I die for love;
But for me love shine only in the distance, like a friendly star!

"Ventured and won"
Is engraved upon my sword!
"Ventured and lost"
Is my sad lot!

But I like this characterization of my lot.
If it falls in battle
Well, let me fall with it.

No man is worthy
Of love's reward,
Nor wins his beloved
By fleeing the fight.

In the hot coals of longing
Is the heart destroyed.
It soon bleeds out its life
In long and deep pain.

But I feel my own wound,
And I love this suffering.
I will leave what happens
To the future.

And indeed the woman
Who so tortured his heart
Was yet loved in fidelity
Even as he died.

SECOND MOVEMENT

Think of what is above, not of what is on earth.

Epistle to the Colossians

The vesper bell recalls the tragedy of the wanderer's life. The memories are of failed hopes and dreams betrayed, yet the vesper bell sounds a new note. The dream will one day be realized. The thought of death is a reminder of final triumph, explored in a series of variations.

Wehmut
Heinrich Hüttenbrenner, D.825
The Vesper bell chimes.
Peace is poured down from the heavens.
The eye clouds with tears,
But does not close.
My youth is wasted.
I am alone and unloved.
Every flower for me has wilted...
This is my complaint!
When I was young
My heart and my world were my joy.
Now that my youth is lost.
My very breath is a waste!
The stream flowing from the rocky spring,
And the mountains cannot love...
Only a heart can do that.
And hearts can be so easily broken by sadness.
Sound, gentle vesper bell,
Throughout this quiet valley.As dawn crowns the day,
So does death crown a life of sorrow!

THIRD MOVEMENT

We are children of no slave, but of a free woman...so stand firm and do not submit to the yoke of slavery!

Epistle to the Galatians

Enlivened by the anticipation of final triumph this wanderer joyfully recommits himself to freedom and love. This commitment is intensely earthy. "Before the heart slows" this wanderer must create his freedom. Here is a joyful but strong-willed warrior, one newly invigorated by his certainty of transcendental victory, who accepts his role as knight-protector to his beloved, and courageously pursues his goal. This wanderer demands the spirit of the birds.

Flucht
Karl Lappe, D.825
I want to live out of doors.
Death dwells enclosed in a box!
See the sunset
Reflecting upon the hillside...
Life blooms out of doors.
Misery stays inside.
...
Hurry then, run outside
Before the heart slows.
I need the light and the space!
...
I want to live out of doors!

Dear bird, let us both fly away,
Driven aloft by nature!

DerTanz
Kolumban Schnitzer von Meerau D.826
Young people dance and dream of parties and banquets;
But when they have them they complain of pains in head and heart;
Their heaven has disappeared!
"Oh make me sound just once more!"...
Their cry as they implore the heavens!

Piano Sonata in C major (Unfinished), D.840

1825

The night is pregnant with the mystrery. It is a paradox presenting in its darkness a glimpse of the new age of light. The *Piano Sonata in C Major D.840* is a quasi-liturgical work, one uniquely crafted to introduce a group into an experience of the rose cross mystery. It celebrates an ascent to the higher consciousness through music and the mystery of the night. The stars are symbols of the universe of values that co-exists with the universe of ideas. For this wanderer they are divine invitations to transcendence. This night world is alive and vibrant.

There is no ideology, no set of ideals, no science, no commandments, no book, no single man or woman in whom the divine fullness is fully and permanently realized. No messiah, no sacrament, no incarnation of the divine is that fullness. No definition of God, no scientific theory, no religion, no political system escape this limitation. So the higher consciousness, with its shadowy experience of that fullness, is ever searching for what embraces yet transcends every experience. Longing is its trademark. This recognition of limits to each and every experience of the divine invitation co-exists with the reality of incarnations of that divinity. The higher consciousness recognizes incarnations of the divine and follows their call. But the higher consciousness also recognizes that every incarnation must be measured against a fullness which calls us yet further in the spiritual ascent. In Christian terms this means that we can and do rejoice in the divine incarnation of two thousand years ago, but realize with St. Paul that the fullness remains transcendental.

Night here is an invitation to the higher consciousness of this hidden higher world. In the clarity of midday ideas we see much yet miss something essential. This hidden reality is suggested by the night. When earth's shapes are muted, divine truth can be felt. This sensitivity to deeper truth is expressed in the first movement of this sonata.

The *Piano Sonata in C Major* is only a torso. The last two movements were left incomplete. The first movement in particular is finished and awesome. Schubert effectively creates a magical setting in which a wanderer encounters in the night the mystery at the heart of his life. The night song helps us feel the star-shine and soft light of the moon, and in magical light it awakens us to awareness of the better world. We sense the thrill of its invitation, even though we remain pilgrims and far from home. We are immersed in a prefiguration of the better world, a kind of mystical celebration of the inner secret of the life experience. But then in the development section the very same mystery is celebrated as it is realized in interpersonal love. As the wanderer unites with others in love the mystery appears. Foul winds, contradictions, disappear. We are each on our way, invited into the pleroma.

Early in the same year Schubert set three poems by Sir Walter Scott which may be the inspiration for the Second, and the incomplete Third, and Fourth Movements. The Secxond Movement is inspired by the poem *Lied der Anna Lyle*, set by Schubert as D 830. The recognition of the parting of the lovers suggests Schubert' relationship with Theresa Grob.

FIRST MOVEMENT

Above all reigns the fountain of light, the truth of truths, the God of gods,
for all is full of divinity, truth and goodness.

Giordano Bruno

The night dawns in its immensity, and covers the earth with its magic. As edges are blurred, freedom appears. Slowly, solemnly, majestically, night ascends. The wanderer invites us to share with him the special moment. The sharing will be through song and mystical imagination. In a hymn reminiscent of Orpheus the wanderer rejoices in the night, its peace, its luminosity, its stars, its love-bonding, its living invitation to transcendence.

In the wisdom tradition night is a sacred time, a foretaste of the better world, an experience of its call, a symbol of the mystery. Through this music we can experience this. In the development section the focus shifts from the radiance of the night to the radiance of love. Closer and closer does the spiritual ascent bring us to others climbing the same mountain. Together with the wanderer we stand, awestruck by the mystery of the better world, sacramentalized in the transfigured night. We gasp in awe at the monumental universe of love that envelops us.

Nachtmusik
Karl Sigmund Freiherr von Seckendorf, D 848
I will play for you a song on my flute,
In sounds rich and sweet, to harp accompaniment…

It will be a song of nocturnal joy.
Come outside to joyous freedom
In the evening's twilight enchantment.
...
Look. All now sleep under the watchful eye of the moon.
Worries disappear.
The country is cradled in sleep...
Cradled in love.
...
Don't delay. Get up!
All of the stars joyously wait for you!
They are kind to good people,
And sprinkle golden treasure from their distant vaults.
...
Come and join us!
Here no false wind will blow,
So be greeted in darkness!
Night unites us ever closer,
When one holds his friend's hand.
...
So with flute and harp in sweet harmony,
Come, share our joy and join our group.
In the night's stillness
Your eye may be blessed and your heart fulfilled.

SECOND MOVEMENT

Here is sad resignation to the pain of the winter's journey of life

Lied der Anna Lyle, ***Annot Lyle's song***

Andrew MacDonald, quoted in Walter Scott, *The Legend of Montrose.* The translation used by Schubert in D.830 was attributed by Deutsch to Sophie May, but it cannot be traced.

Wert thou, like me, in life's low vale,
With thee how blest, that lot I'd share;
With thee I'd fly wherever gale
Could waft, or bounding galley bear.
But parted by severe decree,
Far different must our fortunes prove;
May thine be joy - enough for me
To weep and pray for him I love.
The pangs this foolish heart must feel,
When hope shall be forever flown,
No sullen murmur shall reveal,
No selfish murmurs ever own.

Nor will I through life's weary years,
Like a pale drooping mourner move,
While I can think my secret tears
May wound the heart of him I love.

Piano Sonata in A minor, D.845

1825

In this majestic sonata, the ascent to the rose cross mystery leads through the agony of unrequited love to a sublime disposition of peace underlying the pain. The yearning of the alienated wanderer for the absent dream maiden is set in stark contrast to his hope for love's fulfillment. He is painfully aware of the chasm that separates him from the world of his dreams. His life has the character of an exile. It is a prison out of which he must go if he is to find his complete freedom. In feeling his way through the mists of life he encounters sacraments of divine invitation in the stars and flowers which grace his (or her) path. He anticipates the end of his journey as the consummation rather than the nullification of these loves. This piano sonata is a celebration of an exile's painful ascent. The emergence out of darkness into light presented in the *Wanderer Fantasy* and in the *Piano Sonata in A Major D 959* is here an analogue of the archetypal passage through death to transfiguration.

The wanderer (who is the composer's alter-ego as well as our own) is a stranger in a foreign land, wild and savage. He wants the peace of his true home, but lacks the power to gain it. He has tried to find that peace in his wandering, but in vain. Here is the Gnostic hero, locked in darkness, but alive with a divine spark, and hungry for the fullness of light. This sonata tells the tale of his liberation.

The first movement reveals the wanderer's savage need for love and its absence in his life. He wishes that he could sing with the birds, join the symphony of nature praising God. Yet he feels cut off from beauty, unable to sing, for his springtime has not yet come. What can be done to free the spirit and the voice of this one who would sing with nature? The adequate resolution is both an artistic obligation and the personal need of the composer.

It is clear that Schubert finds his artistic confrontations with life's challenge liberating. Freedom will be won and re-won over these last years of his life and seems conditioned by the honesty with which he admits and expresses the grueling pains and fears of his life experience. The higher consciousness evidenced in the last three movements would be unintelligible apart from the authenticity of the sorrow expressed in the first movement.

The second movement has two parts, each with a separate poem as its inspiration. First, through a musical setting of a Schlegel poem the wanderer is called to nourish his spirit in nature. Nature is at peace in her eternal rhythms. Starting here the wanderer, aware of the power residing within himself, is called upwards to courage and constancy in the midst of his winter's journey. A second poem by Schlegel introduces a new spirit altogether. The wanderer, engaged in a love ascent, becomes aware, in mystical premonition, of the love fulfillment that he is sure awaits him. Once again sorrow is transfigured in a higher consciousness.

The third movement celebrates going home as if it were a ride on horseback. The passage is through darkness to light, a symbol of dying and new life. In the process of going home this wanderer has a job to do. He is a knight, a creator of beauty, who must woo his beloved through faithful commitment to his task. Thus must he turn from enchanting distractions, and renew his commitment to celebrations of the great romance. He races ahead towards love's radiant light.

In the fourth movement Schubert sets Pyrker's great German hymn, praising God in his presence throughout creation. Here is the composer's artistic resolution of the dilemma posed in the first movement. We note just how successful are Schubert's efforts to free himself from despair and find new life through an awareness of divine invitation. Rather than seeing the life experience as hopeless, rather than mind-numbing bitterness in the face of pain and sorrow, his wanderer finds liberation of spirit and sings his thanks to God. Conditioned by the embrace of his "sorrow" Schubert's wanderer can celebrate life.

FIRST MOVEMENT

Tell the one I love most that I sicken, suffer, and die.

John of the Cross

A wandering theme is sounded. Then follows the expression of pain, persistent, insistent, always there. The wanderer has been deprived of the love that alone makes his life worthwhile. He cannot sing with the birds, cannot rejoice with the spring, but identifies with nature in the wild, on the move, ever restless, longing for the beyond. Will he find his peace…ever?

Im Walde

Ernst Schulze, D 834

I wander over peaks and valleys,
Through meadows of green.

And with me wanders... my pain!
It never leaves me,
If I crossed the wide ocean,
That pain would be there!

How many flowers bloom in the meadows!
I don't notice them.
Only one flower can I see,
Wherever I go.
How often have I reached for it,
Yet never, ever has it been mine.

How beautifully the birds sing
Amid the branches.
How glad I would be to sing with them...
But I stay silent and sad,
The joy of love and the pain of love
Avoid one another.

High in the sky, as if winged,
The clouds fly by.
I hear the lapping of waters,
Gently upon the shore.
Stirred by the breeze
Clouds and waters cavort.

But I wander back and forth
Through all kinds of weather,
And never can I find
What I crave.
Oh longing of love! Oh pain of love!
When will this wanderer find peace?

SECOND MOVEMENT

May the eyes of your hearts be enlightened... that you may experience the hope of your calling and the riches of your inheritance.

Epistle to the Ephesians

The inner life of the wanderer is here the guide, pointing beyond this life to a better one. In premonitions and memories he finds hope for the realization of dreams. He commits himself courageously and firmly to fidelity to the invitation. The hope becomes thrilling anticipation. The wanderer's sense of the coming love-victory grows. A mystical communication binds the lovers as they draw ever nearer to their transcendental goal.

Abendlied fur die Entfernte
August Wilhelm von Schlegel, D 856

Look forth, eyes of mine, out upon the valley.
There you still find life's riches!
Delight in the beams of the moon,
And in the sacred peace.

Listen undisturbed, my heart.
Hark to the gentle music,
Which from afar, for joy and woe,
Enfolds you.

When premonition and memory
Are united in our experience,
The door is open to the twilight shadows
Of the gently whispering spirit.

Were we not able to enhance
This life with our dreams of the better one,
How colorless, how dark, how dull
Would our existence be!

Our heart, hopes, and trusts, and believes
Even in the face of death.
It joyfully lives in the present
And considers itself rich in blessings.

The wealth that it creates for itself
No misfortune can destroy.
It lives and moves with warmth and strength,
Under providential care, and in hope.

And when in the night and fog
All else perishes
The heart will treasure its every battle
And will win its own shield.

With noble constancy in adversity
It suffers its fate at night;
Thus I fall asleep and waken to
the new dawn,
If not in heavenly joy, at least in peace.

...

Widerschein
August Wilhelm von Schlegel, D 855
The spring sun's ever-rudiant smile
Is morning dawn to all my hopes.
I hear a whisper in the western breeze,
A sign full of the bliss to come.
I'm coming, past valleys and hills,
Oh sweet bringer of my bliss!
On the rapid wings of song,
The lover sends greetings over to you!

Accept love's greeting from your friend.
He, without love returned, swore
To worship you for ever and ever;
As steady, as sure as nature herself.
He looks to his lode star;
And, like a solitary boatman, listens…
In hope that out of the celestial darkness
The sound of that distant star might be heard.

THIRD MOVEMENT

Think of what is above, not of what is on earth.
Epistle to the Colossians

This wanderer no longer walks. Horse-mounted he rides swiftly through the night, with dangers on every side, single-mindedly committed to his goal of returning home. That home is love's fulfillment… and sure he is sure of reaching tt.

Auf der Brucke
Ernst Schulze, D 853
My fine steed, trot without rest
Through night and rain!
Do not fear bush or thicket.
Don't shy at the wild country.
The forest is indeed thick,
But in the end it will open.
A distant glow of welcome
Will light up the dark valley.

I ride swiftly over mountains and meadows,
High on your back,
And could easily stop to enjoy the world,

To see new, enchanting sights.
How many bright eyes now attract me,
Promising peace, love and joy!
Yet I canter on, without rest...
Back, back to my pain.

For three days I have been away
From the one to whom I am bound.
For three days the sun and stars,
The earth and heavens disappeared.
The joy and anguish she resolved
Were again in turmoil and conflict.
For three days I felt only the anguish,
But the joy I lacked.
Now all over the land
Birds seek a better, warmer home!
Is it possible for true love
Not to do the same?
And though the way is dark and full of mystery,
My longing is awake and watchful,
And I race ahead
In sweet anticipation!

FOURTH MOVEMENT

If you embrace in your thought all things at once, times, places, substances, qualities, quantities, you may understand God.

Corpus Hermeticum

The world sparkles with the glory of the Lord! It reverberates with his might! Thunder and lightning blaze forth with divine power. But even more glorious and powerful is the kindness of God as he leans down to the wanderer and lovingly calls him home.

Die Allmacht
Johann Ladislaus Pyrker, D 852
Great is Jehovah, the Lord!
Heaven and earth proclaim his might!
You can hear it in the thundering tempest,
And the cascading roar of the waterfall.
You can hear it in the whisper of the green forest.
You can see it in the golden fields of corn,
In the splendor of the flowers,
In the majesty of the starry heavens.
Terrifying sounds his thunder!

Horrifying is the flame of his lightning!
But still more does your heart
Reveal Jehovah's might
When it reaches up longingly in prayer,
And trusts in his love and mercy.
Great is Jehovah, the Lord!

Piano Sonata in D major, D.850

1825

The dream maiden is the symbol of the triumph of love, the reconciliation of contradictions in the *mysterium magnum*. She represents the wholeness, the Being who becomes incarnate in the Becoming of his life. She is the rose cross mystery. This fullness, this Divine Sophia, this union of messianic light-bringing and sophianic beauty, has been an aura that accompanies his experience of certain women in his life. The aura can disappear because Becoming unites both Being and non-being. Yet the wanderer lives with the attraction of the divine presence that gives meaning to the sorrow. The joy in the mystical vision must co-exist with savage pain in the disappearance of its incarnation. Through the experience of the divine presence the wanderer and his beloved are called to a higher world. The wanderer commits himself to that world with courage and fidelity. In the face of life's agonizing contradictions the wanderer anticipates love's triumph. In this outlandishly beautiful and metaphysically profound piano sonata the harsh reality of life is set in contrast with the divine invitation that illuminates the man/woman romance.

There is divine presence in human love. Becoming occurs as opposites unite. In the union Being is reflected. Sexual love is the icon here. Troubadours and Minnesingers celebrated this incarnation of God. In the works of the great German mystics the sublime disposition, the experience of Being as the condition for the experience of Becoming, is an invitation to love's fulfillment. Henry Suso wrote:

> *Lord, I consider your loving invitation from the Book of Wisdom saying, "Come to me, you who desire me; with my fruits you will be filled... I am the Mother of fair love... My spirit is sweeter than honey, my inheritance above honey and the honeycomb... Noble wine and sweet music give the heart joy, but my wisdom exceeds both.*

The experience of divinity through love finds expression symbolically through the romance of a dream maiden who was incarnate for the composer in a real woman in his life. He expresses all of this in the *Piano Sonata in D Major*. As much as any Schubert composition this sonata expresses the *sehnsucht*, the longing of the wanderer, as he struggles through the contradictions of this world toward the divine harmony of a better one.

The first movement focuses upon the savage and painful drive of the wanderer towards love's fulfillment in the incarnation of his dream maiden. That drive leads to and through death itself in its ascent to a better world. There is cruel separation from her. The burning, yearning, other-seeking flame of love is almost physically present in this movement, and drives the wanderer to seek the beloved by passing through the narrow fissure of death. Here Eros leads beyond the self to the desired other. This music is not pretty. It flames, yearns, suffers, and shouts. It originates as an agonized craving for eternal harmony in a world split into opposites. An incarnation of that harmony has briefly flamed into life. But now it has disappeared. The clash between the love and the unspecified forces that would supress it is catastrophic, yet something priceless in the love survives.

The second movement, a miracle of mystical beauty, is bathed in transcendental hope and love for the dream maiden. Love transfigures the life of the wanderer here in a premonition of otherworldly fulfillment. The transfiguration is pure magic, a union of spirits. The wanderer ascends to a higher world through union with the Beloved. The vision reorders all in the wanderer's life. The star-touch of the composer, the bliss of his higher consciousness, is sublime, leaving us "at peace above the pain."

In the third movement the anxiously beating heart of the wanderer, wed to the vision but fearing its loss, is called to courageous endurance. The suffering of one who lives his life of love in a world of power, who lives his life of clemency in a world of violent retribution, who lives his life of hope in a world doomed to death, is intense. Yet he is encouraged to adopt a star-view of the life experience. Problems can be transformed by light from afar.

The fourth movement is a thrilling conclusion to this magnificent sonata. In radiant joy it celebrates in joyful hope the apotheosis of divine wisdom that is the dream maiden. The pathway to this ending takes us through a serious meditation upon the central role played by love in the wanderer's life. The music celebrates this triumphant romance as the archetypal cosmic mystery in beguilingly joyful simplicity.

FIRST MOVEMENT

> *If I might glimpse my beloved, talk with her! So much beauty is hidden within her! Is she divine or human?*
>
> *Henry Suso*

The *Sehnsucht* here is demonic, driving, elemental. It has brought the wanderer to his love, and then to his pain. Feverish, frantic, this yearning is a flame burning within, never to be quenched, never satisfied short of its goal, which lies beyond death.

Fülle der Liebe
Friedrich Schlegel, D.854
Unsatisfied longing tears my heart,
Making life a sorrow.
Pain serves to awaken the longing,
And love draws me straight to my goal.

A flame of love calls us to life.
Calls us to unite in God.
A flame indeed is the driving force...
Strong, clear, eternal!

We reached for our love, for the union of our lives.
But then fell a sword of separation
And the searing pain of love's insatiable longing.

In the spirit's depths dwells her image,
For the separation like death cannot be right!.
Many tears revealed the painful yearning,
A love that follows her through even death!
In waves of love the spirit moves,
And when the beloved is gone the heart is shattered.

SECOND MOVEMENT

Heavenly stars, children of the night, in you we see our fate, shining through night's mantle of darkness.

Orphic Hymn

A star announces the mystery. Somehow the yearning will be satisfied! The wanderer has a mystical premonition of the intense beauty that awaits him. The union of the wanderer with his beloved is suggested in the magic of this music.

Fülle der Liebe cont'd
But a star then appears in the heavens,
And there, surely we will be together.

Upon earth the eyes are moist with tears,
Yet all around I am bathed in the heavenly apparition.

Its magic overcomes me.
It orders all in my life...

As if by mystic power of spirits
Uniting soul to soul.

Although indeed my heart is broken,
I remain at peace above all the pain.

THIRD MOVEMENT

She was distant, yet near, far above yet low, present yet hidden.
Henry Suso

The thundering heart is bid: "Be silent!" The dream of love cannot be satisfied short of the union beyond death. Pain and hope make of life neither heaven nor hell. The wandering is a winter's journey, a pilgrimage that is meaningful due to transcendental invitation.

An Mein Herz
Ernst Schulze, D.860
My heart, at last be silent!
Why are you so wildly beating?
Only a command from heaven
Can make me leave her now!

Your youth
Brought you only pain.
But because she was pleased,
Let it be forgotten.

Although she never understood
Your pain-filled love,
You were faithful to her...
And God has seen it.

We must courageously endure
Although the tears flow.
We dream of the beautiful times,
Now long passed.

When you see the blossoms appearing,
And birds singing aloft,
Shed a furtive tear, perhaps,
But complain no more!

For high above, the stars eternal
Move round in golden light,
Twinkling in joy from afar…
Unbothered by our problems, here!

FOURTH MOVEMENT

Today, as my burning heart desires, I shall embrace you!
Henry Suso

The wanderer jauntily strides through life, encouraged by the anticipation of his coming love feast. This feast seems almost upon him. He sends his love to the beloved along with a ringing pledge of fidelity. This beloved controls his life.

Wiederschein
August Wilhelm Schlegel, D.855
The spring sun's ever-radiant smile
Is morning dawn to all my hopes.
I hear a whisper in the western breeze,
The sigh so full of bliss to come.
I'm coming, past valleys and hills,
O, sweet bestower of my bliss!
On the rapid wings of song,
The lover sends greeting over to you!

Accept love's greeting from your friend.
He, without love returned, swore
To worship you for ever and ever,
As steady, as sure as nature herself.
He looks to his lodestar,

And, like a solitary boatman, listens
In hope that, out of the celestial darkness,
The sound of that distant star might be heard.

String Quartet in G major, D.887

June 1826

In Schubert's final quartet, the composer with consummate artistry leads us deep into the valley of death and despair only to celebrate a triumphant ascent into the higher world of the great mystery. The ascent is measured by the descent. The wanderer lives in a world where the hope for a new dawn has dimmed, indeed it has almost vanished. Here indeed is the dark night of the soul. There seems to be no further reason to live. The beloved, the new dawn of society, is to be found only beyond this life. Yet once again the wanderer embraces his painful and seemingly meaningless life.

The poetry inspiring this quartet suggests what is found in the music: a plunge into the agony of alienation and the loss of the Beloved. Paradoxically in and through the sorrow there is life-transfiguring invitation. Alienation is harrowing but no less real is the inner vision that is the backbone of all of Schubert's art. A voyager in one world, a citizen of another, his wanderer finds it difficult to play the games required. In his inner life there are whispers from the better world, intimations of beauty, inviting, reminding, refreshing. In the outer world there is pain and frustration. The contrast between the two worlds is starkly expressed in this string quartet which begins with the setting of a Saturnine poem by Jakob Craigher about a gravedigger. This is Schubert's first instrumental setting of this poem. A second setting will be the first movement of the *Piano Trio in E Flat* D.927. In both works the wanderer or grave digger finds the pain of life in the lower world unbearable. And in both settings the higher consciousness of the mystery transfigures in beauty the stormy sky. The despairing readiness to leave this life evokes memories of Schubert's setting of the poem *Lebenstraum* by Gabriele von Baumberg fifteen year earlier in which the poetess cried: "I have dedicated my life, my every joy to you and you alone, o regal God of the Sun. Now in return give me everlasting life!" The desire to transcend this world of pain, to move on in his great journey, is intense in the composer. Again and again he will give voice to it in these last two and a half years of his life.

In the *Quartet for Strings in G Major* Schubert is severely depressed in his reflections upon his present life. He is obviously in pain, obviously filled with dread at the prospect of carrying on indefinitely in a life which has lost its flavor, a life without the enrichment of love and without public understanding of his artistic achievements. The mystical homeland of peace beckons with mystical poignancy. There is where the pain will stop. There is where the beloved will be found. Here is the dark-winged angel that tormented him, yet gave his art such unparalleled sweep. Such sentiments lie at the root of *Winterreise* and other masterpieces of 1827 and 1828.

In the second movement the contrast between the two worlds takes the form of meditations upon longing and upon the inner tumult of the wanderer. It is clear from the words of the poem that the character of the better world is determined by the presence of the beloved. In life she is far away, meaning over there, on the other side. There, in that mysterious, unknowable existence beyond life, the wanderer will find the satisfaction of his longing.

The third movement is a mystical premonition of the better world. The clear light of day, the logic of this world, gives way to the shadows of night, pregnant with divine beauty. Schober's poem provides a nocturnal vision, anticipating the realization of dreams. As in *Nachtmusik* D.848 night prefigures eternity and love's triumph.

The fourth movement is a wild depiction of the madness of earthly life in contrast with the peace and order of the higher life. Earthly madness plays in circles, one dream driving out another, all hope being false, all promises failing. For the Gnostic the better world can be touched at every point in life. Here it is touched by way of contrast with the tortured life of the alienated wanderer. Understanding this movement centers upon a comprehension of Schubert's definitive transcendence of the "tracelessly flying" dream of earthly happiness. This might seem like ultimate pessimism. It is not. The divine invitation to transcend this world does not despise the crazed and disordered world; it transfigures it.

FIRST MOVEMENT

You shall be abandoned both by God and the whole world, persecuted by friends and enemies. Everything you undertake will go awry.

Henry Suso

Life is pain. The wanderer looks in horror and despondency at the rubble that is now his life. Death comes all too slowly. "Come and close my eyes!" Mystically the grave changes from the absurd end to the promising beginning. It becomes the pathway to the homeland of peace. The wanderer envisions sinking and rising, dying and awakening to life. Despair and hope rub against one another…and the sublime disposition is born. Once again an experience of the unspeakably beautiful is conditioned upon a transcendence of earthly systems.

Totengräbers Heimweh
Jakob Nikolaus von Craigher de Jachelutta, D.842
Oh race of men! Oh life! To what purpose? To dig! To bury!
Day and night, again and again,
The driving, the searching... and for what?
"Lower him into the grave, deep, deep down!"
Oh destiny of men, oh dreadful task,
I can stand it no longer!

When, my hour of peace, will you sound for me?
Death, come and close my eyes!
Life is, alas, so dreary.
The grave is so friendly, so cool!
But who will lay me in it?

I am alone... so terribly alone!
I have been abandoned by everyone, bound solely to death.
I stand on the brink of life, holding a cross,
And stare with desire into the deep, deep grave!

Oh homeland of peace, world of the blessed,
I am bound to you with a mystical tie.
From away in the distance comes the glimmer of eternal light!
The stars disappear! My eyes dim!
I sink! I sink! Dear ones, I come!

SECOND MOVEMENT

...a thirst for eternal unity in light
Pseudo Dionysius

This wanderer is an alien, an exile from his true homeland. That homeland, his "better world," the land where his beloved awaits, is "over there," "on the other side." But here, in this world, his head spins; his stomach burns as he waits to go home.

Lied der Mignon
Johann Wolfgang von Goethe, D.877 no. 4
Only one who knows longing
Can understand my pain.
I am alone, cut off

From all friends.
I look up to the heavens…
Up towards eternity!
And, alas! The one who knows and loves me is far away.
My head spins! My stomach burns!
Only the one who knows longing can understand my pain.

THIRD MOVEMENT

I shall sing of night, Mother of gods and men.
Orphic Hymn

Magically, mystically the dusky night world of the wanderer is transfigured. His world of pain, his exile, is cleansed of its poisons and beauty reigns in freedom. The power that so transforms the world of darkness into a world of priceless beauty is the power of love. Yet the wanderer must return from his liberating vision to his exile.

Mondenschein
Franz Schober, D.875
The magic flower of the moon smiles,
And soulfully invites our dusky night world
To a paradise of love.

Vanquished by sleep's power
Worry, guilt and pain are gone.
Only gentle beauty reigns,
In spiritual freedom.

Look there! The fields are new!
The old earth is gone.
I see a garden of silver, with perfumed scents,
Bathed in golden mist and magical light.
Man's spirit, free of daily concerns,
Is enveloped in a cloud of sweet yearning.
In peace it enjoys the heavenly life.

But the song of the nightingale
Reminds our dream-filled hearts of the world of daily concerns.
Into the midst of that heaven, her call awakens
The deepest pain, the pain of love.

FOURTH MOVEMENT

> *Contradictions to beauty…enable the soul, which longs for things above, to ascend to them.*
>
> *Pseudo Dionysius*

Alone, apart from the invitation to the better world, this world with its clashing "absolutes" in religion, race, and politics, its endless parade of false gods, is chaotic and absurd. By itself it consists of dreams tracelessly flying, madness playing in circles. To live this life as if it were itself the end is monumental folly.

Tiefes Leid
Ernst Schulze, D.876

I am of all peace forsaken,
Drifting now on wildest floods!
Only in one place peace is certain,
That's the place where all's at rest.

Though the winds may roar in terror,
Though the cold rains may pour down,
I prefer to live in peace
Over a life on the fickle earth.

Our earthly life consists of dreams tracelessly flying…
One driving the next one out…
Madness playing in circles,
Each one hears, yet none remains.

Never do false hopes recede!
Never do yearning, fearing and worry abate!
But those all-peaceful, so-pale departed ones,
They never promise or deny.

PIANO SONATA IN G MAJOR, D.894

October 1826

The *mysterium magnum* in which we are all united, is here a tangible presence. The hope in this piano sonata seems to be a direct response to the despair in the *String Quartet In G Major D.887*. While the experience of the mystery was never absent in the string quartet, it takes on a note of resilience. There is a new taste for life in this piano sonata. The wanderer ascends out of the emptiness of daily worries into a higher world. This Hermetic magician stands astride the opposing worlds of darkness and light, making them touch and deriving power from the union. He will use that power for further creation.

In this sonata darkness, grief, and pain are no longer deadening traps for the spirit but are seen against the background of gentle beauty, gardens of silver and perfumed scents, a universe in which Eros yearns and is satisfied. This experience is invitational. Sadly it is also transient. The transfiguration of the inner life through the fleeting contact with the higher world gives the wanderer both the strength to go on and hope for the future.

The first movement leaves no doubt about the momentous nature of what is happening. Two worlds touch in surreal beauty. But the poem carries the wanderer through the experience to its other side; he must return to the pain-filled world. This movement gives him a taste of transcendental freedom, then takes it away, replacing it with the anxiety-laden, love-deprived life commitment which is his responsibility to pursue.

The second movement focuses upon the pain of that life commitment. Life is agony because the beloved has gone. The wanderer sings a sad song of unsatisfied longing and fidelity towards the lost love. He is sustained by hopes for the better world beyond death where the longing will be satisfied. Love's pain has eternal significance.

In the third movement the agonized wanderer anticipates love's triumph. He calls to the beloved, "Arise"! And the lark sings at the gate of heaven. The same poem inspires the third movement of the posthumous *Piano Sonata in A Major D.959*. There the lark's song awakens the wanderer to eternal life and love. Here however the bird's song awakens him to the continuing pain of the spiritual ascent. This wanderer tastes the better world, yet is aware of the moral and artistic challenges that still lie ahead. His artistic goal is to clothe in music the experience of the wanderer as he approaches death. Perhaps it is this awareness that gives to the song of the lark its somewhat irritating character.

In the fourth movement setting of *Nachthelle* there is an unclouded and thrilling foretaste of the better world. Its life spirit pulses within the wanderer, lifting him to a higher existence. For a priceless moment it takes over, raising a hymn that breaks the chains of earthly life in a transfiguration experience. There is no stress, no fear, no concern, just sublime freedom and joy. Set upon this mystical pathway by the magic of a moonlit night, this wanderer is overcome by an awareness of the inner light that erupts from him in his art.

Schubert was uniquely gifted with an awareness of divine invitation. He perceived his life responsibility as a call to celebrate its light, allowing its rays to transform the earth through music. He thought that this responsibility demanded that he express the meeting between heaven and earth up to the very point of his own death. This awareness is evident from poetry set when he was fourteen years old in his setting of the poem *Lebenstraum* by Gabriele von Baumberg. But now, at the end of the year 1826, he knows that the most trying part of the challenge has arrived. His art will explore experiences that unite the composer with everyone else...the experiences of suffering and dying. Schubert's art is a treasure for anyone enduring the disappearance of earthly hope, love, and life. In the darkest shadows of the night his wanderer finds promise of a radiant dawn.

FIRST MOVEMENT

Amid the deepest shadow the mysteries pour overwhelming light!
Pseudo Dionysius

Two worlds, one of love and light, the other of sorrow and darkness, touch and the prison world of the wanderer is illuminated. Darkness changes into light as a new world appears. Heavenly freedom unleashes the reign of beauty. Yet the higher world for Schubert summons to a challenging future. With the abrasively insistent nightingale it orders him back to deal with intractable reality.

Nachthelle
Franz Schober, D.875
The moon smiles upon our night world,
And transforms our dusky night world
Into a paradise of love.

Vanquished by sleep's power
Worry, guilt and pain are gone.
Spiritual freedom rules the world
In gentle beauty!

Look there! The fields are new!
The old earth has disappeared!
I see a garden of silver, with perfumed scents,
Bathed in golden mist and magical light.
Man's spirit breaks free!
In a cloud of sweet yearning
It tastes the life of heaven !

But the piercing call of the nightingale
Reminds our dream-filled hearts
of harsh reality.
Into the midst of that heaven
Her call awakens the deepest pain…
The need for love!

SECOND MOVEMENT

I tasted; now I hunger and thirst! You touched me and I burn for your peace!

Saint Augustine

The wanderer has given his heart to the full incarnation of his immortal beloved, his transcendental bride. She is the better world that is partially realized and partially but a dream in this one. She is invitation, the meaning of his life. No other can take her place. She is an ideal both brought to unique perfection yet uniquely betrayed in any woman. Through union with her he finds the hidden God.

Hippolits Lied
Johanna Schopenhauer, D.890
Leave me alone, though I am in agony!
Leave me alone, and quietly go away!
I dream of her at night… see her in the dawn…
She is ever with me!

How can you think that I could find peace with you?
She has stolen my peace!
Where she is, there must I be…
In this life, or beyond it!

Do not deny this consideration to my heart.
It has only one problem…
It lives only to die.
It has never concealed that.

Leave me alone. I can only think of her.
I can only dream as she does.
Apart from her there is no heaven for me!

In life and in death,
In the better world as in this one,
In times of joy and in pain of separation,
I'm hers alone!

THIRD MOVEMENT

…incongruities are often suitable for lifting our minds to the spiritual!
Pseudo Dionysius

Harshly falls the wake-up song of the lark upon the wanderer's ears. It stridently calls him to the challenge of the new age and to its beauty.

Ständchen
William Shakespeare, D.889
Hark! Hark! The lark at heaven's gate sings,
And Phoebus 'gins arise,
His steeds to water at those springs
On chalice'd flowers that lies;

And winking Mary-buds begin
To ope their golden eyes:
With every thing that pretty is,
My lady sweet, arise!
Arise, arise!

FOURTH MOVEMENT

There you will show me what my soul has been seeking.
John of the Cross

Transfiguration! Its radiant promise is what the wanderer has to share. Nighttime magic transports the wanderer into the better world of inner light. Illumination transforms the night! It is radiant inside the wanderer, free, without care, rich, noble. It demands to find voice in his creations. It must come out enriching others! Here is a foretaste of the divine life, the rose at the center of life's cross.

Nachthelle
Johann Gabriel Seidl, D.892
The night is clear and pure,
Of brightest glory!
The houses are wondrous
In their silvery veil.

The brightness is mysteriously within me…
So full, so over-flowing.
It pulses inwardly, free and limpid,
With no anguish, no cares.

I cannot keep within me
This wealth of light!
It will come out. It must come out,
Bursting the last chains!

The night is clear and pure,
Of brightest glory!

RONDO FOR PIANO AND VIOLIN, D.895

1826-1827

Come, beautiful, inviting goddess. I call to you with sacred words and a pure heart. Orphic Hymn

The contradiction-reconciling mystery of life is a romance. The messianic wanderer seeks his bride. The wanderer needs his dream maiden to make him whole. The wanderer here is a hero, a knight dedicated to this Beloved and deserving of her favors. Through imaginative creativity he must be messianic in bringing light to the world in the service of his Beloved. In this self portrait Schubert is the wanderer-knight who presents himself to Sophia for transcendental acceptance. In his own eyes he has done what he has set out to do. His noble deeds, his music, are his love offerings. This hero has played his part nobly in the great romance. He stands before his beloved, confidant of her love.

The theme of the wanderer as a singing hero, as a Troubadour, bringing a love offering to the Eternal Beloved is fundamental to Schubert. The *Arpeggione Sonata* and the *Piano Sonata in E Flat for Four Hands* are two earlier indications of this. Schubert's vision of himself as an artist was much the same as was that of Beethoven and Wagner. They saw themselves as heaven-sent warriors, divinely aflame with a messianic role to play, mediating between heaven and earth, lifting minds and hearts up to a higher world in ways new and powerful. Schubert here seems to see himself as coming to the end of his road,. The love offering to his beloved is laid at her feet, and he anticipates that she will graciously accept it and reward the lover who acted with such heroism.

The knight-wanderer returns to sing beneath his beloved's bower and offers to her the fruits of his courage and skill. This is done in the form of a song...and what a song! Joy, knightly courage, devotion are celebrated. He pleads that she unbar the gate. Death approaches. It is time to accept and grant her favors to this knight who has served her with heroic fidelity.

Romanze des Richard Löwenherz
Original (given below) by Walter Scott, German used by Schubert by Karl Ludwig Müller, D.907
High deeds achieved of knightly fame,
From Palestine the champion came;
The cross upon his shoulders borne,
Battle and blast had dimm'd and torn.
Each dint upon his batter'd shield
Was token of a foughten field;
And thus, beneath his lady's bower,
He sang, as fell the twilight-hour:—

"Joy to the fair!—thy knight behold,
Return'd from yonder land of gold:
No wealth he brings, nor wealth can need,
Save his good arms and battle-steed;
His spurs, to dash against a foe,
His lance and sword to lay him low;
Such all the trophies of his toil,
Such—and the hope of Tekla's smile!

"Joy to the fair! whose constant knight
Her favour fired to feats of might;
Unnoted shall she not remain,
Where meet the bright and noble train,
Minstrel shall sing and herald tell—
"Mark yonder maid of beauty well,
"Tis she for whose bright eyes was won
The listed field of Askalon!

"Note well her smile!—it edged the blade
Which fifty wives to widows made,
When, vain his strength and Mahound's spell,
Iconium's turban'd Soldan fell.
Seest thou her locks, whose sunny glow
Half shows, half shades, her neck of snow?
Twines not of them one golden thread,
But for its sake a Paynim bled.

"Joy to the fair!—my name unknown.
Each deed and all its praise thine own;
Then, oh unbar this churlish gate,

The night dew falls, the hour is late.
Inured to Syria's glowing breath,
I feel the north breeze chill as death;
Let grateful love quell maiden shame,
And grant him bliss who brings thee fame."

ADAGIO FOR PIANO AND STRINGS, D.897

The power of this holy night dispels all evil, washes guilt away, restores lost innocence, bring mourners joy!

The Exultet

The rose cross mystery embraces both the hidden world and the one that we grasp with clear ideas. The wanderer must unite the two. Here he stands alone under the moon and stars and his consciousness expands to embrace the universe that appears at night but is hidden in the clear light of day. This "Adagio" is not a restful nightsong but a celebration of monumental awakening. Using the same poem that inspired the fourth movement of the *Piano Sonata in G Major* the composer celebrates the transfiguration of one world by another. The music begins restfully enough with a night experience. But magical peace is only the introduction to an alchemy of a high quality indeed. All of the pent-up desire for love, all of the anticipation of transcendental fulfillment, all of the majestic power of Eros is here in a priceless vision of the spiritual ascent. The moonlit night is an invitation to transcend nature. The great mystery of the rose cross lies within the wanderer but its outline can be detected in the world "out there". Portentously the inner brightness is proclaimed, its control over this wanderer everywhere dominant. The wealth of inner light will soon break the last chains, and the wanderer will ascend to the light source from which the moon and the transfigured night receive their beauty.

Nachthelle
Johann Gabriel Seidl, D.897
The night is clear and pure, of bright glory.
The houses are wondrous in their silvery veils.
The brightness is mysteriously within me…
So full, so over-flowing.

It pulses inwardly, free and limpid,
With no anguish, no cares.

I cannot keep within me
This wealth of light!
It will come out. It must come out,
Bursting the last chains!

The night is clear and pure,
Of brightest glory!
The houses are wondrous
In their silvery veils.

PIANO TRIO IN B FLAT, D.898

Spring 1828

Eternal Wisdom to the Servant (Wanderer): Now raise you eyes. See where you belong. Your home is paradise. Here you are a stranger, an exile. As a pilgrim hurries home where his friends await him with longing and love, so should you hasten to you true fatherland.

Henry Suso

The *mysterium magnum* is experienced through Becoming. The mystery is intensely personal and is uniquely experienced in interpersonal Becoming. Our wanderer has emerged from the depths of the winter's journey and sings of the transcendental triumph of love. The mythical expression of this is consummate union with the dream maiden. That triumph beckons mysteriously from beyond death. The mystery reaches its dramatic apex as death is celebrated as the pathway to life and love. A higher consciousness of this life-transforming, archetypal mystery is reached in this piano trio in three images: first death-transfiguration; second a mystical presence of the physically absent dream maiden; and finally spring. The wanderer relishes this core of the mystery with joy and hope.

It is thought by some that perhaps this piano trio was composed in the Spring of 1828, together with the *Piano Trio in E Flat* (D.927).. Thematically this new chronology makes good sense. These two works seem to form a larger unity, a kind of cycle. While the *Piano Trio in E Flat* depicts the wanderer battling despair but emerging from sorrow and regaining spiritual equilibrium, the *Piano Trio in B Flat* simply exults in this triumph. In the *Piano Trio in B Flat* death is not a terrorizing enemy but a highway to love's triumph. There is an unrestricted and joyful realization of new life and freedom. This triumph begins with a celebration of victory over death. Then it turns to a priceless sensual celebration of the divine invitation in its magical joy. The dark night of the soul, so harrowingly experienced in *the Piano Trio in E Flat*, is nowhere to be seen.

The first movement presents an ascent to the higher consciousness through the passage through death to transfiguration. The sacred hour of death is celebrated as the point of moving from pain to joy. The wanderer will pass from one world into another as time is swept up into eternity. In focus is the triumphant nature of the passage. The drama of the struggle is expressed as it was in the first movement of the *Unfinished Symphony*. Verse by verse the poem is invested with rich, deep meaning by the composer.

In the second movement the setting of *Im Frühling* is unspeakably beautiful. The higher consciousness emanates from the luminescent beauty of a girl who has disappeared. Through the plastic medium of music the composer expresses the ascent to a transcendental realization of this love. Bathed in the light of the mystery the wanderer casts sorrow aside. This is done mythically in setting the Second Verse of the poem, implying that the romance is somehow eternal and inviting the wanderer into its bliss. Again there is no question about the outcome of the adventure. The battle is already won; sublime peace illuminates the life of the wanderer.

In the third movement the wanderer's sublime joy is one with the love that radiates from the sun and fills nature, one with the peace that emanates from the stars. The poetry used here was set as songs in October of 1815, the same month as the settings that inspire the fourth movement. In 1815 the composer was deeply in love with Theresa Grob and anticipated marrying her. It is this joy that is re-captured in 1826 when Theresa has disappeared from his life.

The fourth movement celebrates the triumph of the sublime disposition. This wanderer has emerged from the Hell expressed in the first two movements of the *Piano Trio in E Flat* (D.929) and in *Die Winterreise*. The intensity of suffering in that Hell reveals just how immense a triumph is this joy, peace, and freedom. Now in this fourth movement the wanderer laughs at death and revels in the joy and peace of the sublime disposition. The composer raises his arm in artistic and personal triumph.

Schubert's reach back to October of 1815 for the poems set in the last two movements is of some consequence. In 1815 and in early 1816 the love between the composer and Theresa Grob was both intense and promising. Joy in nature seemed linked to the joy of love and Schubert sang of May-time, Spring, and love in song after song. But now it is 1828. The Beloved has married someone else. The hope for artistic acceptance has been frustrated; death is approaching. Still the wanderer sings! The miracle of the higher consciousness reigns supreme over a life that has been and is being challenged by sorrow. Love triumphs and transfigures the universe! The drama of this restoration of the sublime disposition is accentuated by the fact that the composer reaches back to that very time when he was most happy, before the tragic separation, and experiences in memory and premonition the divine image in nature at a time when this would seem to be impossible.

FIRST MOVEMENT

In the middle of the night, while all things were wrapped in silence, a secret word was spoken to me. It came stealthily, like a thief. It is the nature of a word to reveal what is hidden.

Meister Eckhart

We join the wanderer in a struggle with death, a struggle at times taxing, but with no hint of despair, no thought of final tragedy. Here is the mentality of the composer of *Lazarus* in which the sublime disposition dominates the experience of dying. The musical movement is overall an expression of definitive emergence from darkness. The sublime disposition that is being won is joy-filled as the soul is carried heavenwards. Celestial harmonies are heard and the wonders of the wanderer's life are transfigured. Differing aspects of the experience are brought into musical focus. Here is a warrior's victory, his ascent to peace.

Todsmusik
Franz Schober, D.758
At the sacred hour of death,
When I shall leave this earth,
And in pain fight my last battle,
Holy spirits, bless me
A final time with your peaceful melody, your pure harmony,
Ease the pain in my heart, torn by its fatal wound.

Free my simple and tortured spirit in this last battle of life.
Sweep it aloft, and upon your wings carry it into eternal light!
Then will the sweet, heavenly harmonies envelop me,
And the chains I have escaped will become light, and fall away!

I will see all the wonders of life which brought me such joy,
All the beauty which bloomed in my life will stand transfigured before me!
Every star that sparkled for me as a friend
In the sultry darkness of my winter's journey,

Every flower that graced my path…will be there!
And those fearful minutes, when I am in anguish,
Will be accompanied by joy-filled anticipation!
And I will see all things transfigured!
So will I surrender my life in the radiance of wondrous joy!

SECOND MOVEMENT

Man, having seen nature's beauty reflected in the water, loved her… and burning with love they were united!

Corpus Hermeticum

Here is the mystery…a memory, a sublime premonition, and the transfiguration of life. Love breaks through the limits of space and time. The great romance sweeps all of creation into the spiritual ascent. The wanderer follows his beloved in their quest for one another and for eternal life. Redemption is at this point an adventure of the heart with sexuality as the archetype. The wanderer in a sacred moment at a spring revels in the illumination.

Im Frühling
Ernst Schulze, D.882
Quietly I sit on the hillside.
The sky is so blue!
A gentle breeze plays in the green valley
Where in the early spring
I was once so very happy.

I walked by her side,
So much in love, so close to her!
And deep in the dark mountain spring
I could see heavenly beauty, bright and blue…
And in those heavens, I saw her!

Springtime beauty graces blossoms and flowers;
But not every blossom means the same to me.
I like to pick flowers where she picked them.

Everything is once again as it was then,
The flowers, the fields…
The sun shines just as brightly,
And no less enchanting is the reflection of the sky
There in the spring…

But will and desire change.
Happiness can give way to conflict.
Forever love's happiness can flee,
And only the love remains…
The love, and alas the pain!

If only I were a little bird
Over there on the sloping meadow,
I could stay in the branches
And sing a sweet song of her
The whole summer long!

THIRD MOVEMENT

What is this coming up from the desert,
Like a column of smoke
Laden with myrrh, with frankincense,
And with the perfume of every exotic dust?
Song of Songs

Physical and spiritual worlds unite. Love reigns supreme in nature. No longer is there darkness. Winter is over. The joyful life of May that seemed so definitively lost to the wanderer has been restored. He is one with the better world. The stars and galaxies all celebrate the God who invites.

Die Macht der Liebe
Johann Nepomuk von Kalchenberg, D.308
Whenever I look
Love triumphs! I can see it!
Every bush, every budding flower
At its core is sealed by love.

Love fills, warms, renews, adorns
Every living thing.
The earth, the heavens, each creature
Live by virtue of love,
And therein are fulfilled.
...

Die Sternenwelten
Johann Georg Fellinger, D.307
Above the clouds in majesty
Is the mysterious world of space,
Blessed by the suns radiance
Each star following its course.

The stars are spread far and wide
Like a numberless army,
Sending their joyful light far and wide
Celebrating the glory of God.

FOURTH MOVEMENT

When love speaks, the voice of all the gods
Make heaven drowsy with the harmony!
Giordano Bruno

The very May that once awakened the wanderer to the pursuit of the spiritual ascent through sensuality and joy had disappeared. But now it is luminous with transcendence in its return. Sorrow and death rule no longer. The wanderer is no longer a cripple but strong and free. All sorrow, including death, is part of the triumphant ascent. This wanderer, fortified by sublime powers, laughs at death. He is one with the stars, one with the divine word that enlivens nature, one with his God, one with life and love.

Skolie
Johann Ludwig Ferdinand von Deinhardstein, D.306
In the warmth of the May morning
Rejoice in the blooming of life,
Quickly, before the fragrance passes,
If the heart is grieved,
The spirits in our glasses and our friendship
Can easily solve the problem.

Swiftly can joy bestow its kiss upon us,
Yet when death approaches, that joy can disappear.
So then, must we tremble in fear?
In a girl's soft lips is the water of life!
He who loves life laughs at death!
...

Mein grūss an den Mai
Johann Ludwig Ferdinand von Deinhardstein, D.305
Oh May, with your heavenly flowers, your spring,
Your ocean of joys, I welcome you!
Amid all joy-filled creation
I sing your welcome!

Your breath enlivens the dull air
Transforming mountains, valleys, and meadows.
Fragrant breezes softly caress us
In the radiant joy of the blue day.

Impromptus Opus 90, D.899

October 1827

Each of Schubert's sonatas celebrates lyrically the dramatic ascent into the *mysterium magnum*. The setting and arrangement of the poems inspiring the movements give unmistakeable clues to the intelligent craftsmanship celebrating the ascent.. The impromptus are a bit different from the sonatas. There is a looser connection between the poems. In *Opus 90* there is nevertheless a thread of unity, whether by design or by chance. The poetry celebrates a romance between heaven and earth. This romance controls the wanderer, dictating what he does. This appears in the *First Impromptu*. In the *Second Impromptu* the absence of an enlivening heaven, the absence of Sophia, ravages the life and sanity of the wanderer, setting him adrift in a whirlwind of superficiality and emptiness, damning him to unbearable agony. We hear a foreshadowing of *Die Winterreise*. But the pain is eased and the higher consciousness made accessible by the sorrow and resignation expressed in the *Third Impromptu*. For Schubert the pathway to a higher consciousness of the rose cross mystery and involvement in its romance always includes coming to terms with the past. This can mean the forgiveness of offenses. It also can mean, as here, the acceptance of sorrow as the price of love. And in the *Fourth Impromptu* memories and premonitions of the bliss of love lend hope and meaning to the higher consciousness of the wanderer in the face of present sorrow. This set of piano pieces is a work of immense intensity and sacred promise. It draws back the veil upon life at its most painful point and shows to us the light of redemption. The four impromptus constitute an epic journey of the soul.

FIRST IMPROMPTU

Render thyself, oh goddess, unto pity!
Open, oh lady, the portals of thine eyes,
And look on me if thou wouldst give me death!
Giordano Bruno

Heavenly stars solemnly guide and control the life of the wanderer. They are sacraments of a higher order, an order of light and love, penetrating the darkness of this world. They convey divine invitation. That same invitation shines through the eyes of the beloved, alive with the luminous possibility of the spiritual ascent in love. With a voice sometimes regal and commanding, sometimes lyrical and beguiling, they speak to the wanderer and to us. They define for him the immensity of the mystery in which he is immersed.

L'Incanto degli Occhi
Pietro Metastasio, D.902, No. 1
My life belongs to you, heavenly stars!
Like distant gods, you control my destiny...
To your desire I will respond!

You inspire my courage as you sparkle in joy.
But when you are sad I am atremble!

SECOND IMPROMPTU

They who think wrongly say:...Our lives will pass away like a cloud, and be dispersed like mist!
Book of Wisdom

This magical piece begins in confusion that leads to despair. A poem that seems farcical betrays the loveless state of the unwise wanderer. There is no divine invitation in his life. Love is not a possibility. Schubert expresses the emptiness of his age and ours in this depiction of a loveless search for a wife expressed in the wild meanderings of the piano. Then inspired by a second poem by Metastasio the composer reveals the horror and agony that follows upon the loss of interplay between worlds, a loss so overwhelming as to suggest the madness of *Die Winterreise* and the Heine settings..

Il modo di prender Moglie
Pietro Metastasio, D.902
No more delay...I will do it!
I must find a wife.
Why? I know the answer;
I marry for money...I still lack that!

I say it again, my interest is money!
Some dullards are mad about women.
You must excuse me, but they are fools!
One marries for love..others marry for other reasons.
This one is commanded to do so!
That one is afraid of gossip…
"Is it really so—or not?"
But with all my problems of wallet and heart
I will marry as if a wife were medicine for an ailment.
I proclaim it loudly:I follow a noble tradition!
I am marrying for cash…
The girl has nothing to do with it!

…

Il Traditor deluso
Pietro Metastasio D.902 No. 2 1827
Oh God, I am afraid!
I feel terror, wild despair, break into a cold sweat!
Escape? But where? How can I ?
Oh God, what is happening to me?

All around me the air is on fire!
The earth shudders and disappears!
In this darkness what horrors engulf me!
What beasts hold me prey!
What monsters have me in their power!

THIRD IMPROMPTU

Out of the depth I cry to you, oh Lord!
Psalm 130

Resignation, the sad acceptance of unavoidable tragedy, is often the only pathway to peace. Out of the depths of his life from which true love and true wisdom have been removed the wanderer cries for redemption …and finds it. The only return to the sublime disposition is through resignation and acceptance of his sad lot. The tears of this resignation roll away the mountain of grief that has so destroyed his peace. Here in this miracle of music is the miracle of repentance and rebirth.

Das Weinen
Karl Gottfried von Leitner, D.926
Comforting are the tears flowing from the sacred well
As from a healing spring…bitter, hot, and bright.

Therefore anguished heart, so full of pain,
If you desire peace immerse yourself in this spring.

There lives in these same waters a secret, wondrous force
That is a balm for wounds that hurt you.
It will ease your pain, lift and roll away the ponderous burden
That now crushes your heart.

FOURTH IMPROMPTU

By the power of a lover's hope let warmth return to the air; free us from the winter's cold…so that we both in happy amazement may see our mistress sitting on the grass in the shadow of her own upraised arms.

Petrarch

A love sonnet for Schubert as for Giordano Bruno, and Petrarch can express the interplay between worlds, an interplay celebrated in the Zohar. In this impromptu memories of love combine with the anticipation of future fulfillment. Human sensuality has made divine love incarnate. The awakening to the truth of divine invitation has transfigured the experience of this wanderer. Yet he is aware that the completion of the trial is not yet. He is still separated from the earthly beloved who has opened to him the gates of paradise.

Heimliches Lieben
Karoline Louise von Klenke, D.922
Ah, when your lips touch mine,
I am transfigured by joy.
Apprehension seizes me!
My bosom heaves!
My eyes come alive, my cheeks redden,
My heart pulses with deepest joy.
My mind reels, driven to ecstasy by your lips.
It cannot, cannot be calm!
My life itself seems suspended at this moment.

In your sweet, soft, rose-like mouth
I am lost. I am enveloped in your Loving arms.

Ah, if only my spirit might transcend itself
to find its fulfillment wholly in you!
Yet our lips, so bright with their love,
Must sadly part.

Variations on a Theme from Herold's "Marie", D.908

February 1827

The queenship of Sophia lies at the heart of the rose cross mystery. She is divinely human. In this set of variations Schubert celebrates Sophia's coronation. The music celebrates the hope and joy of the wanderer who anticipates the end of his long journey. The immortal beloved appears in majestic beauty. Each successive variation serves to express an aspect of that beauty, as noted in Shakespeare's poem.

This work serves as an admirable conclusion to other Schubert works for piano, four hands, such as the *Fantasy* or the *Piano Sonata in E Fla*t D.840 and the *Piano Sonata In E Flat for Four Hands* D.823. Artists who wish to create their own fantasies in a spirit faithful to that of the composer can and should take advantage of the unity indicated by the inspiring poetry. In the other works the painful yearning of the wanderer is in sharp focus. Here however the sorrow is gone. The woman whose divine beauty has awakened a yearning for the light beyond the stars finally appears.

She must be my beloved, and I shall be her servant, Oh God!
Henry Suso

Slowly, simply the vision of the divine Sophia appears. Quickly we become aware of the majestic nature of the occasion. The radiant beauty of the beloved is celebrated as regal, captivating, and overpowering. She is a thrilling presence in whom is divinity, the mark of heavenly favor. She comes as the wanderer's bride. Her eyes are for him alone, and he joyfully celebrates her triumphant coronation. In her triumph is his own.

An Silvia
William Shakespeare, D.891

Who is Silvia, tell me now
Whom all of Nature praises?
Tender, sweet, I saw her coming,
She leaves the mark of heavenly favour;
All things are subject unto her.

Is she fair, and good withal?
For charm doth please like virtue;
Love dwells within her sparkling eyes,
And there so blind, so holy,
Tarries in sweetest peace.

Thus to Silvia's name I sing now
And chant her holy praises;
She possesses all the graces
Even heaven did endow:
Silver strings sweep at her crowning.

Piano Trio in E flat, D.929

October 1827

For Beethoven, Schubert, Wagner and others, the highest art should celebrate the *mysterium magnum* that transfigures the life experience. In this supreme piano trio the composer sings of the transfiguration of life by the rose cross mystery. The mysterious promise of a luminous night world turns darkness into light. The contradiction between the pain of the wanderer's life and the promise of a dimly apprehended better world is resolved by an ascent to the sublime disposition of peace and hope in the face of mind-numbing sorrow. The savage contradictions and agonies of this world are the seemingly implausible gateway to something quite different, something foreshadowed in the muted joys of a night world, a transfigured halfway house between the object of our longing and the bitter experiences of life. In the end Schubert's wanderer sings a monumental hymn of praise for the God who invites in and through the darkness of this world to the triumph of light and love in a better one. Here is an ascent to a higher consciousness that is anticipated in lines by Henry Suso:

> *The more bitterly you have suffered, the more nobly will you be received.*

Friedrich Schiller observed that peace and joy can persist in the face of outer tragedy and he called this state the "sublime". He recalled that the biblical Job once wealthy, became impoverished. Nonetheless Job possessed mystical peace due to his inner life. It is the sublime in this sense that Franz Schubert celebrates in a cycle of two piano trios composed in 1827. The first of these trios, if not chronologically then at least in a dramatic sense, is the *Piano Trio in E Flat* (D.929), composed in the midst of work on *Die Winterreise*. The agony of the wanderer in his long winter's journey is captured in the first two movements. All the depths of sorrow and despair in the song cycle are here; but here too is redemption and the contradiction of the despair. The wanderer in his agony looks inward to the invitation that centers his life experience and finds a moral ballast. The last two movements of the trio in E Flat and the entire *Piano Trio in B Flat,* D.898, celebrate in various ways the otherworldly joy of the wanderer that brings peace even as he plods along this thorny path.

The power of the inner life to transfigure the life experience and transform ugly tragedy into a triumph of freedom and the sublime disposition was clearly on the composer's mind. In the *Piano Trio in B Flat* Schubert celebrated an archetypal triumph over sorrow. The pathway to that celebration is the *Piano Trio in E Flat*. In the first movement of the *Piano Trio in E Flat* we have a wanderer, an incarnation of the supernal Shekhinah, who is alienated, longs for death, uttering the cry of one who suffers such pain that continued existence seems impossible. The movement follows in the tracks of *Die Winterreise*. The wanderer/ has no thought of a creative commitment to the world, no capacity for it. He exists in a lifeless world, a world of darkness and alienation. The transcendental promise of death is inaccessible. But this movement does what the song cycle did not do. It gives the wanderer a taste of transcendence, a taste of the light that will banish the darkness. He senses joy, beauty, and freedom as the backdrop to his alienation and sorrow. While *Die Winterreise* is unrelenting in its tale of woe, the piano trio paints a picture the fullness of which is a more complete expression of the composer life view. The sorrow is transfigured through the higher consciousness. The wanderer suffers the agony of the exiled Shekhinah. But like her he also experiences the messianic invitation to ascend to something quite different.

The second movement is unusual for Schubert in that the musical theme is from a folksong, the Sweedish, "Se solen junker". The movement is also inspired by the words of the folksong, a poem that he did not set as a Lied. The instrumental setting of the poem is true to the words and spirit of that poem, but the composer flies in a higher world than did the poet. In this stumbling, lurching victim is the exiled, alienated Shekhinah... everyone at some time in life. Horror, weakness, despair, insanity are palpable. This wanderer cannot bear life and seems ready for suicide, screaming out his farewells to this earth. Here is a universe devoid of messianic redemption. The intensity of the agony is such that one cannot imagine how redemption is possible. Yet it is axiomatic for Schubert that the stars cannot be reached other than by descending into the valley of death. Only in sorrow's dark night does the dawn of new life appear...and the new life begins in this movement with the transfiguration of the falling octaves into rising ones. The task at hand is to honestly face the ruins of life and accept the present invitation. Once this wanderer does this a new world appears. For this reason his farewell is an angry shout, rejecting any illusions about hopes for this world. Through the prism of his sickness he dimly foresees his own death combined with the impossibility of finding love in this world.

The third movement is a song of redemption. It is a sublime night-dawning song in which the wanderer has a taste of the world of the Divine Sophia, a world of light, not darkness, a world of loving unity, not alienation and war. The song is made possible by the rejection of illusion. The wanderer exults in a new peace, a new surge of life that transfigures even this world of darkness. Here is a triumph of love as the wanderer ascends towards his goal. Indeed it is still night and light comes only from the moon and stars. But hope, joy, and love have replaced terror, sorrow, and paralysis. This transformation is sudden, not gradual, just as it is in the transition between the Second and Third Movements of the *Piano Sonata in A Major, D.959*.

The fourth movement is a German psalm concluding the rite of awakening. It celebrates the illumination of the wanderer with a mighty hymn of praise for the God who reveals himself in the counterbalances of Nature and in the complexities and contradictions of the human drama. We are one with the trees, the corn, and the flowers in their odyssey. We unite with the stars and then with the earth as it passes from nourishing rain, through the storm, to once again experience new life and peace in the gentle rain-shower. But then the music takes another step and ascends beyond nature into the uniquely personal realm of the great romance. The wanderer, profoundly moved, looking through tears, trusts in the divine invitation. This is depicted with profound spirituality and consummate artistry. In its original but unauthorized form the movement was a majestic and powerful transfiguration of sorrow into joy arising from the reconciliation of the opposites of nature and the inner life in the spiritual ascent. In the music Nature's power combines with the ascent of the soul in sheer white magic. The transition from the storm's power to gentle nurturing rain is Hermetically paired with the transition from painful yearning to loving trust. Nature and the human heart could not be more powerfully and more felicitously united. This appears most clearly in the recording by the Altenberg Trio of the work as originally submitted by Schubert but rejected because of its length by the publishers. This trio is not, like the *String Quintet*, a swan-song, although the First and Second Movements might lead one to think so. It celebrates transfigured life according to a wedding of Pagan and Christian wisdom. In a prefiguring of the posthumous *Piano Sonata in C Minor D.958* the wanderer, trapped in sorrow, is renewed, emerging out of slavery to creative freedom.

FIRST MOVEMENT

> *Lead us beyond unknowing and light, up to the farthest, highest peak of mystic Scripture, where the mysteries of God's word lie, simple, absolute, unchangeable in the brilliant darkness of hidden silence. Amid the deepest shadow they shine in overwhelming light.*
>
> *Pseudo-Dionysius*

These lines by one of the most influential of all Christian mystics prepare us for the paradoxical mystery celebrated in the two piano trios. We ascend out of a cloud of unknowing into light and joy. The ascent begins, however, in a cold, dark night of the soul. Only by immersion in this night will our wanderer stand in the place where he can experience the dawn.

The despair of *Die Winterreise* opens the movement. Horror at what life has become, savage rejection of this misbegotten, misshapen world, gives way to insistent demands for the escape offered by the grave. The music screams of alienation as the wanderer looks morosely into the mystery of death and resurrection where he finds the living invitation to his true homeland. Descent and ascent are strangely connected.

Totengräbers Heimweh
Jakob Nikolaus von Craigher de Jachelutta, D.842
Oh race of men! Oh life! To what purpose?
To dig! To bury!
Day and night, again and again,
The driving, the searching…and for what?
For what?
"Lower him into the grave, deep, deep down!"
Oh destiny of men, Oh dreadful task,
I can stand it no longer!

When, hour of peace, will you sound for me?
Death! Come and close my eyes.
Life is, alas, so dreary.
The grave is so friendly, so cool!
But who will lay me in it?

I am alone. So terribly alone.
I have been abandoned by everyone,
Bound solely to death.
I stand on the brink of life, holding a cross,
And stare with desire into the deep, deep grave.

Oh homeland of peace, world of the blessed,
I am bound to you with a mystical tie.
From away in the distance comes rays of eternal light!
The stars disappear, my eyes dim!
I sink! I sink! Dear ones, I Come!

SECOND MOVEMENT

One dark night…I went out unseen…

John of the Cross

The dream maiden's betrayal has robbed life of its meaning. Yet the condition for the higher consciousness is resigned acceptance of the "now" as an intensely personal call to the wanderer. Before the illuminating acceptance the wanderer must face the night with its terrors, its aloneness. Here he plods sadly, stoically on his way. Worldly hopes are set aside as he bids farewell to his faithless, earthly bride. Here again is the spiritual message of *Die Winterreise*, the key to redemption: the hope of the wanderer must not remain within the narrow confines of this world.

Translation of the Sweedish folksong "Se solen junker"
See the sun going down behind the high mountain tops.
O beautiful Hope,you flee for the dark shadows of the night.
Farewell! Farewell!Farewell Ah!
The friend forgot his faithful, beloved,
His faithful beloved!

THIRD MOVEMENT

Even though this happy night impoverishes them and empties them of all possessions and natural affection, it does so only that they might reach out divinely to the enjoyment of all earthly and heavenly things with a general freedom of spirit.

John of the Cross

Now comes a lively song of nocturnal joy that celebrates the dawn of a higher consciousness even while the wanderer is imprisoned in exile. Here is a night world, an eve on which a new dawn is anticipated. It is where the opera *Alfonso und Estrella* begins. The earth is in shadow, but the light of the better world shines. This wanderer lives no longer according to the rules of the day. The sun has set and everything is different. Peace reigns supreme. Golden treasures flow from starry vaults. The wanderer lives by day in a lesser world. But in his inner life he is elevated to a higher and better one and is united with others who anticipate a supreme dawn.

Nachtmusik
Karl von Seckendorf, D.848
I will play for you a song on my flute,
In sounds rich and sweet, to harp accompanishment…
It will be a song of nocturnal joy.
Come outside and take joy
In the evening's twilight enchantment.
Look. All now are asleep
Under the watchful eye of the moon.
Our worries disappear.
The country all around is cradled in sleep…
Cradled in love.

Don't delay. Get up!
All of the stars joyously wait for you!
They are kind to good people,
Sprinkling golden treasure from distant vaults.

Come and join us!
On our quiet path no false wind will blow,
So be greeted here in the darkness!
Night unites us ever closer
When one holds his friend's hand.

So with flute and harp in sweet harmony
Come, share our joy and join our group.
In the night time stillness.
Your eye will be blessed and your heart fulfilled.

FOURTH MOVEMENT

> *Hymns are sung by the first ranks of angels whose gloriously transcendent enlightenment is thereby made manifest. Some of these hymns, if one may use perceptible images, are like the "sound of many waters" as they proclaim "Blessed be the Lord". Others thunder the great song "Holy, holy, holy is the Lord God of Hosts. The whole earth is full of his glory."*
>
> *The Pseudo Dionysius*

Here is a mighty celebration of the Divine Sophia. She is the perfect image of God. Her immensity is whispered in the forest night and the life-giving rain, thundered in the heavenly galaxies and storms. In the tradition of Gnostic-Christianity the composer makes his music the mouthpiece of Nature singing its praise of the Source of divine invitation who creates, saves, and loves through the intertwining of opposites. In harmony with principalities and powers, with the divine that sparkles throughout the universe, Schubert raises a cosmic hymn of praise to both the body and soul of Sophia. He sings of the interplay of dramas that unite heaven to earth. The beauty of the flowers is complemented by the titanic sweep of the stars. The power of the storm is resolved in the gentle rain. Immersed in these mighty contradictions and often at their mercy the wanderer pursues his archetypal journey that will lead through death to life. Transcending the counterbalances of nature that constitute Sophia's "body" there is her soul's ascent that passes through profound sorrow in its pilgrimage to the better world. Sophia's wisdom is not merely the power to recognize and participate in nature's tensions, but immersion in something far greater. The agonized wanderer responds to this painful, hope-filled paradox with trust. Here is the core of the great romance. In a supreme symbiosis of the Cabala and Christian mysticism the natural counterbalances of storm and gentle, quiet forest and heavenly splendor complement and re-enforce the still greater mystery of the spiritual ascent out of despair to trust in the love of the hidden God.

Die Allmacht
Johann Ladislaus Pyrker, D.852
Great is Jehovah, the Lord!
Heaven and earth proclaim his might.
You can hear it in the thundering tempest,
In the cascading roar of the waterfall.
You can hear it in the whisper of the green forest.
You can see it in the golden fields of corn,
In the splendor of the flower;
In the majesty of the starry heavens.

Terrifying sounds his thunder!
Horrifying is the flame of his lightening!
But still more does your heart
Reveal Jehovah's might
When it reaches upwards in prayer;
And looking through its tears trusts in his love and mercy.
Great is Jehovah, the Lord!

Fantasy for Piano and Violin, D.934

December 1827

In the face of all sorrow the mystery-illuminated life of the wanderer is a triumph. In this splendid fantasy the wanderer exults in the joy of his higher consciousness of the *mysterium tremendum* that we are calling the rose cross mystery. The dream maiden will be his. While that expectation exists in tension with the agony of lost love hope has transfigured pain. Once more Schubert employs a unique musical form, the fantasy, to express an intimate and paradoxical personal experience. Once more we have a tone poem that celebrates the joy of the wanderer's life. The agony of the wanderer is paired with a dramatic realization of Schiller's sublime disposition. The wanderer is ascending to his true home… the transfiguration of the human by the divine. It is a love triumph that unites heaven and earth.

The *Fantasy for Piano and Violin* was inspired by poems that five years earlier (between August and November of 1822) had been set as Lieder or a part song. Here in 1827 is a re-incarnation of the ideas hat inspired the *Unfinished Symphony*.The scene for the celebration is set with music inspired by Bruchmann's *Schwestergrūss* in an atmosphere of intense mystery. The spiritual ascent of the soul from a lower to a higher world is in focus. The soul ascends to the divine life of true wisdom. Out of the darkness and gloom, out of the clouds and mist of the earth she rises, clothed in light, obviously of different substance than the graves and fog around her. She is luminous with divine light. Then, in a revelation of what the finishing of the symphony would have been, comes a hymn of praise for the divine inviter. God looks lovingly upon his creatures and breathes life into them. The soul responds with a psalm of praise. While the earth remains darkened, the dialogue proceeds in celestial joy, radiant in love's mystery. In Part Three, a set of variations is the heart of the work. Based upon the poem *Sei mir gegrūsst* they express first a descent into sorrow, but then a dramatic ascent out of love's betrayal into the light of love's transcendental realization. Here is where the mature Schubert differs from the younger one. The development is through pain to a transfigured present and thrilling future. The beloved, who is perhaps still Theresa and/or Karoline Esterhazy, and just as surely the divine Sophia, the eternal feminine, the immortal beloved, is the feminine face of the alluring, inviting God. In this critical section Schubert employs music to capture and transcend the words of the poem. The beloved can be reached only by accepting and transcending the sorrow.. Finally through a second setting of the poem *Des Tages Weihe* the wanderer joyfully declares his gratitude to the crucified Logos, who has led the way through death to life. Love is once again triumphant.

PART ONE

Alas, dear heart, tell me where comes all love and charm?
Does it not all flow from the Divine Source?

Henry Suso

Mysteriously, portentously the apparition appears, a symbol of the soul, rising out of the mist and calling the wanderer's attention upwards to the higher world of the sublime. She is called to rise high above the moon and stars.

Schwestergrüss
Franz Bruchmann, D.762
In the moonlight I wander to and fro
Looking at dead bones and quiet graves.
Floating as a ghostly breath,
Flickering by, like flame and smoke,
A shape rises out of the swirling mists,
Flowing past me without sin or falsehood,
With eyes blue and sincere,
As in the fields of heaven, as if in God's bosom.

A white sheet covers the vision.
In her soft hand springs a lily,
And in ghostly whisper she speaks to me:
I am wafted now in pure light.
I see the moon and sun at my feet,
And live in bliss, in the angels' embrace.
But your breast, child of man, can never know
All the pleasure that I experience.

PART TWO

God does not want to rob us of pleasure. He wants to arouse in us the desire for infinity.

Henry Suso

A song of joy erupts from the marveling wanderer. He praises the great God whose majestic power creates and sustains the universe, the stars and galaxies, and reaches down in love to the earth, bringing forth everywhere an explosion of beauty, creativity and life. This is the God who is inviting the spirit to ascend.

Gott in der Natur
Ewalt Christian von Kleist, D.757
Great is the Lord! Great is the Lord!
The heavens are his castle.
The storm his carriage, thunder and
Lightening his royal steeds...
Great is the Lord! Great is the Lord!
Morning's red light is but a reflection
Of his brilliance.
Compared with that splendor
The setting sun is but a spark.
He looks down in love upon the earth,
And it takes on life, blossoming in joy.
He reproves it, and rocks burst aflame,
While sea and sky tremble.
Praise the Almighty Lord.
Starry lights in his castle, majesty of the sun,
Blaze triumphantly in his name,
While we on earth sing his glory!

PART THREE

At daybreak, when thou ariseth on the horizon.. Thou drivest away the darkness...

Ancient Egyptian Hymn

This wanderer lives in darkness and sorrow. The light of his life is gone. Only memories survive, memories and a mystical hope. Yet love is not limited by space and time, but unites lovers in their separation and promises more in the future. The divine invitation to life transforms sorrow into joy.

Sei mir gegrüsst
Friedrich Ruckert, D.741
You are now torn from me, from my kisses...
Accept my love! Accept my kiss!
You can be reached only by my dreams...
Accept my love! Accept my kiss!

The hand of love once gave you to my heart.
Now from my breast
It has wrenched you away. With my tears
Accept my love. Accept my kiss.

In spite of the distance, the savage separation
Between us,
In spite of jealous fate,
Accept my love. Accept my kiss.

In the joyful springtime of our love
You welcomed me with love and a kisses…
So now, from the burning passion within me,
Accept my love, Accept my kiss.

The spirit of love transcends space and time.
I am with you, you are with me.
I hold you in my arms…
Accept my love. Accept my kiss.

PART FOUR

Her crown is eternity!
Henry Suso

The child of love, symbol of the soul, reappears. She ascends to a higher world, announcing the good news of divine love.

Schwestergrüss, (continued)
Thus the air resounds, and the wind sighs.
The child of heaven calls to the stars.
And before she flees, white of face,
She transforms herself, as if incandescent.
In pure flame she rises.
Without pain or grief, to the angelic choir.
Night envelopes the holy place,
And, filled with divinity, I sing the good news.

PART FIVE

Powers within me, sing to the One, the All!
Corpus Hermeticum

A new psalm of praise and thanksgiving erupts from the wanderer. The Ruler of Destiny invites him to transcend this world with its limitations, its betrayals of love. All sorrow is forgotten. Joy and love are everywhere triumphant and reign supreme.

> ***Des Tages Weihe,***
> Anon., D.763
> *You, Ruler of Destiny,*
> *Look down upon a heart full of thanks.*
> *Joy has given us new life,*
> *The old pain is now forgotten.*
> *Through the mist beams your splendid majesty,*
> *Shining as a crown of stars!*
> *Out of love for your father,*
> *You emptied a chalice of sorrow.*
> *Ruler of Destiny, look down upon me,*
> *Upon a heart full of thanks.*
> *Far and wide be praised your triumphant love!*

Impromptus Opus 135, D.935

October 1827

These impromptus, like those of *Opus 90*, constitute a loosely connected and unique Schubertian work of art inspired by the rose cross mystery. They are hymns to the romance between the feminine face of God, the Divine Sophia, and the wanderer. First she is hidden, only a memory, yet her attraction is erotic and powerful. In the second of these impromptus she is a mother, a figure from the distant past, still radiant in her effect upon the wanderer. She has awakened him to the meaning of life and will shepherd him through death. In the third impromptu the wanderer's knight-like fidelity to this wisdom is in focus. And finally the wanderer revels in the life of courage and joy that true wisdom brings.

FIRST IMPROMPTU

> *...the fourth furor, coming from Venus, turns and transforms the spirit of man into a god by the ardor of love and renders him entirely like God, a true image.*
>
> *Giordano Bruno*

Eros is godly. He leads the wanderer to the Divine Sophia, awakening a desire that earth will certainly disappoint. The desire reaches to the throne of God. Eros then must be savored in the spiritual ascent. Yet divine love does not always fare well in its incarnations. This is the "sorrow" of the wanderer as the soul reaches beyond itself for higher life..

Heimliches Lieben
Karoline Louise von Klenke, D.922
Ah, when your lips touch mine,

I am transfigured by joy.
Apprehension seizes me!
My bosom heaves!
My eyes come alive, my cheeks redden,
My heart pulses with deepest joy.
My mind reels, driven to ecstasy by your lips.
It cannot, cannot be calm!
My life itself seems suspended at this moment.
In your sweet, soft, rose-like mouth I am lost.
I am enveloped in your loving arms.

Ah, if only I might become spirit
To become one with you!
Yet our lips, bright with love, must part.
This body of mine is not made spirit by your kiss...
And your heart, stirred by passion,
Dares not beat aloud for me!

SECOND IMPROMPTU, OPUS 135

For man is the image of God, at least who by the furor of Venus has been made like to God and lives only in the highest reaches of the Mind.
Giordano Bruno

Like an infant, the wanderer lies bound and helpless in his present state. Archetypal memories of primordial happiness lead him to an anticipation of recapturing the bliss and "going home".

Vor Meiner Wiege
Karl Gottfried von Leitner, D.927
Here, here is the narrow crib
Where once I lay as an infant...
Feeble, helpless, speechless,
Opening my lips only to cry.

I could hold nothing with my tiny hands,
Was tightly bound as a prisoner.
My small feet were useless, as if lame,
Until my mother lifted me to her breast...

Then I laughed, and I looked up to her as I drank...
......She sang to me of roses and angels...
She sang and she rocked, lulling me to sleep
With a loving kiss, closing my eyes.

She drew over me a silken green cover,
Closing me in a cool, heavenly world.
Where can I find again that peaceful world?
Perhaps when the green of the grass covers me!

Oh mother, dear mother, please stay longer!
Who else can sing so beautifully to me of the angels?
Who else can so lovingly close my eyes with a kiss,
As I lie down for my longest, last, and deepest sleep.

THIRD IMPROMPTU

Behold now standing before you the man who has pierced the air and penetrated the sky, wended his way amongst the stars and overpassed the margins of the world...

Giordano Bruno

Through a series of variations we explore with the wanderer-monk his pilgrimage through life, undertaken under the banner of the cross. Divine providence takes the form of a continuous invitation that leads him to dare to be free. In the face of threatening death he must chart his course and sail his ship into the promised land. The pathway will lead from one world into a better one.

The composer infuses the musical setting with echoes of his own experience, seeing himself as a spiritual pilgrim, confidant that the pathway of the wisdom tradition leads to the Promised Land.

Der Kreuzzug
Karl Gottfried von Leitner, D.932
The monk stands in his cell
By the gray window molding,
An army of knights marches
In shining armor over the meadow.

They sing pious songs
In harmonious, solemn voice.
Above them is unfurled
The silken banner of the Cross.

At the sea's edge they board a stately ship...
It sails away over the green water,...
And is soon no bigger than a swan.

The monk stands there at the window
Watching it all the while.

"I am, like them, also a pilgrim,
Although I remain at home."

"Life leads through perilous seas
And burning desert sands.
My journey is also a crusade
Into the promised land."

FOURTH IMPROMPTU

Acteon had absorbed divinity into himself...
Giordano Bruno

Wisdom and sexuality constitute a major tension that this composer feels he must resolve. In the *Fifth Symphony* that resolution seems to have been a major effort to minimize the role of sensuality in the life of his wanderer. Here the importance of the sensual and the blatantly sexual is suggested. They play and essential role in wisdom. Wisdom is the underground river, the water of life. It springs up to enrich its possessor with real life. Here is Schubert's tribute to the source of life's hope and joy. This tribute comes at an important time. Death has been a constant companion for five years. Within little more than a year it will make its definitive claim. At times like this it loses its terror. Schubert's wisdom is evident in the sublime disposition that he realizes artistically and mystically in the face of death in each successive masterpiece.

In this impromptu, the wanderer proclaims his readiness to die. This is a critical point in gnosis. Courageous wisdom triumphs over terror. The composer is able to sing this song mocking the emptiness of a life devoid of the mystery because of the nourishing role of sensuality in his life.

Lebensmut
Ludwig Rellstab, D.937
Courage boils in the blood!
The fountain of life erupts in glistening silver.
And before the moment passes,
Before the spirit deadens,
Drink boldly from the sparkling waters!

Dare to act with courage! Don't hesitate.
Fortune ebbs and flows.
Unless you act you will never taste the magical fruit.
If you crave joy,
You must dare to make the bold leap!

Courageously embrace even death when the moment is right.
Take your full goblet and knock it against the cup of death.

Peace with death unlocks the prison cell of life.
New dawns will appear!
Welcome death with brazen courage!

Symphony No. 10 in D major, D.936

November 1828

I belong to what is above.
The Gospel of John

The great drama of ascent into the *mysterium magnum* is reaching its definitive moment. Life for this wanderer has been a romance of a mystical presence symbolized in a dream maiden and made incarnate in real women in his life. Now at the end of life the dream maiden who has been the inspiration for his every achievement awaits him. In these late works of the composer's last year the theme of emerging out of the contradiction between Being and Becoming through an awakening to love's transcendental invitation is predominant. In this relic of a symphony, unfinished due to the death of the composer, a wanderer stands at the great divide. That divide separates him from the dream maiden. Approaching it he sings his song of plaintive yearning and then anticipates an utterly new spring. Inviting him, attracting him, beguiling him from the "other side" is the image of his immortal beloved, who awakens him to life's meaning yet for now is beyond his reach. So Schubert creates this hymn of love for the Divine Sophia. He sings of his pain in separation from her and his anticipation of final union.

The profound but simple beauty of Schubert's genius is evident throughout this symphony. At its beginning the wanderer stands atop the mountain of life and looks out over death's dark valley...and he sings. His song is the cosmic song, mysterious, penetrating far down into that darkness, and echoing clearly back to the singer, an echo that carries with it intimations of cosmic fulfillment. This art extends even into the yawning mouth of death itself. It sings of yearning for the beloved who is over there, on the other side, in eternal transcendence, unity. As is appropriate to a dying man the pain, the pain of the yearning first inspires his song; but then he experiences heaven's acceptance of his prayer. Hope supplants sorrow yet one more time.

The second movement develops the same poetry but stops short of celebrating the coming of spring, leaving that for the third movement. It expresses such intense longing for the dream maiden that both wanderer and the listener are ready for a heavenly acceptance of the song.

In the third movement the wanderer's thoughts turn to going home. "Spring is coming; spring my joy!" The wanderer is preparing himself to ascend finally to a higher, transcendental, luminous state of being, to "wander away". The solemnity of death is present here. Fear resonates in the music, but joyful hope is dominant. Once again the sublime disposition triumphs and the better world becomes incarnate.

We have this unfinished symphony in its present, performance-ready state due to Brian Newbould of the University of Hull in Great Britain. Because the composition was interrupted by the death of the composer, it was necessary for Newbould to exercise some creativity in its completion. The work of this great Schubertian as it stands is completely faithful to Schubert's sketches. For both his scholarship and creativity we owe Nebould an enormous debt of thanks.

FIRST MOVEMENT:

One dark night, fired with love's urgent longing… ah, the sheer grace!…I went out unseen, my house being now completely still.

John of the Cross

For this wanderer a song expresses the mystery. The song from the mountain peak penetrates far down into the darkness and then echoes back. Here is commerce between two worlds, between heaven and earth. The song of the exile is echoed in like intensity in the response of the earth. The yearning is for reunion with the heavenly bride, the ideal of creation, "over there, on the other side" where contradictions are reconciled and heaven and earth are one. The song is a lament so profound, so heavenly in its acceptance of life's truth that redemption follows. Spring comes at last!

Der Hirt auf dem Felsen
Wilhelm Müller/ F.Schubert? D.965
When I stand upon the mountain peak,
I look down into the valley so deep, so dark…
And I sing!

Up from the distant blackness the echo rises…
From out of the depths of the earth.

The further my cry reaches
The clearer is the echo from the depths.

My beloved is so distant,
so far away,
And I so yearn for Her...
Over there...
on the other side!

In deep grief am I torn.
I have no joy in life...
No hope here upon the earth.
I am so alone.

So plaintive is the cry in the woods,
So tortured is the voice in the night,
That the prayer ascends to Heaven with divine power.

Spring is coming!
Spring, my joy!
Even now I prepare...
to wander away!

SECOND MOVEMENT:

Where beloved, have you gone, leaving me in agony?...I went out seeking you, but I found you nowhere!

John of the Cross

In another of his sublime swan songs, Schubert descends deeply into the sorrow of the life experience, its contradiction to the heart's desires. Once again he addresses conflict in order to celebrate the mystery of life.

Der Hirt auf dem Felsen (continued)
My beloved is so distant,
so far away,
And I so yearn for Her...
Over there...
on the other side!

The further my cry reaches
The clearer is the echo from the depths

I am so alone here!.

So plaintive is the cry in the woods,
So tortured is the voice in the night,
That the prayer ascends to Heaven with divine power.

THIRD MOVEMENT

The Father ceaselessly begets his Son, and, what is more, he begets me as his Son...begetting me in his own nature, his own being!
Meister Eckhart

Joyfully the wanderer anticipates the "new spring", the end of the spiritual ascent, the definitive union with his divine Sophia, his eternal bride. Redemption, homecoming, the triumph of love approach. The divine soul that was cast into earth's darkness and there was exiled in a long winter's journey, is about to go home. The way leads through death and is not without its fearsome aspect, but joyful anticipation reigns supreme. The divine word, the god-song, flung far into the darkness, is about to be reunited with its divine source in a final triumph of love.

Der Hirt auf dem Felsen (continued)
Spring is coming!
Spring, my joy!
Even now do I make myself ready...
Ready to wander away!

My beloved is so distant, so far away,
And I so yearn for Her...
Over there...on the other side!

The further my cry reaches
The clearer is the echo out of the depths.

Spring is coming!

FANTASY FOR PIANO FOUR HANDS IN F MINOR, D.940

January to April 1828

She was suspended high above him on a throne of clouds.
She shone as the morning star and dazzled as the glittering sun.
Henry Suso

The divine invitation into the mystery that is a living presence in the wanderer's life and gives his life its ultimate meaning is symbolized for this wanderer in a dream maiden whose incarnations have been damnably transient. In this superb fantasy the mystery of life is experienced through the prism of a romance of the dream maiden. The higher consciousness that graces this monumental and tragic work is a blend of creativity, peace, and pain. The "work" of this wanderer is the musical celebration of the dream maiden. Here that celebration is bathed in a divine light, despite the presence of pain, and despite its inability to make the dream real. The Divine Sophia, the perfect harmony of creation, union with the Beloved, is so transcendentally sublime as to be beyond reach. And yet the wanderer reaches out in song. The better world that Karoline Esterhazy and Theresa Grob made incarnate for the composer has sadly disappeared. The divine feminine, the light of his life, the star-like goal of all his longing, can be captured in dreams and in poetry. It can be touched by the work, the song, of the wanderer; but he needs more. The dream maiden hovers above his consciousness, breathing life into it. He sings of her among the great ladies. He sings of her laughing, high in the Alpine meadows. He sings of her, snow white in the blue waters of the sea, gaily, deliciously reaching out to him, the alluring, thrilling incarnation of divine invitation. The dream/song makes her physical absence all the more bitter...so bitter that the wanderer finds life almost unbearable. And still the dream/song goes on, causing pain, yet giving strength for this winter's journey.

Sie in jedem Leide
Karl Gottfried von Leitner D.896

I take up my harp.
And following my deepest longing…
I dream of you.
Beloved, you must know it…
Without these songs
I would be indeed lost!

As I sing I think of hermit's cells,
Of castles and tournaments…
And there among the great ladies,
With their hats and furs,
High upon the balcony I see you!

As I sing of the towering mountains,
Winds blowing far above the town's tumult,
It is you who fill the mountains with your singing,
And the small wooden hut with your joy!

If I sing of the beautiful water maidens
Playing alone in the moonlight,
Swimming in the sea,
You are there among them,
Gliding through the blue waters…
Stretching your snow white arms out to me!

How close you are to me, my beloved,
In the rose-tinted land of dreams and poetry…
But, ah, in life, so bitter, so tragic,
We are separated by the cruel hand of savage fate!

Taking up my harp…I dream of you!

Symphony No. 9 in C major, D.944

1825 and 1828

As deer long for running water so does my soul long for you, my God!
Psalm 42

The wedding of the divine self and the divine other is the culmination of the great mystery. This is achieved paradoxically by passing through joy and sorrow, triumph and catastrophe, life and death to transfiguration. Schubert presents this sublime archetypal myth of the wanderer that is the very cornerstone of the Egyptian and Greek mysteries and of Judaic and Christian mysticism in this majestic symphony. Worlds are in a tension that is sometimes horrifying. Tragedy comes to the wanderer, yet the invitation is alive. As always in Schubert's instrumental works the wanderer, inspired by hope, encounters contradiction. But that is transfigured in a spiritual ascent.

The first movement begins with a noble annunciation of the homeland theme that will resonate throughout this movement in a mystical invitation to the wandering hero. In dreams he sees that home, the idealized cottage of true love. He feels its mystery, its shimmering beauty. This symbol has titanic power and grandeur. Then the attention shifts to mystical reminders of that homeland envisioned as an Alpine paradise. The experience is laced with divine invitation. Memories and premonitions together present that homeland to the wanderer and he thinks of it with irresistible yearning.

The second movement uses Schober's poem to envision first the travels of a wanderer and then his catastrophic descent into the terrifying contradiction to his hopes and dreams. This descent is followed by an ascent to the true homeland. This wanderer is a stranger in a foreign land, a Gnostic hero, homeless, penniless. His beloved has left long ago and he despairs of achieving his life's goals. But hope is born in the depths of the catastrophe. Through the indescribably beautiful setting of *Die Mutter Erde,* the second poem inspiring this movement, death and failure cease to terrify and become the flip side of transcendence, which allures and beguiles the wanderer, leading him to light.

In the third movement it is the new and higher life of love that is celebrated as a taste of transcendence. A poem by Schiller inspires a musical meditation upon the contrast between the life of the liberated wanderer, and the greed that controls the lower world. The wanderer has a grim realization that the lower world attempts to destroy the higher one just as rationalistic philosophy seeks to destroy the wisdom tradition. He must be clever and opportunistic. The "flint-hearted gods" bear some resemblance to the demonic forces which buried this composer's mystical work in his own time and which threaten wanderers uniquely in every age. Schubert's only course is to protect his treasure, his immersion in the rose cross mystery, through symbolic art.

The fourth movement is one of praise and gratitude for the life-giving mystery whereby we awaken to divine invitation and follow it through sorrows and joys to a transcendental triumph of love. The mystery is experienced in the stars, the roar of cascading falls, the whisper of the forest, the awesome power of thunder and lightning, and through the resolution of the storm in the gentle rain (a Schubert addition not found in the poem). All of nature sings its praise of the Creator. But a celebration yet more powerful is sounded by the human heart as, looking through tears of sorrow, it seeks and finds its loving inviter. Just as he does in the fourth movement of the *Wanderer Fantasy*, the third movement of the *Piano Sonata in A Minor, D.845*, and the fourth movement of the *Piano Trio in E Flat* Schubert expresses an analogy between the spiritual ascent of the wanderer and the movement of nature. Nature is rich in beauty, staggering in power, an eruption at every point of divine life. But yet more powerful is the intensely personal drama of the wanderer in his or her ascent through life and its contradictions to God. Again and again in this Finale the music affirms with massive force the majesty of God expressed first in nature, and then in the spiritual ascent of the wanderer.

FIRST MOVEMENT:

What a great miracle is Man...he sees the poverty of that part of himself that is only human, and places his trust in the divinity of the other part.
Corpus Hermeticum

In ghostly majesty the horns announce the wanderer's inner bond to his true homeland. He yearns to return to it. In his heart is its undying image. In his exile the wanderer listens for mystical "awakeners", reminders of its beauty. He finds them in songs of the Alps and in memories of the good people there. Nature and these people are sacramentally alive with the life of the higher world.

Das Heimweh
Johann Ladislaus Pyrker D.851
Ah, the child of the mountains

Has ever a filial love for his homeland!
A flower, torn from its Alpine bed, wilts…
So he, taken from his mountains, suffers.

Always he can see the beloved cottage
Where he was born, standing in the green, flowery meadow.
He can see the dark majesty of the fir trees…
The sheer rock ascent above him…
And mountain upon mountain standing in towering majesty,
Radiant in the crimson glow of sunset.
All this will never leave him. But, alas, that beloved cottage,
In the light of sunset, stands before him…
And all else disappears!

Anxiously he listens. Did he hear
The cattle lowing from the woods!
Did he hear the call of the shepherd?
Did he hear the yodel of the milk maid…
That yodel echoes joyously the songs of the Alps…
And it echoes again and again within him.

The fields in the valley have no appeal to him.
He leaves the town, all alone…
And looks in agony at the distant hills of home…
There he is drawn with irresistible yearning!

SECOND MOVEMENT

Unless the grain of wheat falls to the earth and dies, it remains just a grain of wheat.

The Gospel of John

The wanderer progresses through life, at first with a jaunty step, only to experience the inevitable contradiction between opposing worlds, a shattering, breathtaking pain. The experience does not stop there but continues into thrilling transcendental anticipation of the mysterious end of the journey. Here is the wanderer's life in joy, in graphic horror, and in the unmatched beauty of subliminal hope.

Pilgerweise
Franz Schober D.789
I am a wanderer upon this earth.
I go from house to house.
Please, in friendliness and good spirits,
Give me your gift of love!

With open sympathy
And a handshake
You could refresh my spirit
And ease its pain, so long endured.

Do not think that in return
I will do you a service.
Rather I will shower your doorway
With wreathes of blue flowers.

I will play my zither
And sing you a song.
Perhaps that seem to you rather silly,
Of not much value at all.

To me it is necessary;
It is my wealth
As it is to every wanderer.
This you cannot understand.

Your wealth is different,
Yiu can easily replace it.
In the amplitude of your riches
Your better world is secure.

But I, in my wandering,
Struggling with pilgrim stick in hand,
See my fortune disappear
As thread parts from thread in my clothes!

So I live on handouts
From moment to moment.
Won't you, without anger, give me some food?
For you it will be pleasant, for me bliss.

I am a wanderer on the earth.
I go from house to house.
Please, in friendliness and good spirit,
Give me your gift of love!

…

Die Mutter Erde
Friedrich Leopold zu Stolberg-Stolberg D.788
The day of life can be long and full of sorrow;
The life-transfiguration of death is fresh and cool;

Like a gentle breeze seeping through the leaves,
It ushers all of us to our final peace.

The moon shines, the dew falls
Over graves as over flowery fields.
The tears of loved ones also fall…
Aglow with the soft light of hope.

All of us, great and small,
Are welcomed to the bosom of Mother Earth!
And would we but observe her beauty,
Her bosom would hold no terror for us.

THIRD MOVEMENT

Heavenly Aphrodite…you have yoked the world. You give birth to all, to everything: heaven, earth, and even the depths of the sea.
Orphic Hymn

Woman can be the incarnation of the divine invitation to transfigure one world by another. She can be that spiritually. She can be that physically. She can be a living sacrament, bringing heaven to earth. In her inviting eyes the wanderer can taste paradise. Divine life approaches as his bride, the opposite, the other, who is a divine emanation just as he himself is. Union with her is the womb of the better world, the place where redemption begins.

Das Geheimnis
Friedrich Schiller D.793
She would not so much as whisper…
There were too many who could hear!
I could ask only her eyes…
And I well understood what they said.
So now my cozy woodland hide-away,
I quietly enter your peace.
Hide the lovers in your green leaves
From the prying eyes of the world!

From afar the day drives ahead
In its business and frenzy.
I can make out the ring of the hammer
Through the sounds of many voices,
Each man struggling for his daily portion,
Out of the meager largesse of the flint-hearted gods.
Still, without demanding anything, the gods
Lay this greatest treasure in my lap!

Some people do not understand
The enchantment of true love.
These people can only destroy the enchantment,
For they do not share it.
Their world has no place for such mystery,
And they seek it out to destroy it.
Thus we must quickly snatch it
Lest the opportunity be lost.
So tiptoe quietly, noiselessly
Into the night's blessed stillness,
And quickly vanish
From the sight of threatening eyes.
Gentle stream, wrap yourself round us
As if you were an ocean,
Protecting us with your might.
Defend this, our holy sanctuary!

FOURTH MOVEMENT:

Let all nature listen to the hymn.
I sing of the Lord of Creation, the All, the One..
Open heavens! Listen to my song!
Corpus Hermeticum

The storm, the cascading falls, the stars and galaxies all participate in the awakening to divine invitation, the catastrophic contradiction, and transfiguration. This passage is the mystery. It is the prize. More quietly do the forests, the fields of corn, and the flowery meadows proclaim this same mystery, a universal imaging of an ascent to the life of God. Yet more than all of nature does the soul express this mystery in its often painful ascent to God in response to divine invitation. Christians and non-Christians of every kind unite in the celebration.

Die Allmacht
Ladislaus Pyrker D.852
Great is Jehovah, the Lord!
Heaven and earth proclaim his might!
You can hear it in the thundering tempest,
In the cascading roar of the waterfall.
You can hear it in the whisper of the green forest.
You can see it in the golden fields of corn,
In the splendor of the flower,
In the majesty of the starry heavens.

Terrifying sounds his thunder!
Horrifying is the flame of his lightening!
But still more does your heart
Reveal Jehovah's might
When it reaches upwards in prayer;
And trusts in his love and mercy.
Great is Jehovah, the Lord!

KLAVIERSTÜCKE, D.946

May 1828

Awareness of the rose cross mystery colors the depictions of the wanderer's pain at the absence of the dream maiden as well as his awakening to her mystical invitation. Hidden in these thrilling piano works is the paradox of the spiritual ascent. With the wanderer we plunge into the waters of wisdom and find everything transfigured. The *Klavierstücke* in carefully-crafted unity reveal a fantasy-like structure in which the central experience of Gnostic-Christianity, of Jewish Cabalism, and of the pagan mysteries is expressed. The scene is set for the drama of the inner life with an instrumental realization of the poem *Herbst*. The pathway to gnosis begins in sorrow. With Saturnine depression the wanderer turns away from earthly illusions. In the First Piece the bleakness of Schubert's actual sorrow is reflected. Yet the sorrow will be redemptive. And even in this first movement there is the promise of future bliss. First the reminder comes as a glimpse of the past. Then it becomes a precious mystical ascension out of Saturn into a higher world.

The Second Piece, inspired by the poem *Widerschein*, is pure magic. Originally set as a Lied in 1818, Schubert transposed the poem into another key in 1828, presumably in preparation for this instrumental setting. Here he is able to explore freely its mystical potential. The piece begins by telling what seems to be a simple story. But then the inner world appears and sublime gnosis is achieved. All this happens as the wanderer, awaiting his beloved, sees her reflection in the waters (symbolic of the better world) and is enraptured in mystical anticipation. He has waited, but she is late, indeed hiding. The water, like the night, is a fact-clouding, wisdom-awakening condition as it was in the four-part song *Der Gondelfahrer* and in the song cycle *Die Schöne Müllerin*. Here our wanderer is both frightened and attracted by the waters of the mystery. Ultimately he is simply enchanted by its otherworldly beauty.

The Third Piece is a psalm setting breathing the same Cabalistic higher consciousness that we find in the part songs *Miriam's Siegegesang D.942, Psalm 92, D.953,* and in the *Rondo for Four Hands in A Major D.953* in which God, who invites the wanderer up out of his sorrow and into the better world, is given praise and thanks.

FIRST PIECE

> *Thus we say that it is good to die in God so that He may give us instead that being which is better than life.*
>
> *Meister Eckhart*

Relentlessly cold winds blow away the dreams of summer as the pure life of the spirit is stifled by earth's darker powers. The coming winter is prefigured in the clouds and disappearing stars. Hopes and memories of earthly love have vanished like rose blossoms blown away by the wind. Earthbound dreams bloom but briefly, then disappear without a trace. Yet in the midst of these disturbing thoughts the wanderer has a brief vision of the peace of the past summer and the distant spring.

Herbst
Ludwig Rellstab D.945
The winds howl a cold song of death.
The field is barren;
The trees stripped bare.

Oh, field of flowers,
Oh, sun-soaked meadow,
You disappear as do all dreams in life!
The clouds rush by, so dark and gray.
Even the stars are gone along with their heavenly blue.
Just as the stars desert the sky,
So does hope abandon us in life.

Days of spring, graced with rose buds,
Once with you I pressed by darling to my breast.
But cold winds from the hills have blown this all away...
Thus each year the roses of love must perish!
...

Die Nacht
Friedrich Wilhelm Krummacher D.983a
How beautiful you are,
Loving, silent, heavenly peace!
See the bright stars wander

Through the pastures of the sky
And look down upon us,
Soundless in their blue distance!

How beautiful you are,
Loving, silent, heavenly peace!
Gentle spring quietly draws near
The earth's tender breast,
Bedecking the brooks with moss,
The fields with flowers!

SECOND PIECE

Then man...having seen this form reflected in the water, loved her and wished to dwell with her.

Corpus Hermeticum

The theme is redemption, a sublime vision of hope. The wanderer finds the fulfillment of his dreams in this mystical vision of his beloved, seen shimmering through the waters. She is divine invitation, a living mystery, an incarnation of transcendental beauty. Found in life, yet never finally possessed there, she hides, revealing herself magically in the water, symbol of the Pleroma, the Better World.

Widerschein
Franz Xaver von Schlechta D.949
The fisherman stands on the bridge...
His beloved is late.
Impatiently he looks into the brook...
And daydreams.

She is hiding in the lilac,
And he sees the reflection
Clearly in the water...
Even more clearly than in life!

He sees her!
He recognizes the ribbons
And her sweet smile!
And he grabs on the railing
Lest he drawn down into the water!

THIRD PIECE

> *You are light and life, like God the father of whom man was born. If you know yourself, you will return to life!*
>
> *Corpus Hermeticum*

A sparkling psalm of praise and thanksgiving is sung by the wanderer to the God above all of nature. This God invites the wanderer through human events but calls higher to fuller life. This Psalm follows upon the meditation upon Sophia. She channeled divine invitation to the wanderer. He turns now in thanksgiving and praise to the source of that invitation, the font of his hope and joy.

Psalm 92
D.953
How wondrous it is to thank you eternal God,
To sing your name, Most High!
In the morning we extol your kindness.
In the evening we extol your faithfulness.
Our lyre and psaltery sing their praise.
We thank you with our harps.
Lord and God, your works give me delight,
How great they are!
How deep are your divine thoughts!
The fool cannot understand this.
Unthinking people are puzzled…
The evil seem to triumph…
But they shall go down…for ever.
For you are eternal, O God!
Eternal! Eternal!

Allegro for Four Hands "Lebensturm", D.947

May 1828

What then shall be said of him who has found a way to mount up to the sky?
He has released the human spirit and set knowledge at liberty!
Giordano Bruno

The wanderer must mount the pathway to the stars by actions that are often terrifying. He must put himself on the line, accepting death as the price of his creative immersion in the mystery. *Lebensturm* is a musical depiction of the wanderer as a skipper, a symbol surely of the composer in the middle of one of the most productive creative periods in musical history. Benjamin Brittin called this period of about eighteen months the most important in musical history. The drama of Schubert's spiritual ascent was reaching its climax. Death was drawing near and he knew it. A job still had to be done. He had to sing his song of dying as no one had ever sung it before.

Wildly the sea thunders, the winds howl, the sails and halyards snap and spit, all a thrilling, terrifying call, demanding that the wanderer set out on a journey that will end in his death. Here is the wanderer's artistic task, his mystical challenge. No other can stand beside him. He is a warrior, a knight, and must face his challenge alone. Courageously does he accept the challenge, turning resolutely away from the dream of earthly love in order to answer the call from and to a better world.

Schiffers Scheidelied
Franz Schober D.910
The waves thunder upon the shore;
The wind billows the sails

And sings in the foam-flecked waves.
I hear its wild song.
It beckons me to leave.
Calling to distant shores.
The boat tosses impatiently at anchor.
And out there into the distance, so endlessly far,
You, my beloved, must not venture.
How quickly my stars can vanish!
How fast does the breeze turn into a storm.
Were you with me, threatened by death,
How could I fight my battles?
Better let me go!
Free even your heart of me!
I know not if I will survive and return victorious.
These very waves which now sound so benign
May indeed draw me into their depths.
Yes, let me sail knowing that in this world I am alone.
Then, before all terrifying danger and unspeakable peril
I shall stand in courage.
Then in my game with terror I might indeed be victorious.
As long as I have command of my senses I need not fear.
I do not wish to die nor to succumb to death…
For how could I wish to leave a world
That holds such heaven as you!

Rondo for Four Hands in A major, D.951

December 1826

I will sing in praise of the Lord of Creation, the All, the One!
Corpus Hermeticum

Here is the wanderer, elevated by his experience of the paradoxical *mysterium magnum* and at peace with his life. As the Psalmist sang his thanksgiving to God in *Psalm Ninety-two* the composer (through the wanderer) sings his thanksgiving to God for leading him to the gateway to paradise. The passage through contradiction has led to the sublime disposition. In this noble work for four hands Schubert simply luxuriates in it.

In this psalm setting, inspired by Schubert's Jewish friends, we have a peace-filled meditation upon the goodness of the Divine Inviter and the trustworthiness of the divine invitation. This gnostic Christianity sees man as a spark of the divine, whose hunger for life and dream of love is not a sour joke by nature, but a promise of destiny. The yearning of the human heart is not delusory, but the beginning of a great love adventure.

Psalm 92
D.953
How wondrous it is to thank you eternal God,
To sing your name, most high!
In the morning we extol your kindness,
In the evening your faithfulness.
Our lyre and psaltery sing their praise.
We thank you with our harps.
Lord and God, your works give me delight,

Happily I sing of your works.
How great they are!
How deep are your divine thoughts!
The fool cannot understand this.
Unthinking people are puzzled…
The evil seem to triumph…
But they shall go down…for ever.
For you are eternal, Oh God!
Eternal! Eternal!

String Quintet in C major, D.956

September 1828

We say that it is good to die in God so that he may give us instead that Being which is better than life... One ought to be glad to surrender to dying and death, so that the better Being may be his portion.

Meister Eckhart

The wanderer's life, illuminated by the rose cross mystery, has reached its definitive conclusion. The wanderer stands face to face with death. Fear challenges his peace. The final victory demands this confrontation. Schubert's *String Quintet* salutes the coming of this fearsome yet sacred climax of the drama. As the wanderer faces his own imminent death he experiences both the mind-numbing dread and the unspeakable beauty of the spiritual ascent. Now, more than ever, the divine life that permeates nature fortifies him, raising him above his fear, calming him, and creating hope and freedom.

Supreme artistry measures itself to the spiritual elevation of the wanderer. Pure magic arises out of the interplay between musicians, evocative of the tension between Nature and spirit, the unmatched horses of the Platonic dialogues. The sublime in nature exists in a Schelling-like counterbalance with the interpersonal sublime. But Schubert's celebration of this counterbalance is not the product of books. It is autobiographical and absolutely authentic. In reflecting on what Schubert achieves here the lines set in February of 1815 in the Lied *Auf einen Kirchhof* D.151 when the composer was eighteen come to mind:

Like a flame will you shine in your dying, giving light like a sunset, like the radiant splendor of the evening, like music reaching the heavens...

These lines were given a second setting in the last movement of the *Piano Sonata in E Major D.157.* The composer of this otherworldly *String Quintet* is measuring his creation to his own personal experience of divine invitation.

Here is a revelation of the composer's personal experience of the contradiction-reconciling life of the spirit as it nears its definitive passage to the new age. He knew exactly what he was doing. The first movement is prayer expressed musically first as an ascent, the reaching of the soul for the divine source of its invitation. Then the music expresses a descent of grace from God to the wanderer. The beauty of this ascent and descent, this sublime interplay between heaven and earth, give substance to the words of *Die Allmacht* set in the *Piano Trio in E Flat,* (D.927):

> But still more (than all of nature) does your heart reveal the might of God, when it reaches up in painful, agonized yearning, and trusts in his love and mercy..

From the very beginning of the movement we are immersed in the great romance between heaven and earth through the setting of A. Schmidl's poem *Hymnus an den Heiligen Geist*, set as a part song D.948 first in May 1828 and then revisited in October, the month before he died. The composer uses a second poem, set earlier also as a part song, to intensify the experience of sacred peace. Here the peace of the stars and of spring unites with spiritual peace in an utterly magical, mystical experience of cosmic harmony. Schmidl's poem includes a petition for the strength necessary for the wanderer to complete his course and return home.

The second movement in a magical interplay of inner and outer worlds assigns to the different musicians themes inspired by the above two poems. The trusting prayer for divine help unites with the peace of the stars and of spring. As was the case in the first movement of the *Trout Quintet*, the experience of nature's sublime blends with a personal experience of divine initiation through the interplay of two different poems. One of the poems, *Das Grab*, was also used in the earlier quintet. The peace of nature is one with an inner illumination. The majestic brilliance and order of the stars and galaxies along with the blossoms of spring are counterpoint to a background of both the prayer and fear-filled alarm of the wanderer who faces death. This second movement differs from the First in that it is more than a musical narration of the tension between nature and spirit. It is a musical working out of the interplay through the interplay between musicians. The two inspiring poems are expressed simultaneously. Prayer, despair, and hope interact. As in the Ninth Symphony, the *Piano Trio in E Flat*, and the posthumous *Piano Sonata in A Major;* the descent into despair is every bit as compelling as the consequent ascent in faith. The need of the wanderer is crushing. But the divine response is to extend divine peace found both in nature and in the human heart to the wanderer as a supreme transfiguring force. Here is redemption realized.

In the third movement the composer expresses his faith in the redemptive drama he experiences both in Nature and in his own destiny. "Spring is coming! Spring my joy!" The inspiring poetry consists of one of the three poems found in the Lied The Shepherd on the Rock. Counterbalancing this is the silent, dark face of death, expressed in a second poem, the same poem used to inspire the development section of the first movement of the Trout Quintet. Life triumphs in the completion of life's drama. Once again the joy is counterbalanced by a vivid and frightening anticipation of death. And once again hope prevails.

The Finale is a thrilling conclusion, not merely to the musical work, but to the myth of the wanderer and to the composer's life. The party that is ending is the life of the composer. He expresses satisfaction with how he has lived it. He contemplates his "going to the grave" with peace and gentle humor.

FIRST MOVEMENT:

Soul: Ah Love, Thou hast consumed my very flesh and blood!
Love: Thereby art thou illuminated and raised up to God!
Mechthild of Magdeburg

Solemnly we stand with the composer before his God, the one who invites, who comforts, who strengthens. The wanderer knows that the invitation now calls to a transition that frightens and excites beyond all others. In the great romance of life it has always been this divine inviter who has bestowed ultimate meaning upon the event, gracing it with mysterious hope, transfiguring it with an otherworldly beauty. Now the wanderer speaks directly to that inviter in a plea for peace.

Hymnus an den Heiligen Geist
A. Schmidl D.948
Oh Lord my God!
Hear my prayer,
Which reaches longingly
Up to You in Your mercy.
Gaze upon me, oh comforter,
Give heavenly peace to my heart!

Die Nacht
Friedrich Wilhelm Krummacher D.983c
How lovely you are,
Gentle, loving, heavenly peace!
You pervade the heavenly fields of light;
From distant heights descending silently upon our world!

How lovely you are,
Gentle, loving, heavenly peace!
You rest upon the earth's warm breast
In the blossoms of spring!
In silver streams, leaves and flowers!

Hymnus an den Heiligen Geist *(continued)*
Fill me with strength and courage!
Do not abandon me on my path!
Lead me home...to what is good and just.

SECOND MOVEMENT:

You give to us your own Spirit, the Power of powers, the Perfection of all things.
Nicholas of Cusa

The sublime moment for the wanderer, who is mystically in the presence of the divine invitation experienced in the stars and in spring blossoms, now becomes sublime on a more personal level. The wanderer is immersed in the night. Divine peace envelops him. The stars through plucked strings beam their heavenly light onto the earth's warm breast. Fortified by this heaven in Nature he gives voice to his own feelings. He cries out his need to share that otherworldly peace. At the point of utter catastrophe that peace dawns. The very heaven that fills nature's night illuminates the life of the wanderer. His inner turmoil, fears, agonies, need for help and comfort are transfigured in the all-conquering divine love that shines in the stars and erupts in the blossoms of spring. The contradiction between nature's peace and the wanderer's agony has opened the door to a sublime experience of divine invitation.

Hymnus an den Heiligen Geist
Alois Schmidl, D.948
Oh Lord my God!
Hear my prayer,
Which reaches longingly
Up to You in Your mercy.
Gaze upon me, oh comforter,
Give heavenly peace to my heart!

Die Nacht
Friedrich Wilhelm Krummacher D.983c
How lovely you are,
Gentle, loving, heavenly peace!
You pervade the heavenly fields of light;
From distant heights descending silently upon our world!

How lovely you are,
Gentle, loving, heavenly peace!
You rest upon the earth's warm breast
In the blossoms of spring!
In silver streams, leaves and flowers!

Hymnus an den Heiligen Geist *(continued)*
Fill me with strength and courage!
Do not abandon me on my path!
Lead me home...to what is good and just.

THIRD MOVEMENT

I am the bright morning star...
Yes, I am coming soon!
Book of Revelation

Here the wanderer is a hunter seeking eternal life. That life takes the form of spring. It is coming. It is the wanderer's joy! The hunt begins in joyful anticipation. Then, as in the second movement, the focus changes to the challenge to mind and heart that dying poses. The poetry, probably written by the composer, expresses alienation and despair. As he looks around he finds that this world is not where his heart is, not where his hope lies. But life returns in the anticipation of coming joy.

Der Hirt auf dem Felsen
Wilhelm Muller/ F.Schubert (?), D.965
Spring is coming!
Spring, my joy!
Now at last I am free...
Ready to wander away!

Das Grab
Johan Gaudenz von Salis-Seewis, D.663
The grave is deep and quiet...
Its darkness conceals a land of deep mystery...
No songs of nightingales... only the flowers of the bereaved...
Widows wring their hands and orphans weep...in vain...
Yet nowhere else does the heart find peace and go home...
Storm-tossed hearts find little peace until they stop beating...

FOURTH MOVEMENT:

I call upon Daimon…O blessed one, drive painful cares away…
Bring a glorious, sweet, and noble end to life!
Orphic Hymn

In the fourth movement, Schubert, the wanderer, is now at the end of his creative life. He has translated his dream into a career of composition, and fashioned in his art precisely what he intended, transfiguring the life experience from beginning to end by virtue of the wisdom tradition. The vision of life as a spiritual ascent is brought to completion. The godliness of the human experience, the divine joy present throughout life, even in its sorrows, has triumphed time after time in his work. It has stood up against tragedy of every kind, and now stands triumphant even in the face of death. It is Schubert's ultimate triumph to realize artistically the victory of the sublime disposition in the face of death itself.

Zur guten Nacht
Johann Friedrich Rochlitz, D.903
Listen, the hour chimes
To end our party.
It tells each to go home
After he has emptied his glass,
Thanked our host,
And sung this song, to its end.
So empty the glass,
And thank the host,
Then sing the song to its end.
We will go away happy.
What we have heard and seen
And done, none can fault.
And that which we experienced
United us to one another and to art!
It gives us joy.
Yes. That which we experienced,
That which united us
To one another and to art, give us joy.
So sleep well. Dream like brides.
Soon we will meet again!
And if one of us
Finds his peace in the grave,
Sing to him a tender "Good Night."
Yes, if one of us
Finds his peace in the grave
Sing to him a tender "Good Night."

The Posthumous Piano Sonatas

August 1828

What is the secret wisdom, the commitment to the *mysterium tmagnum,* so treasured by the mystics, that shines through Schubert's art? We find at its core the divine invitation, experienced and embraced indirectly, as contradictions are reconciled. We symbolize this subtle and elusive mystery as a rose cross. Meister Eckhart described it thus:

> *The wise man said: "In the middle of the night, while all things were wrapped in silence, a secret word was spoken to me. It came stealthily, like a thief." What does he mean by a word that is secret or hidden? It is the nature of a word to reveal what is hidden. It opened and shone before me as if it were revealing something and made me conscious of God, and thus it was called a word. Furthermore it was not clear to me what it was, because it came with stealth like a whisper trying to explain itself through the stillness. See, as long as it is concealed men will always be after it. It appears and disappears, which means that we shall plead and sigh for it.*

A higher consciousness of the mystery was expressed by Plato and sparkles within the Egyptian and Greek mysteries, Judaism, Islam, Buddhism, Hinduism, and Christianity. But the mystery disappears within them as often as it reveals itself. The elusive reality is experienced in the movement through contradiction upwards in response to the divine invitation to a higher harmony. This ascent can be reduced to no formula, institution, belief, or law. It embraces yet transcends them all.

Schubert's view of the *mysterium magnum* was a continuation of the long and noble Platonic tradition. But Schubert's grasp of the mystery was in some ways unique. The incorporation of Eros into the spiritual ascent is a bridge over what in the Augustinian tradition was considered unbridgeable. For Schubert romance defined life. The romance of a dream maiden in her incarnations inspired some of the greatest art ever created. We follow that romance with the help of poetry. There is no magical geometry of sound that can pretend to divine transcendence, just as there is no political order or philosophy, no ideology or system, no religion or art form, that does not betray divine life even as it expresses it. The *mysterium magnum* beckons from behind the contradictions of the "now", the present moment with its joys and sorrows. It is a personal invitation, experienced indirectly, in the tensions between opposites like idea and intuition, poetry and music, sorrow and joy, death and new life. The invitation to penetrate those walls is never lacking. A higher consciousness of this romance of the mystery is the pearl of divine life. By it everything human is transfigured.

This romance of the mystery is especially evident in special clusters of works. One of these is a series of piano sonatas completed three months before the composer died but inspired by poems set as Lieder one or two years earlier. In these sonatas Schubert tells once more the story of the spiritual ascent of his wanderer. And once again the opposition is between hope for a triumph of love on one hand and a bitter and frustrating life experience on the other. He begins this particular story, not at the beginning, but in the middle. The beloved has disappeared. Artistic creation seems impossible. The bitter sorrow that inspired *Die Winterreise* is deadening. If anything the devastation of spirit in the song cycle is intensified in these sonatas. The agony is that of a rejected lover, one betrayed by a human and a divine beloved. Only after this confession of misery can the healing takes place. As it does Schubert sings his song of redemption one last time. There is nothing cheap about it; tragedy and despair are given their due. And the victory is utterly authentic. It is convincing because it is real.

Piano Sonata in C minor, D.958

The drama of the spiritual ascent into the *mysterium mgnum* begins in darkness and ends in light. We begin this epic journey in darkness. The incarnation of divine beauty has disappeared. The experience of the mystery begins in this *Piano Sonata in C Minor* with the "sorrow" of the wanderer who is almost paralyzed by grief at the loss of his dream maiden. He has gambled everything in the effort to bring heavenly joy to earth. Schubert had given up marriage and artistic compromises that might have made him wealthy. This effort appears to him to have been a complete failure. The composer had been rejected as a suitor and in important ways as an artist. Although he was respected as a highly talented composer his greatest contributions were not recognized when he was alive nor are they understood today. He bore the burden of painful alienation as his prize

Schubert had set the poem *Der Atlas* as a Lied in *Schwanengesang*. Now it inspires a catastrophic plunge into despair in the first movement of this sonata. Earlier, when marriage was possible, he had decided to pursue a lonely course of artistic creativity, and cut himself off from his beloved. He had been aware of his own creative power and knew that he could fashion a musical expression of the higher consciousness such as never before seen on this earth. Yet no one seemed capable of ascending to it or even understanding it. Some of those who understood it best chose to oppose or ignore it. His wager was apparently a disaster. He had given up the girl he loved and his health as well to create something that society was incapable of appreciating or even understanding. No one wanted it. Now, alone and facing death, he experienced a dark night of the soul. Had he been betrayed by Sophia, his Immortal Beloved. He had given up everything. And for what?

In *Mignons Gesang*, the poem inspiring the second movement, the wanderer in agonized despair fixes his eye upon his transcendental goal and turns decisively away from dreams of earthly joys. He puts aside the illusion that his world could be redeemed by his art. Earthly Fate is utterly untrustworthy. What alone can give meaning to his life in this world is its transfiguration by a higher world.

The third movement of this sonata, inspired by *Das Weinen,* begins to reap the rewards of a change from worldly dreams to transcendental ones. In the new context anger is transformed into sadness. Tears of resignation lead to the awakening of new life just as they did in the fourth movement of the *Piano Trio in E Flat* and in the *Third Inpromptu Opus 90*. The bitter and destructive rage evident in the first movement has changed into a healing spring. Mysteriously with this change a wondrous redemptive force is unleashed. It is precisely the commitment to the transcendental font of life's invitation that brings strength. Now the diseased paralysis ends as the wanderer-creator re-awakens.

In the last movement based upon *Lebensmut*, the wanderer re-commits himself to his creative task. In spite of the disappearance of the dream maiden and in spite of the world's obtuseness with respect to his art he has re-discovered the higher consciousness and new life. He turns with renewed strength to the task that awaits him.

The *Piano Sonata in C Minor* is a testament to the composer's fidelity in his life's work, a testament coming only three months before death. Surely the temptation to give it all up must have been strong, but the powers within him were even stronger. The creative urge could not be overwhelmed even by his awareness that what he was about was politically incorrect and religiously unorthodox precisely because of its intensity and purity.

FIRST MOVEMENT:

> *Hear me, Eumenides...of terrifying visage, of paralyzing insanity, dark and frightful...it is you upon whom I call to bring me the sublime disposition.*
>
> *Orphic Hymn*

Crushed by failure, burdened by contempt, the wanderer roars in pain and rebellious anger. He reflects that he wanted heaven on earth, yet found only hellish agony. His hopes were all for nothing and he grumbles and stumbles under his unbearable load. Even his mind is disintegrating in this Saturnine prison.

Der Atlas
Heinrich Heine D.957

I am Atlas doomed,
Carrying the world of pain upon my shoulders.
I stagger under what I cannot bear;
My heart strained to breaking!
Proud heart you did this!
You gambled for heavenly joy or the agony of the damned...
And you have won your agony!

SECOND MOVEMENT

Lead us up beyond unknowing and light, up to the supreme peak of the holy word.

Pseudo Dionysius

The wanderer's vision shifts from earth to the better world. Its shape is deliberately indistinct, felicitously blurred in the language of poetry. But the dream is alive. His interest is not in clear ideas in which to believe, but in redemptive hope. He is invited to where the breeze is soft, the sky heavenly. His loved ones are there. And there he must go.

Mignons Gesang
Johann Wolfgang von Goethe, D.877 no1
Have you seen the house? Its roof rests upon noble columns.
The great hall sparkles, the rooms gleam!
The marble statues stand and look at me:
What has happened to you, dear child?
Have you seen it?
There, there, I want to go there with you, Oh my protector!

Have you seen the mountain with its steep, misty path?
The mule feels his way in the clouds,
While in the chasm lives the monster serpent's brood.
The cliffs are sheer; the water cascades.
Have you seen it?
There, there, our road lies. Oh let us go!

Have you seen the land where the lemon tree blooms?
Amid dark leaves, the golden oranges glow.
A soft breeze is gift of the heavenly sky.
The myrtle stands peacefully, the laurel majestic.
Have you seen it?
There! There! I want to go there with you, Oh my beloved!

THIRD MOVEMENT:

When will you hear and answer me, gentle Father?...As I was sitting there in sorrow the celestial court came to console me, intoning a heavenly dance.

Henry Suso

Rebellious anger has become sad resignation and the miracle of rebirth begins. Consolation refreshes the spirit of the wanderer, drawing him out of despair and back into life. Once again the wanderer finds the divine by accepting the divine invitation that lies at the heart of the "now". He looks into the depths of his sorrow, plumbs its depths, and there discovers the new life and strength he needs to go on.

> ***Das Weinen***
> Karl Gottfried von Leitner D.926
> *Comforting are the tears*
> *Flowing from the sacred well,*
> *As from a healing spring…*
> *Bitter, hot and bright!*
> *Therefore anguished heart,*
> *If you desire peace*
> *Immerse yourself in this spring.*
>
> *There lives in these same waters*
> *A secret and wondrous force,*
> *That is for wounds that hurt you*
> *A soothing oil.*
>
> *It softens your ailments,*
> *And grips and lifts and rolls*
> *Away the stone-like burden*
> *That seemed to crush your heart.*

FOURTH MOVEMENT:

> *No one has such powers but he who has cohabited with the elements, vanquished nature, mounted higher than the heavens, elevating himself above the angels to the archetype itself.*
>
> *Cornelius Agrippa*

Now life is changed! No longer is the wanderer despondent. New life is an experience of freedom and world-transforming power. This wanderer can once again do his creative work in the world. "Speed and courage" are reawakened. He turns to face this climax of life's challenging invitation.

> ***Lebensmut***
> Ernst Schulze, D.883
> *Oh, how the forces of youthful life flow through mind and heart!*
> *I feel everything within me come alive…doubly sensitive to joy and pain.*
>
> *It is impossible to hold the spirits within me!*
> *Be my rulers for suffering or for joy!*
> *This delaying, this yearning which vainly pulses within me,*
> *These sighs, these tears which only pride can stifle,*

This pointless struggle, this fight without strength,
Without hope, without fulfillment…
They have stolen my youth.

Let my speed and courage now awaklen!
Sound the battle horn for my sleeping spirit!
I dreamed and rested long enough.
Far too long was I in prison.
Here is neither hell nor heaven,
Neither frost nor desert heat.
So up and go into battle!
With renewed strength brave the floods!

Piano Sonata in A major, D.959

The *mysterium magnum* is a paradox, uniting a descent into sorrow and death with an ascent to love and life. A special symbol of the mystery is the Easter drama of passing through death to life. Schubert creates a miracle of Christian cabalism in this sonata by presenting an experience of this absolute core of Catholicism as it is realized in the wanderer's love of his dream maiden. The girl who made the alluring, elusive dream maiden incarnate has disappeared, taking with her the wanderer's happiness. Yet her invitational allure is still alive and redemptive. Schubert's consciousness of the rose cross mystery again and again plunges deeply into the tragedy of life and into death itself, only to ascend to the joy and peace of the sublime disposition and new life. This wisdom magician forges his sublime art out of the contradictory elements of hope and despair and in doing so celebrates the paradoxical secret of life.

The wanderer here is a lover in search of his beloved. She has disappeared. Yet she awaits him, he is sure, transcendentally, mysteriously, beyond this life. And her invitation transfigures his life. In this monumental sonata the wanderer, after descending into despair, rises from what is surely close to madness by virtue of a definitive shift in orientation from earthly dreams to the divine invitation that transcends and transfigures them in both joys and sorrows.

The first movement sounds the theme of painful alienation. The dream maiden has disappeared. The wanderer is a pilgrim/prisoner of this world, tortured by the clash between his dream of love and harsh reality. His art has been nothing but a prolonged song of love, love for the hidden God who invites, love for the girl in whom the invitation becomes incarnate, love for nature in which the life experience is seen macrocosmically, love for the society which his art has the power to enrich. Yet this love has brought only frustration and sorrow. The contrast between the beauty of the love and the pain encountered in its pursuit is expressed powerfully in the development section where the last two verses of the poem are interpreted instrumentally.

The second movement unites us with the wanderer in his trek through life. That journey inspired by Schober's *Pilgerweise* proceeds ominously to a terrifying plunge of nearly four octaves in which life itself seems to disintegrate. The reverberations of the disintegration of the body are symbolized by the separation of thread from thread of his clothes. This symbol was used by Porphery, a student of Plotinis, to symbolize the terrorizingly gradual loss of life. Finally the wandering theme that opened the movement is repeated, now with a surrealistic character, since the wanderer has been graced with a measure of peace that raises him above the pain.

The third movement salutes Sophia's crowning as Queen of Love's Kingdom. William Shakespeare's *Hark! Hark! The Lark!* provides the inspiration for a song of otherworldly joy in its vision of love's triumph. Here is Sophia, the beloved, the eternal bride, envisioned at the very gates of heaven. This lark sings for Schubert at the gate of heaven. The triumphing sun begins its ascent. And the flowers form chalices out of which the horses drink. With the blossoms the lady fair is bid, "Arise!" Literally faithful to the poem, but with a pietism that would perhaps have astounded the poet, Schubert celebrates the triumph of love.

In the fourth movement the splendid poem, *Im Frühling*, inspires a celebration of peace and hope gained by the awareness of transcendental invitation. The presence of this invitation beckoning through tragedy and death is suggested poetically through the image of the blue heavens subsuming the turbulent dark spring waters. And in those heavens is the vision of the beloved. The several dramatic musical settings of this redemptive moment at the spring, especially in the development section, constitute the core of this magical movement. Due to this redemptive hope the spring day on the hillside retains its beauty, even though the girl has disappeared.

The Piano Sonata in A Major is a monumental celebration of the passage through death, figuratively and literally, to transfigured life. The sonata contrasts a hopeless life without wisdom and ultimately death itself (Movements One and Two) with the peace and hope and new life of the wise wanderer (Movements Three and Four). The wanderer's life, even its terror and despair, is transfigured by opening the human spirit to divine invitation.

FIRST MOVEMENT:

Extinguish this burning agony, since there is no one else with the power to do so.

John of the Cross

Octave descents set an ominous tone for this sonata movement. The wanderer in alienation pursues his seemingly endless trek through mountains and wild country. He passes by sunny fields, feeling one with nature in its barrenness and chaos. He is mercilessly driven by inner longing for an unreachable beloved. The beauty of May wrings from him the tortured question: "Joy of love, will I never experience you again?

Über Wildemann
Ernst Schulze, D.884
The winds sweep through the fir trees.
The streams rush through the valley.
I wander on through woods and snow,
Mile after mile, from mountain to mountain.

Life in the open valley
Rises to accept the sun's rays.
But I rush by in a frenzy!
I am more comfortable with winter.

In the green meadows and sunny fields
I can only see my own anguish.
Life everywhere, even in the rocks, is erupting,
While the one who is life to me closes her heart.

Oh love, love, breath of May!
You bring the tender shoots from tree and bush.
The birds sing in the green tree tops.
The spring bubbles in your gentle breezes.

But love, you make me wander in sorrow,
Through howling winds on rocky paths.
Oh joy of Spring, joy of Spring
Will I never experience you again?

SECOND MOVEMENT:

Boundless Fates…you march toward men whose goals are as noble as their hopes are vain; you bring them to the valley of death.

Orphic Hymn to the Fates

On and on the wanderer trudges in his exile, looking for signs of friendship, signs of his homeland. He offers in return songs of that homeland, songs that keep his own spirit alive. In his trek he encounters mind-shattering tragedy, yet continues on his way, not without a hint that he is in some way above it all.

Pilgerweise
Franz Schober, D.789
I am a wanderer upon this earth.
I go from house to house.

Please, in friendliness and good spirits,
Give me your gift of love!

With open sympathy and a handshake
You could refresh my spirit,
And ease its pain, so long endured.

In return I will do you no service,
Except to shower your doorway with blue flowers.

I will play my zither,
Sing you a song.

Perhaps that seems rather silly,
But to me and to other wanderers it is life itself.

You have wealth that can be replaced
Your better world is secure.

Yet I, in my wandering,
With stick in hand,
See my fortune disappear......
As thread parts from thread in my clothes!

So I live on handouts from moment to moment;
Won't you, without anger, give me some food?
You will be gratified; for me it is bliss.

I am a wanderer on the earth.
I go from house to house.
Please, in friendliness and good spirit.
Give me your gift of love!

THIRD MOVEMENT

Let us rejoice and be glad...for the wedding day of the lamb has come. His bride is ready!

Book of Revelation

Everything has changed! The change does not develop. It cannot be attributed to the wanderer. It is, as Schiller insisted, a gift. In radiant expectancy the wanderer stands at the threshold of the better world in which love is triumphant. The lark sings "at heaven's gate." She announces imminent victory in the spiritual ascent, the definitive union with Sophia. The wanderer is coming home to love's triumph. The immortal beloved awakens from sleep, and together with all things beautiful, with May, with birds, meadows, and flowers welcomes the wanderer home.

Ständchen
William Shakespeare, D.882
Hark! Hark! The lark at heaven's gate sings,
And Phoebus' gins arise,
His steeds to water at those springs
On chalice'd flowers that lies.

And winking Mary-buds begin
To ope their golden eyes;
With every thing that pretty is,
My lady sweet, arise!
Arise, arise!

FOURTH MOVEMENT:

Here among the waters...he sees the most beautiful figure and face...beyond all imagining...

Giordano Bruno

In hushed tones memories of love are stirred. The union between the wanderer and his beloved began in a past time of blossoms and May. It was then that he discovered Sophia, and the mystery began. He saw the heavens reflected in the spring, and in those heavens he saw her. Now the promise of that earlier May might seem to have disappeared. Yet strangely it remains. The past is prologue and the heavens still beckon, offering the pearl of wisdom. That pearl has given its peace and restored all things in the earthly journey to radiant beauty. Sophia reigns in her kingdom of love.

Im Frühling
Ernst Schulze, D.882
Quietly I sit on the hillside.
The sky is so blue!
A gentle breeze plays in the green valley
Where once in the early spring
I was so very happy.

I walked by her side,
So much in love, so close to her!
And deep in the dark mountain spring
I could see heavenly beauty, bright and blue...
And in those heavens, I saw her!

Springtime beauty graces all the flowers;
But not every one means the same to me.
I pick flowers where she did.

Everything is still as it was then,
The flowers, the fields;
The sun is just as bright;
And no less enchanting are the heavens there in the spring.

But minds can change;
Happiness can become pain;
Love's bliss can disappear;
Then only the love remains…
The love, and alas the pain!

If only I were a bird in the meadow,,
I could sit in the treetop,
And sing a sweet song of her…
All the summer long!

Piano Sonata in B flat, D.960

The rose cross mystery that defines life in the wisdom tradition has reached its point of final definition. The wanderer is on his way towards the life-culminating wedding with the dream maiden and, through her, with the hidden God. Consciousness of the divine invitation guides him home. The wanderer anticipates the conclusion of life's drama. At last life's great romance reaches its dramatic apogee. The third and final piano sonata that celebrates this ultimate reconciliation of opposites in this mighty cycle is the *Piano Sonata in B Flat Major*. The composer, sensing the nearness of death, sets his wanderer on his way to final union with his eternal bride. The passage through death begins. Just as the *Unfinished Symphony* D.759 was an expression of liberating gnosis at the point of death, so too is this piano sonata. Here, as in the unfinished *Symphony in D Major D.936* and in the *String Quintet* D.957, Schubert is fulfilling the artistic and mystical commitment made much earlier in the *Piano Sonata in E Major D.157*, the *Unfinished Symphony*, the *Wanderer Fantasy*, the *Grand Duo for Four Hands*, and the unfinished *Symphony in E* of 1825. His life's invitation was to celebrate the life-giving mystery even to the point of death. He has done this through a romance of the Divine Sophia, the perfect image of God, expressed creatively and uniquely through his musical myth of the wanderer. This sublime sonata begins with a solemn declaration of leaving the earth. Death is greeted at times with rhapsodic hope, at other times with the fearsome rumblings of terror. The fear coexists with a consciousness of the mystery that gives life its meaning. In the development section the new world dawns with appropriate drama and beauty. The wanderer knows the paradoxical immensity of the moment, sometimes solemn and dignified, sometimes anticipating freedom, sometimes horrified.

The second movement grows out of a prayer set first as a part song. In it the wanderer's spirit reaches upwards to God, begging for final peace in dying, much as he did in *Todesmusik* in 1822. The prayer is for personal courage and for the experience of divine presence. The prayer secures a victory of hope over fear.

The third movement is *Psalm 92,* the same psalm that inspired the *Rondo for Four Hands in A Major D.951* just a few months earlier. The lyre and psaltery sing the praises of the eternal God, the source of the divine invitation, even as the psalmist/wanderer/composer stands on the doorstep of eternity. This movement is then a prayer of praise, sung at the end of life, in which the wanderer unites his voice to all of nature in thanking the one who brought him into being and is calling him home.

In the fourth movement the composer, as if on horseback and plunging ahead towards final victory, sings of his wild present and thrilling future. His forest "is indeed thick", the night dark, but he feels the "glow of welcome" that lights up the valley. His eternal bride, the divine Sophia, awaits him. He has been away from her for "three days", but quite soon he will find her again, ascending to love's fullness and to the joy, the freedom, the love that have been so elusive in these last years of his life.

In Schubert's life-view the wanderer, Everyman, is potentially a hero, endowed with a divine spark, godly in a world strange to such divinity. In this world God's image, the divine Sophia, appears, awakening him or her to life's meaning. Thus the wanderer is called to a celestial marriage with an eternal spouse, the "self" called to unite with the "other", the "earth" called to transfiguration by "heaven". This great romance transforms life. As in the opera *Alfonso und Estrella* true wisdom is realized in a consciousness of life's mystery. That consciousness means a commitment to the wedding of opposites as the pathway of the spiritual ascent, a wedding symbolized by a man and woman in love.

Consciousness of the mystery created a chasm between Schubert and both the Enlightenment and traditional Christianity. But it was critical and central to his art. Without it there is no Schubert, no art. For Schubert, the opposites of the "transcendental" and the "earthly" need one another; they become what they should be only when they work in harmony.

FIRST MOVEMENT:

> *Then I saw a new heaven and a new earth…and the holy city, dressed as a bride..!*
>
> *Book of Revelation*

This last part of the wanderer's journey is otherworldly, sacred. The wanderer approaches the time of the great transition, the movement from one world to another. He thinks ahead, anticipating freedom, joy, and love's triumph. He prays once again as he did in the *Unfinished Symphony* that the beauty contacted in his youth will be eternally his.

Lied der Mignon
Johann Wolfgang von Goethe D.877 no. 3
I am on my way, leaving this beautiful earth
For the mysterious afterworld.
I will spend a time at peace......
Then I will see all things transfigured!

I will leave the veil,
The sash, and the wreath behind me.
The spirits of the heavenly world
Do not limit love to man and wife.
No clothes, no cloak
Will hide the transfigured body.

My life has been free of work and responsibility,
Yet I have deeply suffered.
From my suffering I have become old before my time.
Oh, make me eternally young!

SECOND MOVEMENT

You, splendor of love, flow into the heart of the beloved; pour yourself into the very being of the soul!

Henry Suso

In solemn prayer the wanderer's spirit reaches longingly up to the inviter. As the peace of the better world descends upon him he asks for continued strength and courage as his hour approaches.

Hymnus an den Heiligen Geist
Alois Schmidl D.964
Lord my God!
Hear my prayer
That longs for You in Your goodness.
Gaze upon me, oh comforter,
Give heavenly peace to my heart!
Fill me with strength and courage in faith.
Do not abandon me on my path!
Lead me to what is good and just.
O Lord, do not abandon me!

THIRD MOVEMENT

Let us rejoice and be glad. Let us give him glory, for the wedding day of the Lamb has come. The bride is now ready.

Book of Revelation

A hymn of joyful praise erupts from the wanderer who sings in thanksgiving to the one who is calling him home. This divine inviter, this hidden God, cannot be understood, but rather can be touched by the wonder and paradox of the invitation to transcend contradiction. The wanderer sings in praise of the Ultimate Other, in whom heaven and earth, joy and sorrow, death and resurrection are reconciled, and in whom the wanderer finds himself.

Psalm 92
D.953
How wondrous it is to thank you eternal God,
To sing to your name, Most high!
In the morning we extol your kindness.
In the evening we extol your faithfulness.
Our lyre and psaltery sing their praise.
We thank you with our harps.
Lord and God, your works give me delight,
Happily I sing of your works.
How great they are!
How deep are your divine thoughts!
The fool cannot understand this,
Unthinking people are puzzled.
The evil seem to triumph…
But they shall go down…for ever.
For you are eternal, O God!
Eternal! Eternal!

FOURTH MOVEMENT

Now I discover your promised truth, O sweet Love…Give me your crown of pearls and stay with me. Be my possession that I may eternally rejoice in you.

Jacob Boehme

This wanderer, now mounted on horseback, the human illuminated by the divine, inspired with the anticipation of going home, rides boldly into the night's darkness, aware that soon it will be brightened by the light of welcome! For "three days" he has been away from his true home, has been in exile. Now he draws ever nearer to the fulfillment of his dream, to the divine freedom and love for which he was born. His immortal bride, his divine Sophia, awaits him. She will at last present to him her pearl. He rides on in "sweet anticipation."

Auf der Bruck
Ernst Schulze D.853
My fine steed, trot without rest
Through night and rain!
Do not fear bush or thicket.
Don't shy at the wild country.
The forest is indeed thick,
But in the end it will open.
A distant glow of welcome
Will light up the dark valley.
I ride swiftly over mountains and meadows
High on your back,
And could easily stop to enjoy the world,
To see new, enchanting sights.
How many bright eyes would attract me,
Promising peace, love and joy!
Yet I canter on, without rest…
Back, back to my pain.
For three days I have been away
From the one to whom I am bound.
For three days the sun and stars,
The earth and heavens disappeared.
The joy and anguish she resolved
Were again in turmoil and conflict.
For three days I felt only the anguish,
But the joy I lacked.
Now all over the land
Birds seek a better, warmer home!
Is it possible for true love
Not to do the same?
And though the way is dark and full of mystery,
My longing is awake and watchful,
And I race ahead in sweet anticipation.

Conclusion

Underlying the art of Schubert is an experience of the *mysterium magnum,* the point at which man touches God. This mystery challenges the world view that Western Civilization has chosen to inherit from the Greeks. A broader and deeper world-view recognizes that at the heart of experience is a creative tension between transcendental Being and bi-polar Becoming. That bi-polarity defines our experience of life as an involvement in value tension, either in its conflict or reconciliation. Both the evil twins, nihilism and fundamentalism, the bastard progeny of human blindness, distort this mystery. Nihilism denies the reality of transcendental Being, making life absurd. Fundamentalism negates the importance of bi-polar Becoming, denigrating the sacred nature of creative problem solving.

For the wise wanderer who embraces the *mysterium magnum* the paradoxical romance of the hidden God through the intensification of values and the creative resolution of their conlicts is the core concern of life. That romance is a painful, joyful, doubting, trusting, mistake-filled, probing ascent through the mists of consciousness towards a dimly sensed goal. The ascent is towards Being through bi-polar Becoming. For the wise wanderer every holy book, every law, every church pronouncement, every human adventure, all of Nature is a part of this Becoming, offering indirect, limited, partially valid, partially misleading experiences of that goal. The ethic of the wanderer is to ascend through courage, humility, brains, and effort, through trial and error, ever self-correcting, towards the partially hidden but trustworthy source of divine invitation. That invitation calls the wanderer into and through what is to what can be.

Christianity at its best, like Judaism, Islam, Buddhism, and Hinduism at their best, is an incarnation of this *mysterium magnum*. As the Jewish Shekhinah is symbol of the ascent of the people of God out of contradiction to the unity of Sophia, so is the Christian Church the living symbol of that same ascent. Conditioning the fidelity of each religion to the mystery is a recognition of limitation. No person, no church, no scripture, no philosophy, no racial ideology, no principle, no set of principles, no enthusiasm, no conviction... nothing gives us an experience of the *mysterium magnum* without simultaneously betraying it. While indirect and imperfect experiences of the mystery are quite real and necessary in our lives, those experiences simultaneously limit and thus betray their source. Revelation, sacred scripture, the lives of Buddha and Jesus, the life of the church...any church, parents, children, heroes...all bring to us priceless and unique experiences of the great mystery. But they are only handmaidens to the ongoing romance between the wanderer and the transcendental and hidden God. Conditioning the health of these and other orthodoxies is a recognition of their inadequacy in making incarnate the rose cross mystery.

In 1841 Bulwer Lytton wrote about the split between the false wisdom of rationalism and the revolutionary wisdom that transfigures life by reconciling contradictions. In the allegorical novel *Zanoni, A Rosicrucian Tale he* told the story of two initiates from an ancient Chaldean brotherhood who came to have diametrically opposed ideas about true wisdom. Both had survived thousands of years by virtue of their dispassionate, ultra-cerebral knowledge of causal relationships, their science, their philosophy. Both had mastered the power to survive. Both could control Nature. The insights of both reached back beyond recorded time. In many respects their wisdoms were identical. But one of these brothers, Zanoni, stepped beyond the wisdom that they shared. He committed the ultimate heresy. He fell in love with a woman. In doing so he transcended causality and power relationships. He discovered a whole new metaphysical universe, indeed he discovered his true self through the love of his polar opposite. He found himself willing to die for her. In this limit-shattering experience he found true wisdom, more ancient even than what he had shared with his brother. The supreme wisdom that now graced his life awakened in him a higher consciousness of the meaning of life and a happiness of which he had never dreamed. Death was no longer the ultimate evil. Rationalism was embraced but transformed by the rose cross mystery. He had entered a new age.

Zanoni had embraced the *mysterium tremendum*. The ascent out of darkness (the rationalist's universe of value conflict) into light (the broader universe of love) was for him at once a horizontal embrace of opposites (e.g. man and woman) and a vertical embrace of the romance between heaven and earth. Although Zanoni, the archetypal wanderer, is a fool in the eyes of his rationalistic brother, in reality he is wise. He has surrendered neither his science nor his reason. He has found their true meaning within the larger context of love. He has been caught up in the great romance through self-transcendence in union with the other. That self-transcendence means an acceptance of life, love, and death as steps in a love drama that is unique for each wanderer. In embracing this drama Zanoni is set free, illuminated by the light of Being. Zanoni has touched God.

Zanoni's challenge is that of every man, every woman, the challenge to our world, yesterday, today, and tomorrow. Each wanderer is born into a chaotic asylum of ideologies in conflict. The wanderer is set free in only one way, through a radical expansion of the inner life, an immersion in the *mysterium magnum*. Conflicts are creatively reconciled in new and higher realities. The experience wrenches the wanderer out of chaotic insanity and frees him or her like an agonized bird to ascend to a new reality.

True wisdom is perennially politically incorrect, anathema to both fundamentalism and nihilism. History is for the most part a rejection of its core mystery. Certainly the twenty-first century is hosting a devastating annihilation of it. In place of the love ascent that is open to transcendental invitation and therefore to an embrace of opposites there has been a chaotic mélange of insane religious, racial, and national movements and enthusiasms, each deeming itself an absolute, each seeking to annihilate its opposite. As I write, the United States of America is tragically a world leader in this insanity. Islamic fundamentalism, Zionism, and Christian fundamentalism vie with one another in destructive power.

The great challenge before society is to empower individual wanderers in sufficient numbers to romance the *mysterium magnum* in a new age. More and more wanderers within each orthodoxy must be empowered, philosophically, religiously, and politically to explore, embrace, and then transcend actual separation in quest of an ideal unity. This paradoxical empowerment requires among other things a liturgy. The art of Schubert can help in a unique way. With utter authenticity it celebrates with consummate beauty the great mystery that is the soul of life. The reader has already seen that Schubert's liturgy consists centrally of a series of musical parables, his instrumental works, in which he celebrates in a multitude of conflict situations an ascent into the *mysterium magnum*. The ascent was his theme in masterwork after masterwork. For him life's prison consists of "dreams tracelessly flying, madness playing in circles" (*String Quartet in G D.887*). But his wanderer is called out of this madhouse to a higher world, to a "new age". His wanderer, like Zanoni, experiences the call to freedom through an alluring woman. Like Zanoni he discovers that the ascent leads paradoxically and inevitably through the valley of death. He gradually awakens to the life-giving mystery.

The fearsome prison of value conflict and the hope for illuminated freedom are experienced by everyone. What will the response be? All men and women are wanderers. The pathway to freedom demands transcending both fundamentalism and nihilism in an embrace of the rose cross mystery. For every wanderer the starting point is a lower world of slavery to powerlessness in a chaotic universe. But the end point can be a higher world. For mystery adepts such as Schubert, Novalis, and others the hidden God draws art, religion, philosophy, and politics upwards to ever more intense self-realizations in ever higher unities. The *mysterium magnum*, the root of Christianity, Judaism, and the Enlightenment, calls them all to their transcendental realizations in the unity, freedom, joy, and love of the hidden God.

Acknowledgments

The path leading to this book has been a long one. It began early in life with a love of Schubert that drove me at the age of seven to look for a birthday present for my mother, asking for "the symphony that you always hear" (the "Unfinished"). My enthusiasm began to take a creative form thirty-five years ago after Betty, my wife, encouraged me to invest in the Lieder recordings of Dietrich Fischer Dieskau. First the music and then the poetry captivated me. It was clear that the music emanated out of the inner sense of the poem. The thought occurred that the same inspirational process might explain the music development in the instrumental works. So I tried to find correlations between the instrumental works and the poems set as songs. The process took time and the patience of my family and friends. Successes in finding correlations were inflicted on family, relatives, and friends. But they endured it all with understanding and generosity.

My immersion in the mystery through Catholicism was and is obviously important to me. It was through the genius of Eugene Walsh at St. Mary's Seminary in Baltimore and through the genius of Josef Fuchs, S.J. at the Gregorian University in Rome, both now deceased, that the profound humanity of the *mysterium magnum* was unveiled for me... in a way that was a healthful challenge to orthodoxy, but always in harmony with it. Friends such as José Neistein, formerly of the Brazilian Cultural Institute and Steven Ackert, Music Director of the National Gallery of Art have been encouraging and helpful with suggestions. My cousin and friend, Joe Walshe, and my friends, Roger Sorrentino and David Nace, have read the manuscript and offered valuable insights. Friends and relatives beyond counting have endured my Lieder singing and have responded with good humor and kindness to the project. Especially helpful has been the retirement community at the Chevy Chase House in Washington, D.C.. These wonderful people have for fifteen years listened to my Schubert presentations and responded with both mind and heart. And more recently Professor Clopper Almon of Maryland University has given me immense assistance in developing presentations of the interlacing of poetry and music in this remarkable art and has given invaluable help in preparing this manuscript. To all of these fine people, and most especially to my wife and daughters, the true inspirations for this work, whose patience has been endless and whose generosity boundless, I offer profound thanks and love. Betty's labor-intensive preparations for the Schubertiades held at our home have made them a joy for me as well as for the guests.